Around the World Bicycle - Volume From Teheran To Yokohama

Thomas Stevens

Alpha Editions

This Edition Published in 2021

ISBN: 9789355759146

Design and Setting By
Alpha Editions
www.alphaedis.com
Email – info@alphaedis.com

As per information held with us this book is in Public Domain.
This book is a reproduction of an important historical work.
Alpha Editions uses the best technology to reproduce historical
work in the PR-same manner it was first published to preserve its
original nature. Any marks or number seen are left intentionally to
preserve its true form.

TABLE OF CONTENTS

FROM TEHERAN TO YOKOHAMA	- 1 -
CHAPTER I	- 2 -
CHAPTER II	- 16 -
CHAPTER III	- 29 -
CHAPTER IV	- 46 -
CHAPTER V	- 60 -
CHAPTER VI	- 79 -
CHAPTER VII	- 99 -
CHAPTER VIII	- 119 -
CHAPTER IX	- 135 -
CHAPTER X	- 147 -
CHAPTER XI	- 157 -
CHAPTER XII TAKEN BACK TO PERSIA	- 174 -
CHAPTER XIII	- 196 -
CHAPTER XIV	- 222 -
CHAPTER XV	- 243 -
CHAPTER XVI	- 262 -
CHAPTER XVII	- 289 -
CHAPTER XVIII	- 316 -
CHAPTER XIX	- 340 -
CHAPTER XX	- 354 -

ITINERARY GIVING THE NAME AND DATE OF
EACH SLEEPING-POINT ON THE BICYCLE TOUR
AROUND THE WORLD

FROM TEHERAN TO YOKOHAMA

CHAPTER I

THE START FROM TEHERAN

The season of 1885-86 has been an exceptionally mild winter in the Persian capital. Up to Christmas the weather was clear and bracing, sufficiently cool to be comfortable in the daytime, and with crisp, frosty weather at night. The first snow of the season commenced falling while a portion of the English colony were enjoying a characteristic Christmas dinner of roast-beef and plum-pudding, at the house of the superintendent of the Indo-European Telegraph Station, and during January and February, snow-storms, cold and drizzling rains alternated with brief periods of clearer weather. When the sun shines from a cloudless sky in Teheran, its rays are sometimes uncomfortably warm, even in midwinter; a foot of snow may have clothed the city and the surrounding plain in a soft, white mantle during the night, but, asserting his supremacy on the following morning, he will unveil the gray nakedness of the stony plain again by noon. The steadily retreating snow line will be driven back-back over the undulating foot-hills, and some little distance up the rugged slopes of the Elburz range, hard by, ere he retires from view in the evening, rotund and fiery. This irregular snow-line has been steadily losing ground, and retreating higher and higher up the mountain-slopes during the latter half of February, and when March is ushered in, with clear sunny weather, and the mud begins drying up and the various indications of spring begin to put in their appearance, I decide to make a start. Friends residing here who have been mentioning April 15th as the date I should be justified in thinking the unsettled weather at an end and pulling out eastward again, agree, in response to my anxious inquiries, that it is an open spell of weather before the regular spring rains, that may possibly last until I reach Meshed.

During the winter I have examined, as far as circumstances have permitted, the merits and demerits of the different routes to the Pacific Coast, and have decided upon going through Turkestan and Southern Siberia to the Amoor Valley, and thence either follow down the valley to Vladivostok or strike across Mongolia to Pekin—the latter route by preference, if upon reaching Irkutsk I find it to be practicable; if not practicable, then the Amoor Valley route from necessity. This route I approve of, as it will not only take me through some of the most interesting country in Asia, but will probably be a more straightaway continuous land-journey than any other. The distance from Teheran to Vladivostok is some six thousand miles, and, well aware that six thousand miles with a bicycle over Asiatic roads is a task of no little magnitude, I at once determine upon taking advantage of the fair March weather to accomplish at least the first six hundred miles of the journey between Teheran and Meshed, one of the holy cities of Persia.

The bicycle is in good trim, my own health is splendid, my experience of nearly eight thousand miles of straightaway wheeling over the roads of three continents ought to count for something, and it is with every confidence of accomplishing my undertaking without serious misadventure that I set about making my final preparations to start. The British Charge d'Affaires gives me a letter to General Melnikoff, the Russian Minister at the Shah's court, explaining the nature and object of my journey, and asking him to render me whatever assistance he can to get through, for most of the proposed route lies through Russian territory. Among my Teheran friends is Mr. M———, a lively, dapper little telegraphist, who knows three or four different languages, and who never seems happier than when called upon to act the part of interpreter for friends about him.

Among other distinguishing qualities, Mr. M———shines in Teheran society as the only Briton with sufficient courage to wear a chimney-pot hat. Although the writer has seen the "stove-pipe" of the unsuspecting tenderfoot from the Eastern States made short work of in a far Western town, and the occurrence seemed scarcely to be out of place there, I little expected to find popular sentiment running in the same warlike groove, and asserting itself in the same destructive manner in the little English community at Teheran. Such, however, is the grim fact, and I have ventured to think that after this there is no disputing the common destiny of us Anglo-Saxons, whatever clime, country, or government may at present claim us as its own. Having seen this unfortunate headgear of our venerable and venerated forefathers shot as full of holes as a colander in the West, I come to the East only to find it subjected to similar indignities here. I happen to be present at the wanton destruction of Mr. M———'s second or third importation from England, see it taken ruthlessly from his head, thrust through and through with a sword-stick, and then made to play the unhappy and undignified part of a football so long as there is anything left to kick at. More than our common language, methinks—more than common customs and traditions—more than all those characteristic traits that distinguish us in common, and at the same time also distinguish us from all other peoples—more than anything else, does this mutual spirit of destructiveness, called into play by the sight of a stove-pipe hat, prove the existence of a strong, resistless undercurrent of sympathy that is carrying the most distant outposts of Anglo-Saxony merrily down the stream of time together, to some particular end; perchance a glorious end, perchance an ignominious end, but certainly to an end that will not wear a stove-pipe hat.

Mr. M————'s linguistic accomplishments include a fair knowledge of Russian, and he readily accompanies me to the Russian Legation to interpret. The Russian Legation is situated down in the old Oriental quarter (birds of a feather, etc.) of the city, and, for us at least, necessitated the employment of a guide to find it. On the way down, Mr. M————, who prides himself on a knowledge of Russian character, impresses upon me his assurance that General Melnikoff will turn out to be a nice, pleasant sort of a gentleman. "All the better-class Russians are delightfully jolly and agreeable, much more agreeable to have dealings with than the same class of people of any other country," he says, and with these favorable comments we reach the legation and send up my letter. After waiting what we both consider an unnecessarily long time in the vestibule, a full-faced, sensual-looking, or, in other words, well-to-do Persian-looking individual, in the full costume of a Persian nobleman, comes out, bearing my letter unopened in his hand. Bestowing upon us a barely perceptible nod, he walks straight on past, jumps into a carriage at the door, and is driven off.

Mr. M————looks nonplussed at me, and I suppose I looked equally nonplussed at him; anyhow, he proceeds to relieve his feelings in language anything but complimentary to the Russian Minister. He's the—well, I've met scores of Russians, but—him, queer! I never saw a Russian act half as queer as this before, never!"

"Small prospect of getting any assistance from this quarter," I suggest.

"Seems deucedly like it," assents Mr. M————. "I said, just now, that, being a Russian, he was sure to be courteous and agreeable, if nothing else; but it seems as if there are exceptions to this rule as to others;" and, talking together, we try to find consolation in the thought that he may be merely eccentric, and turn out a very good sort of fellow after all. While thus commenting, a liveried servant presents himself and motions for us to follow him in the wake of the departing carriage. Following his guidance a short distance through the streets, he leads us into the court-yard of a splendid Persian mansion, delivers us into the charge of another liveried servant, who conducts us up a broad flight of marble stairs, at the top of which he delivers us into the hands of yet a third flunky, who now escorts us into the most gorgeously mirrored room it has ever been my fortune to see. The apartment is perfectly dazzling in its glittering splendor; the floor is of highly polished marble, the walls consist of mirror-work entirely, as also does the lofty, domed ceiling; not plain, large squares of looking-glass, but mirrored surfaces of all shapes and sizes, pitched at every conceivable angle, form niches, panels, and geometrical designs—yet each separate piece plays well its part in working out the harmonious and decidedly pretty effect of the whole. All the furniture the large apartment boasts is a crimson-and-gold divan or two, a few strips of rich carpet, and an ebony stand-table, inlaid with mother-of-pearl; but suspended from the ceiling are several magnificent cut-glass chandeliers. At night, when these Persian mirrored rooms are lit up, they present a scene of barbaric splendor well calculated to delight the eye of the sumptuous Oriental; every tiny square of glass reflects a point of light, and every larger one reproduces a chandelier; for every lamp he lights, the Persian voluptuary finds himself surrounded by a thousand.

Seated on a divan toward one end of this splendid room, with an open box of cigarettes before him, is the man who a few minutes ago passed us by on the other side and drove off in his carriage. Offering us cigarettes, he bids us be seated, and then, in very fair English (for he has once been Persian Minister to England), introduces himself as "Nasr-i-Mulk," the Shah's Minister for Foreign Affairs; the same gentleman, it will be remembered, to whom I was introduced on the morning of my appearance before the Shah. (Vol. I.) I readily recognize him now, and he recognizes me, and asks me when I am going to leave Teheran; but in the gloomy vestibule of the other palace, my own memory of his face and figure was certainly at fault. It turns out, after all, that the wretch whom we paid to guide us to the Russian Legation, in his ignorance guided us into the Persian Foreign Office.

"I knew—yes, dash it all! I knew he wasn't the Russian Minister the moment I saw him," says Mr. M———as we take our departure from the glittering room. His confidence in his knowledge of Russian character, which a moment ago had dropped down to zero, revives wonderfully upon discovering our ludicrous mistake, and, small as he is, it is all I can do to keep up with him as we follow the guide Nasr-i-Mulk has kindly sent to show us to the Russian Legation. A few minutes' walk brings us to our destination, where we find, in the person of General Melnikoff, a gentleman possessing the bland and engaging qualities of a good diplomatist in a most eminent degree.

"Which is Mr. Stevens?" he exclaims, with something akin to enthusiasm, as he advances almost to the door to meet us, his face fairly beaming with pleasure; and, grasping me warmly by the hand, he proceeds to express his great satisfaction at meeting a person, who had "made so wonderful a journey," etc., etc., and etc. Never did Mr. Pickwick beam more pleasantly at the deaf gentleman, or regard more benignantly Master Humphrey's clock, than the Russian Minister regards the form and features of one whom, he says, he feels "honored to meet." For several minutes we discuss, through the medium of Mr. M———, my journey from San Francisco to Teheran, and its proposed continuation to the Pacific; and during the greater part, of the interview General Melnikoff holds me quite affectionately by the hand. "Wonderful!" he says, "wonderful! nobody ever made half such a remarkable journey; my whole heart will go with you until your journey is completed."

Mr. M———looks on and interprets between us, with a fixed and confident didn't-I-tell-you-so smile, that forms a side study of no mean quality. "There will be no trouble about getting permission to go through Turkestan?" I feel constrained to inquire; for such excessive display of affection and bonhommie on the Russian diplomat's part could scarce fail to arouse suspicions. "Oh dear, no!" he replies. "Oh dear, no! I will telegraph to General Komaroff, at Askabad, to remove all obstacles, so that nothing shall interfere with your progress." Having received this positive assurance, we take our leave, Mr. M———reminding me gleefully of what he had said about the Russians being the most agreeable people on earth, and the few remaining clouds of doubt about getting the road through Turkestan happily dissipated by the Russian Minister's assurances of assistance.

Searching through the bazaar, I succeed, after some little trouble, in finding and purchasing a belt-full of Russian gold, sufficient to carry me clear through to Japan; and on the morning of March 10th I bid farewell to the Persian capital, well satisfied at the outlook ahead. While packing up my traps on the evening before starting, it begins raining for the first time in ten days; but it clears off again before midnight, and the morning opens bright and promising as ever. Six members of the telegraph staff have determined to accompany me out to Katoum-abad, the first chapar-station on the Meshed pilgrim road, a distance of seven farsakhs. "Hodge-podge," the cook, and Meshedi Ali, the gholam, were sent ahead yesterday with plenty of substantial refreshments and sun-dry mysterious black bottles— for it is the intention of the party to remain at Katoum-abad overnight, and give me a proper send-off from that point to-morrow morning.

Some little delay is occasioned by a difficulty in meeting the fastidious tastes of some of the party as regards saddle-horses; but there is no particular hurry, and ten o'clock finds me bowling briskly through the suburbs toward the Doshan Tepe gate, with four Englishmen, an Irishman, and a Welshman cantering merrily along on horseback behind.

"Khuda rail pak Kumad!" (May God sweep your road!), All Akbar had exclaimed as I mounted at the door, and as we pass through the city gate the old sentinel, when told that I am at last starting on the promised journey to Meshed on the asp-i-awhan, supplements this with "Padaram daromad!" (My father has come out!), a Persian metaphorical exclamation, signifying that such wonderful news has had the effect of calling his father from the grave.

The weather has changed again since early morning; it is evidently in a very fitful and unsettled mood; the gray clouds are swirling in confusion about the white summit of Demavend as we emerge on the level plain outside the ramparts, and fleecy fugitives are scudding southward in wild haste. Imperfect but ridable donkey-trails follow the dry moat around to the Meshed road, which takes a straight course southeastward from the city and is seen in the distance ahead, leading over a sloping pass, a depression in the Doshan Tepe spur of the Elburz range. The road near the city is now in better condition for wheeling than at any other time of the year; the daily swarms of pack-animals bringing produce into Teheran have trodden it smooth and hard during the ten days' continuous fine weather, while it has not been dry sufficiently long to develop into dust, as it does later in the season. Our road is level and good for something over a farsakh, after which comes the rising ground leading gently upward to the pass. The gradient is sufficiently gentle to be ridable for some little distance, when it becomes too rocky and steep, and I have to dismount and trundle to the summit. The summit of the pass is only about nine miles from the city walls, and we pause a minute to investigate a bottle of homemade wine from the private cellar of Mr. North, one of our party, and to allow me to take a farewell glance at Teheran, and the many familiar objects round about, ere riding down the eastern slope and out of sight.

Teheran is in semi-obscurity beneath the same hazy veil observed when first approaching it from the west, and which always seems to hover over it. This haziness is not sufficiently pronounced to hide any conspicuous building, and each familiar object in the city is plainly visible from the commanding summit of the pass. The different gates of the city, each with its little cluster of bright-tiled minars, trace at a glance the size and contour of the outer ditch and wall; the large framework of the pavilion beneath which the Shah gives his annual tazzia (representation of the religious tragedy of Hussein and Hassan), denuded of its canvas covering, suggests from this distance the naked ribs of some monster skeleton. The square towers of the royal anderoon—which the Shah professes to believe is the tallest dwelling-house in the world—loom conspicuously skyward above the mass of indefinable mud buildings and walls that characterize the habitations of humbler folk, but perhaps happier on the whole than the fair occupants of that seven-storied gilded prison.

Hundreds of women-wives, concubines, slaves, and domestics are understood to be dwelling within these palace walls in charge of sable eunuchs, and the fate of any female whose bump of discretion in an evil moment fails her, is to be hurled headlong from the summit of one of the anderoon towers—such, at least, is the popular belief in Teheran; it may or may not be an exaggeration. Some even assert that the Shah's chief object in building the anderoon so high was to have the certainty of this awful doom ever present before its numerous inmates, the more easily to keep them in a submissive frame of mind. Off to the right, below our position, is the Doshan Tepe palace, a memorable spot for me, where I had the satisfaction of first introducing bicycle-riding to the notice of the Persian monarch. Off to the left, the Parsee "tower of silence" is observed perched among the lonely gray hills far from human habitation or any traversed road; on a grating fixed in the top of this tower, the Guebre population of Teheran deposit their dead, in order that the carrion-crows and the vultures may pick the carcass clean before they deposit the whitened bones in the body of the tower.

Having duly investigated the bottle of wine and noticed these few familiar objects, we all remount and begin the descent. It is a gentle declivity from top to bottom, and ridable the whole distance, save where an occasional washout or other small obstacle compels a dismount. The wind is likewise favorable, and from the top of the pass the bicycle outdistances the horsemen, except two who are riding exceptionally good nags and make a special effort to keep up; and at two o'clock we arrive at Katoum-abad. Katoum-abad consists of a small mud village and a half-ruined brick caravansarai; in one of the rooms of the latter we find "Hodge-podge" and Me-shedi Ali, with an abundance of roast chickens, cold mutton, eggs, and the before-mentioned mysterious black bottles.

The few Persian travellers in the caravansarai and the villagers come flocking around as usual to worry me about riding the bicycle, but the servants drive them away in short order. "We want to see the sahib ride the aap-i-awhan," they explain,-no doubt thinking their request most natural and reasonable. "The sahib won't let you see it, nor ride on it this evening," reply the servants; and, given to understand that we won't put up with their importunities, they worry us no more. "Oh, that I could get rid of them thus readily always!" I mentally exclaim; for I feel instinctively that the farther east I get, the more wretchedly worrying and inquisitive I shall find the people. We arrive hungry and thirsty, and in condition to do ample justice to the provisions at hand. After satisfying the pressing needs of hunger, we drink several appropriate toasts from the contents of the mysterious black bottles—toasts for the success of my journey, and to the bicycle that has stood by me so well thus far on my journey, and promises to stand by me equally as well for the future.

About four o'clock two of the company, who have been thoughtful enough to bring shotguns along, sally forth in quest of ducks. They come plodding wearily back again shortly after dark, without any game, but with deep designs on the credulity of the non-sporting members of the company. In reply to the general and stereotyped query, "Shoot anything?"

one of the erring pair replies, "Yes, we shot several canvas-backs, but lost them in the reeds; didn't we, old un?" "Yes, five," promptly asserts "old un," a truthful young man of about three-and-twenty summers. After this, the silence for the space of a minute is so profound that we can hear each other think, until one of the company, acting as spokesman for the silent reflections of the others, inquires, "Anybody know of any reeds about Katoum-abad?" Some one is about to reply, but sportsman No. 1 artfully waives further examination by heaping imprecations on the unkempt head of a dervish, who at this opportune moment commences a sing-song monotone, in a most soul-harrowing key, outside our menzil doorway.

A slight drizzling rain is falling when the early riser of the company wakes up and peeps out at daybreak next morning, but it soon ceases, and by seven o'clock the ground is quite dry. The road for a mile or so is too lumpy to admit of mounting, as is frequently the case near a village, and my six companions accompany me to ridable ground. As I mount and wheel away, they wave hats and send up three ringing cheers and a "tiger," hurrahs that roll across the gray Persian plain to the echoing hills, the strangest sound, perhaps, these grim old hills have ever echoed; certainly, they never before echoed an English cheer.

And now, as my friends of the telegraph staff turn about and wend their way back to Teheran, is as good a time as any to mention briefly the manner in which these genial lightning-jerkers assisted to render my five months' sojourn in the Persian capital agreeable. But a few short hours after my arrival in Teheran, I was sought out by Messrs. Meyrick and North, who no sooner learned of my intention to winter here, than they extended a cordial invitation to join them in their already established bachelors' quarters, where four disconsolate halves of humanity were already messing harmoniously together. With them I took up my quarters, and, under the liberal and wholesome gastronomic arrangements of the establishment, soon acquired my usual semi-embon-point condition, and recovered from that gaunt, hungry appearance that the hardships and scant fare of the journey from Constantinople had imparted. The house belonged to Mr. North, and he managed to give me a little room to myself for literary work, and, under the influence of a steady stream of letters and papers from friends and well-wishers in England and America, that snug little apartment, with a round, moon-like hole in the thick mud wall for a window, soon acquired the den-like aspect that seems inseparable from the occupation of distributing ink.

Three native servants cooked for us, waited on us, turned up missing when wanted for anything particular, cheated us and each other, swore eternal honesty and fidelity to our faces, called us infidel dogs and pedar sags behind our backs, quarrelled daily among themselves over their modokal (legitimate pickings and stealings—ten per cent, on everything passing through their hands), and meekly bore with any abuse bestowed gratuitously upon them, for an aggregate of one hundred and thirty kerans a month—and, of course, their modokal. Some enterprising members of the colony had formed themselves into a club, and imported a billiard-table from England; this, also, was installed in Mr. North's house, and it furnished the means for many an hour of pleasant diversion. Like all Persian houses, the house was built around a square court-yard. Mr. North had also a pair of small white bull-dogs, named, respectively, "Crib" and "Swindle." The last-named animal furnished us with quite an exciting episode one February evening. He had been acting rather strangely for two or three days; we thought that one of the servants had been giving him a dose of bhang in revenge for having worried his kitten, and that he would soon recover; but on this particular day, when out for a run with his owner, his strange behavior took the form of leaping impulsively at Mr. North, and, with seemingly wild frolic, seizing and shaking his garments. When Mr. North returned home he took the precautionary measure of chaining him up in the yard. Shortly afterward, I came in from my customary evening walk, and, all unconscious of the change in his behavior, went up to him; with a half-playful, half-savage spring he seized the leg of my trousers, and, with an evidently uncontrollable impulse, shook a piece clean out of it. He became gradually worse as the evening wore away; the wild expression of his eyes developed in an alarming manner; he would try to get at any person who showed himself, and he made night hideous with the fearful barking howl of a mad dog. Poor Swindle had gone mad; and I had had a narrow escape from being bitten. We lassoed him from opposite directions and dragged him outside and shot him. Swindle was a plucky little dog, and so was Crib; one day they chased a vagrant cat up on to the roof; driven to desperation, the cat made a wild leap down into the court-yard, a distance of perhaps twenty feet; without a moment's hesitation, both dogs sprang boldly after her, recking little of the distance to the ground and the possibility of broken bones.

Sometimes the colony drives dull care and ennui away by indulging in private theatricals; this winter they organized an amateur company, called themselves the "Teheran Bulbuls," and, with burnt-corked faces and grotesque attire, they rehearsed and perfected themselves in "Uncle Ebenezer's Visit to New York," which, together with sundry duets, solos, choruses, etc., they proposed to give, an entertainment for the benefit of the poor of the city. When the Shah returned from Europe, he was moved by what he had seen there to build a small theatre; the theatre was built, but nothing is ever done with it. The Teheran Bulbuls applied for its use to give their entertainment in, and the Shah was pleased to grant their request. The mollahs raised objections; they said it would have a tendency to corrupt the morals of the Persians. Once, twice, the entertainment was postponed; but the Shah finally overruled the bigoted priests' objections, and "Uncle Ebenezer's Visit to New York" was played twice in Nasr-e-Deen's little gilded theatre a few days after I left, with great success; the first night, before the Shah and his nobles and the foreign ambassadors, and the second night before more common folk. The two postponements and my early departure prevented me from being on hand as prompter. The winter before, these dusky-faced "bul-buls" had performed before a Teheran audience, and one who was a member at that time tells an amusing story of the individual who acted as prompter on that occasion. One of the performers appeared on the stage sufficiently charged with stage-fright to cause him to entirely forget his piece. Expecting every moment to get the cue from the prompter's box, what was his horror to hear, after waiting what probably seemed to him about an hour, instead of the cue, in a hoarse whisper that could be distinctly heard all over the room, the comforting remark, "I say, Charlie, I've lost the blooming place!"

The American missionaries have a small chapel in Teheran, and on Sunday morning we sometimes used to go; the little congregation gathered there was composed of strange elements collected together from far-off places. From Colonel F _____, the grizzled military adventurer, now in the Shah's service, and who was also with Maximilian in Mexico, to the young American lady who is said to have turned missionary and come, broken-hearted, to the distant East because her lover had died a few days before they were to be married, they are an audience of people each with a more or less adventurous history. It is perfectly natural that it should be so; it is the irrepressible spirit of adventure that is either directly or indirectly responsible for their presence here.

Half an hour after the echoes of the three cheers and the "tiger" have died away finds me wet-footed and engaged in fording a series of aggravating little streams, that obstruct my path so frequently that to stop and shed one's foot-gear for each soon becomes an intolerable nuisance. I should think I can lay claim, without exaggeration, to crossing fifty of these streams inside of ten miles. A good-sized stream emerges from the Elburz foot-hills; after reaching the plain it follows no regular channel, but spreads out like an open fan into a gradually widening area of small streams, that play their part in irrigating a few scattering fields and gardens, and are then lost in the sands of the desert to the south. Situated where it can derive the most benefit from these streams is the village of Sherifabad, and beyond Sherifabad stretches a verdureless waste to Aivan-i-Kaif. On this desert, I sit down, for a few minutes, on one of those little mounds of stones piled up at intervals to mark the road when the trail is buried beneath the winter snows; a green-turbaned descendant of the Prophet, bestriding a bay horse, comes from the opposite direction, stops, dismounts, squats down on his hams close by, and proceeds to regale himself with bread and figs, meanwhile casting fugitive glances at the bicycle. Presently he advances closer, gives me a handful of figs, squats down closer to the bicycle, and commences a searching investigation of its several parts.

"Where are you going?" he finally asks. "Meshed." "Where have you come from?" "Teheran." With that he hands me another handful of figs, remounts his horse, and rides away without another word. Inquisitiveness is seen almost bristling from the loose sleeves and flowing folds of his sky-blue gown, but his over-whelming sense of his own holiness forbids him holding anything like a lengthy intercourse with an unhallowed Ferenghi, and, much as he would like to know everything about the bicycle, he goes away without asking a single question about it.

Shortly after parting company with the sanctimonious seyud, I encounter a prosperous-looking party of dervishes. Some of them are mounted on excellent donkeys, and for dervishes they look exceptionally flourishing and well to do. As I ride slowly past, they accost me with their customary "huk yah huk," and promise to pray Allah for a safe journey to wherever I am going, if I will only favor them with the necessary backsheesh to command their good offices.

There are some stretches of very good road across this desert, and I reach Aivan-i-Kaif near noon. There has been no drinkable water for a long distance, and, being thirsty, my first inquiry is for tea. "There is a tchai-khan at the umbar (water-cistern), yonder," I am told, and straightway proceed to the place pointed out; but "tchai-khan neis" is the reply upon inquiring at the umbar. In this manner am I promptly initiated into one peculiarity of the people along this portion of the Meshed pilgrim road, a peculiarity that distinguishes them from the ordinary Persian as fully as the shaking of their heads for an affirmative reply does the people of the Maritza Valley from other people of the Balkan Peninsula. They will frequently ask you if you want a certain article, simply for the purpose of telling you they haven't got it. Whether this queer inconsistency comes of simon-pure inquisitiveness, to hear what one will say in reply, or whether they derive a certain amount of inquisitorial pleasure from raising a person's expectations one moment so as to witness his disappointment the next, is a question I prefer to leave to others, but more than once am I brought into contact with this peculiarity during the few brief hours I stay at Aivan-i-Kaif. It is not improbable that these people are merely carrying their ideas of politeness to the insane length of holding out the promise of what they think or ascertain one wants, knowing at the same time their inability to supply it.

It is threatening rain as I pick my way through a mile or so of mud ruins, tumble-down walls, and crooked paths, leading from the umbar to the house of the Persian telegraph-jee, who has been requested, from Teheran, to put me up, and, in view of the threatening aspect of the weather, I conclude to remain till morning. The English Government has taken charge of the Teheran and Meshed telegraph-line, during the delimitation of the Afghan and Turkestan boundary, and, besides guaranteeing the native telegraph-jees their regular salary-which is not always forthcoming from the Persian Government-they pay them something extra. In consequence of this, the telegraph-jees are at present very favorably disposed toward Englishmen, and Mirza Hassan readily tenders me the hospitality of the little mud office where he amuses himself daily clicking the keys of his instrument, smoking kalians, drinking tea, and entertaining his guests. Mr. McIntire and Mr. Stagno are somewhere between here and Meshed, inspecting and repairing the line for the English Government, for they received it from the Persians in a wretched, tumble-down condition, and Mr. Gray, telegraphist for the Afghan Boundary Commission, is stationed temporarily at Meshed, so that, thanks to the boundary troubles, I am pretty certain of meeting three Europeans on the first six hundred miles of my journey.

Mirza Hassan is hospitable and well meaning, but, like most Persians, he is slow about everything but asking questions. Being a telegraph-jee, he is, of course, a comparatively enlightened mortal, and, among other things, he is acquainted with the average Englishman's partiality for beer. One of the first questions he asks, is whether I want any beer. It strikes me at once as a rather strange question to be asked in a Persian village, but, thinking he might perchance have had a bottle or two left here by one of the above-mentioned telegraph-inspectors, I signify my willingness to sample a little. True to the peculiar inconsistency of his fellows, he replies: "Ob-i-jow neis" (beer, no). If he hasn't ob-i-jow, however, he has tea, and in about an hour after my arrival he produces the samovar, a bowl of sugar, and the tiny glasses in which tea is always served in Persia.

Visitors begin dropping in as usual, and, before long, hundreds of villagers are swarming about the telegraph-khana, anxious to see me ride. It is coming on to rain, but, in order to rid the telegraph-office of the crowd, I take the bicycle out. Willing men carry both me and the bicycle across a stream that runs through the village, to smooth ground on the opposite side, where I ride back and forth several times, to the wild and boisterous delight of the entire population.

In this manner I succeed in ridding the telegraph-office of the crowd; but there is no getting rid of the visitors. Everybody in the place who thinks himself a little better than the ragamuffin ryots comes and squats on his hams in the little hut-like office, sips the telegraph-jee's sweetened tea, smokes his kalians, and spends the afternoon in staring wonderingly at me and the bicycle. Having picked up a little Persian during the winter, I am able to talk with them, and understand them, rather better than last season, and, Persian-like, they ply me mercilessly with questions. Often, when some one asks a question of me, Mirza Hassan, as becomes a telegraphies, and a person of profound erudition, thoughtfully saves me the trouble of replying by undertaking to furnish the desired information himself. One old mollah wants to know how many farsakhs it is from Aivan-i-Kaif to Yenghi Donia (New World-America); ere I can frame a suitable reply, Mirza Hassan forestalls my intentions by answering, in a decisive tone of voice that admits of no appeal, "Khylie!" "Khylie" is a handy word that the Persians always fall back on when their knowledge of great numbers or long distances is vague and shadowy; it is an indefinite term, equivalent to our word "many." Mirza Hassan does not know whether America is two hundred farsakhs away or two thousand, but he knows it to be "khylie farsakhs," and that is perfectly satisfactory to himself, and the white-turbaned questioner is perfectly satisfied with "khylie" for an answer.

A person from the New World is naturally a rara avis with the simple villagers of Aivan-i-Kaif, and their inquisitiveness concerning Yenghi Donia and Yenghi Donians fairly runs riot, and shapes itself into all manner of questions. They want to know whether the people smoke kalians and ride horses—real horses, not asps-i-awhans-in Yenghi Donia, and whether the Valiat smoked the kalian with me at Hadji Agha. Mirza Hassan explains about the kalian and horses; he enlightens his wondering auditors to the extent that Yenghi Donians smoke nargilehs and chibouques instead of kalians, and he contemptuously pooh-poohs the idea of them keeping riding-horses when they are clever enough to make iron horses that require nothing to eat or drink and no rest. About the question of the Heir Apparent smoking the kalian with me he betrays as lively an interest as anybody in the room, but he maintains a discreet silence until I answer in the negative, when he surveys his guests with the air of one who pities their ignorance, and says, "Kalian neis."

A lusty-lunged youngster of about three summers has been interrupting the genial flow of conversation by making "Rome howl" in an adjoining room, and Mirza Hassan fetches him in and consoles him with sundry lumps of sugar. The advent of the limpid-eyed toddler leads the thoughts and questions of the company into more domestic channels. After exhaustive questioning about my own affairs, Mirza Hassan, with more than praiseworthy frankness and becoming gravity, informs me that, besides the embryo telegraphjee and sugar-consumer in the room, he is the happy father of "yek nim" (one and a half others). I cast my eye around the room at this extraordinary announcement, expecting to find the company indulging in appreciative smiles, but every person in the room is as sober as a judge; plainly, I am the only person present who regards the announcement as anything uncommon.

After an ample supper of mutton pillau, Mirza Hassan proceeds to say his prayers, borrowing my compass to get the proper bearings for Mecca, which I have explained to him during the afternoon. With no little dismay he discovers that, according to my explanations, he has for years been bobbing his head daily several degrees east of the holy city, and, like a sensible fellow, and a person who has become convinced of the infallibility of telegraph instruments, compasses, and kindred aids to the accomplishment of human ends, he now rectifies the mistake.

Everybody along this route uses a praying-stone, a small cake of stone or hardened clay, containing an inscription from the Koran. These praying-stones are obtained from the sacred soil of Meshed, Koom, or Kerbela, and are placed in position on the ground in front of the kneeling devotee during his devotions, so that, instead of touching his forehead to the carpet or the common ground of his native village, he can bring it in contact with the hallowed soil of one of these holy cities. Distance lends enchantment to a holy place, and adds to the efficacy of a prayer-stone in the eyes of its owner, and they are valued highly or lightly according to the distance and the consequent holiness of the city they are brought from. For example, a Meshedi values a prayer-stone from Kerbela, and a Kerbeli values one from Meshed, neither of them having much faith in the efficacy of one from his own city; familiarity with sacred things apparently breeds doubts and indifference. The prayer-stone is reverently touched to lips, cheeks, and forehead at the finish of prayers, and then carefully wrapped up and stowed away until praying-time comes round again. To a sceptical and perhaps irreverent observer, these praying-stones would seem to bear about the same relation to a pilgrimage to Meshed or Kerbela as a package of prepared sea-salt does to a season at the sea-side.

CHAPTER II

PERSIA AND THE MESHED PILGRIM ROAD

It rains quite heavily during the night, but clears off again in the early morning, and at eight o'clock I take my departure, Mirza Hassan refusing to allow his son and heir to accept a present in acknowledgment of the hospitality received at his hands. The whole male population of the village is assembled again at the spot where their experience of yesterday has taught them I should probably mount; and the house-tops overlooking the same spot, and commanding a view of the road across the plain to the eastward, are crowded with women and children. The female portion of my farewell audience present quite a picturesque appearance, being arrayed in their holiday garments of red, blue, and other bright colors, in honor of Friday, the Mohammedan Sabbath.

Pour miles of most excellent camel-path lead across a gravelly plain, affording a smooth, firm, wheeling surface, notwithstanding the heavy rains of the previous night; but beyond the plain the road leads over the pass of the Sardara Kooh, one of the many spurs of the Elburz range that reach out toward the south. This spur consists of saline hills that present a very remarkable appearance in places; the rocks are curiously honey-combed by the action of the salt, and the yellowish earthy portion of the hills are fantastically streaked and seamed with white. A trundle of a couple of miles brings me to the summit, from which point I am able to mount, and, with brake firmly in hand, glide smoothly down the eastern slope. After descending about a mile, I am met by a party of travellers who give me friendly warning of deep water a little farther down the mountain. After leaving them, my road follows down the winding bed of a stream that is probably dry the greater part of the year; but during the spring thaws, and immediately after a rain-storm, a stream of brackish, muddy water a few inches deep trickles down the mountain and forms a most disagreeable area of sticky salt mud at the bottom. The streak this morning can more truthfully be described as yellow liquid mud than as water, and both myself and wheel present anything but a prepossessing appearance in ten minutes after starting down its grimy channel. I am, however, congratulating myself upon finding it so shallow, and begin to think that, in describing the water as nearly over their donkeys' backs, the travellers were but indulging their natural propensity as subjects of the Shah, and worthy followers in the footsteps of Ananias.

About the time I have arrived at this comforting conclusion, I am suddenly confronted by a pond of liquid mud that bars my farther progress down the mountain. A recent slide of land and rock has blocked up the narrow channel of the stream, and backed up the thick yellow liquid into a pool of uncertain depth. There is no way to get around it; perpendicular walls of rock and slippery yellow clay rise sheer from the water on either side. There is evidently nothing for it but to disrobe without more ado and try the depth. Besides being thick with mud, the water is found to be of that icy, cutting temperature peculiar to cold brine, and after wading about in it for fifteen minutes, first finding a fordable place, and then carrying clothes and wheel across, I emerge on to the bank formed by the land-slip looking as woebegone a specimen of humanity as can well be imagined. Plastered with a coat of thin yellow mud from head to foot, chilled through and through, and shivering like a Texas steer in a norther, feet cut and bleeding in several places from contact with the sharp rocks, and no clean water to wash off the mud! With the assistance of knife, pocket-handkerchief, and sundry theological remarks which need not be reproduced here, I finally succeed in getting off at least the greater portion of the mud, and putting on my clothes. The discomfort is only of temporary duration; the agreeable warmth of the after-glow exhilarates both mind and body, and with the disappearance of the difficulty to the rear cornea the satisfaction of having found it no harder to overcome.

A little good wheeling is encountered toward the bottom of the pass, and then comes an area of wet salt-flats, interspersed with saline rivulets—those innocent-looking little streamlets the deceptive clearness of which tempts the thirsty and uninitiated wayfarer to drink. Few travellers in desert countries but have been deceived by these innocuous-looking streamlets once, and equally few are the people who suffer themselves to be deceived by their smooth, pellucid aspect a second time; for a mouthful of either strongly saline or alkaline water from one of them creates an impression on the deceived one's palate and his mind that guarantees him to be wariness personified for the remainder of his life. Since a certain experience in the Bitter Creek country, Wyoming, the writer prides himself on being able to distinguish drinkable water from the salty or alkaline article almost as far as it can be seen, and a stream about which the least suspicion is entertained is invariably tasted with gingerly hesitancy to begin with.

Soon after noon I reach the village of Kishlag, where a halt of an hour or so is made to refresh the inner man with tea, raw eggs, and figs—a queer enough bill of fare for dinner, but no more queer than the people from whom it is obtained. Some of my readers have doubtless heard of the Milesian waiter who could never be brought to see any inconsistency in asking the guests of the restaurant whether they would take tea or coffee, and then telling them there was no tea, they would have to take coffee. The proprietor of the little tchai-khan at Kishlag asks me if I want coffee, and then, in strict conformity with the curious inconsistency first discovered and spoken of at Aivan-i-Kaif, he informs me that he has nothing but tea. The country hereabout is evidently the birthplace of Irish bulls; when the ancestors of modern Handy Andys were running wild on the bogs of Connemara, the people of Aivan-i-Kaif and Kishlag were indulging in Irish bulls of the first water.

The crowd at Kishlag are good-natured and comparatively well-behaved. In reply to their questionings, I tell them that I am journeying from Yenghi Donia to Meshed. The New World is a far-away, shadowy realm to these ignorant Persian villagers, almost as much out of their little, unenlightened world as though it were really another planet; they evidently think that in going to Meshed I am making a pilgrimage to the shrine of Imam Riza, for some of them commence inquiring whether or no Yenghi Donians are Mussulmans.

The weather-clerk inaugurates a regular March zephyr in the east, during the brief halt at Kishlag; and in addition to that doubtful favor blowing against me, the road leading out is lumpy as far as the cultivated area extends, and then it leads across a rough, stony plain that is traversed by a network of small streams, similar to those encountered yesterday at Sherifabad. To the left, the abutting front of the Elburz Mountains is streaked and frescoed with salt, that in places vies in whiteness with the lingering-patches of snow higher up; to the right extends the gray, level plain, interspersed with small cultivable areas for a farsakh or two, beyond which lies the great dasht-i-namek (salt desert) that comprises a large portion of the interior of Persia.

Wild asses abound on the dasht-i-namek, and wandering bands of these animals occasionally stray up in this direction. The Persians consider the flesh of the wild donkey as quite a delicacy, and sometimes hunt them for their meat; they are said to be untamable, unless caught when very young, and are then generally too slender-limbed to be of any service in carrying weights. Wild goats abound in the Elburz Mountains; the villagers hunt them also for their meat, but the flesh of the wild goat is said to contribute largely to the prevalence of sore eyes among the people. The Persian will eat wild donkey, wild goat, and the flesh of camels, but only the very poor people—people who cannot afford to be fastidious—ever touch a piece of beef; gusht-i-goosfang (mutton) is the staple meat of the country.

The general aspect of the country immediately south of the Elburz Mountains, beyond the circumscribed area of cultivation about the villages, is that of a desert, desolate, verdureless, and forbidding. One can scarcely realize that by simply crossing this range a beautiful region is entered, where the prospect is as different as is light from darkness. An entirely different climate characterizes the Province of Mazanderan, comprising the northern slopes of these mountains and the Caspian littoral. With a humid climate the whole year round, and the entire face of the country covered with dense jungle, the northern slopes of the Elburz Mountains present a striking contrast to the barren, salt-frescoed foot-hills facing the south hereabout. Here, as at Resht, the moisture from the Caspian Sea does for the province of Mazanderan what similar influences from the Pacific do for California. It makes all the difference between California and Nevada in the one case, and Mazanderan and the desert-like character of Central Persia in the other.

In striking and effective contrast to the general aspect of death and desolation that characterizes the desert wastes of Persia—an effect that is heightened by the ruins of caravansaries or villages, that are seldom absent from the landscape—are the cultivated spots around the villages. Wherever there is a permanent supply of water, there also is certain to be found a mud-built village, with fields of wheat and barley, pomegranate orchards, and vineyards. In a country of universal greenness these would count for nothing, but, situated like islands in the sea of sombre gray about them, they often present an appearance of extreme beauty that the wondering observer is somewhat puzzled to account for; it is the beauty of contrast, the great and striking contrast between vegetable life and death.

These impressions are nowhere more strongly brought into notice than when approaching Aradan, a village I reach about five o'clock. Like almost all Persian towns and villages, Aradan has evidently occupied a much larger area at one time than it does at present; and the mournful-looking ruins of mosques, gateways, walls, and houses are scattered here and there over the plain for a mile before reaching the present limits of habitation. The brown ruins of a house are seen standing in the middle of a wheat-field; the wheat is of that intense greenness born of irrigation and a rich sandy soil, and the mud ruins, dead, desolate, and crumbling to dust, look even more deserted and mournful from the great contrast in color, and from the myriad stems of green young life that wave and nod about them with every passing breeze. The tumble-down windows and doorways form openings through which the blue sky and the green waving sea of vegetation beyond are seen as in a picture, and the ruined mud mosque, its dome gone, its windows and doorways crumbled to shapeless openings, seems like a weather-beaten skeleton of Persia's past, while the ever-moving waves of verdant life about it, seem to be beating against it and persistently assailing it, like waves of the sea beating against an isolated rock.

While engaged in fording a stream on the stony plain between road. The shagird-chapar is with them, on a third "bag of bones," worse, if possible, than the others. Taking the world over, there is perhaps no class of horses that are, subject to so much cruelty and ill-treatment as the chapar horses of Persia, With back raw, ribs countable a hundred yards away, spavined, blind of an eye, fistula, and cursed with every ill that horseflesh in the hands of human brutes is subject to, the chapar horse is liable to be taken out at any hour of the day or night, regardless of previous services being but just finished. He is goaded on with unsparing lash to the next station, twenty, or perhaps thirty miles away, staggering beneath the weight of the traveller, or his servant, with ponderous saddlebags.

This chapar, or post-service, is established along the great highways of travel between Teheran and Tabreez, Teheran and Meshed, and Teheran and Bushire, with a branch route from the Tabreez trail to the Caspian port of Enzeli; the stations vary from four to eight farsakhs apart. Not all the chapar horses are the wretched creatures just described, however, and by engaging beforehand the best horses at each station along the route, certain travellers have made quite remarkable time between points hundreds of miles apart. In addition to horses for himself and servants, the traveller is required to pay for one to carry the shagird-chapar who accompanies them to the next station to bring back the horses. The ordinary charge is one keran a farsakh for each horse. It wouldn't be a Persian institution, however, if there wasn't some little underhanded arrangement on hand to mulct the traveller of something over and above the legitimate charges. Accordingly, we find two distinct measurements of distance recognized between each station—the "chapar distance" and the correct distance. If, for instance, the actual distance is six farsakhs, the "chapar distance" will be seven, or seven and a half; the difference between the two is the chapar-jee's modokal; without modokal there is no question but that a Persian would feel himself to be a miserable, neglected mortal.

Aradan is another telegraph control station, and Mr. Stagno informs me that the telegraph-jee is looking forward to my arrival, and is fully prepared to accommodate me over night; and, furthermore, that all along the line the people of the telegraph towns are eagerly anticipating the arrival of the Sahib, with the marvellous vehicle, of which they have heard such strange stories. Aradan is reached about five o'clock; the road leading into the village is found excellent wheeling, enabling me to keep the saddle while following at the heels of a fleet-footed ryot, who voluntarily guides me to the telegraph-khana. The telegraph-jee is temporarily absent when I arrive, but his farrash lets me inside the office yard, spreads a piece of carpet for me to sit on, and with commendable thoughtfulness shuts out the crowd, who, as usual, immediately begin to collect. The quickness with which a crowd collects in a Persian town has to be seen to be fully comprehended. For the space of half an hour, I sit in solitary state on the carpet, and endure the wondering gaze and the parrot-like chattering of a thin, long row of villagers, sitting astride the high mud wall that encloses three sides of the compound, and during the time find some amusement in watching the scrambling and quarrelling for position. These irrepressible sight-seers commenced climbing the wall from the adjoining walls and houses the moment the farash shut them out of the yard, and in five minutes they are packed as close as books on a shelf, while others are quarreling noisily for places; in addition to this, the roof of every building commanding a view into the chapar-khana compound is swarmed with neck-craning, chattering people.

Soon the telegraph-jee puts in an appearance; he proves to be an exceptionally agreeable fellow, and one of the very few Persians one meets with having blue eyes. He appears to regard it as quite an understood thing that I am going to remain over night with him, and proceeds at once to make the necessary arrangements for my accommodation, without going to the trouble of extending a formal invitation. He also wins my eternal esteem by discouraging, as far as Persian politeness and civility will admit, the intrusion of the inevitable self-sufficients who presume on their "eminent respectability" as loafers, in contradistinction to the half-naked tillers of the soil, to invade the premises and satisfy their inordinate curiosity, and their weakness for kalian, smoking and tea-drinking at another's expense. After duly discussing between us a samovar of tea, we take a stroll through the village to see the old castle, and the umbars that supply the village with water. The telegraph- gee cleared the walls upon his arrival, but the housetops are out of his jurisdiction, and before starting he wisely suggests putting the bicycle in some conspicuous position, as an inducement for the crowd to remain and concentrate their curiosity upon it, otherwise there would be no keeping them from following us about the village. We set it up in plain view on the bala-khana, and returning from our walk, are amused to find the old farrash delivering a lecture on cycling.

The fortress at Aradan is the first one of the kind one sees when travelling eastward from Teheran, but as we shall come to a larger and better preserved specimen at Lasgird, in a couple of days, it will, perhaps, be advisable to postpone a description till then. They are all pretty much alike, and were all built to serve the same purpose, of affording shelter and protection from Turkoman raiders. The Aradan umbars are nothing extraordinary, except perhaps that the conical brick-work roofs are terraced so that one can walk, like ascending stairs, to the summit; and perhaps, also, because they are in a good state of repair —asufficiently unusual thing in a Persian village to merit remark. These umbars are filled by allowing the water to flow in from a street ditch connecting with the little stream to which every village owes its existence; when the umbar is full, a few spadefuls of dirt shut the water off.

The chief occupation of the Eastern female is undoubtedly carrying water; the women of Oriental villages impress the observant Occidental, as people who will carry water-worlds may be created and worlds destroyed; all things else may change, and habits and costumes become revolutionized by the march of time, but nothing will prevent the Oriental female from carrying water, and carrying it in huge earthenware jugs! At any hour of the day—I won't speak positively about the night—women may be seen at the unbars filling large earthenware jugs, coming and going, going and coming. I don't remember ever passing one of these cisterns without seeing women there, filling and carrying away jars of water. No doubt there are occasional odd moments when no women are there, but any person acquainted with village life in the East will not fail to recognize this as simply the plain, unvarnished truth. As the ditch from which the umbar is filled not infrequently runs through half the length of the village first, the personal habits of a Mohammedan population insure that it reaches the umbar in anything but a fit condition for human consumption. But the Koran teaches that flowing water cannot be contaminated or defiled, consequently, when he takes a drink or fills the village reservoir, your thoroughbred Mussulman never troubles his head about what is going on up-stream. The Koran is to him a more reliable guide for his own good than the evidence of all his seven senses combined.

Stagnant pools of water, covered, even this early in the season (March 12th), with green scum, breed fever and mosquitoes galore in Aradan; the people know it, acknowledge it readily, and suffer from it every summer, but they take no steps to remedy the evil; the spirit of public enterprise has dwindled to such dimensions in provincial Persia, that it is no longer equal to filling up a few fever-breeding pools of water in the centre of a village. The telegraph-jee himself acknowledges that the water-holes cause fever and mosquitoes, but, intelligent and enlightened mortal though he be in comparison with his fellow-villagers, when questioned about it, he replies: "Inshalla! the water don't matter; if it is our kismet to take the fever and die, nothing can prevent it; if it is our kismet not to take it, nothing can give it to us." Such unanswerable logic could only originate in the brain of a fatalist; these people are all fatalists, and—as we can imagine—especially so when the doctrine comes in handy to dodge doing anything for the public weal.

All Persian villages, except those clustered about the immediate vicinity of a large city, have some peculiarity of their own to offer in the matter of the people's dress. The pantaloons of any Persian village are not by any means stylish garments, according to Western ideas; but the male bipeds of

Aradan have something really extraordinary to offer, even among the many startling patterns of this garment met with in Eastern lands. To note the quantity of material that enters into the composition of a pair of Aradan pantaloons, would lead an uninitiated person into thinking the people all millionaires, were it not likewise observed that the material is but coarse blue cotton, woven and dyed by the wearer's wife, mother, or sister. One of the most conspicuous features about them is that their shape—if they can truthfully be said to have any shape—seems to be a wild, rambling pattern of our own ideas concerning the shape this garment ought to assume. The legs, instead of being gathered, Oriental fashion, at the ankles, dangle loosely about the feet; and yet it is these same legs that are the chief distinguishing feature of the pants. One of the legs, cut off and sewed up at one end, would make the nicest kind of an eight-bushel grain sack; rather too wide, perhaps, in proportion to the depth, to make a shapely grain sack, but there is no question about the capacity for the eight bushels. No doubt these people would be puzzled to say why they are wearing yards and yards of stuff that is not only useless, but positively in the way, except that it has been the fashion in Aradan from time immemorable to do so. These simple Persian peasants, when they make any pretence of sprucing up, probably find themselves quite as much enslaved by fashion as our very fastidious selves; a wide difference betaken ourselves and them, however, being, that while they cling tenaciously to some prehistoric style of garment, and regard innovations with abhorrence, fashion demands of us to be constantly changing.

The Aradan telegraph-jee is a young man skin-full of piety, rejoicing in the possession of a nice little praying-carpet, a praying-stone from holy Kerbela, the holiest of all except Mecca, and he owns a string of beads of the same soul-comforting material as the stone. During his waking hours he is seldom without the rosary in his hand, passing the holy beads back and forth along the string; and five times a day he produces the praying-stone from its little leathern pouch and goes through the ceremony of saying his prayers, with becoming earnestness. At eventide, when he spreads his praying-carpet and places the little oblong tablet from Kerbela in its customary position, preparatory to commencing his last prayers for the day, it is furthermore ascertained by the compass that he has been pretty accurate in his daily prostrations toward Mecca. With all these enviable advantages—the praying-carpet, the praying-stone, the holy rosary, and the happy accuracy as regards Mecca—the Aradan telegraph-jee is a Mussulman who ought to feel tolerably certain of a rose-garden, a gurgling rivulet, and any number of black-eyed houris to contribute to his happiness in the paradise he hopes to enter beyond the tomb.

Indications have not been wanting during the day that the weather is in anything but a settled condition, and upon waking in the morning I fancy I hear the pattering music of the rain. Fortunately it proves to be only fancy, and the telegraph-jee, assuming the part of a weather-prophet, reassures me by remarking, "Inshalla, am roos, baran neis" (Please God, it will not rain to-day). Being a Persian, he says this, not because he has any particular confidence in his own predictions, but because his idea of making himself agreeable is to frame his predictions by the measurement of what he discovers to be my wishes.

The road into Aradan led me through one populous cemetery, and the road out again leads me through another; beyond the cemetery it follows alongside a meandering streamlet that flows, sluggishly along over a bed of deep gray mud. The road is lumpy but ridable, and I am pedalling serenely along, happy in the contemplation of better roads ahead than I had yesterday, when one of those ludicrous incidents happen that have occurred at intervals here and there all along my journey. A party of travellers have been making a night march from the east, and as we approach each other, a wary kafaveh-carrying mule, suspicious about the peaceful character of the mysterious object bearing down toward him, pricks up his ears, wheels round, and inaugurates confusion among his fellows, and then proceeds to head them in a determined bolt across the stream. Unfortunately for the women in the kajavehs, the mud and water together prove to be deeper than the mule expected to find them, and the additional fright of finding himself in a well-nigh swamped condition, causes him to struggle violently to get out again. In so doing he bursts whatever fastenings may have bound him and his burden together, scrambles ashore, and leaves the kajavehs floating on the water!

The women began screaming the moment the mule wheeled round and bolted, and now they find themselves afloat in their queer craft, these characteristic female signals of distress are redoubled in energy; and they may well be excused for this, for the kajavehs are gradually filling and sinking; it was never intended that kajavehs should be capable of acting in the capacity of a boat. The sight of their companion's difficulties has the effect of causing the other mules to change their minds about crossing the stream, and almost to change their minds about indulging in the mulish luxury of a scare; and fortunately the charvadars of the party succeed in rescuing the kajavehs before they sink. Nobody is injured, beyond the women getting wet; no damage is done worth mentioning, and as the two heroines of the adventure emerge from their novel craft, their garments dripping with water, their doleful looks are rewarded with unsympathetic merriment from the men. Few have been my wheeling days on Asian roads that have not witnessed something in the shape of an overthrow or runaway; so far, nobody has been seriously injured by them, but I have sometimes wondered whether it will be my good fortune to complete the bicycle journey around the world without some mishap of the kind, resulting in broken limbs for the native and trouble for myself.

After a couple of miles the road and the meandering stream part company, the latter flowing southward and the road traversing a flat, curious, stone-strewn waste; an area across which one could step from one large boulder to another without touching the ground. Once beyond this, and the road develops into several parallel trails of smooth, hard gravel, that afford as good, or better, wheeling than the finest macadam. While spinning at a highly satisfactory rate of speed along these splendid paths, a small herd of antelopes cross the road some few hundred yards ahead, and pass swiftly southward toward the dasht-i-namek. These are the first antelopes, or, for that matter, the first big game I have encountered since leaving the prairies of Western Nebraska. The Persian antelope seems to be a duplicate of his distinguished American relative in a general, all-round sense; he is, if anything, even more nimble-footed than the spring-heeled habitue of the West, possesses the same characteristic jerky jump, and hoists the same conspicuous white signal of retreat. He is a decidedly slimmer-built quadruped, however, than the American antelope; the body is of the same square build, but is sadly lacking in plumpness, and he seems to be an altogether lankier and less well-favored animal. For this constitutional difference, he is probably indebted to the barren and inhospitable character of the country over which he roams, as compared with the splendid feeding-grounds of the—Far West. The Persians sometimes hunt the antelope on horseback, with falcons and greyhounds; the falcons are taught to fly in advance and attack the fleeing antelopes about the head, and so confuse them and retard their progress in the interest of the pursuing hounds and horsemen.

The little village of Deh Namek is reached about mid-day, where my ever-varying bill of fare takes the shape of raw eggs and pomegranates. Deh Namek is too small and unimportant a place to support a public tchai-khan; but along the Meshed pilgrim road the villagers are keenly alive to the chance of earning a stray keran, and the advent of one of those inexhaustible keran-mines, a "Sahib," is the signal for some enterprising person, sufficiently well-to-do to own a samovar, to get up steam in it and prepare tea.

East of Deh Namek, the wheeling continues splendid for a dozen miles, traversing a level desert on which one finds no drinkable water for about twenty miles. Across the last eight miles of the desert the road is variable, consisting of alternate stretches of ridable and unridable ground, the latter being generally unridable by reason of sand and loose gravel, or thickly strewn flints. More antelopes are encountered east of Deh Namek; at one place, particularly, I enjoy quite a little exciting spurt in an effort to intercept a band that are heading across my road from the Elburz foot-hills to the desert. The wheeling is here magnificent, the spurt develops into a speed of fourteen miles an hour; the antelopes see their danger, or, at all events, what they fancy to be danger, and their apprehensions are not by any mean lessened by the new and startling character of their pursuer. Wild antelopes are timid things at all times, and, as may be readily imagined, the sight of a mysterious glistening object, speeding along at a fourteen or fifteen mile pace to intercept them, has a magical effect upon their astonishing powers of locomotion. They seem to fly rather than run, and to skim like swallows over the surface of the level plain rather than to touch the ground; but they were some distance from the road when they first realized my terrifying presence, and I am within fifty yards of the band when they flash like a streak of winged terror across the road. These antelopes do not cease their wild flight within the range of my powers of observation; long after the mousy hue of their bodies has rendered their forms indistinguishable in the distance from the sympathetic coloring of the desert, rapidly bobbing specks of white betray the fact that their supposed narrow escape from the vengeful pursuit of the bicycle has given them a fright that will make them suspicious of the Meshed pilgrim road for weeks.

"Deh Namek" means "salt village;" and it derives its name from the salt flats that are visible to the south of the road, and the general saline character of the country round about. Salt enters very largely into the composition of the mountains that present a solid and fantastically streaked front a few miles to the north; and the streams flowing from these mountains are simply streams of brine, whose mission would seem to be conveying the saline matter from the hills, and distributing it over the flats and swampy areas of the desert. These flats are visible from the road, white, level, and impressive; like the Great American Desert, Utah, as seen from the Matlin section house, and described in a previous chapter (Vol. I.), it looks as though it might be a sheet of water, solidified and dead.

At the end of the twenty miles one comes to a small and unpretentious village and an equally small and unpretentious wayside tchai-khan, both owing their existence to a stream of fresh water as small and unpretentious as themselves. Beyond this cheerless oasis stretches again the still more cheerless desert, the rivulets of undrinkable salt water, the glaring white salt-flats to the south, and the salt-encrusted mountains to the north. The shameless old party presiding at the tchai-khan evidently realizes the advantages of his position, where many travellers from either direction, reaching the place in a thirsty condition, have no choice but between his decoction and cold water. Instead of the excellent tea every Persian knows very well how to make, he serves out a preparation that is made, I should say, chiefly from camelthorn buds plucked within a mile of his shanty; he furthermore illustrates in his own methods the baneful effects of being without the stimulus of a rival, by serving it up in unwashed glasses, and without noticing whether it is hot or cold.

Much loose gravel prevails between this memorable point and Lasgird, and while trundling laboriously through it I am overtaken by a rain-storm, accompanied by violent wind, that at first encompasses me about in the most peculiar manner. The storm comes howling from the northwest and advances in two sections, accompanied by thunder and lightning; the two advancing columns seem to be dense masses of gray cloud rolling over the surface of the plain, and between them is a clear space of perhaps half a mile in width. The rain-dispensing columns pass me by on either side with muttering rolls of thunder and momentary gleams of lightning, enveloping me in swirling eddies of dust and bewildering atmospheric disturbances, but not a drop of rain. It is plainly to be seen, however, that the two columns are united further west, and that it behooves me to don my gossamer rubbers; but before being overtaken by the rain, the heads of the flying columns are drawn together, and for some minutes I am surrounded entirely by sheets of falling moisture and streaming clouds that descend to the level plain and obscure the view in every direction; and yet the clear sky is immediately above, and the ground over which I am walking is perfectly dry. After the first violent burst there is very little wind, and the impenetrable walls of vapor encompassing me round about at so near a distance, and yet not interfering with me in any way, present a most singular appearance. While appreciating the extreme novelty of the situation, I can scarce say in addition that I appreciate the free play of electricity going on in all directions, and the irreverent manner in which the nickeled surface of the bicycle seems to glint at it and defy it; on the contrary, I deem it but an act of common discretion to place the machine for a short time where the lightning can have a fair chance at it, without involving a respectful non-combatant in the destruction. In half an hour the whole curious affair is over, and nothing is seen but the wild-looking tail-end of the disturbance climbing over a range of mountains in the southeast.

The road now edges off in a more northeasterly course, and by four o'clock leads me to the base of a low pass over a jutting spur of the mountains. At the base of the spur, a cultivated area, consisting of several wheat-fields and terraced melon-gardens, has been rescued from the unproductive desert by the aid of a bright little mountain stream, whose wild spirit the villagers of Lasgird have curbed and tamed for their own benefit, by turning it from its rocky, precipitous channel, and causing it to descend the hill in a curious serpentine ditch. The contour of the ditch is something like this: ~~~~~~~~~~; it brings the water down a pretty steep gradient, and its serpentine form checks the speed of its descent to an uniform and circumspect pace. The road over the pass leads through a soft limestone formation, and here, as in similar places in Asia Minor, are found those narrow, trench-like trails, worn by the feet of pilgrims and the pack-animal traffic of centuries, several feet deep in the solid rock. On a broad cultivated plain beyond the pass is sighted the village of Lasgird, its huge mud fortress, the most conspicuous object in view, rising a hundred feet above the plain.

CHAPTER III

PERSIA AND THE MESHED PILGRIM ROAD

A mile or so through the cultivated fields brings me to the village just in time to be greeted by the shouts and hand-clapping of a wedding procession that is returning from conducting the bride to the bath. Men and boys are beating rude, home-made tambourines, and women are dancing along before the bride, clicking castanets, while a crowd of at least two hundred villagers, arrayed in whatever finery they can muster for the occasion, are following behind, clapping their hands in measured chorus. This hand-clapping is, I believe, pretty generally practiced by the villagers all over Central Asia on festive occasions. As a result of riding for the crowd, I receive an invitation to take supper at the house of the bridegroom's parents. Having obtained sleeping quarters at the chapar-khana, I get the shagird-chapar to guide me to the house at the appointed hour, and arrive just in time for supper. The dining-room is a low-ceiled apartment, about thirty feet long and eight wide, and is dimly lighted by rude grease lamps, set on pewter lamp-stands on the floor.

Squatting on the floor, with their backs to the wall, about fifty villagers form a continuous human line around the room. These all rise simultaneously to their feet as I am announced, bob their heads simultaneously, simultaneously say, "Sahib salaam," and after I have been provided with a place, simultaneously resume their seats. Pewter trays are now brought in by volunteer waiters, and set on the floor before the guests, one tray for every two guests, and a separate one for myself. On each tray is a bowl of mast (milk soured with rennet—the "yaort" of Asia Minor), a piece of cheese, one onion, a spoonful or two of pumpkin butter and several flat wheaten cakes. This is the wedding supper. The guests break the bread into the mast and scoop the mixture out with their fingers, transferring it to their mouths with the dexterity of Chinese manipulating a pair of chop-sticks; now and then they take a nibble at the piece of cheese or the onion, and they finish up by consuming the pumpkin butter. The groom doesn't appear among the guests; he is under the special care of several female relations in another apartment, and is probably being fed with tid-bits from the henna-stained fingers of old women, who season them with extravagant and lying stories of the bride's beauty, and duly impress upon him his coming matrimonial responsibilities.

Supper eaten and the dishes cleared, an amateur luti from among the villagers produces a tambourine and castanets, and, taking the middle of the room, proceeds to amuse the company by singing extempore love songs in praise of the bride and groom to tambourine accompaniment and pendulous swayings of the body. Pretending to be carried away by the melodiousness and sentiment of his own productions, he gradually bends backward with hands outstretched and castanets jingling, until his head almost touches the floor, and maintains that position while keeping his body in a theatrical tremor of delight. This is the finale of the performance, and the luti comes and sets his skull-cap in front of me for a present; my next neighbor, the bridegroom's father, takes it up and hands it back with a deprecatory wave of the hand; the luti replies by promptly setting it down again; this time my neighbor lets it remain, and the luti is made happy by a coin.

Torchlight processions to the different baths are now made from the house of both bride and groom, for this is the "hammam night," devoted to bathing and festivities before the wedding-day. Torches are made with dry camelthorn, the blaze being kept up by constant renewal; a boy, with a lighted candle, walks immediately ahead of the bridegroom and his female relations, and a man with a farnooze brings up the rear. Nobody among the onlookers is permitted to lag behind the man with the farnooze, everybody being required to either walk ahead or alongside. The tambourine-beating and shouting and hand-clapping of the afternoon is repeated, and every now and then the procession stops to allow one or two of the women to face the bridegroom and favor him with an exhibition of their skill in the execution of the hip-dance.

The bridal procession is coming down another street, and I stop to try and obtain a glimpse of the bride; but she is completely enveloped in a flaming red shawl, and is supported and led by two women. There seems to be little difference in the two processions, except the preponderance of females in the bride's party; everything is arranged in the same order, and women dance at intervals before the bride as before the groom.

It begins raining before I retire for the night; it rains incessantly all night, and is raining heavily when I awake in the morning. The weather clears up at noon, but it is useless thinking of pushing on, for miles of tenacious mud intervene between the village and the gravelly desert; moreover, the prospect of the fine weather holding out looks anything but reassuring. The villagers are all at home, owing to the saturated condition of their fields, and I come in for no small share of worrying attention during the afternoon. A pilgrim from Teheran turns up and tells the people about my appearance before the Shah; this increases their interest in me to an unappreciated extent, and, with glistening eyes and eagerly rubbing fingers, they ask "Chand pool Padishah?" (How much money did the King give you?) "I showed the Shah the bicycle, and the Shah showed me the lions, and tigers, and panthers at Doshan Tepe," I tell them; and a knowing customer, called Meshedi Ali, enlightens them still further by telling them I am not a luti to receive money for letting the Shah-in-Shah see me ride. Still, luti or no luti, the people think I ought to have received a present. I am worried to ride so incessantly that I am forced to seek self-protection in pretending to have sprained my ankle, and in returning to the chapar-khana with a hypocritical limp. I station myself ostensibly for the remainder of the day on the bala-khana front, and busy myself in taking observations of the villagers and their doings.

Time was, among ourselves, or more correctly, among our ancestors, when blood-letting was as much the professional calling of a barber as scraping chins or trimming hair, and when our respected beef-eating and beer-drinking forefathers considered wholesale blood-letting as a well-nigh universal panacea for fleshly ills. In travelling through Persia, one often observes things that suggest very strikingly those "good old days" of Queen Bess. The citizens of Zendjan offering the Shah a present of 60,000 tomans, as an inducement not to visit their city, as they did when he was on his way to Europe, has a true Elizabethan ring about it, a suggestion of the Virgin Queen's rabble retinue travelling about, devouring and destroying, and of justly apprehensive citizens, seeing ruin staring them in the face, petitioning their regal mistress to spare them the dread calamity of a royal visit.

The ancient Zoroastrian barber, no doubt, bled his patients and customers on the public streets of Persian towns, for the benefit of their healths, when we pinned our pagan faith on Druidical incantations and mystic rites and ceremonies; his Mussulman descendants were doing the same thing when we at length arrived at the same stage of enlightenment, and the Persian wielder of razor and tweezers to-day performs the same office as belonging to his profession. From my vantage point on the bala-khana of the Lasgird chapar station, I watch, with considerable interest, the process of bleeding a goodly share of the male population of the village; for it is spring-time, and in spring, every Persian, whether well or unwell, considers the spilling of half a pint or so of blood very necessary for the maintenance of health.

The village barber, with his arms bared, and the flowing, o'er-ample legs of his Aradan-Lasgird pantaloons tucked up at his waist, like a washerwoman's skirt, a bunch of raw cotton in lieu of lint under his left arm, and his keen-edged razor, looks like a man who thoroughly realizes and enjoys the importance of the office he is performing, as from the bared arm or open mouth of one after the other of his neighbors he starts the crimson stream. The candidates for the barber's claret-tapping attentions bare their right arms to the shoulder, and bind for each other a handkerchief or piece of something tightly above the elbow, and the barber deftly slits a vein immediately below the hollow of the elbow-joint, pressing out the vein he wishes to cut by a pressure of the left thumb. The blood spurts out, the patient looks at the squirting blood, and then surveys the onlookers with a "who-cares?—I-don't" sort of a grin. He then squats down and watches it bleed about a half-pint, occasionally working the elbow-joint to stimulate the flow. Half a pint is considered about the correct quantity for an adult to lose at one bleeding; the barber then binds on a small wad of cotton.

Now and then a customer gives the barber a trifling coin by way of backsheesh, but the great majority give nothing. In a mere village like Lasgird, these periodical blood-lettings by the barber are, no doubt, regarded as being all in the family, rather than of professional services for a money consideration. The communal spirit obtains to a great extent in village life throughout both Asia Minor and Persia; nevertheless backsheesh would be expected in Persia from those able to afford it. Some few prefer being bled in the roof the mouth, and they all squat on their hams in rows, some bleeding from the arm, others from the mouth, while the inevitable crowd of onlookers stand around, gazing and giving advice. While the barber is engaged in binding on the wad of cotton, or during any interval between patients, he inserts the handle of the razor between his close-fitting skull-cap and his forehead, letting the blade hang down over his face, edge outward; a peculiar disposition of his razor, that he would, no doubt, be entirely at a loss to account for, except that he is following the custom of his fathers. As regards the customs of his ancestors, whose trade or profession he invariably follows, the Asiatic is the most conservative of mortals. "What was good enough for my father and grandfather," he says, "is certainly good enough for me;" and earnestly believing in this, he never, of his own accord, thinks of changing his occupation or of making improvements.

Later in the afternoon I descend from the bala-khana and take a strolling look at the village, and with the shagird-chapar for guide, pay a visit to the old fortress, the conspicuous edifice seen from the trail-worn limestone pass. Forgetting about my subterfuge of the sprained ankle, I wander forth without the aforementioned limp; but the people seem to have forgotten it as completely as I had; at all events, nobody makes any comments. A ripple of excitement is caused by a two-storied house collapsing from the effects of the soaking rains, an occurrence by no means infrequent in the spring in a country of mud-built houses. A crowd soon appears upon the scene, watching, with unconcealed delight, the spectacle of tumbling roof and toppling wall, giving vent to their feelings in laughter and loud shouts of approval, like delighted children, whenever another bulky square of mud and thatch comes tumbling down. Fortunately, nobody happens to be hurt, beyond the half-burying in the debris of some donkeys, which are finally induced to extricate themselves by being vigorously bombarded with stones. No sympathy appears to be given on the part of the spectators, and evidently nothing of the kind is expected by the tenants of the tumbling house; the wailing women, and the look of consternation on the face of the men who barely escaped from the falling roof, seem to be regarded by the spectators as a tomasha (show), to be stared at and enjoyed, as they would stare at and enjoy anything not seen every day; on the other hand, the occupants of the house regard their misfortune as kismet.

Returning to the chapar-ktiana, I get the shayird to pilot me into and round about the fortress. It is rapidly falling to decay, but is still in a sufficiently good state of preservation to show thoroughly its former strength and conformation. The fortress is a decidedly massive building, constructed entirely of mud and adobe bricks, a hundred feet high, of circular form, and some two hundred yards in circumference. The disintegrated walls and debris of former towers form a sloping mound or foundation about fifty feet in height, and from this the perpendicular walls of the castle rise up, huge and ugly, for another hundred feet. Following a foot-trail up the mound-like base, we come to a low, gloomy passage-way leading into the interior of the fort. A door, composed of one massive stone slab, that nothing less than a cannon-shot would shatter, guards the entrance to this passage, which is the only accessible entrance to the place. Following it along for perhaps thirty yards, we emerge upon a scene of almost indescribable squalor—a scene that instantly suggests an overcrowded "rookery" in the tenement-house slums of New York. The place is simply swarming with people, who, like rabbits in an old warren, seem to be moving about among the tumble-down mud huts, anywhere and everywhere, as though the old ruined fortress were burrowed through and through, or that the people now moved through, over, under, and around the remnants of what was once a more orderly collection of dwellings, having long forsaken regular foot-ways.

The inhabitants are ragged and picturesque, and meandering about among them, on the most familiar terms, are hundreds of goats. Although everything is in a more or less dilapidated condition, huts or cells still rise above each other in tiers, and the people clamber about from tier to tier, as if in emulation of their venturesome four-footed associates, who are here, we may well imagine, in as perfect a paradise as vagrom goatish nature would care for or expect. At a low estimate, I should place the present population of the old fortress at a thousand people, and about the same number of goats. In the days when the bold Turkoman raiders were wont to make their dreaded damans almost up to the walls of Teheran, and such strongholds as this were the only safeguard of out-lying villagers, the interior of Lasgird fortress resembled a spacious amphitheatre, around which hundreds of huts rose, tier above tier, like the cells of a monster pigeon-house, affording shelter in times of peril to all the inhabitants of Lasgird, and to such refugees as might come in. At the first alarm of the dreaded man-stealers' approach, the outside villagers repaired to the fortress with their portable property; the donkeys and goats were driven inside and occupied the interior space, and the massive stone door was closed and barricaded. The villagers' granaries were inside the fortress, and provisions for obtaining water were not overlooked; so that once inside, the people were quite secure against any force of Turkomans, whose heaviest arms were muskets.

The suggestion of an amphitheatre, as above described, is quite patent at the present day, in something like two or three hundred tiered dwellings; in the days of its usefulness there must have been a thousand. Thanks to the Russian occupation of Turkestan, there is no longer any need of the fortress, and the present population seem to be occupying it at the peril of having it some day tumble down about their ears; for, massive though its walls most certainly are, they are but mud, and the people are indifferent about repairs. Failing to surprise the watchful villagers in their fields or outside dwellings, the baffled marauders would find confronting them fifty feet of solid mud wall without so much as an air-hole in it, rising sheer above the mound-like foundation, and above this, tiers of rooms or cells, from inside which archers or musketeers could make it decidedly interesting for any hostile party attempting to approach. This old fortress of Lasgird is very interesting, as showing the peaceful and unwarlike Persian ryot's method of defending his life and liberty against the savage human hawks that were ever hovering near, ready to swoop down and carry him and his off to the slave markets of Khiva and Bokhara. These were times when seed was sown and harvest garnered in fear and trembling, for the Turkoman raiders were adepts at swooping down when least expected, and they rode horses capable of making their hundred miles a day over the roughest country. (Incredible as this latter fact may seem, it is, nevertheless, a well-known thing in Central Asia that the Turkoman's horse is capable of covering this remarkable distance, and of keeping it up for days.)

A thunder-storm is raging violently and drenching everything as I retire for the night, dampening, among other things, my hopes of getting away from Lasgird for some days; for between the village and the gravelly, and consequently always traversable, desert, are some miles of slimy clay of the kind that in wet weather makes an experienced cycler wince to think of crossing. The floor of the bala-khana forms once again my nocturnal couch; but the temperature lowers perceptibly as the night advances and the rain continues, and toward morning it changes into snow. The doors and windows of my room are to be called doors and windows only out of courtesy to a rude, unfinished effort to imitate these things, and the floor, at daybreak, is nicely carpeted with an inch or so of "the beautiful snow," and a four-inch covering of the same greets my vision upon looking outside.

Determined to make the best of the situation, I remove my quarters from the cold and draughty bala-khana to the stable, and send the shagird-chapar out in quest of camel-thorn, bread, eggs, and pomegranates, thinking thus to obtain the luxury of a bit of fire and something to eat in comparative seclusion. This vain hope proves that I have not even yet become thoroughly acquainted with the Persians. No sooner does my camel-thorn blaze begin to crackle and the smoke to betray the whereabouts of a fire, than shivering, blue-nosed villagers begin to put in their appearance, their backs humped up and their bare ankles and slip-shod feet adding not a little to the general aspect of wretchedness that seems inseparable from Persians in cold weather.

And these are the people who, during a gleam of illusory sunshine yesterday, were so nonchalantly parting with their blood—of which, by the by, your bread and cucumber eating, and cold water drinking Persian has little enough, and that little thin enough at any time. These rag-bedecked, shivering wretches hop up on the raised platform where the fire is burning and squat themselves around it in the most sociable manner; and under the thawing process of passing their hands through the flames, poking the coals together, and close attention to the details of keeping it burning, they quickly thaw out in more respects than one. Fifteen minutes after my fire is lighted, the spot where I anticipated a samovar of tea and a pomegranate or two in peace, is occupied by as many Persians as can find squatting room, talking, shouting, singing, and kalian-smoking, meanwhile eagerly and expectantly watching the preparations for making tea. Preferring to leave them in full possession rather than be in their uncongenial midst, I pass the time in promenading back and forth behind the horses. After walking to and fro a few times, the, to them, singular performance of walking back and forth excites their easily-aroused curiosity, and the wondering attention of all present becomes once again my unhappy portion. An Asiatic's idea of enjoying himself in cold weather is squatting about a few coals of fire, making no physical exertion whatever beyond smoking and conversing; and the spectacle of a Ferenghi promenading back and forth, when he might be following their example of squatting by the fire, is to them a subject of no little wonder and speculation.

The redeeming feature of my enforced sojourn at Lasgird is the excellence of the pomegranates, for which the place is famous, and of which there seems an abundance left over through the winter. A small quantity of seedless pomegranates, a highly valued variety, are grown here at Lasgird, but they are all sent to Teheran for the use of the Shah and his household, and are not to be obtained by anyone. It has been a raw, disagreeable day, and at night I decide to sleep in the stable, where it is at least warmer, though the remove is but a compromise by which one's olfactory sensibilities are sacrificed in the interest of securing a few hours' sleep.

An unexpected, but none the less welcome, deliverance appears on the following morning in the shape of a frost, that forms on the sticky mud a crust of sufficient thickness to enable me to escape across to the welcome gravel beyond the Lasgird Plain ere it thaws out. Thus on the precarious path of a belated morning frost, breaking through here, jumping over there, I leave Lasgird and its memories of wedding processions, and blood-letting, its huge mud fortress, its pomegranates, and its discomforts.

Three miles of mostly ridable gravel bring me to another village, and to four miles of horrible mud in getting through its fields and over its ditches. A raw wind is blowing, and squally gusts of snow come scudding across the dreary prospect—a prospect flanked on the north by cold, gray hills, and the face of nature generally furrowed with tell-tale lines of winter's partial dissolution. While trundling through this village, both myself and bicycle plastered to a well-nigh unrecognizable state with mud, feeling pretty thoroughly disgusted with the weather and the roads, an ancient-looking Persian emerges from a little stall with a last season's muskmelon in hand, and advancing toward me, shouts, "H-o-i" loud enough to wake the seven sleepers. Shouting "H-o-i!!" at a person close enough to hear a whisper, as loud as though he were a good mile away, is a peculiarity of the Persians that has often irritated travellers to the pitch of wishing they had a hot potato and the dexterity to throw it down their throats; and in my present unenviable condition, and its accompanying unenviable frame of mind, I don't mind admitting that I mentally relegated this vociferous melon-vender to a place where infinitely worse than hot potatoes would overtake him. Knowing full well that a halt of a single minute would mean a general mustering of the population, and an importuning rabble following me through the unridable mud, I ignore the old melon-man's foghorn efforts to arrest my onward progress; but he proves a most vociferous and persistent specimen of his class. Nothing less than a dozen exclamation points can give the faintest idea of how a "hollering" Persian shouts "H-o-i."

Seven miles over very good gravel, and my road leads into the labyrinth of muddy lanes, ditches, and water-holes, tumble down walls, and disorderly-looking cemeteries of the suburbs of Semnoon. In traversing the cemeteries, one cannot help observing how many of the graves are caved in by the rains and the skeletons exposed to view. Mohammedans bury their dead very shallow, usually about two feet, and in Persia the grave is often arched over with soft mud bricks; these weaken and dissolve after the rains and snows of winter, and a cemetery becomes a place of exposed remains and of pitfalls, where an unwary step on what appears solid ground may precipitate one into the undesirable company of a skeleton. By the time Semnoon is reached the day has grown warmer, and the sun favors the cold, dismal earth with a few genial rays, so that the blooming orchards of peach and pomegranate that brighten and enliven the environs of the city, and which suggest Semnoon to be a mild and sheltered spot, seem quite natural, notwithstanding the patches of snow lying about. The crowds seem remarkably well behaved as I trundle through the bazaar toward the telegraph office, the total absence of missiles being particularly noticeable. The telegraph-jee proves to be a sensible, enlightened fellow, and quite matter-of-fact in his manner for a Persian; apart from his duty to the Governor and a few bigwigs of the place, whom it would be unpardonable in him to overlook or ignore, he saves me as much as possible from the worrying of the people.

Prince Anushirvan Mirza, Governor of Semnoon, Damghan, and Shahrood, is the Shah's cousin, son of Baahman Mirza, uncle of the Shah, and formerly Governor of Tabreez. Baahman Mirza was discovered intriguing with the Russians, and, fearing the vengeance of the Shah, fled from the country; seeking an asylum among the Russians, he is now—if not dead—a refugee somewhere in the Caucasus. But the father's disgrace did not prejudice the Shah against his sons, and Prince Anushirvan and his sons are honored and trusted by the Shah as men capable of distinguishing between the friends and enemies of their country, and of conducting themselves accordingly.

The Governor's palace is not far from the north gate of the city, and after the customary round of tea and kalians, without which nothing can be done in Persia, he walks outside with his staff to a piece of good road in order to see me ride to the best advantage. (As a specimen of Persian extravagance—to use a very mild term—it may be as well to mention here as anywhere, that the Governor telegraphed to his son, acting as his deputy at Shahrood, that he had ridden some miles with me out of the city!)

During the evening one of the Governor's sons, Prince Sultan Madjid Mirza, comes in with a few leading dignitaries to spend an hour in chatting and smoking. This young prince proves one of the most intelligent Persians I have met in the country; besides being very well informed for a provincial Persian, he is bright and quick-witted. Among the gentlemen he brings in with him is a man who has made the pilgrimage to Mecca via "Iskenderi" (Alexandria) and Suez, and has, consequently, seen and ridden on the Egyptian railway. The Prince has heard his description of this railway, and the light thus gained has not unnaturally had the effect of whetting his curiosity to hear more of the marvellous iron roads of Frangistan; and after exhausting the usual programme of queries concerning cycling, the conversation leads, by easy transition, to the subject of railways.

"Do they have railways in Yenghi Donia?" questioned the Prince.

"Plenty of railways; plenty of everything," I reply.

"Like the one at Iskenderi and Stamboul?"

"Better and bigger than both these put together a hundred times over; the
Iskenderi railroad is very small."

Nods and smiles of acquiescence from Prince and listeners follow this statement, which show plainly enough that they consider it a pardonable lie, such as every Persian present habitually indulges in himself and thinks favorably of in others.

"Railroads are good things, and Ferenghis are very clever people," says the Prince, renewing the subject and handing me a handful of salted melon seeds from his pocket, meanwhile nibbling some himself.

"Yes; why don't you have railroads in Iran? You could then go to Teheran in a few hours."

The Prince smiles amusingly at the thought, as though conscious of railroads in Persia being a dream altogether too bright to ever materialize, and shaking his head, says: "Pool neis" (we have no money).

"The English have money and would build the railroad; but, 'Mollah neis' —Baron Reuter?—you know Baron Reuter—' Mollah neis,' not 'pool neis.'"

The Prince smiles, and signifies that he is well enough aware where the trouble lies; but we talk no more of railroads, for he and his father and brothers belong to the party of progress in Persia, and the triumph of priests and old women over the Shah and Baron Reuter's railway is to them a distressful and humiliating subject.

The late lamented O'Donovan, of "To the Merve" fame, used to make Semnoon his headquarters while dodging about on the frontier, and was personally known to everyone present. Semnoon is celebrated for the excellence of its kalian tobacco, and O'Donovan was celebrated in Semnoon for his love of the kalian. This evening, in talking about him, the telegraph-jee says that "when he pulled at the kalian he pulled with such tremendous eagerness that the flames leaped up to the ceiling, and after three whiffs you couldn't see anybody in the room for smoke!"

The telegraph-jee's farrash builds a good wood fire in a cozy little room adjoining the office; blankets are provided, an ample supper is sent around from the telegraph-jee's house, and what is still better appreciated, I am left to enjoy these substantial comforts without so much as a single spectator coming to see me feed; no one comes near me till morning.

The morning breaks cold and clear, and for some six miles the road is very fair wheeling; after this comes a gradual inclination toward a jutting spur of hills; the following twenty miles being the toughest kind of a trundle through mud, snow-fields, and drifts. This is a most uninviting piece of country to wheel through, and it would seem but little less so to traverse at this time of the year with a caravan of camels, two or three of these animals being found exhausted by the roadside, and a couple of charvadars encountered in one place skinning another, while its companion is lying helplessly alongside watching the operation and waiting its own turn to the same treatment. It is said to be characteristic of a camel that, when he once slips down, cold and weary, in the mud, he never again tries to regain his feet. The weather looks squally and unsettled, and I push ahead as rapidly as the condition of the ground will permit, fearing a snow-storm in the hills.

About three p.m. I arrive at the caravansarai of Ahwan, a dreary, inhospitable place in an equally dreary, inhospitable country. Situated in a region of wind and snow and bleak, open hills, the wretched serai of Ahwan is remembered as a place where the keen, raw wind seems to come whistling gleefully and yet maliciously from all points of the compass, seemingly centring in the caravansarai itself; these winds render any attempt to kindle a fire a dismal failure, resulting in smoke and watery eyes. Here I manage to obtain half-frozen bread and a few eggs; after an ineffectual attempt to roast the latter and thaw out the former, I am forced to eat them both as they are; and although the sun looks ominously low, and it is six farsakhs to the next place, I conclude to chance anything rather than risk being snow-bound at Ahwan. Fortunately, after about five miles more of snow, the trail emerges upon a gravelly plain with a gradual descent from the hills just crossed to the lower level of the Damghan plain. The favorable gradient and the smooth trails induce a smart pace, and as the waning daylight merges into the soft, chastened light of a cloud-veiled moon, I alight at the village and serai of Gusheh.

There are at the caravansarai a number of travellers, among them a moujik of the Don, travelling to Teheran and beyond in company with a Tabreez Turk. The Russian peasant at once invites me to his menzil in the caravansarai; and although he looks, if anything, a trifle more indifferent about personal cleanliness than either a Turkish or Persian peasant, I have no alternative but to accept his well-meant invitation. At this juncture, when one's thoughts are swayed and influenced by an appetite that the cold day and hard tugging through the hills have rendered well-nigh uncontrollable, a prosperous-looking Persian traveller, returning from a pilgrimage to Meshed with his wives, family, and servitors, quite a respectable-sized retinue, emerges from the seclusion of his quarters to see the bicycle.

Of course he requests me to ride, sending his link-boys to bring out all the farnoozes to supplement fair Luna's coy and inefficient beams; and after the performance, the old gentleman promises to send me round a dish of pillau. In due time the promised pillau comes round, an ample dish, sufficient to satisfy even my present ravenous appetite, and after this he sends round tea, lump sugar, and a samovar. The moujik turns to and gets up steam in the samovar, and over tiny glasses of the cheering but non-intoxicating beverage, he sings a Russian regimental song, and his comrade, the Tabreez Turk, warbles the praises of Stamboul. But although they make merry over the tea, methinks both of them would have made still merrier over something stronger, for the moujik puts in a good share of the evening talking about vodka consumed at Shahrood, and smacking his lips at the retrospective bliss embodied in its consumption; while the Turk from Tabreez catches me aside and asks mysteriously if my packages contain any "raki" (arrack). Like the Ah wan caravansarai, the one at Gusheh seems to draw the chilly winds from every direction, and I arise from a rude couch, made wretchedly uncomfortable by draughts, the attacks of insects, and the persistent determination of a horse to use my prostrate form as a rest for his nose-bag, to find myself the possessor of a sore throat.

Persian travellers are generally up and off before daylight, and the clicking noise (Persian curry-combs are covered with small rings that make a rattling noise when being used) of currying horses begins as early as three o'clock. The attendants of the old gentleman of happy remembrance in connection with last night's pillau and samovar, have been busy for two hours, and his taktrowan and kajauehs are already occupied and starting, when by the first gleam of awakening dawn I mount and wheel eastward. A shallow, unbridged stream obstructs my path but a short distance from Gusheh, and I manage to get in knee-deep in trying to avoid the necessity of removing my footgear; I then wander several miles off my road to an outlying village. This happy commencement of a new day is followed by a variable road leading sometimes over stony or gravelly plains where the wheeling varies through all the stages of goodness, badness, and indifference, and sometimes through grazing grounds and cultivable areas adjoining the villages.

Scattered about the grazing and arable country are now small towers of refuge, loop-holed for defense, to which ryots working in the fields, or shepherds tending their flocks, fled for safety in case of a sudden appearance of Turcoman marauders. But a few years ago men hereabouts went to plough, sow, or reap with a gun slung at their backs, and a few of them reaching the shelter of one of these compact little mud towers were able, through the loop-holes, to keep the Turcomans at bay until relief arrived. The towers are of circular form, about twenty feet high and fifteen in diameter; the entrance is a very small doorway, often a mere hole to crawl into, and steps inside lead to the summit; some are roofed in near the top, others are mere circular walls of mud. On grazing grounds a lower wall often encompasses the tower, fencing in a larger space that formed a corral for the flocks; the shepherds then, while defending themselves, were also defending their sheep or goats. In the more exposed localities these little towers of refuge are often but a couple of hundred yards apart, thickly dotting the country in all directions, while watch-towers are seen perched on peaks and points of vantage, the whole scene speaking eloquently of the extraordinary precautions these poor people were compelled to adopt for the preservation of their lives and property. No wonder Russian intrigue makes headway in Khorassan and all along the Turco-inan-Perso frontier, for the people can scarcely help being favorably impressed by the stoppage of Turcoman deviltry in their midst, and the wholesale liberation of Persian slaves.

The town of Damghan is reached near noon, and I am not a little gratified to learn that the telegraph-jee has been notified of my approach, and has stationed his farrash at the entrance to the bazaar, so that I should have no trouble in finding the office. This augurs well for the reception awaiting me there, and I am accordingly not surprised to find him an exceptionally affable youth, proud of a word or two of English he had somehow acquired, and of his knowledge of how to properly entertain a Ferenghi. This latter qualification assumes the eminently practical, and, it is needless to add, acceptable form of a roast chicken, a heaping dish of pillau, and sundry other substantial proofs of anticipatory preparations. The telegraph-jee takes great pleasure in seeing roast chicken mysteriously disappear, and the dish of pillau gradually diminish in size; in fact, the unconcealed satisfaction afforded by these savory testimonials of his cook's abilities give him such pleasure that he urges me to remain his guest for a day and rest up. But Shahrood is only forty miles away, and here I shall have the pleasure of meeting Mr. McIntyre, before mentioned as line-inspector, who is making his temporary headquarters at that city. Moreover, angry-looking storm-dogs have accompanied the sun on his ante-meridian march to-day, and such experience as mine at Lasgird has the effect of making one, if not weather-wise, at least weather-wary.

In approaching Damghan, long before any other indications of the city appear, twin minarets are visible, soaring above the stony plain like a pair of huge pillars; these minars belong to the same mosque, and form a conspicuous landmark for travellers and pilgrims in approaching Damghan from any direction; at a distance they appear to rise up sheer from the barren plain, the town being situated in a depression. Six farsakhs from Damghan is the village of Tazaria, noted in the country round about for the enormous size of the carrots grown there; the minarets of Damghan and the extraordinary size of the Tazaria vegetables furnish the material for a characteristic little Eastern story, current among the inhabitants.

Finding that people came from far and near to see the graceful minarets of Damghan, and that nobody came to see Tazaria, the good people of that neglected village became envious, and they reasoned among themselves and said: "Why should Damghan have two minarets and Tazaria none?" So they gathered together their pack-donkeys, their ropes and ladders, and a large company of men, and reached Damghan in the silence and darkness of the night, intending to pull down and carry off one of the minarets and erect it in Tazaria. The ropes were fastened to the summit of the minar, but at the first great pull the brick-work gave way and the top of the tall minaret came tumbling down with a crash and clatter, killing several of its would-be removers. The Damghan people turned out, and after hearing the unhappy Tazarians' laments, some sarcastic citizen gave them a few carrot-seeds, bidding them go home and sow them, and they could grow all the minarets they wanted. The carrots grew famously, and the villagers of Tazaria, instead of the promised minarets, found themselves in possession of a new and useful vegetable that fetched a good price in the Damghan bazaars. The Damghanians, meeting a Tazarian ryot coming in with a donkey-load of these huge carrots, cannot resist twitting him regarding the minars; but the now practical Tazarians no longer mourn the absence of minarets in their village, and when twitted about it, reply: "We have more minarets than you have, but our minarets grow downward and are good to eat."

During the afternoon I pass many ruined villages and castles, said to have been destroyed by an earthquake many years ago. Some few natives find remunerative employment in excavating and washing over the dirt and debris of the ruined castles, in which they find coins, rubies, agates, turquoise, and women's ornaments; sometimes they unearth skeletons with ornaments still attached. The sun shines out warm this afternoon, and its genial rays are sufficiently tempting to induce the jackals to emerge from their hiding-places and bask in its beaming smiles on the sunny side of the ruins. Wherever there are ruins and skeletons and decay in Eastern lands—and where are there not?—there also is sure to be found the prowling and sneakish-looking jackal.

Shelter, and the usual rude accommodation, supplemented on this occasion by a wandering luti and his vicious-looking baboon, as also a company of riotous charvadars, who insist on singing accompaniments to the luti's soul-harrowing tom-toming till after midnight, are obtained at the caravansarai of Deh Mollah. From Deh Mollah it is only a couple of farsakhs to Shahrood, and after the first three miles, which is slightly upgrade and not particularly smooth, it is downgrade and very fair wheeling the remainder of the distance. The road forks a couple of miles from Shahrood, and while I am entering by one road, Mr. McIntyre is leaving on horseback by the other to meet me, guessing, from word received from Damghan, that I must have spent last night at Deh Mollah, and would arrive at Shahrood this morning.

Only those who have experienced it know anything of the pleasure of two Europeans meeting and conversing in a country like Persia, where the habits and customs of the natives are so different, and, to most travellers, uncongenial, and only to be tolerated for a time.

I have met Mr. McIntyre in Teheran, so we are not total strangers, which, of course, makes it still more agreeable. After the customary interchange of news, and the discussion of refreshments, Mr. McIntyre hands me a telegram from Teheran, which bears a date several days old. It is from the British Legation, notifying me that permission is refused to go through the Turcoman country; an appendage from the Charge d'Affaires suggests that I repair to Astrakhan and try the route through Siberia. And this, then, is the result of General Melnikoff's genial smiles and ready promises of assistance; after providing myself with proper money and information for the Turkestan route, on the strength of the Russian Minister's promises, I am overtaken, when three hundred miles away, with a veto against which anything I might say or do would be of no avail!

Sultan Ahmed Mirza, a sou of Prince Anushirvan, is deputy governor of Shahrood, responsible to his father; and ere I have arrived an hour the usual request is sent round for a "tomasha," the word now used by people wanting to see me ride, and which really means an exhibition. His place is found in a brick court-yard with the usual central tank, and the airy rooms of the building all opening upon it, and once again comes the feeling of playing a rather ridiculous role, as I circle awkwardly around the tank over very uneven bricks, and around short corners where an upset would precipitate me into the tank—amid, I can't help thinking, "roars of laughter." The Prince is very lavish of his flowery Persian compliments, and says, "You English have now left nothing more to do but to bring the dead back to life." In the court-yard my attention is called to a set of bastinado poles and loops, and Mr. McIntyre asks the Prince if he hasn't a prisoner on hand, so that he can give us a tomasha in return for the one we are giving him; but it is now the Persian New Year, and the prisoners have all been liberated.

Here, gentle reader, in Shahrood—but it now behooves us to be dark and mysterious, and deal in hints and whispers, for the Persian proprieties must not be ruthlessly violated and then as ruthlessly exposed to satisfy the prying curiosity of far off Frangistan that would never do.

Behold, then, Mr. McIntyre absent; behold all male humans absent save myself and a couple of sable eunuchs, whose smooth, whiskerless faces betray inward amusement at the extreme novelty of the situation, and we all alone between the high brick walls that encircle the secrecy of an inner court—and yet not all alone, fortell it in whispers—some half-dozen shrouded female forms are clustered together in one corner. Yashmaks are drawn aside, and plump oval faces and bright eyes revealed, faces brown and soft of outline, eyes black, large and lustrous, with black lines skillfully drawn to make them look still larger, and lashes deeply stained to impart love and languor to their wondrous depths. Whisper it not in Gath, and tell it not in the streets of Frangistan, that the wondrous asp-i-awhan has proved an open sesame capable of revealing to an inquisitive and all-observant Ferenghi the collective charms of a Persian swell's harem!

We can imagine these ladies in the seclusion of the zenana hearing of the Ferenghi and his wonderful iron horse, and overwhelmed with feminine curiosity, with much coaxing and promising, obtaining reluctant consent for a strictly secret and decorous tomasha, with covered faces and no one present but the attendant eunuchs and the Ferenghi, who, fortunately, will soon leave the country, never to return. Mohammedan women are merely overgrown children, and the promise of strict decorousness is forgotten or ignored the moment the tomasha begins; and the fun and the wickedness of removing their yashmaks in the presence of a Ferenghi is too rare an opportunity to be missed, and, no doubt, furnishes them with material for amusing conversation for many a day after. Rare fun these ladies think it to uncover their olive faces and let the Ferenghi see their beauty; the eunuchs are generally indulgent to their charges whenever they can safely be so, and on this occasion they content themselves with looking on and saying nothing. After seeing me ride, the ladies cluster boldly around and examine the bicycle, chatting freely among themselves the while concerning its capabilities; but some of the younger ladies regard me with fully as much curiosity as the bicycle, for never before did they have such an opportunity of scrutinizing a Ferenghi.

And now, while granted the privilege of this little revelation, we must be very careful not to reveal the secret of whose harem we have seen unveiled, and whose inner court our paran wheels have pressed; for the whirligig of time brings about strange things, and apparently trifling things that have been indiscreetly published by travellers in books at home, have sometimes found their way back to the far East, and caused embarrassment and chagrin to people who treated them with hospitality and respect.

CHAPTER IV

THROUGH KHORASSAN

Shahrood is at the exit from the mountains of the caravan route from Asterabad, Mazanderan, and the Caspian coast. The mountains overlooking it are bare and rocky. A good trade seems to be done by several firms of Russian-Armenians in exporting wool, cotton, and pelts to Russia, and handling Russian iron and petroleum. But for the iniquitous method of taxation, which consists really of looting the producing classes of all they can stand, the volume of trade here might easily be tenfold what it is.

Shahrood is, or rather was, one of the "four stations of terror," Mijamid, Miandasht, and Abassabad being the other three, so called on account of their exposed position and the consequent frequency of Turcoman attacks. Even nowadays they have their little ripples of excitement; rumors of Turcoman raids are heard in the bazaars, and news was brought in and telegraphed to Teheran a week ago that fifteen thousand sheep had been carried off from a district north of the mountains. Word comes back that a regiment of soldiers is on its way to chastise the Turcomans and recover the property; what really will happen, will be a horde of soldiers staying there long enough to devour what few sheep the poor people have left, and then returning without having seen, much less chastised, a Turcoman. The Persian Government will notify the Russian Minister of the misdoings of the Turcomans, and ask to have them punished and the sheep restored; the Russian Minister will reply that these particular Turcomans were Persian subjects, and nothing further will be done.

Mr. McIntyre is a canny Scot, a Royal Engineer, and weighs fully three hundred pounds; but with this avoirdupois he is far from being inactive, and together we ramble up the Asterabad Pass to take a look at the Bostam Valley on the other side. The valley isn't much to look at; no verdure, only a brown, barren plain, surrounded on all sides by equally brown, barren mountains. In the evening the Prince sends round a pheasant, and shortly after calls himself and partakes of tea and cigarettes,

I accept Mr. McIntyre's invitation to remain and rest up, but only for another day, my experience being that, when on the road, one or two days' rest is preferable to a longer period; one gets rested without getting out of condition. We take a stroll through the bazaar in the morning, and call in at the wine-shop of a Russian-Armenian trader named Makerditch, who keeps arrack and native wine, and sample some of the latter. In his shop is a badly stuffed Mazanderaii tiger, and the walls of the private sitting-room are decorated with rude, old-fashioned prints of saints and scriptural scenes. It is now the Persian New Year, and bright new garments and snowy turbans impart a gay appearance to the throngs in the bazaar, for everybody changed his wardrobe from tip to toe on eid-i-noo-roos (evening before New Year's Day), although the "great unwashed" of Persian society change never a garment for the next twelve months. Considering that the average lower-class Persian puts in a good share of this twelve months in the unprofitable process of scratching himself, one would think it must be an immense relief for him to cast away these old habiliments with all their horrid load of filth and vermin, and don a clean, new outfit; but the new ones soon get as thickly tenanted as the old; and many even put the new garments on over certain of the old ones, caring nothing for comfort and cleanliness, and everything for appearance. The Persian New Year's holiday lasts thirteen days, and on the evening of the thirteenth day everybody goes out into the fields and plucks flowers and grasses to present to his or her friends.

Governors of provinces who retain their position in consequence of having sent satisfactory tribute to the Shah, and ruled with at least a semblance of justice, get presents of new robes on New Year's Day, and those who have been unfortunate enough to lose the royal favor get removed: New Year's Day brings either sorrow or rejoicing to every Persian official's house.

The morning of my departure opens bright and warm after a thunderstorm the previous evening, and Mr. McIntyre accompanies me to the outskirts of the city, to put me on the right road to Mijamid, my objective point for the day, eleven farsakhs distant. The streets are, of course, muddy and unridable, and ere the suburbs are overcome a messenger overtakes us from the Prince, begging me to return and drink tea with him before starting.

"Tell the Prince, the sahib sends salaams, but cannot spare the time to return," replies my companion, who knows Persian thoroughly. "You must come," says the messenger, "for the Khan of Bostam has arrived to pay the New Year's salaam to the Prince, and the Prince wants you to show him the bicycle."

"'Must come!' Tell the Prince that when the sahib gets fairly started, as he is now, with his bicycle, he wouldn't turn back for the Shah himself."

The messenger looks glum and crestfallen, as though very reluctant to return with such a message, a message that probably sounds to him strangely disrespectful, if not positively treasonable; but he sees the uselessness of bandying words, and so turns about, feeling and looking very foolish, for he addressed us very boldly and confidently before the whole crowd when he overtook us.

A few small streams have to be crossed on leaving Shahrood for the east; splendid rivulets of clear, cold water in which there ought to be trout. After these streams the road launches at once on to a level camel-thorn plain, the gravelled surface of which provides excellent wheeling. An outlying village and caravanserai is passed through at a couple of farsakhs, where, as might be expected in the "district of terror," are hundreds of the little towers of refuge. This village would be in a very exposed position, and it looks as though it is but just now being rebuilt and repopulated after a period of ruin and desertion. Beyond this village the towers of refuge and other signs of human occupation disappear; the uncultivated desert reigns supreme on either hand; but the wheeling continues fairly good, although a strong headwind somewhat impedes my progress. Beyond the level plain and the lower hills to the north are the snowy heights of the Elburz range; a less ambitious range of mountains forms a barrier some twenty miles to the south, and in the distant southeast there looms up a dark, massive pile that recalls at a glance memories of Elk Mountain, Wyoming; though upon a closer inspection there is no doubt but that the densely wooded slopes of our old acquaintance of the Rockies would be found wanting.

Twenty miles of this level plain is traversed, and I find myself gazing curiously at a range of mica-flecked hills off to the right. These hills present a very curious appearance; the myriads of flakes of mica scattered all about glitter and glint in the bright sunlight as if they might be diamonds, and it requires but an easy effort of the imagination to fancy one's self in some strange, rich land of the "gorgeous East," where precious jewels are scattered about like stones. These mica-spangled hills bear about the same relation to what one's imagination might conceive them to be as the "gorgeous East" as it actually exists does to the "gorgeous East" we read of in fairytales.

Beyond the mica hills, I pass through a stretch of abandoned cultivation, where formerly existed fields and ditches, and villages with an abundance of portable property tempted Turkoman raiders to guide their matchless chargers hither. But small outlying settlements hereabout were precarious places to live in, and the persistent damans generally caused them to be abandoned entirely from time to time.

The road has averaged good to-day, and Mijamid is reached at four o'clock. Seeking the shelter of the chapar-khana, that devoted building is soon surrounded by a new-dressed and accordingly a good-natured and vociferous crowd shouting—"Sowar shuk! sowar shuk! tomasha! tomasha!"

As I survey the grinning, shouting multitude from my retreat on the roof, and note the number of widely-opened mouths, the old wicked thoughts about hot potatoes and dexterity in throwing them persist in coming to the fore. Several scrimmages and quarrels occur between the chapar-jee and his shagirds, and the crowd, who persist in invading the premises, and the tumult around is something deafening, for it is holiday times and the people feel particularly self-indulgent and disinclined for self-denial. In the midst of the uproar, from out the chaotic mass of rainbow-colored costumes, there forms a little knot of mollahs in huge snowy turbans and flowing gowns of solid blue or green, and at their head the gray-bearded patriarchal-looking old khan of the village in his flowered robe of office from the governor. These gay-looking, but comparatively sober-sided representatives of the village, endeavor to have the crowd cease their clamorous importunities—an attempt, however, that results in signal failure—and they constitute themselves a delegation to approach me in a respectful and decorous manner, and ask me to ride for the satisfaction of themselves and the people.

The profound salaams and good taste of these eminently respectable personages are not to be resisted, and after satisfying them, the khan promises to provide me with supper, which at a later hour turns up in the form of the inevitable dish of pillau.

Two miles on the road next morning and it begins raining; at five miles it develops into a regular downpour, that speedily wets me through. A small walled village is finally reached and shelter obtained beneath its ample portals, a place that seems to likewise be the loafing-place of the village. The entrance is a good-sized room, and here on wet days the men can squat about and smoke, and at the same time see everything that passes on the road. The village is defended by a strong mud wall some thirty feet high, and strengthened with abutting towers at frequent intervals; the only entrance is the one massive door, and inside there is plenty of room for all the four-footed possessions of the people; the houses are the usual little mud huts with thatched beehive roofs, built against the wall. The flocks of goats and sheep are admitted inside every evening, and taken out again to graze in the morning; the appearance of the interior is that of a very filthy, undrained, and utterly neglected farmyard, and as no breath of wind ever passes through it, or comes any nearer the ground than the top of the thirty-foot wall, living in its reeking, pent-up exhalations must be something abominable.

Such a place as this in Persia would be fairly swarming with noxious insect life, of which fleas would be the most tolerable variety, and two-thirds of the people would be suffering from chronic ophthalmia. This little village, doubtless, had enough to do a few years ago to maintain its existence, even with its remarkably strong walls; and on the highest mountain peaks round about they point out to me their watch-towers, where sentinels daily scanned the country round for the wild horsemen they so much dreaded. Four men and three women among the little crowd gathered about me here, are pointed out as having been released from slavery by the Russians, when they captured Khiva and liberated the Persian slaves and sent them home. Every village and hamlet along this part of the country contains its quota of returned captives who, no doubt, entertain lively recollections of being carried off and sold.

Soon after my arrival here, a little, weazen-faced, old seyud, in a threadbare and badly-faded green gown, comes hobbling through the rain and the mahogany-colored slush of the village yard to the gate. Everybody rises respectfully as he comes in, and the old fellow, accustomed to having this deference paid him by everybody about him, and wishing to show courtesy to a Ferenghi, motions for me to keep seated. Seeing that I had no intention of rising, this courtesy was somewhat superfluous, but the incident serves to show how greatly these simple villagers are impressed with the idea of a seyud's superiority, to say nothing of the seyud's assumption of the same. They explain to me that the little, unwashed, unkempt, and well-nigh unclad specimen of humanity examining the bicycle is a seyud, with the manner of people pointing out a being of unapproachable superiority. Still, looking at the poor old fellow's rags, and remembering that it is new year and the time for a change of raiment, one cannot help thinking, "Old fellow, you evidently come in for more resect, after all, than material assistance, and would, no doubt, willingly exchange a good deal of the former for a little of the latter." Still, one must not be too confident of this; the bodily requirements of a wrinkled old seyud would be very trifling, while his egotism would, on the other hand, be insufferable. This is a grazing village chiefly, and the gravelly desert comes close up to the walls, so that there is no difficulty about pushing on immediately after it ceases raining.

Two farsakhs of variable wheeling through a belt of low hills and broken country, and two more over the level Miandasht Plain, and the caravanserai of Miandasht is reached. Here the village, the telegraph office and everything is enclosed within the protecting walls of an immense Shah Abbas caravanserai, a building capable of affording shelter and protection to five thousand people. In the old—and yet not so very old—dangerous days, it was necessary, for safety, that travellers and pilgrims should journey together through this section of country in large caravans, otherwise disaster was sure to overtake them; and Shah Abbas the Great built these huge caravanserais for their accommodation. In deference to the memory of this monarch as a builder of caravanserais all over the country, any large serai is nowadays called a Shah Abbas caravanserai, whether built by him or not. Certainly not less than three hundred pack-camels, besides other animals, are resting and feeding, or being loaded up for the night march as I ride up, their myriad clanging bells making a din that comes floating across the plain to meet me as I approach.

Miandasht is the first place in Khorassan proper, and among the motley gathering of charmdars, camel-drivers, pilgrims, travellers, villagers and hangers-on about the serai, are many Khorassanis wearing huge sheepskin busbies, similar to the head-gear of the Roumanians and Tabreez Turks of Ovahjik and the Perso-Turkish border. Most of these busbies are black or brown, but some affect a mixture of black and white, a piebald affair that looks very striking and peculiar.

The telegraph-jee here turns out to be a person of immense importance in his own estimation, and he has evidently succeeded in impressing the same belief upon the unsophisticated minds of the villagers, who, apparently, have come to regard him as little less than "monarch of all he surveys." True, there isn't much to survey at Miaudasht, everything there being within the caravanserai walls; but whenever the telegraph-jee emerges from the seclusion of his little office, it is to blossom forth upon the theatre of the crowd's admiring glances in the fanciful habiliments of a la-de-da Persian swell. Very punctilious as regards etiquette, instead of coming forth in a spontaneous manner to see who I am and look at the bicycle, he pays me a ceremonious visit at the chapar-khana half an hour later. In this visit he is preceded by his farrash, and he walks with a magnificent peacock strut that causes the skirts of his faultless roundabout to flop up and down, up and down, in rhythmic accompaniment to his steps. Apart from his insufferable conceit, however, he tries to make himself as agreeable as possible, and after tea and cigarettes, I give him and the people a tomasha, at the conclusion of which he asks permission to send in my supper.

The room in which I spend the evening is a small, dome-roofed apartment, in which a circular opening in the apex of the dome is expected to fill the triple office of admitting light, ventilation, and carrying off smoke from the fire; the natural consequence being that the room is dark, unventilated, and full of smoke. Now and then some determined sightseer on the roof fills this hole up completely with his head, in an effort to peer down through the smoke and obtain a glimpse of myself or the bicycle, or a mischievous youngster, unable to resist the temptation, drops down a stone.

The shagird-chapar here is a man who has been to Askabad and seen the railroad; and when the inevitable question of Russian versus English marifet (mechanical skill) comes up, he endeavors to impress upon the open-mouthed listeners the marvellous character of the locomotive. "It is a wonderful atesh-gharri" (fire-wagon), he would say, "and runs on an awhan rah (iron road); the charvadar puts in atesh and ob. It goes chu, chu! chu!! ch-ch-ch-chu-ch-u-u-u!!! spits fire and smoke, pulls a long-khylie long-caravan of forgans with it, and goes ten farsakhs an hour." But in order to thoroughly appreciate this travelled and highly enlightened person's narrative, one must have been present in the smoke-permeated room, and by the nickering light of a camel-thorn fire have watched the gesticulations of the speaker and the rapt attention of the listeners; must have heard the exclamations of "Mashal-l-a-h!" escape honestly and involuntarily from the parted lips of wonder-stricken auditors as they endeavored to comprehend how such things could possibly be. And yet there is no doubt that, five minutes afterward, the verdict of each listener, to himself, was that the shagird-chapar, in describing to them the locomotive, was lying like a pirate—or a Persian—and, after all, they couldn't conceive of anything more wonderful than the bicycle and the ability to ride it, and this they had seen with their own eyes.

It is the change of the moon, and a most wild-looking evening; the sun sets with a fiery forge glowing about it, and fringing with an angry border the banks of darksome clouds that mingle their weird shapes with the mountain masses to the west, the wind sighs and moans through the archways and menzils of the huge caravanserai, breathing of rain and unsettled weather. These warning signals are not far in advance, for a drenching rain soaks and saturates everything during the night, converting the parallel trails of the pilgrim road into twenty narrow, silvery streaks, that glisten like trails of glass ahead, as I wheel along them to meet the newly-risen sun. It is a morning of hurrying, scudding clouds and fitful sunshine, but fresh and bracing after the rain; a country of broken hills and undulating road is reached in an hour; the broken hills are covered with blossoming shrubs and green young camel-thorn, in which birds are cheerily piping.

Six farsakhs bring me to Abbasabad, the last of the four stations of terror. A lank villager is on the lookout a couple of miles west of the place, the people having been apprised of my coming by some travellers who left Miandasht yesterday evening. Tucking the legs of his pantaloons in his waistband, leaving his legs bare and unencumbered, he follows me at a swinging trot into the village, and pilots me to the caravanserai. The population of the place are found occupying their housetops, and whatever points of vantage they can climb to, awaiting my appearance, their curiosity having been wrought to the highest pitch by their informant's highly exaggerated accounts of what they might expect to see. The prevailing color of the female costume is bright red, and the swarms of these gayly-dressed people congregated on the housetops, and mingled promiscuously with the dark gray of the mud walls and domes, makes a picture long to be remembered.

And long also to be remembered is the reception awaiting me inside the caravanserai yard—the surging, pushing, struggling, shouting mob, among whom I notice, with some wonderment and speculation, a far larger proportion of blue-eyed people than I have hitherto seen in Persia. Upon inquiry it is learned that Abbasabad is a colony of Georgians, planted and subsidized here by Shah Abbas the Great, as a check on the Turkomans, whose frequent alamans rendered the roads hereabout well-nigh impassable for caravans. These warlike mountaineers were brought from the Caucasus and colonized here, with lands, exemption from taxes, and given an annual subsidy. They were found to be of good service as a check on the Turkomans, but were not much of an improvement upon the Turkomans themselves in many respects. As seen in the caravanserai to-day, they seem a turbulent, headstrong crowd of people, accustomed to be petted, and to do pretty much as they please.

At the caravanserai is a traveller who says he hails from the Pishin Valley, and he produces a certificate in English, recommending him as a stone mason. The certificate settles all doubts of his being from India, for were one to meet an Hindostani in the classic shades of purgatory itself, he would immediately produce a certificate recommending him for something or other. As the crowd surge and struggle for some position around me where they can enjoy the exquisite delight of seeing me sip tiny glasses of scalding hot tea, prepared by the enterprising individual who met me two miles out, the Pishin Valley man tries to look amused at them, and to rise superior to the situation, as becomes a person to whom a Sahib, and whatever wonderful things he may possess, are nothing extraordinary. The crowd seem very loath to let such an extraordinary thing as the bicycle and its rider depart from among them so soon, although at the same time anxious to see me speed along the smooth, straight trails that fortunately lead directly from the caravanserai eastward. Scores of the shouting, yelling mob race, bare-footed and bare-legged, over the stones and gravel alongside the bicycle, until I can put on a spurt and out-distance them, which I take care to do as soon as practicable, thankful to get away and eat the bread pocketed in disgust at the caravanserai in the peace and quietude of the desert.

Beyond Abbasabad my road skirts Mazinan Lake to the north, passing between the slimy mud-flats of the lake shore and the ever-present Elburz foot-hills, and then through several wholly ruined or partially ruined villages to Mazinan, where I arrive about sunset, my wheel yet again a mass of mud, for the Mazinan lake country is a muddy hole in spring. A drizzling rain ushers in the dusky shades of the evening, as I repair to the chaparkhana, a wretched hole, in a most dilapidated condition. The balakhana is little better than being out of doors; the roof leaks like a colander, the windows are mere unglazed holes in the wall, and the doors are but little better than the windows. It promises to be a cold, draughty, comfortless night, and the prospects for supper look gloomy enough in the light of smoky camel-thorn and no samovar to make a cup of tea.

Such is the cheerless prospect confronting me after a hard day's run, when, soon after dark, a man arrives with a thrice-welcome invitation from a Russian officer, who he says is staying at the caravanserai. The officer, he says, has pillau, kabobs, wine, plenty of everything, and would be glad if I would bring my machine and come and accept his hospitality for the night. Under the circumstances nothing could be more welcome news than this; and picturing to myself a pleasant evening with a genial, hospitable gentleman, I take the bicycle down the slippery and broken mud stairway, and follow my guide through drizzling rain and darkness, over ditches and through miry byways, to the caravanserai.

The officer is found squatting, Asiatic-like, on his menzil floor, his overcoat over his shoulders. He is watching his cook broiling kabobs for his supper. It is a cheery, hopeful prospect, the glowing charcoal fire sparkling in response to the vigorous waving of half a saddle-flap, the savory, sizzling kabobs and the carpeted menzil, in comparison with the dreary tumble-down place I have just left. My first impression of the officer himself, however, is scarcely so favorable as my impression of the picture in which he is set—the picture as just described; a sinister leer characterizes the expression of his face, and what appears like a nod, with an altogether unnecessary amount of condescension in it, characterizes his greeting. Hopping down to the ground, lamp in hand, he examines the bicycle minutely, and then indirectly addressing the by-standers, he says, "Pooh! this thing was made in Tiflis; there's hundreds of them in Tiflis." Having delivered himself of this lying statement, he hops up on the menzil front again and, without paying the slightest attention to me, resumes his squatting position at the fire, and his occupation of watching the preparations of his cook. Nothing is more evident to me than that he had never before seen a bicycle, and astounded at this conduct on the part of an officer who doubtless thinks himself a civilized being, even though he might not understand anything of our own conception of an "officer and a gentleman," I begin looking around for an explanation from the fellow who brought me the invitation, thinking there must be some mistake. The man has disappeared and is nowhere to be found.

The chapar-jee accompanied us to the caravanserai, and seeing that this man has bolted, and that the Russian officer's intentions toward me are anything but hospitable, he calls the missing man—or the officer, I don't know which—a pedar suktar (son of a burnt father), and suggests returning to the cold comfort of the bala-khana. My own feelings upon realizing that this wretched, unscrupulous Muscovite has craftily designed and executed this plan for no other purpose but to insult and humiliate one whom he took for granted to be an Englishman, in the eyes of the Persian travellers present, I prefer to pass over and leave to the reader's imagination. After sleeping on it and thinking it over, early next morning I returned to the caravanserai, bent on finding the fellow who brought the invitation, giving him a thrashing, and seeing if the officer would take it up in his behalf. In the morning, the cossacks said he had gone away; whether gone away or hiding somewhere in the caravanserai, he was nowhere to be found; which perhaps was just as well, for the affair might have ended in bloodshed, and in a fight the chances would have been decidedly against myself.

This incident, disagreeable though it be to think of, is instructive as showing the possibilities for mean and contemptible action that may lurk beneath the uniform of a Russian officer. Russian officers as a general thing, however, it is but fair to add, would show up precisely the reverse of this fellow, under similar circumstances, being genial and hospitable to a fault; still, I venture that in no other army in the world, reckoning itself civilized, could be found even one officer capable of displaying just such a spirit as this.

The unwelcome music of pattering rain and flowing water in the concert I have to sit and listen to all the forenoon, and a glance outside is rewarded by the dreariest of prospects. The landscape as seen from my lone and miserable lookout, consists of gray mud-fields and gray mud-ruins, wet and slimy with the constant rains; occasional barley-fields mosaic the dreary prospect with bright green patches, but across them all—the mud-flats, the ruins, and the barley-fields—the driving rain sweeps remorselessly along, and the wind moans dismally. There is only one corner of my room proof against the drippings from the roof, and through the wretched apologies for doors and windows the driving rain comes in. Everything seems to go wrong in this particular place. I obtain tea and sugar, but there is no samovar, and the chapar-jee attempts to make it in an open kettle; the result is sweetened water, lukewarm and smoky. I then send for pomegranates, which turn out to be of a sour, uneatable variety; but worse than all is the dreary consciousness of being hopelessly imprisoned for an uncertain period.

It grows gradually colder, and toward noon the rain changes to snow; the cold and the penetrating snow drive me into the shelter of the ill-smelling stables. It blows a perfect hurricane all the afternoon, accompanied by fitful squalls of snow and hail, and the same programme continues the greater part of the night. But in the morning I am thankful to discover that the wind has dried the surface sufficiently to enable me to escape from my mud-environed prison and its uncongenial associations.

Before getting many miles from Mazinan, I encounter the startling novelty of streams of liquid mud, rolling their thick, yellow flood over the plain in treacly waves, travelling slowly, like waves of molten lava. The mud is only a few inches deep, but the streams overspread a considerable breadth of country, as my road is some miles from where they leave the mountains, and they seem to have no well-defined channels to flow in. A stream of slimy, yellow mud, two hundred yards wide, is a most disagreeable obstacle to overcome with a bicycle; but confined in narrow, deep channels, the conditions would be infinitely worse. It is a dreary and forbidding stretch of country hereabout, the carcasses of camels that have dropped exhausted by the roadside, are frequently passed, and jackals feasting on them slink off at my approach, watch my progress past with evident impatience, and then return again to their feast. Occasional stretches of very fair wheeling are passed over, and at six farsakhs I reach Mehr, the usual combination of brick caravanserai and mud village.

Here a halt is made for tea and such rude refreshments as are obtainable, consuming them in the presence of the usual sore-eyed and miserable-looking crowd; more than one poor wretch appealing to me to cure his rapidly-failing sight. A gleam of warm sunshine brightens my departure from Mehr, and after shaking off several following horsemen, the going seems quite pleasant, the wheeling being very good indeed. The mountains off to the left are variegated and beautiful on the lower and intermediate slopes, and are crested with snow; scudding cloudlets, whose multiform shadows are continually climbing up and over the mountains, produce a pleasing kaleidoscopic effect, and here and there a sunny, glistening peak rises superior to the changeful scenes below.

Sheepskin-busbied shepherds are tending flocks of very peculiar-looking sheep on this plain, the first of the kind I have noticed. The fatty continuation of the body, popularly regarded as an abnormal growth of tail, is wanting; but what is lacking in this respect is amply compensated for in the pendulous ears, these members hanging almost to the ground; they have a goatish appearance generally, and may possibly be the result of a cross. Herds of antelope also frequent this locality, which by and by develops into a level mud-plain that affords smooth and excellent wheeling, and over which I take the precaution of making the best time possible, conscious that a few minutes' rain would render it impassable for a bicycle; and wild wind-storms are even now careering over it, accompanied by spits of snow and momentary squalls of hail.

A lone minar, looming up directly ahead like a tall factory chimney, indicates my approach to Subzowar. The minaret is reached by sunset; it turns out to be a lone shrine of some imam, from which it is yet two farsakhs to Subzowar. The wheeling from this point, however, is very good, and I roll into Subzowar, or, at least, up to its gate, for Subzowar is a walled city, shortly after dark. Sherab (native wine) they tell me, is obtainable in the bazaar, but when I inquire the price per bottle, with a view of sending for one, several eager aspirants for the privilege of fetching it shout out different prices, the lowest figure mentioned being three times the actual price. Being rather indifferent about the doubtful luxury of drinking wine for the amusement of an eagerly curious crowd, which I know only too well beforehand will be my unhappy portion, I conclude to chagrin and disappoint the whole dishonest crew by doing without. One gets so thoroughly disgusted with the ever-present trickery, dishonesty, and prying, unrestrained curiosity of the ragged, sore-eyed and garrulous crowds that gather about one at every halting place, that a person actually comes to prefer a mere crust of bread in peace by a road-side pool to the best a city bazaar affords.

A well-dressed individual makes his salaam and intrudes his person upon the scene of my early preparations to depart, on the following morning, and, when I start, takes upon himself the office of conducting me through the labyrinthian bazaar and to the gate of exit beyond. I am wondering somewhat who this individual may be, and wherefore the officiousness of his demeanor to the crowd at our heels; but his mission is soon revealed, for on the way out he pilots me into the court-yard of the Reis, or mayor of the city. The Reis receives me with the glad and courteous greeting of a person desirous of making himself agreeable and of creating a favorable impression; trays of sweetmeats are produced, and tea is served up in little porcelain cups.

As soon as tea and sweetmeats and kalians appear on the board, mollahs and seyuds mysteriously begin to put in an appearance likewise, filing noiselessly in and taking their places near or distant from the Reis, according to their respective rank and degree of holiness. My observations everywhere in the Land of the Lion and the Sun all tend to the conclusion that whenever and wherever a samovar of tea begins to sing its cheery and aromatic song, and the soothing hubble-bubble of the kalian begins telling its seductive tale of solid comfort and social intercourse, a huge green or white turban is certain to appear on the scene, a robed figure steps out of its slippers at the door, glides noiselessly inside, puts its hand on its stomach, salaams, and drops, as silently as a ghost might, in a squatting attitude among the guests. Hardly has this one taken his position than another one appears at the door and goes through precisely the same programme, followed shortly afterward by another, and yet others; these foxy-looking members of the Persian priesthood always seem to me to possess the faculty of scenting these little occasions from afar and of following their noses to the place with unerring precision.

Upon emerging from the shelter of the city and adjacent ruins, I find myself confronted by a furious head-wind, against which it is quite impossible to ride, and almost impossible to trundle. During the forenoon I meet on the road a disgraced official, in the person of the Asaf-i-dowleh, Governor-General of Khorassan, returning to Teheran from Meshed, having been recalled at New Year's by the Shah to give an account of himself for "oppressing the people, insulting the Prophet, and intriguing with the Russians." The Asaf-i-dowleh made himself very obnoxious to the priests and people of the holy city by arresting a criminal within the place of refuge at Imam Riza's tomb, and by an outrageous devotion to his own pecuniary interests at the public expense. Riots occurred, the mob taking possession of the telegraph-office and smashing the windows, because they fancied their petition to the Shah was being tampered with. A timely rain-storm dispersed the mob and gave time for the Shah's reply to arrive, promising the Asaf-i-dowleh's removal and disgrace. The ex-Governor is in a carriage drawn by four grays; his own women are in gayly gilded taktrowans, upholstered with crimson satin; the women of his followers occupy several pairs of kajavehs, and the household goods of the party follow behind in a number of huge Russian forgans or wagons, each drawn by four mules abreast. Besides these are a long string of pack-camels, mules, and attendants on horseback, forming altogether the most imposing cavalcade I have met on a Persian road. How they manage to get the heavily loaded forgans and the Governor's carriage over such places as the pass near Lasgird is something of a mystery—but there may be another route— at any rate, hundreds of villagers would be called out to assist.

An opportunity also presents this morning of seeing the amount of obstinacy and perverseness that manages to find lodgement within the unsightly curves and angles of a runaway camel. A riding-camel, led by its owner, scares at the bicycle, and, breaking away, leads him a lively chase through a belt of low sand ridges near the road, jolting various packages off his back as he runs. Every time the man gets almost within seizing distance of the rope, the contrary camel starts off again in a long, awkward lope, slowing up again, as though maliciously inviting his owner to try it over again, when he has covered a couple of hundred yards. These manoeuvres are repeated again and again, until the chase has extended to perhaps four miles, when a party of travellers assist in rounding him up; the man then has to re-traverse the whole four miles and gather up the things.

A late luncheon of bread, warm from the oven, is obtained at the village of Lafaram, where I likewise obtain a peep behind the scenes of everyday village life, and see something of their mode of baking bread. The walled village of Lafaram presents a picture of manure heaps, holes of filthy water, mud-hovels, naked, sore eyed youngsters, unkempt, unwashed, bedraggled females, goats, chickens, and all the unsavory elements that enter into the composition of a wretched, semi-civilized community. With bare, uncombed heads, bare-armed, bare-breasted, and bare-limbed, and with their nakedness scarcely hidden beneath a few coarse rags, some of the women are engaged in making and baking bread, and others in the preparation of tezek from cow manure and chopped straw. In carrying on these two occupations the women mingle, chat, and help each other with happy-go-lucky indifference to consequences, and with a breezy unconsciousness of there being anything repulsive about the idea of handling hot cakes with one hand and tezek with the other. The ovens are huge jars partially sunk in the ground; fire is made inside and the jar heated; flat cakes of dough are then stuck in the inside of the jar, a few minutes sufficing for the baking. The hand and arm the woman inserts inside the heated jar is wrapped with old rags and frequently dipped in a jar of water standing by to keep it cooled; the bread thus baked tastes very good when fresh, but it requires a stomach rendered unsqueamish by dire necessity to relish it after seeing it baked.

The plain beyond Lafaram assumes the character of an acclivity, that in four farsakhs terminates in a pass through a spur of hills. The adverse wind blows furiously all day and shows no signs of abating as the dusk of evening settles down over the landscape. A wayside caravanserai is reached at the entrance to the pass, and I determine to remain till morning. Here I meet with a piece of good fortune in a small way, in the shape of a leg of wild goat, obtained from a native Nimrod; a thin rod of iron, obtained from the serai-jee, serves for a skewer, and I spend the evening in roasting and eating wild-goat kabobs, while a youth fans the little charcoal fire for me with the sole of an old geiveh.

CHAPTER V

MESHED THE HOLY

Warning spits of snow accompany my early morning departure from the wayside caravanserai, and it quickly develops into a blinding snow-storm that effectually obscures the country around, although melting as it touches the ground.

A mile from the caravanserai the trails fork, and, taking the wrong one, I wander some miles up the mountains ere discovering my mistake. Retracing my way, the right road is finally taken; but the gale increases in violence, the cold is numbing to unprotected hands and ears, and the wind and driving snow difficult to face. At one point the trail leads through a morass, in which are two dead horses, swamped in attempting to cross, and near by lies an abandoned camel, lying in the mud and wearily munching at a heap of kali (cut barley-straw) placed before him by his owners before leaving him to his kismet; perchance with a forlorn hope that he might pull through and finally regain his feet.

I have a narrow escape from swamping in the treacherous morass myself, sinking knee-deep in the slimy, oozing mud-mass, pulling off my geivehs and having no end of trouble in recovering them.

Shurab is reached about noon, where the customary crowd and customary rude accommodations await me. Quite an unaccustomed luxury, however, is obtained at Shurab—a substance made from grapes, called sheerah, which resembles thin molasses. A communal dish, which I see the chapar-jee and his sliagirds prepare for themselves and eat this evening, consists of one pint of sheerah, half that quantity of grease, a handful of chopped onions and a quart of water. This awful mixture is stewed for a few minutes and then poured over a bowl of broken bread; they then gather around and eat it with their hands—that they also eat it with great gusto goes without saying.

Opium smoking appears to be indulged in to a great extent here, two out of the three chapar men putting in a good portion of their time "hitting" the seductive pipe, and tinkering with their opium-smoking apparatus. They only have one outfit between them; both of them are half blind with ophthalmia, and the bane of their wretched existence seems to be a Russian candle-lamp, with a broken globe, that persists in falling apart whenever they attempt to use it—which, by the by, is well-nigh all the time—in manipulating the opium needle and pipe. Observing them from my rude shake-down, after supper, bending persistently over this broken, or ever-breaking lamp, their sore eyes and shrunken features, the suzzle-suzzle of the opium as they suck it into the primer and inhale the fumes—the indescribable odor of the drug pervading the room—all this would seem to be a picture of an ideal Chinese opium den rather than of a chapar-khana in Persia.

A broken bridge and miles of deep mud not far ahead has been the burthen of information gathered from the villagers during the afternoon, and the chapar-jee urges upon me the necessity of employing men and horses to carry me and the bicycle across these obstructions into Nishapoor. Preferring to take my chances of getting through, however, I pay no heed to these warnings, well aware that the chapar-jee's interest in the matter begins and ends in the fact that he has horses to hire himself.

In imitation of my example yesterday, I wander off the proper road again this morning, taking a road that leads to an abandoned ford instead of to the bridge, a mistake that is probably a very good one to have made when viewed from the stand-point of mud, as my road is at least the shorter one of the two.

A wild-looking, busby-decked crowd of Khorassani goatherds from a neighboring village follow behind me across the level mudflats leading to the stream, vociferously clamoring for me to ride. They shout persistently: "H-o-i! Sowar shuk; tomasha! tomasha!" even when they see the difficult task I have of it getting the bicycle through the mud. I have singled out a big, sturdy goat-herder to assist me across the streams, of which I learn there are two, a mile or thereabout apart, and his compatriots are accompanying us to see us cross, as well as being impelled by prying curiosity to see how many kerans he gets for his trouble. The first stream is found to be arm-pit deep, with a fairly strong current. My sturdy Khorassani crosses over first, to try the bottom, feeling his way with a long-handled spade; he then returns and carries the bicycle across on his head, afterward carrying me across astride his shoulders, landing me safely with nothing worse than wet feet.

A mile of awful saline mud, and stream number two is reached and crossed in a similar manner—although here I unfortunately cross part way over fairly sitting on the water. The water and the weather are both uncomfortably chilly, and my assistant emerges from the second stream with chattering teeth and goose-pimply flesh. A liberal and well-deserved present makes him forget personal discomforts, and, fervently kissing my hand and pressing my palm to his forehead, he tells me there is no more water ahead, and, recrossing the stream, he wends his way homeward again.

Fortunately the road improves rapidly, developing beyond the Nishapoor Valley into smooth, upland camel-trails that afford quite excellent wheeling. The Nishapoor Valley impresses me as about the finest area of cultivation seen in Persia, except, perhaps, the Tabreez Plain; and toward Gadamgah the country gets positively beautiful—at least, beautiful in comparison. Crystal streamlets come purling and gurgling across the road over pebbly beds; and, looking northward for their source, one finds that the usually gray and uninteresting foot-hills have changed into bright, green slopes, on whose cheerful brows are seen an occasional pine or cedar. Overtopping these green, grassy slopes are dark, rugged rocks, and higher still the grim white region of—winter. Somewhere behind these emerald foot-hills, near Gadamgah, are the famous turquoise mines alluded to in the "Veiled Prophet of Khorassan." The mines are worked at the present time, but only in a desultory and unenterprising manner.

Favored with good roads, I succeed in reaching Gadamgah before dark, where, besides a comfortable and commodious caravanserai, and the pleasure of seeing around a number of fine-spreading cedars, one can obtain the rare luxury of pine-wood to build a fire.

Immediately upon my arrival a knowing and respectable-looking old pilgrim, who calls himself a hadji and a dervish from Mazan-deran, rescues me from the annoying importunities of the people and invites me to share the accommodation of his menzil. Augmenting his scanty stock of firewood and obtaining eggs and bread, quite a comfortable evening is spent in reclining beside the blazing pine-wood fire, which is itself no trifling luxury in a country of scanty camel-thorn and tezek. Whenever the prying curiosity of the occupants of neighboring menzils impels them to visit our quarters, to stand and stare at me, my friend the hadji waxes indignant, and, waving a stick of firewood threateningly toward them, he pours forth a torrent of withering and sarcastic remarks. Once, in his wrath, he hops lightly off the menzil floor, seizes an individual twice his own size by the kammerbund, jerks him violently forward, bids him stare until he gets ashamed of staring, and then, turning him round, shoves him unceremoniously away again, pursuing him as he retreats to his own quarters with vengeful shouts of "y-a-h!"

To a few eminently respectable travellers, however, the hadji graciously accords the coveted privilege of squatting around our fire and chatting. Being himself a person who dearly loves the music of his own voice, he holds forth at great length on the subject of himself in particular, dervishes in general, and the Province of Mazanderaii. Like a good many other people conscious of their own garrulousness, the hadji evidently suspects his auditors of receiving his statements with a good deal of allowance; consequently, when impressing upon them the circumstance of his hailing from Mazanderan—a fact that he seems to think creditable in some way to himself—he produces from the depths of his capacious saddlebags several dried fish of a variety for which that province is celebrated, and exhibits them in confirmation of his statements.

It is genuine wintry weather, and with no bedclothes, save a narrow horse-blanket borrowed from my impromptu friend, I spend a cold, uncomfortable night, for a caravanserai menzil is but a mere place of shelter after all. The hadji rises early and replenishes the fire, and with his little brass teapot we make and drink a glass of tea together before starting out.

At daybreak the hadji goes outside to take a preliminary peep at the weather, and returns with the unwelcome intelligence that it is snowing.

"Better snow than rain," I conclude, as I prepare to start, little thinking that I am entering upon the toughest day's experience of the whole journey through Persia.

Before covering three miles, the snow-storm develops into a regular blizzard; a furious, driving storm that would do credit to Dakota. Without gloves, and in summer clothes throughout, I quickly find myself in a most unenviable plight. It is no common snow-storm; every few minutes a halt has to be made, hands buffeted and ears rubbed to prevent these members from freezing; yet foot-gear has to be removed and streams waded in the bitter cold.

The road leads up into a region of broken hills, and the climax of my discomfort is reached, when the blizzard is raging with ever-increasing fury, and the cold has already slightly nipped one finger. While attempting to cross a deep, narrow stream without disrobing, it is my unhappy fate to drop the bicycle into the water, and furthermore to front the necessity of instantly plunging in, armpit deep, to its rescue. When I emerge upon the opposite bank my situation is really quite critical; in a few moments my garments are frozen stiff; everything I have with me is wet; my leathern case, containing the small stock of medicines, matches, writing material, and other small but necessary articles, is full of water, and, with hands benumbed, I am unable to unstrap it.

My only salvation consists in vigorous exercise, and, conscious of this, I splurge ahead through the blinding storm and the fast-deepening snow, fording several other streams, often emerging dripping from the icy water to struggle through waist-deep snow-drifts that are rapidly accumulating under the influence of the driving blast and fast-falling snow. Uncertain of the distance to the next caravanserai, I push determinedly forward in this condition for several hours, making but slow progress. Everything must come to an end, however, and twenty miles from Gadamgah the welcome outlines of a road-side caravanserai become visible through the thickly falling snow-flakes, and the din of many jangling camel-bells proclaims it already occupied.

The caravanserai is found so densely crowded with people, horses, camels, and their loads that it is impossible to at first carry the bicycle inside. Confusion, and more than confusion, reigns supreme; every menzil is occupied, and the whole interior space is a confused mass of charvadars, stoutly vociferating at one another and at the pack-animals lying down, wandering about, or being unloaded.

Leaving the bicycle outside in the snow, I clamber over the humpy forms of kneeling camels, through an intricate maze of mules and over barricades of miscellaneous merchandise, and, making a virtue of dire necessity, invade the menzil of a well-to-do looking traveller. Here, waiving all considerations of whether my presence is acceptable or the reverse, I take a seat beside their fire and forthwith proceed to shed my saturated foot-gear. Under ordinary conditions this proceeding would be nothing less than a piece of sublime assurance; but necessity knows no law, and my case is really very urgent. When I explain to the occupants of the menzil that this nolens volens invasion of their premises is but a temporary arrangement, in the flowery language of polite Persian they tell me that the menzil, the fire, and everything they have is mine.

After the inevitable examination of my map, compass, and sundry effects, I begin to fancy my presence something of an embarrassment, and consequently am not a little gratified at hearing the authoritative voice of my friend the hadji shouting loudly at the charvadars, telling them that he is a hadji and a Mazanderan dervish, for whom they cannot clear the way too quickly. Looking round, I see him appear at the caravanserai entrance with a party of pilgrims, in whose company he has journeyed from Gadamgah. The combined excellences that enter into the composition of a person who is both a dervish and an ex-Mecca pilgrim are of great benefit in securing the respect and consideration of the common herd in Persia; and as, in addition to this, our hadji commands attention by the peculiar tone and volume of his voice when delivering his commands, his tall, angular steed is quickly tied up in a snug and sheltered corner and his saddle-bags deposited on the floor of a fellow-pilgrim's menzil.

Hearing of my arrival, he straightway seeks me out and invites me to share the accommodation of his new-found quarters, not forgetting to explain to the people he finds me with, however, that he is a hadji, a dervish, and that he hails from Mazanderan. I shouldn't be much surprised to see him back up the latter assertion by producing a dried fish from the ample folds of his kammerbund; but these finny witnesses are reserved to perform their role later in the evening.

As the gloom of night envelopes the interior of the caravanserai, and the scores of little brushwood fires smoke and glimmer and twinkle fitfully, the scene appeals to an observant Occidental as being decidedly unique, and totally unlike anything to be seen outside of Persia. Around each little fire, from four to a dozen figures are squatting, each group forming a most social gathering; some are singing, some chatting pleasantly, some quarrelling and arguing violently; some are shouting lustily at each other across the whole width of the serai; all are taking turns at smoking the kalian or sipping tea, or preparing supper. Occasionally a fiery wheel glows through the darkness, from which fly myriads of sparks, looking very pretty as it describes rapid circles. This is a. little wire cage, full of live charcoal, that is being swung round and round like a sling to enliven the coals for priming the kalian. In the middle space, crowded with animals and their loads, the horses, being all stallions, are constantly squealing and fighting; camels, are grunting dolefully, donkeys are braying and bells clanging, and grooms and charvadars are shouting and quarrelling. Taken all in all, the interior of a crowded caravanserai is a decidedly animated place.

The snow-storm subsides during the night, and a clear, frosty morning breaks upon a wintry landscape, in which nothing is visible but snow. The hadji announces his intention of "Inshallah Meshed, am roos" (please God, we will reach Meshed to-day) as he covers up the obtrusive tail of a fish emerging from one of the saddle-bags and prepares to mount. I give him my packages to carry, by way of lightening my burden as much as possible for the struggle through the snow, and promise him a bottle of arrack, upon reaching Meshed, as a reward for thus assisting me through. Arrack is forbidden fruit to a hadji above all things else, so that nothing I could promise him would likely prove more tempting or acceptable, or be better appreciated!

It proves slavish work trundling, tugging, and carrying the bicycle through the deep snow along a half-broken trail made by a few horses, and through deep drifts; but the cold, bracing air is favorable for exertion, and by ten o'clock we reach Shahriffabad, where a halt is made to prepare a cup of tea and to give the hadji's horse a feed of barley. At Shahriffabad we are warned that on the hills between here and Meshed snow will be found two feet deep, streams belly deep to the hadji's horse will have to be forded, and, toward Meshed, mud knee-deep. Conscious that the mud will be "knee-deep" the whole distance, after the disappearance of the snow, this makes us only the more eager to push on while we may.

The sun has by this time become uncomfortably warm, and the narrow trail is fast becoming a miry pathway of mud and slush under the trampling feet of the animals gone ahead, and of villagers' donkeys returning from the city. Mile after mile is devoted to the unhappy task of trundling the bicycle ahead, rear wheel aloft, through mud and slush varying from ankle-deep to worse, occasionally varying the programme by fording a stream.

Late in the afternoon we arrive at the summit of the hills overlooking the Meshed Plain, and the hadji points out enthusiastically the golden dome of Imam Biza's sanctuary; the yellow, glistening goal whose famed sanctity has attracted hosts of pilgrims from all quarters of Central Asia for ages past. The hills hereabout are of a rocky character, and pious pilgrims have gathered into little mounds every loose piece of rock, it being customary for each pilgrim to find a stone and add it to one of these piles upon first viewing the bright golden dome of the holy city from this commanding spot.

Below the rocky paths of this declivity the snow disappears in favor of slippery mud, and the hadji's wearied charger slips and slides about, to the imminent danger of its rider's neck; and all the time the slim Turkoman! steed trembles visibly in terror of the old Mazanderan dervish's whip and his awful threats. Two miles down the bed of the stream, crossing and recrossing it a dozen times, often thigh-deep, and we emerge upon the gently sloping area of the Meshed Plain, with the yellow beacon-light of Meshed glowing in the mellow light of the evening sun six miles away.

The late storm has been chiefly rain in the lower altitude of the plain, and the day's sunshine has partially dried the surface, but leaving it slippery and treacherous here and there. After leaving the bed of the stream the hadji becomes anxious about reaching Meshed before dark, and advises me to mount and put on the speed.

"Inshallah, Meshed yek saat," he says, and so I mount and bid him follow along behind. By vocal suasion and a liberal application of his cruel, triple-thonged, raw-hide whip, he urges his well-nigh staggering animal into a canter, lifting his forefeet clear of the ground seemingly by the bridle at every jump. Suspicious as to his lank and angular steed's sure-footedness under the strain, I take the very laudable precaution of keeping as far from him as possible, not caring to get mixed up in a catastrophe that seems inevitable every time the horse, goaded by the stinging stimulus of the whip and the threats, makes another jump. Not more than a mile of the six is covered when I have ample reason for congratulating myself on taking this precaution, for the horse stumbles, and, being too far gone to recover himself, comes down on his nose, and the "hadji and Mazanderau dervish" is cutting a most ridiculous figure in the mud. His tall lambskin hat flies off and lands in a pool of muddy water some distance ahead; the ponderous saddle-bags, which are merely laid on the saddle, shoot forward athwart the horse's neck, the horse's nose roots quite a furrow in the road, and the horse's owner picks himself up and takes a woeful survey of his own figure. It is needless to say that the survey includes a good deal more real estate than the hadji cares to claim, even though it be the semi-sacred soil of the Meshed Plain.

The poor horse is altogether too tired to attempt to recover his legs of his own inclination; but, regarding him as the author of his ignominious misadventure, the hadji surveys him with a wrathful eye for a moment, mutters a few awful imprecations—imported, no doubt, from Mazanderan—and then attacks him savagely about the head with the whip. In his wrath and determination to make a lasting impression of each blow given, the hadji emphasizes each visitation with a very audible grunt; and, to speak correctly, so does the horse. It goes without saying, however, that master and animal grunt from widely different motives; although, so far as the mere audible performance is concerned, one grunt might almost be an echo of the other.

At length, by adopting a more circumspect pace, we reach the gate of the holy city about sunset without further mishap. The hadji leads the way through a bewildering labyrinth of narrow streets that consist of an open sewage-ditch in the centre, at present full of filth, and a narrow footway of rough, broken, and mud-bespattered cobble-stones on either side. Of course we are followed through these fearful thoroughfares by a surging and vociferous crowd of people such as a Central Asian city alone can produce; but I can this time happily afford to smile at these usually irritating accompaniments to my arrival in a populous city, for ten minutes after entering the gate finds me shaking hands with Mr. Gray, the genial telegraphist of the Afghan Boundary Commission. With a well-guarded gate between our cosey quarters and the shouting mob outside, the evening is spent very pleasantly and quietly, in striking comparison with what it would have been had no one been here to afford me a place of refuge.

Meshed is "the jumping off place" of telegraphy; the electric spider spins his galvanized web no farther in this direction, and the dirge-like music of civilization's—Æolian harp, that, like the roll of England's drum, is heard around the world, approaches the barbarous territory of Afghanistan from two directions, but recoils from entering that fanatical and conservative domain. It approaches from Persia on the one side, and from India on the other; but as yet it only approaches. The drum has already been there; it is only a question of time when the Æolian harp will follow.

It is with lively recollection of Khorassani March weather and the experience of the last few days that, after a warm bath, I array myself in a suit of Mr. Gray's clothing, elevate my slippered feet, "Yenghi Donia fashion," on a pile of Turcoman! carpets, and, abetted by the cheering presence of a bottle of Shiraz wine, exchange my recent experiences on the road for telegraphic scraps of the latest news. How utterly unsatisfactory and altogether wretched seems even the gilded palace of a Persian provincial governor—the meaningless compliments, the salaaming lackeys and empty show of courtesy, when compared with the cosey quarters, the hearty welcome, the honest ring of an Englishman's voice, and the genuineness of everything!

Shortly after my arrival, a gentleman with a coal-black complexion, a retreating forehead, and an overshadowing wealth of lip appears at the door bearing a tray of sweetmeats. Making a profound salaam, he steps out of his slipper-like shoes, enters, and places the sweetmeats on the table, smiling a broad expectant-of-backsheesh smile the while he explains his mission.

"The Sartiep has sent you his salaams and a present of sweetmeats, preparatory to calling round himself," explains mine host; "he is a Persian gentleman, Ali Akbar Khan, at the head of the Meshed telegraph-service, and has the rank of general or Sartiep." The Sartiep himself arrives shortly afterward, accompanied by his favorite son, a budding youth of some eight or ten summers, of whose beauty he feels very justly proud. The Sartiep's son is one of those remarkably handsome boys met with occasionally in modern Persia, and which so profusely adorn old Persian paintings. With soft, girlish features, big, black, lustrous eyes, and an abundance of long hair, they remind one of the beautiful youths of Oriental romance; his fond parent takes him about on his visits and finds much gratification in the admiring remarks bestowed upon the son.

The Sartiep is an ideal Persian official, courteous and complimentary, but never forgetful of Ali Akbar Khan; his full, round figure and sensual Oriental face speak eloquently of mutton pillau and other fattening dishes galore, sweetmeats, cucumbers, and melons; and deep draughts from pleasure's intoxicating cup have not failed to leave their indelible marks. In this particular the Sartiep is but a casually selected sample of the well-to-do Persian official. Leaving out a few notable exceptions, this brief description of him suffices to describe them all.

Following in the train of the Sartiep arrive more servants, bearing dishes of kabobs, herb-seasoned pillau, and various other strange, savory dishes, which, Mr. Gray explains, are considered great delicacies among the upper-class Persians and are intended as a great compliment to me.

Although Mohammedans, and particularly Shiite Mohammedans, are forbidden by their religion to indulge in alcoholic beverages, the average high official in Persia is anything but a sanctimonious individual, and partakes with a keen relish of the forbidden fruit in an open-secret manner. The thin, transparent veil of abstemiousness that the Persian noble wears in deference to the sanctimonious pretensions of the mollahs and seyuds and the public eye at large, is cast aside altogether in the presence of intimate friends, and particularly if that intimate friend is a Ferenghi. Owing to their association in the telegraph-service, mine host and the Sartiep are on the most intimate terms. The Sartiep soon after his arrival intimates, with a humorous twinkle of the eye, that he feels the need of a little medicine. Mr. Gray, as becomes a good physician who knows well the constitutional requirements of his patient, and who knows what to prescribe without even going through the preliminary act of feeling the pulse, produces a pale-green bottle and a tumbler and pours out a full dose of its contents for an adult.

The patient swallows it at a gulp, nibbles a piece of sweetmeat, and strokes his stomach in token of approval.

"What was the medicine you prescribed, Gray?" "High wines," says the physician, "95 proof alcohol; a bottle that the entomologist of the Boundary Commission happened to leave here a year ago; it was the only thing in the house except wine. The patient pronounces it the 'best arrack' he ever tasted; the firier these fellows can get it the better they like it."

"Why, it didn't even make him gasp!"

"Gasp—nonsense; you haven't been in Persia as long as I have yet, or you wouldn't say 'gasp' even at 95% alcohol."

But how polite, how complimentary, these French of Asia are, and how imaginative and fanciful their language! Not having shaved since leaving Teheran, after surveying myself in the glass, I feel called upon, in the interest of fellow-wheelmen elsewhere, to explain to our discerning visitors that all bicyclers are not distinguished from their fellow men by a bronzed and stubby phiz and an all-around vagrom appearance.

The Sartiep strokes his beard and stomach, casts a lingering glance at the above-mentioned green-glass bottle, smiles, and replies: "Having accomplished so wonderful a journey, you are now prettier with your rough, unshaven face than you ever were before; you can now survey yourself in the looking-glass of fame instead of in a common mirror that reflects all the imperfections of ordinary mortals." Having delivered himself of this compliment, the Sartiep's eye wanders in the direction of the 95%

alcohol again, and the next minute is again smacking his lips and complacently stroking his stomach.

In the morning, before I am up, a servant arrives from a Mesh-edi notable named Hadji Mahdi, bringing salaams from his master, and a letter clothed in the fine "apparel diplomatique" of the Orient. The letter, although in reality nothing more than a request to be allowed to come and see the bicycle, reads in substance as follows: "Salaams from Hadji Mahdi—may he be your sacrifice!-to Gray Sahib and the illustrious Sahib who has arrived in Holy Meshed from Teheran, on the wonderful asp-i-awhan, the fame of whose deeds reaches to the ends of the earth. Bismillah! May your shadows never grow less! Your sacrifice's brother, Hadji Mollah Hassan, whose eyes were gladdened by a sight of the asp-i-awhan Sahib at Shahrood, and who now sends his salaams, telegraphs me—his unworthy brother—that upon the Sahib's arrival in Meshed I should render him any assistance he might need. Inshallah, with your permission—may it not be withheld—your sacrifice will be pleased to call and gladden his eyes with a sight of Gray Sahib and the illustrious Sahib his guest."

As might have been expected, the advent of a Ferenghi on so strange a vehicle as a bicycle, arriving in the sacred city of Imam Eiza's sanctuary, arouses universal curiosity; and not only the Sartiep and Hadji Mahdi, but hundreds of big-turbaned Meshedi notables, mollahs, and seyuds are admitted during the day to enjoy the happy privilege of feasting their eyes on the latest proof of the Ferenghis' wonderful marifet,

Upon receipt of the telegram at Shahrood refusing me permission to go through Turkestan, I telegraphed to Mr. Gray, requesting him to obtain leave for me to go to the Boundary Commission Camp, and accompany them back to India, or reach India from the camp alone. Mr. Gray kindly forwarded my request to the camp, and now urges me to consider myself his guest until the return courier arrives with the answer. This turns out to mean a stop-over of seven days, and on the second day immense crowds of people assemble in the street, shouting for me to come out and ride the bicycle. The clamor on the streets renders it impossible for them to transact business in the telegraph office, and several times requests are sent in begging me to appease them and stop the uproar by riding to and fro along the street. An outer door separates the compound in which the house is built from the street, and to prevent the rabble from invading the premises, and the possibility of unpleasant consequences, the Governor-General stations a guard of four soldiers at the door. This precaution works very well so far as the common herd are concerned, but every hour through the day little knots of priestly men in the flowing new garments and spotless turbans representing their Noo Roos purchases, or the lamb's-wool cylinder and semi-European garb of the official, bribe, coerce, or command the guard to let them in.

These persistent people generally stand in a respectful attitude just inside the outer gate, and send word in by a servant that a Shahzedah (relative of the Shah) wishes to see the bicycle. After the first "Shahzedah" has been treated with courtesy and consideration in deference to his royal relative at Teheran, fully two-thirds of those who come after unblushingly proclaim themselves uncles, cousins, or nephews of "His Majesty, the King of Kings and Ruler of the Universe!" The constant worry and annoyance of these people compel us to adopt measures of self-defence, and so, after admitting about a hundred uncles, twice that number of nephews, and Heaven knows how many cousins, we conclude that blood-relations of the Shah are altogether too numerous in Meshed to be of much consequence. Soon after arriving at this conclusion, Mr. Gray's farrash, an Armenian he brought with him from Ispahan, comes in with a message that another Shahzedah has succeeded in getting past the guard and sends in his salaams. "Shahzedah be d———d! Turn him out—put him outside, and tell the guards to let nobody else in without our permission!"

A moment later the farrash re-enters with the look of a man scarcely able to control his risibilities, and says the man and his friends are still inside the gate.

"Why the devil don't you put them out, as you are told, then?"

"He says he is the Padishah's step-father."

"Well, what if he is the Padishah's step-father? It's nothing to be the Shah's step-father; the Shah probably has five hundred step-father's, to say the least—turn him out. No; hold hard; let him stay."

We conclude that a step-father to the king, whether genuine or only a counterfeit, is at least something of a relief after the swarms of nephews, cousins, and uncles, and so order him to be shown in He proves to be a corpulent little man about sixty, who advances up the bricked walk toward us, making about three extra profound salaams to the rod and smiling in a curious, apprehensive manner, as though not quite assured of his reception. About a dozen long-robed mollahs and seyuds follow with timid hesitancy in his wake. Strange to say, he makes no allusion to his illustrious step-son, the King of Kings at Teheran; and plainly betrays embarrassment when Gray mentions the fact of my having appeared before him on the wheel. We conclude that the Shah's step-father and the little group of holy men clubbed together and paid the Persian guard about a keran to let them in, and perhaps another half-keran to the Armenian farrash for not summarily turning them out. He tries very hard, however, to make himself agreeable, and when told about the Russians refusing me the road, exclaims artfully: "I was not an enemy of the Russians before I heard this, but now I am their worst enemy! Suppose the Sahib's iron horse was a wheel of fire, what harm would it do their country even then?"

Our most distinguished caller to-day is Mirza Abbas Khan, C. I. E., a Kandahari gentleman, who has been the British political agent at Meshed for many years. He makes a formal call in all the glory of his official garments, a magnificent Cashmere coat lined with Russian sable and profusely trimmed with gold braid; a servant leads his gayly caparisoned horse, and another brings up the rear with a richly mounted kalian.

Appearances count for something among the people of Northeastern Persia, and Abbas Khan draws a sufficiently large salary to enable him to wear gorgeous clothes, and thereby dim the lustre of his bitter rival, the political agent of Russia.

Abbas Khan is perhaps the handsomest man in Meshed, is in the prime of life, dyes his flowing beard an orthodox red, and possesses most charming manners; in addition to his ample salary he owns the revenue of a village near Meshed, and seems to be altogether the right man in the right place.

Abbas Khan and a friend of his from Herat both agree that the difficulties and dangers of Afghanistan will be likely to prove insurmountable; at the same time promising any assistance they can render me in getting to India, consistent, of course, with Abbas Khan's duties as British Agent. It seems to be a pretty general opinion that Afghanistan will prove a stumbling-block in my path; friends at Teheran telegraph again, advising me to go anywhere rather than risk the dangers to be apprehended in that most lawless and fanatical territory. Nothing can be decided on, however, until the arrival of an answer from the Commission.

In the meantime, the days slowly pass away in Meshed; every day come scores of visitors and invitations to go and ride for the delectation of sundry high officials; ever-present are the crowds in the streets shouting, "Tomasha! tomasha! Sowar shuk!" and the frequent squabbles at the gate between the guard and the people wanting to come in.

Above the din and clamor of the crowd outside there sometimes arise the chanting voices of a party of newly arrived pilgrims making their way joyously through the thronged streets toward the gold-domed sanctuary of Imam Riza, the tomb being situated a couple of hundred yards down the street from our quarters. Sometimes we hear parties of men uttering strange cries and sounding aloud the praises of Imam Riza, Houssein, Hassan, and other worthies of the Mohammedan world, in response to which are heard the swelling voices of a multitude of people shouting in chorus, "Allah be praised! Allah be praised!!" These weird chanters are dervishes, who, with tiger-skin mantles drawn carelessly about them, clubs or battle-axes on shoulder, their long unkempt hair dangling down their backs, look wildly grotesque as they parade the streets of the Persian Mecca.

Meshed is a strange city for a Ferenghi to live in; every day are heard the chanting and singing of newly arriving bands of pilgrims, the strange, wild utterances of dervishes preaching on the streets, and the shouting responses of their auditors. Conspicuous above everything else in the city, as gold is conspicuous from dross, is the golden dome and gold-tipped minarets of the holy edifice that imparts to the city its sacred character. The gold is in thin plates covering the hemispherical roof like sheets of tin; like most Eastern things, its appearance is more impressive from a distance than at close quarters. Grains of barley deposited on the roof by pigeons have sprouted and grown in rank bunches between the thin gold plates, many of which are partially loose, imparting to the place an air of neglect and decay. By resting their feet on the dome of this sacred edifice, the pigeons of Meshed have themselves become objects of veneration; shooting them is strictly prohibited, and a mob would soon be about the ears of anyone venturing to do them harm.

The two most important persons in Meshed are the acting Governor-General of Khorassan, and Mardan Khan, Ex-Governor of Sarakhs and Hereditary Chief of the powerful tribe of Timurees. Of course, the Governor sends his salaams, and invites me to come round to the government konak and favor him with an exhibition. Since our refusal to entertain any more of the "Shah's relations," we find that the worthy and long-suffering Abbas Khan has been worried almost to the verge of despair by requests from all over the city begging the privilege of seeing me ride.

"Knowing that you have been worried in the same way yourselves," says Abbas Kahu, "I have replied to them, 'Is the Sahib a giraffe and I his keeper? Why, then, do you come to me? The Sahib has travelled a long way, and is stopping here to rest, not to make an exhibition of himself."

An exception is of course made in favor of the Governor-General and Mardan Khan. The Government compound is a large enclosure, and to reach the Governor-General's quarters one has to traverse numerous long court-yards connected with one another by long, gloomy passage-ways of brick, where the tramping of the sentinels and the march of retiring and relieving guards resound through the vaults like an echo of mediaeval times.

There is nothing particularly interesting about the Governor's apartments, but Mardan Khan's palace is a revelation of barbaric splendor entirely different from anything hitherto seen in the country. In contradistinction to the dazzling, silvery glitter of the mirror-work and stuccoed halls of the Teheran palaces, the home of the wealthy Timuree Chieftain is distinguished by a striking and lavish display of colored glass, gilt, and tinsel.

Mardan Khan is a valued friend of Mirza Abbas Khan and a man of powerful influence; besides this, he is a pronounced admirer of the Ingilis as against the Oroos, and my reception at his palace almost takes the character of an ovation. News of the great tomasha has evidently been widely spread, crowds of outsiders fill the streets leading to the palace, and inside the large garden are scores of the elite of the city, mollahs, seyuds, official and private gentlemen; the numerous niches of the walls are occupied by groups of closely veiled females. Trundling through this interesting and expectant crowd with Abbas Khan, Mardan Khan issues forth in flowing gown of richest Cashmere-shawl material and gold braid, to greet us and to take a preliminary peep at the bicycle, and to lead the way into his gorgeously colored room of state.

The scene in this room is an ideal picture of the popular occidental conception of the "gorgeous East." Abbas Khan and Mar-dan Khan sit cross-legged side by side on a rich Turcoman rug, salaaming and exchanging compliments after the customary flowery and extravagant language of the Persian nobility. The marvellous pattern and costly texture of Abbas Khan's coat, the gold braid, the Russian sable lining, and the black Astrakhan cylinder he wears, are precisely matched by the garments of Mardan Khan. Twenty or thirty of the most important dignitaries and mollahs of the city are ranged according to their respective rank or degree of holiness around the room; prominent among them is the Chief Imam of Meshed, a very important and influential person in the holy city.

The Chief Imam is a slim-built, sharp-looking individual of about forty summers, with a face pale, refined, and intellectual; hands white and slender as a lady's, and a foot equally shapely and feminine. He wears a monster green turban, takes his turn regularly at the kalian, and passes it on to the next with the easy gracefulness that comes of good breeding; and by his manners and appearance he creates an impression of being a person rather superior to his surroundings.

Liveried pages pass around little glasses of tea, kalians, cigarettes, and sweetmeats, as well as tiny bottles of lemon-juice and rose-water, a few drops of these two last-named articles being used by some of the guests to impart a fanciful flavor to their tea. Now and then a new guest arrives, steps out of his shoes in the hallway, salaams, and takes his proper position among the people already here. Everybody sits on the carpet except me, for whom a three-legged camp-stool has been thoughtfully provided.

Finally, all the guests having arrived, I ride several times around the brick-walks, the strange audience of turbaned priests and veiled women showing their great approval in murmuring undertones of "kylie khoob" and involuntary acclamations of "Mashallah! mash-all-ah!" as they witness with bated breath the strange and incomprehensible scene of a Ferenghi riding a vehicle, that will not stand alone.

Altogether, the great tomasha at Mardan Khan's is a decided success. Scarcely can this be said, however, of the "little tomasha" given to the members of Abbas Khan's own family on the way home. Abbas Khan's compound is very small, and the brick-walks very rough and broken; therefore, it is hardly surprising to me, though probably somewhat surprising to him, when, in turning a corner I execute an undignified header into a bunch of busbies.

The third day after my arrival in Meshed, I received a telegram from the British Charge d'Affaires at Teheran saying: "You must not attempt to cross the frontier of Afghanistan at any point." Two days later the expected courier arrives from the Boundary Commission Camp with a letter saying: "It is useless for you to raise the question of coming to the Commission Camp. In the first place, the Afghans would never allow you to come here; and if you should happen to reach here, you would never be able to get away again."

These two very encouraging missives from our own people seem at first thought more heartless than even the "permission refused" of the Russians. It occurs to me that this "you must not attempt to cross the Afghan frontier" might just as easily have been told me at the Legation at Teheran as when I had travelled six hundred miles to get to it; but the ways of diplomacy are past the comprehension of ordinary mortals.

What, after all, are the ambitions and enterprises of an individual, compared to the will and policy of an empire? No matter whether the empire be semi-civilized and despotic, or free and enlightened, the obscure and struggling individual is usually rated 0000.

Russia—"permission refused." England—paternally—"must not attempt;" cold, offish language this for a lone cycler to be confronted with away up here in the northeast corner of Persia, from representatives of the two greatest empires of the world. What is to be done?

Mr. Gray, returning from the telegraph office later in the evening, finds me endeavoring to unravel the Gordian knot of the situation through the medium of a brown-study. My geographical ruminations have already resulted in a conviction that there is no possible way to unravel it and reach

India with a bicycle; my only chance of doing so is to cut it and abide by the consequences.

"I have just been communicating with Teheran," says Mr. Gray. "Everybody wants to know what you propose doing."

"Tell them I am going down to Beerjand to consult with Heshmet-i-Molk, the Ameer of Seistan, and see if it is possible to get through to Quetta via Beerjand."

"Ever hear of Dadur?" queries Mr. Gray. "Ever hear of Dadur, the place of which the Persians tritely say: 'Seeing that there is Dadur, why did Allah, then, make the infernal regions?' That is somewhere in Beloochistan. You'll find yourself slowly broiling to death on a geographical gridiron if you attempt to reach India down that way."

"Never mind; tell them at Teheran I am going that way anyhow."

Having entered upon this decision, I bid my genial host farewell on April 7th, and mounting at the door, depart in the presence of a well-behaved crowd of spectators. In my pocket is a general letter from the Governor-General of Khorassan to subordinate officials of the province, ordering them to render me any assistance I may require, and another from a prominent person in Meshed to his friend Heshmet-i-Molk, the Ameer of Kain and Governor of Seistan, a powerful and influential chief, with his seat of government at Beerjand.

Couched in the sentimental language of the country, one of these letters concludes with the touching remark: "The Sahib, of his own choice is travelling like a dervish, with no protection but the protection of Allah."

It is a fine bracing morning as I leave the Mecca of Khorassan behind, and the paths leading round outside the walls and moat of the city from gate to gate afford excellent wheeling. The Beerjand trail branches off from the Teheran and Meshed road about a farsakh east of Shahriffabad; for this distance I shall be retraversing the road by which I came, and shall be confronted at every turn of my wheel by reminiscences of dried fish, a Mazanderau dervish, and an angular steed.

The streams that under the influence of the storm ran thigh-deep have now dwindled to mere rivulets, and the narrow, miry trail through the melting snow has become dry and smooth enough to ride wherever the grade permits. The hills are verdant with the green young life of early spring, and are clothed in one of nature's prettiest costumes—a costume of seal-brown rocks and green turf studded with a profusion of blue and yellow flowers.

Shahriffabad is reached early in the afternoon, and the threatening aspect of the changed weather forbids going any farther today.

Shortly after taking up my quarters in the chapar-khana, a party of Persian travellers appear upon the scene, and with them a fussy little man in big round spectacles and semi-European clothes. Scarcely have they had time to alight and seek out quarters than the little man makes his appearance at my menzil door in all the glory of a crimson velvet dressing-cap and blue slippers, and beaming gladsomely through his moon-like spectacles, he comes forward and without further ceremony shakes hands. "Some queer little French professor, geologist, entomologist, or something, wandering about the country in search of scientific knowledge," is the instinctive conclusion I arrive at the moment he appears; and my greeting of "bonjour, monsieur," is quite as involuntary as the conclusion.

"Paruski ni?" he replies, arching his eyebrows and smiling.

"Paruski ni; Ingilis."

"Parsee namifami?"

"Parsee kam-kam."

In this brief interchange of words in the vernacular of the country we define at once each other's nationality and linguistic abilities. He is a Russian and can speak a little Persian. It is difficult, however, to believe him anything else than a little French professor, wise above his generation and skin-full of occult wisdom in some particular branch of science; but then the big round spectacles, the red dressing-cap, and the cerulean leather slippers of themselves impart an air of owlish and preternatural wisdom.

Six times during the afternoon he bounces into my quarters and shakes hands, and six times shakes hands and bounces out again. Every time he renews his visit he introduces one or more natives, who take as much interest in the hand-shaking as they do in the bicycle. Evidently his object in coming round so frequently is to exhibit for the gratification of his own vanity and the curiosity of the Persians, this European mode of greeting, and the profound depth of his own knowledge of the subject.

Later in the evening the women of the village come round in a body to see the Ferenghi and his iron horse, and the wearer of the spectacles, the red cap, and blue slippers, takes upon himself the office of showman for the occasion; pointing out, with a good deal of superficial enthusiasm, the peculiar points of both steed and rider.

Particularly is it impressed upon these woefully ignorant fail-ones, that the bicycle is not a horse, but a machine—a thing of iron and not of flesh and blood.

The fair ones nod their heads approvingly, but it is painfully apparent that they don't comprehend in the least, how, since it is an asp-i-awhan, it can be anything else but a horse, regardless of the material entering into its composition.

When supper-time arrives the chapar-Jee announces his willingness to turn cook and prepare anything I order. Knowing well enough that this seemingly sweeping proposition embraces but two or three articles, I order him to prepare scrambled eggs, bread, and sheerah. An hour later he brings in the scrambled eggs, swimming in hot molasses and grease! He has stirred the grease and molasses together, and in this outlandish mixture cooked the eggs.

Off the main road the country assumes the character of low hills of red clay, across which it would be extremely difficult to take the bicycle in wet weather, but which is now fortunately dry. After three or four farsakhs it develops into a curious region of heterogeneous parts; rocky, precipitous mountains, barren, salt-streaked hills, saline streams, and pretty little green valleys. Here, one feels the absence of any plain, well-travelled road, the dim and ill-defined trail being at times very difficult to distinguish from the branch trails leading to some isolated village. The few people one meets already betray a simplicity and a lack of "gumption" that distinguish them at once from the people frequenting the main road.

CHAPTER VI

THE UNBEATEN TRACKS OF KHORASSAN

During the afternoon I traverse a rocky canon, crossing and recrossing a clear, cold stream that winds its serpentine course from one precipitous wall to another. Mountain trout are observed disporting in this stream, and big, gray lizards scuttle nimbly about among the loose rocks on the bank. The canon gradually dwindles into a less confined passage between sloping hills of loose rock and bowlders, a wild, desolate region through which the road leads gradually upward to a pass.

Part way up this gorge is a rude stone tower about twenty feet high, on the summit of which is perched a little mud hut, looking almost as though it might be a sentry-box. While yet a couple of hundred yards away, a rough-looking customer emerges from the tower and appears to be awaiting my approach. His head is well-nigh hidden beneath a huge Khorassani busby, and he wears the clothes of an irregular soldier. The long, shaggy wool of the sheepskin head-dress dangling over his eyes imparts a very ferocious appearance, and he is armed with the ordinary Persian sword and one of those antiquated flint-lock muskets that are only to be seen on the deserts of the East or in museums of ancient weapons.

Taken all in all, he presents a very ferocious front; he is, in fact, about the most ruffianly-looking specimen I have seen outside of Asiatic Turkey. As I ride up he motions for me to alight, at the same time retreating a few steps toward his humble stronghold, betraying a spirit of apprehension lest, perchance, he might be unwittingly standing in the way of danger. Greeting him with the customary "Salaam aleykum" and being similarly greeted in reply, I dismount to ascertain who and what he is. He retreats another step or two in the direction of his strange abode, and eyes the bicycle with evident distrust, edging off to one side as I turn toward him, as though fearful lest it might come whizzing into his sacred person at a moment's notice like a hungry buzz-saw. In response to my inquiries, he points up toward the pass and offers to accompany me thither for the small sum of "yek keran;" giving me to understand that without his presence it is highly indiscreet to proceed.

Little penetration is required to understand that this is one of the little black-mailing schemes peculiar to semi-civilization, and which, it is perhaps hardly necessary to explain, comes a trifle too late in the chapter of my Asiatic experiences to influence my movements or to replenish the exchequer of the picturesque and enterprising person desirous of shielding me from imaginary harm.

This wily individual is making his living by the novel and ingenious process of trading on the fears and credulity of stray travellers, making them believe the pass is dangerous and charging them a small sum for his services as guard. It is not at all unlikely that he is the present incumbent of an hereditary right to extort blackmail from such travellers along this lonely road as may be prevailed upon without resorting to violence to pay it, and is but humbly following in the footsteps of his worthy sire and still more worthy grandsire.

The pass ahead is neither very steep nor difficult, and the summit once crossed, and the first few hundred yards of rough and abrupt declivity overcome, I am able to mount and wheel swiftly down long gradients of smooth, hard gravel for four or five miles, alighting at the walled village of Assababad in the presence of its entire population.

Some keen-sighted villager has observed afar off the strange apparition gliding swiftly down the open gravel slopes, and the excited population have all rushed out in breathless expectancy to try and make out its character. The villagers of Assababad are simple-hearted people, and both men and women clap their hands like delighted children to have so rare a novelty suddenly appear upon the scene of their usually humdrum and uneventful lives. Quilts are spread for me on the sunny side of the village wall, and they gather eagerly around to feast to the full their unaccustomed eyes. A couple of the men round up a matronly goat and exact from her the tribute of a bowl of milk; others contribute bread, and the frugal repast is seasoned with the unconcealed delight of my hospitable audience.

They are not overly clean in their habits, though, these rude and isolated people; and to keep off prying housewives, bent on satisfying their curiosity regarding the texture of my clothing and the comparative whiteness of my skin, I am compelled to adopt the defensive measure of counter curiosity. The signal and instantaneous success of this plan, resulting in the hasty, scrambling retreat of the women, is greeted with boisterous merriment, by the entire crowd.

I have about made up my mind to remain over-night with the hospitable people of Assababad; but at the solicitation of a Persian traveller who comes along, I conclude to accompany him to a building observable in the distance ahead which he explains is a small but comfortable serai. The good villagers seem very loath to let me, go so soon, and one young man kneels down and kisses my dusty geivehs and begs me to take him with me to Hindostan—strange, unsophisticated people; how simple-hearted, how childlike they seem!

The caravanserai is but a couple of miles ahead, but it is situated in the dip of an extensive, basin-like depression between two mountain ranges, and the last half mile consists of mud and water eighteen inches deep. The caravanserai itself stands on a slight elevation, and is found occupied by a couple of families, who make the place their permanent abode and gain a livelihood by supplying food, firewood, and horse-feed to travellers.

Upon our arrival, a woman makes her appearance and announces her willingness to cater to our wants.

"Noon ass?"

"Yes, plenty of bread."

"Toke-me-morge neis f"

"Neis; loke-me-morge-neis."

"Sheerah ass?"

"Sheerah neis."

"What have you then besides bread?"

For answer the woman points to a few beruffled chickens scratching for grains of barley among a heap of rubbish that has evidently been exploited by them times without number before, and says she can sell us chickens at one keran apiece.

Seeing the absence of anything else, I order her forthwith to capture one for me, and the Persian gentleman orders another. The woman sets three youngsters and a yellow, tailless dog to run down the chickens, and in a few minutes presents herself before us, holding in each hand the plucked and scrawny carcass of a fowl that has had to scratch hard and persistently for its life for heaven knows how many years. One of the chickens is considerably larger than the other, and I tell the Persian gentleman to take his choice, thinking that with himself and his two servants he would be glad to accept the larger fowl. On the contrary, however, he fixes his choice on the smaller one.

Touched by what appears to be a simple act of unselfishness, I endeavor to persuade him to take the other, pointing out that he has three mouths to fill while I have only one. My importunities are, however, wasted on so polite and disinterested a person, and so I reluctantly take possession of the bulkier fowl.

The Persian's servant dissects his master's purchase and stows it away for future use, the three making their supper off bread and a mixture of grease, chopped onions and sheerah from the larder of their saddle-bags. The woman readily accepts the offer of an additional half keran for relieving me of the onerous task of cooking my own supper, and takes her departure, promising to cook it as quickly as possible.

Happy in the contemplation of a whole chicken for supper, I sit around and chat and drink tea with my disinterested friend for the space of an hour. To a hungry person an hour seems an ominously long period of time in which to cook a chicken, and, becoming impatient, the Persian gentleman's servant volunteers to go inside and investigate. I fancy detecting a shadow of amusement passing over the face of the gentleman as his servant departs, and when he returns with the intelligence that the chicken won't be tender enough to eat for another hour, his risibilities get the better of his politeness and he gives way to uncontrollable laughter. Then it is that a gleam of enlightenment steals over my unsuspecting soul and tells me why my guileless fellow-traveller so politely and yet so firmly selected the smallest of the fowls—he is a better judge of Persian "morges" than I. The woman finally turns up, bringing the result of her two hours' culinary perseverance in a large pewter bowl; she has cut the chicken up into several pieces and has been industriously keeping the pot boiling from the beginning. The result of this laudable effort is meat of gutta-percha toughness, upon which one's teeth are exercised in vain; but I make a very good supper after all by breaking bread into the broth. I don't know but that the patriarchal ruler of the roost makes at least the richer broth.

Thin ice covers the water when I leave this caravanserai in the gray of the morning, and the Persian travellers, who nearly always start before daybreak, have already departed. Stories were heard yesterday evening of streams between here and the southern chain of mountains, deep and difficult to cross; and I pull out fully expecting to have to strip and do some disagreeable work in the water. Considerable mud is encountered, and three small streams, not over three feet deep, are crossed; but further on I am brought to a stand by a deep, sluggish stream flowing along ten feet below the level of the ground. Though deep, it is very narrow in places, and might almost be described as a yawning crack in the earth, filled with water to within ten feet of the top.

A little way up stream is a spot fordable for horses, and, of course, fordable also for a cycler; but the prevailing mud and the chilliness of the morning combine to influence me to try another plan. A happy plan it seems at the moment, a credit to my inventive genius, and spiced with the seductive condiment of novelty, the stream is sufficiently narrow at one place to be overcome with a running jump; but people cannot take running jumps encumbered with a bicycle. The bicycle, however, can quickly and easily be taken into several parts and thrown across, the jump made, and the wheel put together again.

Packages, pedals, and backbone with rear wheel are tossed successfully across, but the big wheel attached to fork and handle-bar, unfortunately rolls back and disappears with a splash beneath the water. The details of the unhappy task of recovering this all-important piece of property—how I have to call into requisition for the first time the small, strong rope I have carried from Constantinople—how, in the absence of anything in the shape of a stick, in all the unproductive country around, I have to persuade my unwilling and goose-pimpled frame into the water and duck my devoted head beneath the waves several times before succeeding in passing a slip-noose over the handle—is too harrowing a tale to tell; it makes me shiver and shrink within myself, even as I write.

Beyond the stream the road approaches the southern framework of the plain with a barely discernible rise, and dry, hard, paths afford fair wheeling. Looking back one can see the white, uneven crest of the Elburz Range peeping over the lesser chain of hills crossed over yesterday, showing wondrously sharp and clear in the transparent atmosphere of a more or less desert country.

A region of red-clay hills and innumerable little streams ends my riding for the present, and the road eventually leads into a cul-de-sac, the source of the little streams and the home of spongy morasses whose deceptive mossy surface may or may not bear one's weight. Bound about the cul-de-sac is a curious jumble of rocks and red-clay heights; the strata of the former inclining to the perpendicular and sometimes rising like parallel walls above the earth, reminding one of the "Devil's Slide" in Weber Canon, Utah. A stiff pass leads over the brow of the range, and on the summit is perched another little stone tower; but no valiant champion of defenceless wayfarers issues forth to proffer his protection here—perhaps our acquaintance of yesterday comes down here when he wants a change of air.

From the pass the descent is into a picturesque region of huge rocks and splendid streams that come bubbling out from among them, and farther along is a more open space, a few fields of grain, and the little hamlet of Kahmeh. Stopping here an hour for refreshments, the country again becomes rough and hilly for several miles; the road then descends a rocky slope to the plain, where a few miles ahead can be seen the crenelated walls and suburban orchards and villages of Torbet-i-Haiderie.

Remembering my letter from the Governor-General to subordinate officials, I permit a uniformed horseman, who seems anxious to make himself useful in the premises, to pilot me into the city, telling him to lead the way to the Mustapha's office. Guiding me through the narrow, crowded streets into the still more crowded bazaar, he descants, from his commanding position in the saddle, to the listening crowd, on the marvellous nature of my steed and the miraculous ability required to ride it as he had seen me riding it outside the walls. Having accomplished his vain purpose of attracting public attention to himself through me, and by his utterances aroused the popular curiosity to an ungovernable pitch, he rides off and leaves me to extricate myself and find the Mustapha as best I can.

The ignorant, inconsiderate mob at once commence shouting for me to ride. "Sowar shuk; sowar shuk! tomasha; tomasha!" a thousand people cry in the stuffy, ill-paved bazaar as they struggle and push and surge about me, giving me barely room to squeeze through them. When it is discovered that I am seeking the Mustapha, there is a great rush of the crowd to reach the municipal compound and gain admittance, lest perchance the gates should be closed after I had entered and a tomasha be given without them seeing.

Following along with the crowd, the compound is reached and found to be jammed so tightly with people that the greatest difficulty is experienced in forcing my way through them to the Mustapha's quarters. Nobody seems to take a particle of interest in the matter, save to lend their voices to help swell the volume of the cry for me to ride; nobody in all the tumultuous mob seems capable of the simple reflection that there is no room whatever to ride, not so much as a yard of space unoccupied by human beings. They might with equal propriety be shouting for a fish to swim without providing him with water.

The Mustapha is found seated on the raised floor of his open-fronted office, examining, between whiffs of the kalian, papers brought to him by his subordinates, and I hand him my general letter of recommendation. Taking a cursory glance at the contents, he gives a sweep of his chin toward the bicycle, and says, "Sowar shuk; tomasha." Pointing out the utter impossibility of complying with his request in a badly-paved compound packed to its utmost capacity with people; he looks wearily at the ragged and unruly multitude before him, as though conscious that it would be useless to try and do anything with them, and then giving some order to an officer resumes his official labors.

The officer summons a couple of farrashes, and with long willow switches they flog their way through the crowd, opening a narrow, but instantly filled again, passage for me to follow. Outside the compound the officer practically forsakes me and goes over body and soul to the enemy. Filled with the same dense ignorance and overwhelming desire to see the bicycle ridden, he desires also to gain the approbation of the crowd, and so brings all his powers of persuasion to bear against me. Time and again, while traversing with the greatest difficulty the narrow bazaar in the midst of a surging mob, he faces about and makes the same insane request, shouting like a maniac to make his voice audible above the din of a thousand clamorous appeals to the same purpose. Had I the power to annihilate the whole crazy, maddening multitude with a sweep of the hand, I am afraid they would at this juncture have received but small mercy.

The caravanserai is a big, commodious affair, a quadrangular structure of brick surrounding fully an acre of ground, and with a small open space outside. There is plenty of room to satisfy their insane curiosity here without jeopardizing my own neck, and in a fruitless effort to gratify them I essay to ride. My appearance in the saddle is greeted with wild shouts of exultation, and in their eagerness to come closer and see exactly how the bicycle is propelled and prevented from falling over, they close up in front as well as behind, compelling an instant dismount to prevent disagreeable consequences to myself. Howls of disapproval greet this misinterpreted action, and the officer and farrashes commence flogging right and left to clear a space for another trial.

This time, while circling about in the small amphitheatre, walled around by shouting, grinning human beings, wanton youngsters from the rear shy several stones, and the officer comes near giving me a header by accidentally inserting his willow staff in the front wheel while pointing out to the crowd the action of the pedals and the modus operandi of things in general. The officer evidently regards me as the merest dummy, unable to speak or comprehend a word of the language, or help myself in any way— the result, it is presumed, of some explanation to that effect in the letter— and he stalks about with the proud bearing and self-conscious expression of a showman catering successfully to an appreciative and applauding populace.

The accommodation provided at the caravanserai consists of doorless menzils, elevated three feet above the ground; a walled partition, with an open archway, divides the quarters into a room behind and an open porch in front. Conducting me to one of these free-for-anybody places, which I could just as easily have found and occupied without his assistance, he takes his departure, leaving me to the tender consideration of an overbearing, ragamuffin mob, in whom the spirit of wantonness is already aroused.

I attempt to appeal to the reason of my obstreperous audience by standing on the menzil front and delivering a harangue in such Persian as I have at command.

"Sowar shuk, neis, tomasha, caravanserai neis rah koob neis. Inshalla saba, gitti koob rah Beerjandi, khylie koob lomasha-kh-y-l-ie koob tomasha saba," is the burden of this harangue; but eloquent though it be in its simplicity, it fails to accomplish the desired end. Their reply to it all takes the form of howls of disapproval, and the importunities to ride become more clamorous than ever.

An effort to keep them from taking possession of my quarters by shoving them off the front porch, results in my being seized roughly by the throat by one determined assailant and cracked on the head with a stick by another. Ignorant of a Ferenghi's mode of attack, the presumptuous individual, with his hand twisted in my neck-handkerchief, cocks his head in a semi-sidewise attitude, in splendid position to be dropped like a pole-axed steer by a neat tap on the temple. He wears the green kammerbund of a seyud, however; and even under the shadow of the legations in Teheran, it is a very serious and risky thing to strike a descendant of the Prophet. For a lone infidel to do so in the presence of two thousand Mussulman fanatics, already imbued with the spirit of wantonness, would be little less than deliberate suicide, so a sense of discretion intervenes to spare him the humiliation of being knocked out of time by an unhallowed fist. The stiff, United States army helmet, obtained, it will be remembered, at Fort Sidney, Nebraska, and worn on the road ever since, saves my bump of veneration from actual contact with the stick of number two; and finding me making only a passive resistance, the valiant individual in the green kammerbund relaxes both the severity of his scowl and his grip on my neck gear.

After this there is no use trying to keep them from invading my quarters, and I deem it advisable to stand closely by the bicycle, humoring their curiosity and getting along with them as peaceably as possible. The crowd present is constantly augmented by new arrivals from without; at least two thousand people are struggling, pushing and shouting, some coming forward to invade my menzil, others endeavoring to escape from the crush. While the rowdiest portion of the crowd struggle and push and shout in the foreground of this remarkable scene, little knots of big-turbaned mollahs and better-class citizens are laying their precious heads together scheming against me in the rear. Now and then a messenger in the semi-military garb of a farrash, pushes his way to the front and delivers a message from these worthies, full of lies and deceit. From the top of their shaved and turbaned heads to the soles of their slip-shod feet they are filled with a pig-headed determination to accomplish their object of seeing the bicycle ridden. They send me all sorts of messages, from one of but ordinary improbability, saying that the Mustapha is outside and wants me to come out and ride, to one altogether ridiculous in its wild absurdity, promising me a present of two tomans.

Occasionally a dervish holds aloft the fantastic paraphernalia of his profession, battles his way through the surging human surf, and with his black, ferret-like eyes gleaming with unconscious ferocity through a vision of unkempt hair, thrusts his cocoa-nut alms-receiver under my nose and says, "Huk yah huk!" or "backsheesh!" Shouted at, gesticulated at, intrigued against and solicited for alms all at the same time, and with brain-turning persistency, the classic halls of Bedlam would, in contrast, be a reposeful and calm retreat. Driven by my tormentors almost to the desperate resolve of emptying my six-shooter among them, let the result to myself be what it may, the sun of my persecutions has not reached the meridian even yet. The officer who an hour ago inconsiderately left me to my own resources, now returns with a large party of friends, bent on seeing the same wonderful sight that has seemingly set the whole city in an uproar. He has been about the place collecting friends and acquaintances for the purpose of treating them to an exhibition of my skill on the wheel. The purpose of the officer's return, with his friends, is readily understood by the crowd, and his arrival is announced by a universal roar of "Sowar shuk! tomasha!" as though not one of this insatiable mob had yet seen me ride.

Appearing before the elevated porch of the menzil, he beckons me to "come ahead" in quite an authoritative manner. The peculiar beckoning twist of this presumptuous individual's chin and henna-stained beard summoning me to come out and "perform" reminds me of nothing so much as some tamer of wild animals ordering a trained baboon to spruce himself up and dance for the edification of the circus-going public. Signifying my unwillingness to be thus made a circus of over and over again, the officer beckons even more peremptorily than before, and even makes a feint of coming and fetching me out by force.

As may well be believed, the sum of my patience is no longer equal to the strain, and jerking my revolver around from the obscurity of its hiding-place at my hip to where it can plainly be seen, and laying a hand menacingly on the butt, I warn him to clear off, in a manner that causes him to wilt and turn pale. He leaves the caravanserai at once in high dudgeon. It has been a most humiliating occasion for him, to fall so ignobly from the very high horse on which he just entered with his bosom friends; but it is no more than he rightly deserves.

Shortly after this little incident the part-proprietor of a tchai-khan not far from the caravanserai, proposes that I leave my menzil and come with him to his place. Happy in the prospect of any kind of a change that will secure me a little peace, I readily agree to the proposal and at once take my departure. A few stones are thrown, fortunately without doing any damage, ere the tchai-khan is reached; but once inside, the situation is materially improved.

It soon transpires that the speculative proprietors have conceived the bright idea of utilizing me as an attraction to draw customers to their place of business. Two men are stationed at the door with clubs, and admittance is only granted to likely-looking people who have money to spend on water-pipes and tea. A rival attraction already occupies the field in the person of a Tabreez Turkish luti with a performing rib-nosed mandril and a drum. Now and then, when the crowd with no money to spend becomes too clamorous about the doorway, the luti goes to the assistance of the guards, and giving the mandril the length of his chain, chases the people away.

These wandering troubadours and their performing monkeys are common enough all over Persia, and one often meets them on the road or in the villages; but the bicycle is quite a different thing, and the enterprising Tchan-jees do a roaring business all the evening with customers pouring in to see it and me. The bicycle, the luti, and the mandril occupy the back part of the large room, where several lamps and farnooses envelop this attractive and drawing combination with a garish and stagy glow, so that they can be seen to advantage by the throngs of eager visitors. My own place, as the lion of the occasion, is happily in the vicinity of the samovar, where liberal-minded customers can treat me to cigarettes and tea.

Ridiculous as is my position in the tchai-khan, it is, of course, infinitely superior in point of comfort and freedom from annoyance, to my exposed quarters over at the caravanserai. The luti sings doubtful love songs to the accompaniment of finger-strumming on the drum, and the mandril now and then condescends to stand on its head, grunt loudly in response to questions, spin round and round like a dancing dervish, and otherwise give proof of his intelligence and accomplishments. Its long hair is shorn from the lower portion of its body, but its head and shoulders are covered with a wealth of silvery-grayish hair that overlaps the nakedness of its body and gives it the grotesque appearance of wearing a tippet. The animal's temper is anything but sweet, necessitating the habitual employment of a muzzle to prevent him from biting. Every ten or fifteen minutes, as regular almost as the movements of Father Time, the mandril's bottled discontent at being made to perform seems to reach the explosive point, and springing suddenly at his master, he buries his nose viciously among his clothing in a determined effort to chew him up. This spasmodic rage subsides in horrible grunts of disappointment at being unable to use his teeth, and he becomes reasonably tractable again for another ten minutes.

The luti himself is filled with envy and covetousness at the immense drawing powers of the bicycle; and in a burst of confidence wants to know if I am an "Ingilis lut;" at the same time placing his forefingers together as an intimation that if I am we ought by all means to form a combination and travel the country together. About ten o'clock the khan-jees make me up quite a comfortable shake-down, and tired out with the tough journey over the mountains and the worrying persecutions of the afternoon, I fall asleep while yet the house is doing a thriving trade; the luti singing, the mandril grunting, kalians bubbling, and people talking, all fail to keep me awake.

The mental and physical exhaustion that makes this possible, does not, however, prevent me from falling asleep with a firm determination to leave Torbet-i-Haiderie and its turbulent population too early in the morning for any more crowds to gather. Accordingly, the morning star has scarcely risen above the horizon ere I turn out, waken one of the khan-jees, pocket some bread and depart.

Beyond the streams and villages about Torbet-i-Haiderie, the country develops into a level desert, stretching away southward as far as eye can reach. The trail is firm gravel, the wind is favorable, the morning cool, and the fresh, clear air of the desert exhilarating; under these favorable conditions I bowl rapidly along, overtaking in a very short time night-marching camel-riders that left the city last night. Traces of old irrigating ditches and fields in one or two places tell the tale of an attempt to reclaim portions of this desert long ago; but now the camel-thorn and kindred hardy shrubs hold undisputed sway on every hand. During the forenoon a small oasis is found among some low, shaly hills that give birth to a little stream, and consequent subsistence, to a few families of people; they live together inside a high mud-walled enclosure and cultivate a few small fields of grain. The place is called Kair-abad, and the people mix chopped garlic with their bread before baking it, or sprinkle the dough liberally with garlic seeds.

About 2 p.m. is reached a much larger oasis containing a couple of villages; beyond this are diverging trails with no one anywhere near to ask the way. Choosing the one that seems to take the most southerly course, the trail continues hard and ridable for a few more miles, when it becomes lost in a sea of shifting sand. Firmer ground is visible in the distance ahead, and on it are seen the small black tents of a few families of Eliautes. Considerable difficulty is experienced in getting through the sand; but the width is not great, and the dim trail is recovered on the southern side with the assistance of a chance acquaintance.

This chance acquaintance is an Eliaute goat-herd, whom I unwittingly scared nearly out of his senses, and whose gratitude at finding himself confronting a kindly-disposed human being instead of some supernatural agent of destruction, is very great indeed. He was slumbering at his post, this gentle guardian of a herd of goats, stretched at full length on the ground. Surveying his unconscious form for a moment and carried away by the animal-like simplicity of his face, I finally shout "Hoi!" Opening his eyes with a start and seeing a white-helmeted head surveying him over the top of a weird, bristling object, the natural impulse of this simple-hearted child of the desert is to seek safety in flight. Recovering his head, however, upon hearing reassuring words, he adopts the propitiatory course of rushing impulsively forward and kissing my hand.

Spending his whole life here on the lonely desert in the constant society of a herd of goats, rarely seeing a stranger or meeting anybody to speak to outside the very limited members of his own tribesmen in yonder tents, he seems to have almost lost the power of conversation. His replies are mere guttural gruntings, as though the ever-present music of bleating goats has had the lamentable effect of neutralizing the naturally superior articulation of a human being and dragging his powers of utterance down almost to the ignoble level of "mb-b-a-a."

My small stock of Persian words seems also to be altogether lost upon his warped and blunted powers of understanding, and it is only by an elaborate use of pantomime that I finally succeed in making my wants understood. He possesses the simple hospitable instincts of a child of Nature's broad solitudes; he leads the way for over a mile to put me on the now scarcely perceptible continuation of the trail, and with a worshipfully anxious face he begs of me to go and stay over night at the tents.

My road leads right past the little cluster of black tents; several women outside collecting stunted brushwood greet me with the silent, wondering stare of people incapable of any deeper display of emotion than the animals they daily associate with and subsist upon; half-naked children stare at me in a dreamy sort of way from beneath the tents. Even the dogs seem to have lost their canine propensity to resent innovations; the result, no doubt, of the same dreary, uneventful round of existence, in which the faculty of resentment has become dwarfed by the general absence of anything new or novel to bark at.

The tents of the Eliautes are small and inelegant as compared with the tents of well-to-do Koords, and the physique and general appearance of the Eliautes themselves is vastly inferior to the magnificent fellows that we found loafing about the headquarters of the Koordish sheikhs in Asia Minor and Western Persia.

The trail I am now following is evidently but little used, requiring the tracking instincts of an Indian almost to keep it in view. It leads due southward across the broad, level wastes of the Goonabad Desert, the surface of which affords most excellent wheeling even where there is not the faintest indication of a trail. Much of the surface partakes of the character of bare mud-flats that afford as smooth a wheeling surface as the alkali flats of the West; the surface is covered all over with crisp sun peelings—the thin, shiny surface of mud, baked and curled upward by the fierce heat of the sun, and which now crackle like myriads of dried twigs beneath the wheel. Occasionally I pass through thousands of acres of wild tulips, and scattering bands of antelopes are observed feeding in the distance. The bulbous roots of a great many of the tulips have been eaten by herbivorous animals of epicurean tastes—our fastidious friends, the antelopes, no doubt. The flags are bitten off and laid aside, the tender, white interior of the bulb alone is extracted and eaten, the less tender outside layers being left in the hole. It is a glorious ride across the Goonabad Desert, a ten-mile pace being quite possible most of the way; sometimes the trail is visible and sometimes it is not. With but the vaguest idea of the distance to the next abode of man, or the nature of the country ahead, I bowl along southward, led by the strange infatuation of a pathfinder traversing terra incognita, and rejoicing in the sense of boundless freedom and unrestraint that comes of speeding across open country where Nature still holds her primitive sway.

Twice I wheel past the ruins of wayside umbars, whose now utterly neglected condition and the well-nigh obliterated trail point out that I am travelling over a route that has for some reason been abandoned. A variation from the otherwise universal level occurs in the shape of a cluster of low, mound-like hills, whose modest proportions are made gorgeous and interesting by flakes of mica that glint and glisten in the sunlight as though the hills might be strewn with precious jewels.

The sun is getting pretty low, and no signs of human habitation anywhere about; but the wheeling is excellent, and the termination of the lake-like level is observable in the distance ahead in favor of low hills. Between my present position and the hills the prospect is that of continuous level ground. Imagine my astonishment, then, at shortly finding myself standing on the bank of a stream about thirty yards wide, its yellow waters flowing sluggishly along twenty feet below the surface of the desert. The abrupt nature of its banks, and an evidently unpleasant habit of becoming unfordable after a rain, tell the story of the abandoned trail I have been following. Whether three feet deep or thirty, the thick, muddy character of its moving water refuses to reveal, as, standing on the bank, I ruefully survey the situation.

No time is to be lost in idle speculation, unless I want to stretch my supperless form on the barren, brown bosom of mother earth, and dream the dreary visions conjured up by the clamorous demands of unsatisfied nature; for the sun has well-nigh sunk below the horizon. Clambering down the almost perpendicular bank I succeed, after several attempts, in discovering a passage that can be forded, and so, wrapping my clothing, money, revolver, etc. tightly within my rubber coat, I essay to carry the bundle across. All goes well until I reach a point just beyond the middle of the stream, when the bed of the stream breaks through with my weight and lets me down into a watery cavern to which there appears to be no bottom. The bed of the stream at this point seems to be a mere thin shell, beneath which there are other aqueous depths, and fearful lest the undercurrent should carry me beneath the crust and prevent me recovering myself, I loose the bundle and regain the surface without more ado. The rubber covering preserves the clothes from getting much of a wetting, and I swim and wade to the opposite shore with them without much trouble.

To get the bicycle over, however, looks a far more serious undertaking; for to break through in this way with a bicycle held aloft would probably result in getting entangled in the wheel and held under the water. It would be equally risky to take that important piece of property apart and cross over with it piece by piece, for the loss of any part would be a serious matter here.

Several new places are tried, but this one is the only passage that can be forded. My rope is also too short to be of avail in swimming over and pulling the bicycle across. Finally, after many attempts, I succeed in finding a ford immediately alongside where I had broken through, and after thoroughly testing the strength of the crust by standing and jumping up and down, I conclude to risk carrying the wheel. Owing to the extreme difficulty of following the same line, it is scarcely necessary to remark that every step forward is made with extreme caution and every foot of the riverbed traversed tested as thoroughly as possible, under the circumstances, before fully trusting my weight upon it. Once the crust breaks through again, letting me down several inches; but, fortunately, the second bottom is here but a matter of inches below the first shell, and I am able to recover myself without dropping the bicycle; and the southern bank is reached without further misadventure.

No trail is visible on the crackled surface of the mud-flat across the river, as I continue in a general southward course, hoping to find it again ere it becomes too dark Soon a man riding on a camel is descried some distance off to the right, and deeming it advisable to seek for information at his hands, I shape my course toward him and give chase. Becoming conscious of a strange-looking object careering over the plain in his direction, the man surveys me for a moment from the back of his awkward steed and then steers his ship of the desert in another direction. The lumbering camel is quickly overtaken, however, and the gallant but apprehensive rider makes a stand and threateningly waves me away. Observing the absence of the familiar long-barrelled gun, I persist in my purpose of interviewing him regarding the road, and finally learn from him that the village of Goonabad is eight miles farther south, and that the trail will be easier followed when I reach the hills. Had he been armed with a gun, there would have been more or less risk in approaching him in the dusky shades of evening on so strange a vehicle of travel; but before I depart he alights from his camel for the characteristic purpose of kissing my hand.

A couple of miles brings me to the hills, where my riding abruptly comes to an end; the hills are simply huge waves of sand and dust collected on the shore of the desert and held together by a growth of coarse shrubs. The dim light of the young moon proves insufficient for my purpose of keeping the trail, and the difficulty in trundling through the sand compels me to seek the cold comfort of a night in the desert, after all.

Goonabad appears to be a sort of general rendezvous for wandering tribes of Eliautes that roam the desert country around with their flocks and herds, the tent population of the place far outnumbering the soil-tilling people of the village itself. A complete change is here observable in both the climate and the people; north of the desert the young barley is in a very backward state, but at Goonabad both wheat and barley are headed out, and the sun strikes uncomfortably hot as soon as it rises above the horizon. It is a curious change in so short a distance. The men affect the long, dangling, turban-end of the Afghans and the women blossom forth in the gayest of colors; the people are refreshingly simple-hearted and honest, as compared with the knowing customers along the Teheran-Meshed road.

Sand-hills, scattering fields and villages, and a bewildering time generally, in keeping my course, characterize the experience of the forenoon. The people of one particular village passed through are observed to be all descendants of the Prophet, wearing monster green turbans and green kammerbunds; the women are dressed in white throughout—white socks, white pantalettes, and white shrouds; they move silently about, more like ghostly visitants than human beings. Distinctly different types of people from the majority are sometimes met with—full-bearded, very dark-skinned men, whose bared breasts betray the fact that they are little less hairy than a bison.

Beyond the sand-hills, the villages, and the cultivation is a stony plain extending for sixteen miles, a gradual upward slant to a range of mountains. At the base of the mountains an area of dark-green coloring denotes the presence of fields and orchards and the whereabouts of the important village of Kakh. Beautifully terraced wheat-fields and vineyards, and peach and pomegranate orchards in full bloom, gladden the eyes and present a most striking contrast to the stony plain as the vicinity of Kakh is reached, and another pleasing and conspicuous feature is the dome of a mesjid mosaicked with bright-colored tiles.

The good people of Kakh are inquisitive even above their fellows, if such can be possible, but they are well-behaved and mild-mannered with it. After taking the ragged edge off their curiosity by riding up and down the main thoroughfare of the village, the keeper of a mercantile affair locks the bicycle up in his room, and I spend the evening hobnobbing with him and his customers in his little stall-like place of business. Kakh is famous for the production of little seedless raisins like those of Smyrna. Bushels of these are kicking about the place, and our merchant friend becomes filled with a wild idea that I might, perchance, buy the lot. A moment's reflection would convince him that ten bushels of sickly-sweet raisins would be about the last thing he could sell to a person travelling on a bicycle; but his supply of raisins is evidently so outrageously ahead of the demand that his ambition to reduce his stock obscures his better judgment like a cloud, and places him in the position of a drowning man clutching wildly at a straw.

Considerable opium is also grown hereabouts, and the people make it into sticks about the size of a carpenter's pencil; hundreds of these also occupy the merchant's shelves. He seems to have very little that isn't grown in the neighborhood except tea and loaf-sugar.

Eyots, who were absent in their fields when I arrived, come crowding around the store in the evening, bothering me to ride; the shop-keeper bids them wait till my departure in the morning, telling them I am not a luti, riding simply to let people see. He provides me with a door that fastens inside, and I am soon in the land of dreams.

Early in the morning I am awakened by people pounding at the door and shouting, "A/tab, Sahib-a/tab.'" It is the belated ryots of yesterday eve; thoroughly determined to be on hand and see the start, they are letting me know that it is sunrise.

A boisterous mountain stream, tearing along at racing speed over a rocky bed a hundred and fifty yards wide, provides Kakh with perpetual music, and furnishes travellers going southward with an interesting time getting across. This stream must very frequently become a raging torrent, quite impassable; for although it is little more than knee-deep this morning, the swift water carries down stones as large as a brick, that strike against the ankles and well-nigh knock one off his feet.

Beyond Kakh the trail winds its circuitous way through a mountainous region, following one little stream to its source, climbing over the crest of an intervening ridge and down the bed of another stream. It is but an indistinct donkey trail at best, and the toilsome mountain climbing reminds me vividly of the worst parts of Asia Minor. Toward nightfall I wander into the village of Nukhab, a small place perched among the hills, inhabited by kindly-disposed, hospitable folks.

Having seen the unhappy effect of the Governor-General's letter of recommendation at Torbet-i-Haiderie, and desirous of seeing what effect it might, perchance, have on the more simple-hearted people of Nukhab, I present it to the little, old, blue-gowned Khan of the village. Like a very large proportion of his people, the Khan is suffering from chronic ophthalmia; but he peruses the letter by the glimmer of a blaze of camel-thorn. The intentions of these people were plainly most hospitable from the beginning, so that it is difficult to determine about the effect of the letter.

Willing hands sweep out the quarters assigned for my accommodation, the improvised besoms filling the place with a cloud of dust; the doorway is ruthlessly mutilated to make it large enough to admit the bicycle; nummuds are spread and a crackling fire soon fills the room with mingled smoke and light. The people are allowed to circulate freely in and out to see me, but only the Khan himself and a few of the leading lights of the village are permitted to indulge in the coveted privilege of spending the entire evening in my company. The village is ransacked for eatables to honor their guest, resulting in a bountiful repast of eggs, pillau, mast, and sheerah.

Away down here among the mountains and out of the world, these people see nothing more curious than their next-door neighbors from year to year; they take the most ridiculous interest in such small affairs as my note-book and pencil, and everything about me seems to strike them as peculiar.

The entire village, as usual, assembles to see me dispose of the eatables so generously provided; and later in the evening there is another highly-expectant assembly waiting around, out of curiosity, to see what sort of a figure a Ferenghi cuts at his evening devotions. Poor benighted followers of the False Prophet, how little they comprehend us Christians! Suddenly it seems to dawn upon the mind of the simple old Khan that, being a stranger in a strange land, I might, perchance, be a trifle mixed about my bearings, and so he kindly indicates the direction of Mecca. When informed that the Ingilis never prostrate themselves toward Mecca and say "Allah-il-allah!" they evince the greatest astonishment; and then the strange, unnatural impiousness of people who never address themselves to Allah nor prostrate toward the Holy City, impresses their simple minds with something akin to the feeling entertained among certain of ourselves toward extra dare-devil characters, and they seem to take a deeper and kindlier interest in me than ever. The disappointment at not seeing what I look like at prayers is more than offset by the additional novelty imparted to my person by the, to them, strange and sensational omission.

They seem greatly disappointed to learn that I am going away in the morning; they have plenty of toke-me-morge, pillau, mast, and sheerah, they say—plenty of everything; and they want me to stay with them always. Revolving the matter over in my mind, I am forcibly struck with the calm, reposeful state of Nukhab society; and what a brilliant field of enterprise for an ambitious person the place would be. Turned Mussulman, joined in wedlock to three or four sore-eyed village damsels; worshipped as a sort of strange, superior being, hakim and eye-water dispenser; consulted as a walking store-house of occult philosophy on all occasions; endeavoring to educate the people up to habits of all-round cleanliness; chiding the mothers for allowing the flies to swarm and devour the poor little babies' eyes—all this, for toke-me-morge, pillau, mast, and sheerah, twice or thrice a day! Involuntarily my eye roams over the gladsome countenances of the eligible portion of my female auditors, as though driven by this whimsical flight of fancy to the necessity of at once making a choice. There is only one present with any pretence to comeliness; and embarrassed, no doubt, by the extreme tenderness of the stranger's glance, she shrinks from view behind an aged and ugly person whom I take to be her mother.

Everybody stops to see what a Ferenghi looks like en deshabille, and when I am snugly sandwiched between the quilts provided, they gather about me and peer curiously down into my face.

An enterprising youth is on hand at daybreak making a fire; but it is eight o'clock before I am able to get away; they seem to be mildly scheming among themselves to keep me with them as long as possible.

The trail winds and twists about among the mountains, following in the train of a wayward little stream, then leads over a pass and emerges, in the company of another stream, upon a slanting plateau leading down to an extensive plain. Rounding the last spur of the hills, I find myself approaching a crowd numbering at least a hundred people. Hats are waved gleefully, voices are lifted up in joyous shouts of welcome, and the whole company give way to demonstrations of delight at my approach. A minute later I find myself surrounded by the familiar faces of the population of Nukhab—my road has followed a roundabout course of six or seven miles, and our enterprising friends have taken a short cut over the lulls to intercept me at this point, where they can watch my, progress across the open plain. They have brought along the kind old Kahn's kalian and tobacco-bag, and the wherewithal to make me a parting glass of tea.

Eight or ten miles of fair wheeling across the plain, through the isolated village of Mohammedabad, and the trail loses itself among the rank, dead stalks of the assafoetida plant that here characterizes the vegetation of the broad, level sweep of plain. The day is cloudy, and with no trail visible, my compass has to be brought into requisition; though oft-times finding it useful, it is the first time I have found this article to be really indispensable so far on the tour.

The atmosphere of an assafoetida desert is among those things that can better be imagined than described; the aroma of the fetid gum is wafted to and fro, and assails the nostrils in a manner quite the reverse of "Araby the blest." The plant is a sturdy specimen among the annuals: its straight, upright stem is but three or four feet high, but often measuring four inches in diameter, and it not infrequently defies the blasts of the Khorassan winter and the upheaving thaws of spring, and preserves its upright position for a year after its death. The thick, dead stems and branching tops of last year's plants are seen by the thousands, sturdily holding their ground among the rank young shoots of the new growth.

Mountainous territory is again entered during the afternoon, and shortly after sunset I arrive at a cluster of wretched mud hovels, numbering about two dozen. Here my reception is preeminently commercial and business-like, the people requiring payment in advance for the bread and eggs and rogan provided.

A nonsensical custom among the people of Southern Khorassan is to offer one's food in turn to everybody present and say, "Bis-millah," before commencing to eat it yourself. Although a ridiculous piece of humbug, it is generally my custom to fall in with the peculiar ways of the country, and for days past have invariably offered my food to scores of people whom I knew beforehand would not take it. The lack of courtesy at this hamlet in exacting payment in advance would seem naturally to preclude the right to expect the following of courteous customs in return. In this, however, I find myself mistaken; for my omission to say "Bis-millah" not only fills these people with astonishment, but excites unfavorable comment.

The door-ways of the houses here are entirely too small to admit the bicycle, and that much-enduring vehicle has to take its chances on the low roof with a score or so inquisitive and meddlesome goats that instantly gather around it, as though revolving in their pugnacious minds some fell scheme of destruction. Outside are several camels tied to their respective pack-saddles, which have been taken off and laid on the ground. Before retiring for the night, it occurs to my mind that the total depravity of a goat's appetite bodes ill for the welfare of my saddle, and that, everything considered, the bicycle could, perhaps, be placed safer on the ground; in addition to regarding the saddle as a particularly toothsome morsel, the goats' venturesome disposition might lead them to clambering about on the spokes, and generally mixing things up. So, taking it down, I stand it up against the wall, and place a heap of old pack-saddle frames and camel-trappings before it as an additional precaution. During the night some of the camels break loose and are heard chasing one another around the house, knocking things over and bellowing furiously. Apprehensive of my wheel, I get up and find it knocked over, but, fortunately, uninjured; I then take off the saddle and return it to the tender care and consideration of the goats.

Four men and a boy share with me a small, unventilated den, about ten feet square; one of them is a camel-driving descendant of the Prophet, and sings out "Allah-il-allah!" several times during the night in his sleep; another is the patriarch of the village, a person guilty of cheating the undertaker, lo! these many years, and who snuffles and catches his breath. The other two men snore horribly, and the boy gives out unmistakable signs of a tendency to follow their worthy example; altogether, it is anything but a restful night.

CHAPTER VII

BEERJAND AND THE FRONTIER OF AFGHANISTAN

Thirty miles over hill and dale, after leaving the little hamlet, and behold, the city of Beerjand appears before me but a mile or thereabouts away, at the foot of the hills I am descending. One's first impression of Beerjand is a sense of disappointment; the city is a jumbled mass of uninteresting mud buildings, ruined and otherwise, all of the same dismal mud-brown hue. Not a tree exists to relieve the eye, nor a solitary green object to break the dreary monotony of the prospect; the impression is that of a place existing under some dread ban of nature that forbids the enlivening presence of a tree, or even the redeeming feature of a bit of greensward.

The broad, sandy bed of a stream contains a sluggishly-flowing reminder of past spring freshets; but the quickening presence of a stream of water seems thrown away on Beerjand, except as furnishing a place for closely-veiled females to come and wash clothes, and for the daily wading and disporting of amphibious youngsters. In any other city a part of its mission would be the nurturing of vegetation.

The Ameer, Heshmet-i-Molk, I quickly learn, is living at his summer-garden at Ali-abad, four farsakhs to the east. Curious to see something of a place so much out of the world, and so little known as Beerjand, I determine upon spending the evening and night here, and continuing on to Ali-abad next morning.

There appears to be absolutely nothing of interest to a casual observer about the city except its population, and they are interesting from their strange, cosmopolitan character, and as being the most unscrupulous and keenest people for money one can well imagine. The city seems a seething nest of hard characters, who buzz around my devoted person like wasps, seemingly restrained only by the fear of retribution from pouncing on my personal effects and depriving me of everything I possess.

The harrowing experiences of Torbet-i Haiderie have taught a useful lesson that stands me in good stead at Beerjand. Ere entering the city proper, I enlist the services of a respectable-looking person to guide the way at once where the pressing needs of hunger can be attended to before the inevitable mob gathers about me and renders impossible this very necessary part of the programme. Having duly fortified myself against the anticipated pressure of circumstances by consuming bread and cheese and sheerah in the semi-seclusion of a suburban bake-house, my guide conducts me to the caravanserai, receives his backsheesh, and loses himself in the crowd that instantly fills the place.

The news of my arrival seems to set the whole city in a furore; besides the crowds below, the galched roof of the caravanserai becomes standing room for a mass of human beings, to the imminent danger of breaking it in. So, at least, thinks the caravanserai-jee, who becomes anxious about it and tries to persuade them to come down; but he might as well attempt to summon down from above the unlistening clouds.

Around two sides of the caravanserai compound is a narrow, bricked walk, elevated to the level of the menzil floors; at the imminent risk of breaking my neck, I endeavor to appease the clamorous multitude, riding to and fro for the edification of what is probably the wildest-looking assembly that could be collected anywhere in the world. Afghans, with tall, conical, gold-threaded head-dresses, converted into monster turbans by winding around them yards and yards of white or white-and-blue cloth, three feet of which is left dangling down the back; Beloochees in flowing gowns that were once white; Arabs in the striped mantles and peculiar headdress of their country; dervishes, mollahs, seyuds, and the whole fantastic array of queer-looking people living in Beerjand, travelling through, or visiting here to trade.

Some of the Afghans wear a turban and kammerbund, all of one piece; after winding the long cotton sheet a number of times about the peaked head-dress, it is passed down the back and then ends its career in the form of a kammerbund about the waist. Fights and tumults occur as the result of the caravanserai-jee's attempt to shut the gate and keep them out, and in despair he puts me in a room and locks the door. In less than five minutes the door is broken down, and a second attempt to seclude myself results in my being summarily pelted out again with stones through a hole in the roof.

A Yezdi traveller, occupying one of the menzils—all of which at Beeriand are provided with doors and locks—now invites me to his quarters; locking the door and keeping me out of sight, he hopes by making me his guest to assist in getting rid of the crowd. Whatever his object, its consummation is far from being realized; the unappeased curiosity of the crowds of newly arriving people finds expression in noisy shouts and violent hammering on the door, creating a din so infernal that the well-meaning traveller quickly tires of his bargain. Following the instincts of the genuine Oriental, he conjures up the genius of diplomacy to rid himself of his guest and the annoyance occasioned by my presence.

"If you go outside and ride around the place once more," he says, "Inshallah, the people will all go home."

This is a very transparent proposition—a broad hint, covered with the thin varnish of Persian politeness. No sooner am I outside than the door is locked, and the wily Yezdi has accomplished his purpose of ousting me and thereby securing a little peace for himself. No right-thinking person will blame him for turning me out; on the contrary, he deserves much praise for attempting to take me in.

I now endeavor to render my position bearable by locking up the bicycle and allowing the populace to concentrate their eager gaze on me, perching myself on the roof in position to grant them a fair view. Swarms of people come flocking up after me, evidently no more able to control their impulse to follow than if they were so many bleating sheep following the tinkling leadership of a bellwether or a goat. The caravanserai-jee begs me to come down again, fearing the weight will cause the roof to cave in. well-nigh at my wit's end what to do, I next take up a squatting position in a corner and resign myself to the unhappy fate of being importuned to ride, shouted at in the guttural tones of desert tribesmen, questioned in unknown tongues, solicited for alms and schemed against and worried for this, that, and the other, by covetous and evil-minded ruffians.

"The Ingilis have khylie pool-k-h-y-lie pool!" (much money) says one ferocious-looking individual to his companion, and their black eyes glisten and their fingers rub together feverishly as they talk, as if the mere imagination of handling my money were a luxury in itself.

"He must have khylie pool if he is going all the way to Hindostan-k-h-y-lie pool!" suggests another; and the coveteousness of dozens of keenly interested listeners finds expression in "Pool, pool; the Ingilis have khylie pool."

One eager ragamuffin brings me half-a-dozen sour and shrivelled oranges, utterly worthless, for which he asks the outrageous sum of three kerans; a second villainous-looking specimen worries me continuously to leave the caravanserai and go with him somewhere. I never could make out where.

He looks the veriest cutthroat, and, curious to penetrate the secret of his intentions, and perchance secure something interesting for my note-book, I at length make pretence of acceding to his wishes. Bystanders at once interfere to prevent him enticing me away, and when he angrily remonstrates he is hustled unceremoniously out into the street.

"He is a bad man," they say; "neis koob adam."

Nothing daunted by the summary ejection of this person, a dervish, with the haggard face and wild, restless eyes of one addicted to bhang, now volunteers to take me under his protection and lead me out of the caravanserai to—where? He vouchsafes no explanation where; none, at least, that is at all comprehensible to me. Where do these interesting specimens of Beerjand's weird population want to entice me to? why do they want to entice me anywhere? I conclude to go with the dervish and find out.

The crowd enter their remonstrances again; but the dervish wears the garb of holy mendicancy; violent hands must not be laid on the sacred person of a dervish. Our path is barred at the outer gate of the caravanserai, however, by two men in semi-military uniforms, armed with swords and huge clubs; they chide the dervish for wanting to take me with him, and have evidently been placed at their post by the authorities.

Soon a uniformed official comes in and tries to question me. He is a person of very limited intelligence, incapable of understanding and making himself understood through the medium of the small stock of his native tongue at my command. The linguistic abilities of the strange, semi-civilized audience about us comprise Persian, Turkish, Hindostani, and even a certain amount of Russian; not a soul besides myself knows a single word of English.

After queries have been propounded to me in all these tongues, my intellectual interviewer gives me up in despair, and, addressing the crowd about us, cries out in astonishment: "Parsee neis! Turkchi binmus! Hindostani nay! Paruski nicht! mashallah, what language does he speak?"

"Ingilis! Ingilis! Ingilis!" shout at least a dozen more knowing people than himself.

"Oh, I-n-g-i-l-i-s!" says the officer, condemning his own lack of comprehension by the tone of his voice. "Aha, I-n-g-i-l-i-s, aha!" and he looks over the crowd apologetically for not having thought of so simple a thing before. But having ascertained that I speak English, he now proceeds to treat me to a voluble discourse in simon-pure Persian. Seeing that I fail to comprehend the tenor of the officer's remarks, some of the garrulous crowd vouchsafe to explain in Turkish, others in Hindostani, and one in Russian!

In the absence of a lunatic asylum to dodge into, I fasten on to the officer and get him to take me out and show me the Ali-abad road, so that I can find the way out early in the morning.

Another caravanserai is found located nearer the road leading from the city eastward, and I determine to change my quarters quietly by the light of the moon, leaving the crowd in ignorance of my whereabouts, so that there will be no difficulty in getting through the streets in the morning.

Late at night, when the now quieted city is bathed in the soft, mellow light of the moon, and the crenellated mud walls and old ruins and archways cast weird shadows across the silent streets, with a few chosen companions, parties to the secret of the removal, the bicycle is trundled through the narrow, crooked streets and under arched alleyways, to the caravanserai on the eastern edge of the city.

Seated beneath the shadowy archway of the first caravanserai is a silent figure smoking a kalian; as we open the gate to leave, the figure rises up and thrusts forth an alms-receiver and in a loud voice sings out, "Backsheesh, backsheesh; huk yah huk!" It is the same dervish that was turned back with me by the guards at this same gate this afternoon.

My much-needed slumbers at my new quarters are rudely disturbed—as a son of Erin might, perhaps, declare under similar circumstances—before they are commenced, by the fearful yowling of Beerjand cats. Several of these animals are paying their feline compliments to the moon from different roofs and walls hard by, and their utterances strike my unaccustomed (unaccustomed to the Beerjand variety of cat-music) ears as about the most unearthly sound possible.

Fancying the noise is made by women wailing for the dead, from a striking resemblance to the weird night-sounds heard, it will be remembered, at Bey Bazaar, Asia Minor (Vol. I), I go outside and listen. Many guesses would most assuredly be made by me before guessing cats as the authors of such unearthly music; but cats it is, nevertheless; for, seeing me listening outside by the door, one of the sharers of my rude quarters comes out and removes all doubt by drawing the rude outlines of a cat in the dust with his finger, and by delivering himself of an explanatory "meow." The yowl of a Beerjand cat is several degrees more soul-harrowing than anything inflicted by midnight prowlers upon the Occidental world, and I learn afterward that they not infrequently keep it up in the daytime.

An early start, sixteen miles of road without hills or mountains, but embracing the several qualities of good, bad, and indifferent, and at eight o'clock I dismount in the presence of a little knot of Heshmet-i-Molk's retainers congregated outside his summer-garden, and a goodly share of the population of the adjacent village of Ali-abad. While yet miles away, Ali-abad is easily distinguished as being something out of the ordinary run of Persian villages by the luxuriant foliage of the Ameer's garden. The whole country around is of the same desert-like character that distinguishes well-nigh all this country, and the dark, leafy grove of trees standing alone on the gray camel-thorn plain, derives additional beauty and interest from the contrast.

The village of Ali-abad, consisting of the merest cluster of low mud hovels and a few stony acres wrested from the desert by means of irrigation, the people ragged, dirty, and uncivilized, looks anything but an appropriate dwelling-place for a great chieftain. The summer garden itself is enclosed within a high mud wall, and it is only after passing through the gate and shutting out the rude hovels, the rag-bedecked villagers, and the barren desert, that the illusion of unfitness is removed.

My letter is taken in to the Ameer, and in a few minutes is answered in a most practical manner by the appearance of men carrying carpets, tent-poles, and a round tent of blue and white stripes. Winding its silvery course to the summer garden, from a range of hills several miles distant, is a clear, cold stream; although so narrow as to be easily jumped, and nowhere more than knee-deep, the presence of trout betrays the fact that it never runs dry.

The tent is pitched on the banks of this bright little stream, the entrance but a half-dozen paces from its sparkling water, and a couple of guards are stationed near by to keep away intrusive villagers; an abundance of eatables, including sweetmeats, bowls of sherbet, and dried apricots, and pears from Foorg, are provided at once.

A neatly dressed attendant squats himself down on the shady side of the tent outside, and at ridiculously short intervals brings me in a newly primed kalian and a samovar of tea. Everything possible to contribute to my comfort is attended to and nothing overlooked; and the Ameer furthermore proves himself sensible and considerate above the average of his fellow-countrymen by leaving me to rest and refresh myself in the quiet retreat of the tent till four o'clock in the afternoon.

Reclining on the rich Persian carpet beneath the gayly striped tent, entertained by the babbling gossip of the brook, provided with luxuriant food and watchful attendants, taking an occasional pull at a jewelled kalian primed with the mild and seductive product of Shiraz, or sipping fragrant tea, it is very difficult to associate my present conditions and surroundings with the harassing experiences of a few hours ago. This marvellous transformation in so short a time—from the madding clamor of an inconsiderate mob, to the nerve-soothing murmur of the little stream; from the crowded and filthy caravanserai to the quiet shelter of the luxurious tent; in a word, from purgatory to Paradise—what can have brought it about? Surely nothing less than the good genii of Aladdin's lamp.

A very agreeable, and, withal, intelligent young man, the incumbunt of some office about the Ameer's person, no doubt a mirza, pays me a visit at noon, apparently to supervise the serving up of the—more than bountiful repast sent in from his master's table. My attention is at once arrested by the English coat-of-arms on his sword-belt; both belt and clasp have evidently wandered from the ranks of the British army.

"Pollock Sahib," he says, in reply to my inquiries—it is a relic of the Seistan Boundary Commission.

About four o'clock, this same young man and a companion appear with the announcement that the Ameer is ready to receive me, and requests that I bring the bicycle with me into the garden. The stream flows through a low arch beneath the wall and lends itself to the maintenance of an artificial lake that spreads over a large proportion of the enclosed space. The summer garden is a fabrication of green trees and the cool glimmer of shaded water, rather than the flower-beds, the turf, and shrubbery of the Occidental conception of a garden; the Ameer's quarters consist of an un-pretentious one-storied building fronting on the lake.

The Ameer himself is found seated on a plain divan at the open-windowed front, toying with a string of amber beads; a dozen or so retainers are standing about in respectful and expectant attitudes, ready at a moment's notice to obey any command he may give or to anticipate his personal wants. He is a stoutly built, rather ponderous sort of individual, with a full, rotund face and a heavy, unintellectual, but good-natured expression; one's first impression of him is apt to be less flattering to his head than to his heart. He is a person, however, that improves with acquaintance, and is probably more intelligent than he looks. He seems to be living here in a very plain and unpretentious manner; no gaudy stained glass, no tinsel, no mirror-work, no vain gew-gaws of any description impart a cheap and garish glitter to the place; no gorgeous apparel bedecks his ample proportions. Clad in the ordinary dress of a well-to-do Persian nobleman, Heshmet-i-Molk, happy and contented in the enjoyment of creature comforts and the universal esteem of his people, probably finds his chief pleasure in sitting where we now find him, looking out upon the green trees and glimmering waters of the garden, smoking his kalian, and attending to the affairs of state in a quiet, unostentatious manner. With a refreshing absence of ceremonial, he discusses with me the prospects of my being able to reach India overland. The conversation on his part, however, almost takes the form of trying to persuade me from my purpose altogether, and particularly not to attempt Afghanistan.

"The Harood is as wide as from here to the other side of the lake yonder (200 yards); tund (swift) as a swift-running horse and deep as this house," he informs me.

"No bridge? no ferry-boat? no means of getting across?"

"Eitch" (no), replies the Ameer. "Pull neis, kishti neis."

"Can't it be forded with camels?"

"Shutor neis."

"No village, with people to assist with poles or skins to make a raft?"

"Afghani dasht-adam (nomads), no poles; you might perhaps find skins; but the river is tund-t-u-n-d! skins neis, poles neis; t-u-n-d!!" and the Ameer points to a bird hopping about on the garden walk, intimating that the Harood flows as swiftly as the flight of a bird.

The result of the conference I have been so anxiously looking forward to is anything but an encouraging picture—a picture of insurmountable obstacles on every hand. The deep sand and burning heat of the dreadful Lut Desert intervenes between me and the Mekran coast; the route through Beloochistan, barely passable with camels and guides and skins of water in the winter, is not only impracticable for anything in the summer, but there is the additional obstacle of the spring floods of the Helmund and the Seistan Lake.

The Ameer's description of the Lut Desert and Beloochistan is but a confirmation of my own already-arrived-at conclusions concerning the utter impracticability of crossing either in the summer and with a bicycle; but the wish gives birth to the thought that perhaps he may not unlikely be indulging in the Persian weakness for exaggeration in his graphic portrayal of the difficulties presented by the Harood.

The region between Beerjand and the Harood is on my map a dismal-looking, blankety-blank stretch of country, marked with the ominous title "Dasht-i" which, being interpreted into English, means Desert of Despair. A gleam of hope that things may not be quite so hopeless as pictured is born of the fact that, in dwelling on the difficulties of the situation, the Ameer makes less capital out of this same Desert of Despair than of the Harood, which has to be crossed on its eastern border.

As regards interference from the Legation of Teheran, thank goodness I am now three hundred miles from the nearest telegraph-pole, and shall enter Afghanistan at a point so much nearer to Quetta than to the Boundary Commission Camp that the chances seem all in favor of reaching the former place if I only succeed in reaching the Dasht-i-na-oomid and the Harood.

The result of the foregoing deliberations is a qualified (qualified by the absence of any alternative save turning back) determination to point my nose eastward, and follow its leadership toward the British outpost at Quetta.

"Khylie koob" (very well), replies the Ameer, as he listens to my determination; "khylie koob;" and he takes a few vigorous whiffs at his kalian as though, conscious of the uselessness of arguing the matter any further with a Ferenghi, he were dismissing the ghost of his own opinions in a cloud of smoke.

Shortly after sunrise on the following morning a couple of well-mounted horsemen appear at the door of my tent, armed and equipped for the road. Their equipment consists of long guns with resting-fork attachment, the prongs of which project above the muzzle like a two-pronged pitchfork; swords, pistols, and the brave but antique display of warlike paraphernalia characteristic of the East. One of them, I am pleased to observe, is the genial young mirza whose snuff-colored roundabout is held in place by the "dieu et mon droit" belt of yesterday; his companion is the ordinary sowar, or irregular horseman of the country. They announce themselves as bearers of the Ameer's salaams, and as my escort to Tabbas, a village two marches to the east.

A few miles of plain, with a gradual inclination toward the mountains; ten miles up the course of a mountain-stream-up, up, up to where thawing snow-banks make the pathway anything but pleasant for my escort's horses and ten times worse for a person reduced to the necessity of lugging his horse along; over the summit, and down, down, down again over a fearful trail for a wheelman, or, more correctly, over no trail at all, but scrambling as best one can over rocks, along ledges, often in the water of the stream, and finally reaching the village of Darmian, the end of our first day's march, about 3 p.m.

Darmian is situated in a rugged gulch, and the houses, gardens, and orchards ramble all over the place—with little regard to regularity, although some attempt has been made at forming streets. Darmian and Poorg are twin villages, but a short distance apart, in this same gulch, and are famous for dried apricots, pears, and dried beetroots, and for the superior quality of its sheerah.

Among the absurdities that crop up during the course of an eventful evening at Darmian is the case of a patriarchal villager whose broad and enlightening experience of some threescore years has left him in the possession of a marvellously logical and comprehensive mind. Hearing of the arrival of a Ferenghi with an iron horse, this person's subtle intellect pilots him into the stable of the place we are stopping at and leads him to search curiously therein, with the expectation, we may reasonably presume, of seeing the bicycle complacently munching kah and jow. This is perhaps not so much to be wondered at, when it is reflected that plenty of people hereabout have no conception whatever of a wheeled vehicle, never having seen a vehicle of any description.

The good people of Darmian, as is perhaps quite natural in people near the frontier, betray a pardonable pride in comparing Persia with Afghanistan, always to the prodigious disadvantage of the latter. In the course of the usual examination of my effects, they are immensely gratified to learn from my map that Persia is much the larger country of the two. A small corner of India is likewise visible on the map, and, taking it for granted that the map represents India as fully as it does Persia, the khan, on whom I am unwittingly bestowing the rudiments of a false but patriotic geographical education, turns around, and with swelling pride informs the delighted people that Seistan is larger than India, and Iran bigger than all the rest of the world, he taking it for granted that my map of Persia is a map of the whole world.

More and more fantastic grow the costumes of the people as one gets farther, so to speak, out of civilization and off the beaten roads. The ends of the turbans here are often seen gathered into a sort of bunch or tuft on the top; the ends are fringed or tipped with gold, and when gathered in this manner create a fanciful, crested appearance—impart a sort of cock-a-doodle-doo aspect to the wearer.

Among the most interesting of my callers are three boys of eight to twelve summers, who enter the room chewing leathery chunks of dried beetroot. Although unwashed, "unwiped," and otherwise undistinguishable from others of the same age about the place, they are gravely introduced as khan this, that, and the other respectively; and while they remain in the room, obsequiousness marks the deportment of everybody present except their father, and he regards them with paternal pride.

They are sons of the village khan, and as such are regarded superior beings by the common people about them. It looks rather ridiculous to see grown people bearing themselves in a retiring, servile manner in deference to youngsters glaringly ignorant of how to use a pocket-handkerchief, and who look as if their chief pastime were chewing dried beetroot and rolling about in the dust.

But presently it is revealed that their first visit has been a mere informal call to satisfy the first impulse of youthful curiosity. By and by their fond parent takes them away for half an hour, and then ushers them into my presence again, transformed into gorgeous youths with nice clean faces and wiped noses. Marshalling themselves gravely opposite where I am sitting, they put their hands solemnly on their youthful stomachs, salaam, and gracefully drop down into a cross-legged position on the carpet.

They look like real little chieftains now, both in dress and deportment. Scarlet roundabouts, trimmed with a profusion of gold braid, bedeck their consequential bodies; red slippers embroidered with gold thread cover their feet, and their snowy turbans end in a gold-flecked tuft of transparent muslin that imparts a bantam-like air of superiority. Their father comes and squats down beside me, and, as we sip tea together, he bestows a fond, parental smile upon the three scarlet poppies sitting motionless, with heads slightly bent and eyes downcast, before us, and inquires by an eloquent sweep of his chin what I think of them as specimens of simon-pure nobility.

All through Persia the word "ob" has heretofore been used for water; but linguistic changes are naturally to be expected near the frontier, and the Darmian people use the term "ow." Upon my calling for ob, the khan's attendant stares blankly in reply; but an animated individual in the front ranks of the crowd about the doors and windows enlightens him and me at the same time by shouting out, "Ow! ow! ow!"

The muezzin, calling the faithful to their evening prayers, likewise utters the summons here at Darmian quite differently from anything of the kind heard elsewhere.

The cry is difficult to describe; but without meaning to cast reflections on the worthy muezzin's voice, I may perhaps be permitted to mention that the people are twice admonished, and twice a listening katir (donkey) awakens the echoing voices of the rock-ribbed gulch in vociferous response.

The mother-in-law of the mirza lives at Darmian, and, like a dutiful son, he lingers in her society until nine o'clock next morning. At that hour he turns his horse's footsteps down the bed of the stream, while his comrade guides me for a couple of miles over a most abominable mountain-trail, rejoining the river and the dutiful son-in-law at Foorg. Foorg is situated at the extremity of the gulch, and is distinguished by a frowning old castle or fort, that occupies the crest of a precipitous hill overtopping the village and commanding a very comprehensive view of the country toward the Afghan frontier.

The villages of Darmian and Foorg, looking out upon wild frontier territory, inhabited chiefly by turbulent and lawless tribes-people whose hereditary instincts are diametrically opposed to the sublime ethics of the decalogue have no doubt often found the grim stronghold towering so picturesquely above them an extremely convenient thing.

The escort points it out and explains that it belongs to the "Padishah at Teheran," and not to his own master, the Ameer—a national, as distinct from a provincial, fortification. The cultivated environs of Foorg present a most discouraging front to a wheelman; walled gardens, rocks, orchards, and ruins, with hundreds of water-ditches winding and twisting among them, the water escaping through broken banks and creating new confusion where confusion already reigns supreme. Among this indescribable jumble of mud, water, rocks, ruins, and cultivation, pitched almost at an angle of forty-five degrees, the natives climb about bare-legged, impressing one very forcibly as so many human goats as they scale the walls, clamber over rocks, or wade through mud and water.

A willing Foorgian divests himself of everything but his hat, and carries the bicycle across the stream, while I am taken up behind the mirza. As the mirza's iron-gray gingerly enters the water, an interesting and instructive spectacle is afforded by a hundred or more Foorgians following the shining example of the classic figure carrying the bicycle, for the purpose of being on hand to see me start across the plain toward Tabbas.

Some of these good people are wearing turbans the size of a bandbox; others wear enormous sheep-skin busbies. A number of tall, angular figures stemming the turbid stream in the elegant costumes of our first parents, but wearing Khorassani busbies or Beerjand turbans, makes a bizarre and striking picture.

A gravelly trail, with the gradient slightly in my favor, enables me to create a better impression of a bicycler's capabilities on the mind of the mirza and the sowar than was possible yesterday, by quickly leaving them far in the rear. Some miles are covered when I make a halt for them to overtake me, seeking the welcome shelter of a half-ruined wayside umbar.

An Eliaute camp is but a short distance away, and several sun-painted children of the desert are eagerly interviewing the bicycle when my escort comes galloping along; not seeing me anywhere in view ahead, they had wondered what had become of their wheel-winged charge and are quite relieved at finding me here hobnobbing with the Eliautes behind the umbar.

The mirza's fond mother-in-law has presented him with a quantity of dried pears with half a walnut imbedded in each quarter; during a brief halt at the umbar these Darmian delicacies are fished out of his saddle-bags and duly pronounced upon, and the genial Eliautes contribute flowing bowls of doke (soured milk, prepared in some manner that prevents its spoiling).

High noon finds us at our destination for the day, the village of Tabbas, famous in all the country around for a peculiar windmill used in grinding grain. A grist-mill, or mills, consists of a row of one-storied mud huts, each of which contains a pair of grindstones. Connecting with the upper stone is a perpendicular shaft of wood which protrudes through the roof and extends fifteen feet above it. Cross-pieces run through at right angles and, plaited with rushes, transform the shaft into an upright four-bladed affair that the wind blows around and turns the millstones below.

So far, this is only a very primitive and clumsy method of harnessing the wind; but connected with it is a very ingenious contrivance that redeems it entirely from the commonplace. A system of mud walls are built about, the same height or a little higher than the shaft, in such a manner as to concentrate and control the wind in the interest of the miller, regardless of which direction it is blowing in.

The suction created by the peculiar disposition of the walls whisks the rude wattle sails around in the most lively manner. Forty of these mills are in operation at Tabbas; and to see them all in full swing, making a loud "sweeshing" noise as they revolve, is a most extraordinary sight. Aside from Tabbas, these novel grist-mills are only to be seen in the territory about the Seistan Lake.

The door-way of the quarters provided for our accommodation being too small to admit the bicycle, not the slightest hesitation is made about knocking out the threshold. Every male visible about the place seems eagerly desirous of lending a hand in sweeping out the room, spreading nummuds, bringing quilts, tea, kalians, or something.

A slight ripple upon the smooth and pleasing surface of the universal inclination to do us honor is a sententious controversy between the mirza and a blatant individual who enters objections about killing a sheep. Whether, in the absence of the village khan, the objections are based on an unwillingness to supply the mutton, or because the sheep are miles away on the plain, does not appear; but whatever the objections, the mirza overcomes them, and we get freshly slaughtered mutton for supper.

Tea is evidently a luxury not to be lightly regarded at Tabbas; after the leaves have served their customary purpose, they are carefully emptied into a saucer, sprinkled with sugar, and handed around—each guest takes a pinch of the sweetened leaves and eats it.

The modus operandi of manipulating the kalian likewise comes in for a slight modification here. The ordinary Persian method, before handing the water-pipe to another, is to lift off the top while taking the last pull, and thus empty the water-chamber of smoke. The Tabbasites accomplish the same end by raising the top and blowing down the stem. This mighty difference in the manner of clearing the water-chamber of a hubble-bubble will no doubt impress the minds of intellectual Occidentals as a remarkably important and valuable piece of information. Not less interesting and remarkable will likewise seem the fact that the flour-frescoed proprietors of these queer little Tabbas grist-mills are nothing less than the boundary-mark between that portion of the water-pipe smoking world which blows the remaining smoke out and that portion which inhales it. The Afghan, the Indian, and the Chinaman adopt the former method; the Turk, the Persian, and the Arab the latter.

Yet another interesting habit, evidently borrowed from their uncultivated neighbors beyond the Dasht-i-na-oomid, is the execrable practice of chewing snuff. Almost every man carries a supply of coarse snuff in a little sheepskin wallet or dried bladder; at short intervals he rubs a pinch of this villainous stuff all over his teeth and gums and deposits a second pinch away in his cheek.

Abdurraheim Khan, the chief of several small villages on the Tabbas plain, turns up in the evening. He is the mildest-mannered, kindliest-looking human being I have seen for a long time; he does the agreeable in a manner that leads his guests to think he worships the "Ingilis" people humbly at a distance, and is highly honored in being able to see and entertain one of those very worshipful individuals. Like nearly all Persians, he is ignorant of the Western custom of shaking hands; the sun-browned paw extended to him as he enters is stared at a moment in embarrassment and then clasped between both his palms.

The turban of Abdurraheim Khan is a marvellous evidence of skill in the arranging of that characteristic Eastern head-dress; the snowy whiteness of the material, the gracefulness of the folds, and the elegant crest-like termination are not to be described and done justice to by either word or pen.

In reply to my inquiries, I am glad to find that Abdurraheim Khan speaks less discouragingly of the Harood than did the Ameer at Ali-abad; he says it will be fordable for camels, and there will be no difficulty in finding nomads able to provide me an animal to cross over with.

Some cause of delay, incomprehensible to me, appears to interfere with the continuation of my journey in the morning, most of the forenoon being spent in a discussion of the subject between Abdurraheim Khan and the mirza. About noon a messenger arrives from Ali-abad, bringing a letter from the Ameer, which seems to clear up the mystery at once. The letter probably contains certain instructions about providing me an escort that were overlooked in the letter brought by the mirza.

When about starting, the khan presents me with a bowl of sweet stuff — a heavy preparation of sugar, grease, and peppermint. A very small portion of this lead-like concoction suffices to drive out all other considerations in favor of a determination never to touch it again. An attempt to distribute it among the people about us is interpreted by the well-meaning khan as an impulse of pure generosity on my own part; the result being that he ties the stuff up nicely in a clean handkerchief that an unlucky bystander happens to display at that moment and bids me carry it with me.

An ancient retainer, without any teeth to speak of, and an annoying habit of shouting "h-o-i!" at a person, regardless of the fact that one is within hearing of the merest whisper, is detailed to guide me to a few hovels perched among the mountains, four farsakhs to the southeast, from which point the journey across the Dasht-i-na-oomid is to begin, with an escort of three sowars, who are to join us there later in the evening.

A couple of miles over fairly level ground, and then commences again the everlasting hills, up, up, down, up, down, clear to our destination for the day. While trundling along over the rough foot-hills, I am approached by some nomads who are tending goats near by. Seeing them gather about me, my aged but valiant protector comes galloping briskly up and imperatively waves them away. A grandfatherly party, with a hacking cough, a rusty cimeter, and a flint-lock musket of "ye olden tyme," I fancied "The Aged" merely a guide to show me the road. As I worry along over the rough, unridable mountains, the irritation of being shouted "hoi!" at for no apparent reason, except for the luxury of hearing the music of his own voice, is so annoying that I have about resolved to abandon him to a well-deserved fate, in case of attack.

But now, instead of leaning on me for protection, he blossoms forth at once as not only the protector of his own person, but of mine as well! As he comes galloping bravely up and dismisses the wild-looking children of the desert with a grandiloquent sweep of his hand, he is almost rewarded by an involuntary "bravo, old un!" from myself, so superior to the occasion does he seem to rise.

The little nest of mud huts are found, after a certain amount of hesitation and preliminary going ahead by "The Aged," and toward nightfall three picturesque horsemen ride up and dismount; they are the sowars detailed by the Ameer's orders to Abdurraheim, or some other border-land khan, to escort me across the Desert of Despair.

"The Aged" bravely returns to Tabbas in the morning by himself. When on the point of departing, he surveys me wistfully across a few feet of space and shouts "h-o-i!" He then regards me with a peculiar and indescribable smile. It is not a very hard smile to interpret, however, and I present him with the customary backsheesh. Pocketing the coins, he shouts "h-o-i!" again, and delivers himself of another smile even more peculiar and indescribable than the other.

"Persian-like, receiving a present of money only excites his cupidity for more," I think; and so reply by a deprecatory shake of the head. This turns out to be an uncharitable judgment, however, for once; he goes through the pantomime of using a pen and says, "Abdurraheim Khan." He saw me write my name, the date of my appearance at Tabbas, etc., on a piece of paper and give it to Abdurraheim Khan, and he wants me to do the same thing for him.

The three worthies comprising my new escort are most interesting specimens of the genus sowar; the leader and spokesman of the trio says he is a khan; number two is a mirza, and number three a mudbake. Khans are pretty plentiful hereabouts, and it is nothing surprising to happen across one acting in the humble capacity of a sowar; a mirza gets his title from his ability to write letters; the precise social status of a mudbake is more difficult to here determine, but his proper roosting-place is several rungs of the social ladder below either of the others. They are to take me through to the Khan of Grhalakua, the first Afghan chieftain beyond the desert, and to take back to the Ameer a receipt from him for my safe delivery.

It is a far easier task to reckon up their moral calibre than their social. Before being in their delectable company an hour they reveal that strange mingling of childlike simplicity and total moral depravity that enters into the composition of semi-civilized kleptomaniacs. The khan is a person of a highly sanguine temperament and possesses a headstrong disposition; coupled with his perverted notions of meum and tuum, these qualities will some fine day end in his being brought up with a round turn and required to part company with his ears or nose, or to be turned adrift on the cold charity of the world, deprived of his hands by the crude and summary justice of Khorassan. His eyes are brown and large, and spherical almost as an owl's eyes, and they bulge out in a manner that exposes most of the white. He wears long hair, curled up after the manner of Persian la-de-da-dom, and in his crude, uncivilized sphere evidently fancies himself something of a dandy.

The mirza is quiet and undemonstrative in his manners, as compared with his social superior; and as becomes a person gifted with the rare talent of composing and writing letters, his bump of cautiousness is several degrees larger than the khan's, but is, nevertheless, not large enough to counterbalance the pernicious effect of an inherited and deeply rooted yearning for filthy lucre and a lamentable indifference as to the manner of obtaining it.

The mudbake is the oldest man of the three, and consequently should be found setting the others a good example; but, instead of this, his frequent glances at my packages are, if anything, more heavily freighted with the molecules of covetousness and an eager longing to overhaul their contents than either the khan's or the mirza's.

"Pool, pool, pool—keran, keran, keran," the probable amount in my possession, the amount they expect to receive as backsheesh, and kindred speculations concerning the financial aspect of the situation, form almost the sole topic of their conversation. Throwing them off their guard, by affecting greater ignorance of their language than I am really guilty of, enables me to size them up pretty thoroughly by their conversation, and thus to adopt a line of policy to counteract the baneful current of their thoughts. Their display of cunning and rascality is ridiculous in the extreme; fancying themselves deep and unfathomable as the shades of Lucifer himself, they are, in reality, almost as transparent and simple as children; their cunning is the cunning of the school-boy. Well aware that the safety of their own precious carcasses depends on their returning to Khorassan with a receipt from the Khan of Ghalakua for my safe delivery, there is little reason to fear actual violence from them, and their childish attempts at extortion by other methods will furnish an amusing and instructive study of barbarian character.

The hovel in which our queerly assorted company of eight people sleep —the owners of the shanty, "The Aged," the khan, the mirza, the mudbake, and myself—is entered by a mere hole in the wall, and the bicycle has to stand outside and take the brunt of a heavy thunder-storm during the night. In this respect, however, it is an object of envy rather than otherwise, for myriads of fleas, larger than I would care to say, for fear of being accused of exaggeration, hold high revel on our devoted carcasses all the livelong night. From the swarms of these frisky insects that disport and kick their heels together in riotous revelry on and about my own person, I fancy, forsooth, they have discovered in me something to be made the most of, as a variety of food seldom coming within their province. But the complaining moans of "Ali-Akbar" from "The Aged," the guttural grunts of disapproval from the mirza and the mudbake, and the impatient growls of "kek" (flea) from the khan, tell of their being at least partial companions in misery; but, being thicker-skinned, and withal well seasoned to this sort of thing, their sufferings are less than mine.

The rain has cleared up, but the weather looks unsettled, as about eight o'clock next morning our little party starts eastward under the guidance of a villager whom I have employed to guide us out of the immediate range of mountains, the sowars betraying a general ignorance of the commencement of the route.

My escort are a great improvement as regards their arms and equipments upon "The Aged." Among the three are two percussion double-barrelled shot-guns, a percussion musket, six horse-pistols of various degrees of serviceableness, swords, daggers, ornamental goat's-paunch powder-pouches, peculiar pendent brass rings containing spring nippers for carrying and affixing caps, leathern water-bottles, together with various odds and ends of warlike accoutrements distributed about their persons or their saddles.

"Inshallah, Ghalakua, Gh-al-a-kua!" exclaims the khan, as he swings himself into the saddle. "Inshallah, Al-lah," is the response of the mirza and the mudbake, as they carelessly follow his example, and the march across the Dasht-i-na-oomid begins.

The ryot leads the way afoot, following along the partially empty beds of mountain torrents, through patches of rank camel-thorn, over bowlder-strewn areas and drifts of sand, sometimes following along the merest suggestion of a trail, but quite as frequently following no trail at all. At certain intervals occurs a piece of good ridable ground; our villager-guide then looks back over his shoulder and bounds ahead with a swinging trot, eager to enjoy the spectacle of the bicycle spinning along at his heels; the escort bring up the rear in a leisurely manner, absorbed in the discussion of "pool."

Several miles are covered in this manner, when we emerge upon a more open country, and after consulting at some length with the villager, the khan declares himself capable of finding the way without further assistance. It is a strange, wild country, where we part from our local guide; it looks as though it might be the battleground of the elements. A trail, that is only here and there to be made out, follows a southeasternly course down a verdureless tract of country strewn with rocks and bowlders and furrowed by the rushing waters of torrents now dried up. Jagged rocks and bowlders are here mingled in indescribable confusion on a surface of unproductive clay and smaller stones. On the east stretches a waste of low, stony hills, and on the west, the mountains we have recently emerged from rise two thousand feet above us in an almost unbroken wall of precipitous rock.

By and by the khan separates himself from the party and gallops away out of sight to the left, his declared mission being to purchase "goosht-i" (mutton) from a camp of nomads, whose whereabouts he claims to know. As the commissaire of the party, I have, of course, intrusted him with a sufficient quantity of money to meet our expenses; and the mirza and the mudbake no sooner find themselves alone than another excellent trait of their character conies to the surface. Upon comparing their thoughts, they find themselves wonderfully unanimous in their suspicions as to the honesty of the khan's intentions toward—not me, but themselves!

These worthy individuals are troubled about the khan's independent conduct in going off alone to spend money where they cannot witness the transaction. They are sorely troubled as to probable sharp practice on the part of their social superior in the division of the spoils.

The "spoils!" Shades of Croesus! The whole transaction is but an affair of battered kermis, intrinsically not worth a moment's consideration; but it serves its purpose of affording an interesting insight into the character of my escort.

The poor mirza and the mudbake are, no doubt, fully justified in entertaining the worst opinions possible of the khan; he is a sad scoundrel, on a small scale, to say the least. While they are growling out to each other their grievances and apprehensions, that artful schemer is riding his poor horse miles and miles over the stony hills to the camping-ground of some hospitable Eliaute chieftain, from whom he can obtain goosht-i-goosfany for nothing, and come back and say he bought it.

Several miles are slowly travelled by us three, when, no sign of the khan appearing, we decide upon a halt until he rejoins us. In an hour or so the bizarre figure of the absentee is observed approaching us from over the hills, and before many minutes he is welcomed by a simultaneous query of "chand pool?" (how much money?) from his keenly suspicious comrades, delivered in a ludicrously sarcastic tone of voice.

"Doo Tceran," promptly replies the khan, making a most hopeless effort to conceal his very palpable guilt beneath a transparent assumption of innocence. The mirza and the mudbake make no false pretence of taking him at his word, but openly accuse him of deceiving them. The khan maintains his innocence with vehement language and takes refuge in counter-accusations. The wordy warfare goes merrily on for some minutes as earnestly as if they were quarrelling over their own honest money instead of over mine. The joint query of "chand pool?" gathers an additional load of irony from the fact that they didn't seem to think it worth while to even ask him what he had bought.

Across the pommel of his saddle he carries a young kid, which is now handed to the mudbake to be tethered to a shrub; he then dismounts and produces three or four pounds of cold goat meat. Before proceeding again on our way we consume this cold meat, together with bread brought from last night's rendezvous. By reason of his social inferiority the mudbake is now required to assume the burden of carrying the youthful goat; he takes the poor kid by the scruff of the neck and flings it roughly across his saddle in a manner that causes the gleeful spirits of the khan to find vent in a peal of laughter. Even the usually imperturbable countenance of the mirza lightens up a little, as though infected by the khan's overflowing merriment and the mudbake's rough handling of the young goat. They know each other thoroughly—as thoroughly as orchard-looting, truant-playing, teacher-deceiving school-boys—these three hopeful aspirants to the favor of Allah; they are an amusing trio, and not a little instructive.

CHAPTER VIII

ACROSS THE "DESERT OF DESPAIR"

For some hours we are traversing a singularly wild-looking country; it seems as though the odds and ends of all creation were tossed indiscriminately together. Rocky cliffs, sloping hills, riverbeds, dry save from last night's thunder-storm, bits of sandy desert, strips of alkaline flat or hard gravel, have been gathered up from various parts of the earth and tossed carelessly in a heap here. It is an odd corner in which the chips, the sweepings and trimmings, gathered up after the terrestrial globe was finished, were apparently brought and dumped. There is even a little bit of pasture, and at one point a little area of arable land. Here are found four half-naked representatives of this strange, wild border-land, living beneath one rude goat-hair tent, watching over a few grazing goats and several acres of growing grain.

We arrive at this remarkable little community shortly after noon, and halt a couple of hours to rest and feed the horses, and to kill and cook the unhappy kid slung across the mudbake's saddle. The poor little creature doesn't require very much killing; all the way from where it was given into his tender charge its infantile bleatings have seemed to grate harshly on the mudbake's unsympathetic ear, and he has handled it anywise but tenderly. The four men found here are Persian Eliautes, a numerous tribe, that seem to form a sort of connecting link between the genuine nomads and the tillers of the soil. They are frequently found combining the occupations of both, and might aptly be classed as semi-nomads. Pitching their tents beside some outlying, isolated piece of cultivable ground in the spring, they sow it with wheat or barley, and three months later they reap a supply of grain to carry away with them when they remove their flocks to winter pasturage.

An iron kettle is borrowed to stew the kid in, and when cooked a portion is stowed away to carry with us. The Eliaute quartette contribute bowls of mast and doke, and off this and the remainder of the stewed kid we all make a hearty meal.

More than once of late have I been impressed by the striking, even startling, resemblance of some person among the people of Southern Khorassan, to the familiar face of some acquaintance at home. And, strange it is, but true, that one of these four Eliautes blossoms forth upon my astonished vision as the veritable double of one of America's most prominent knights of the pen and wheel. The gentleman himself, an enthusiastic tourist, and to use his own expression, fond of "walking large," has taken considerable interest in my tour of the world. Can it be—I think, upon first confronting this extraordinary reproduction—can it be, that Karl Kron's enthusiasm has caused him to start from the Pacific coast of China on his wheel to try and beat my time in circumcycling the globe?

And after getting as far as this strange terrestrial chip-pile, he has been so unfortunately susceptible as to fall in love with some slender-limbed daughter of the desert?—has he been captivated by a pair of big, opthamalmia-proof, black eyes, a coy sidewise glance, or a graceful, jaunty style of shouldering a half-tanned goat-skin of doke?

The very first question the nomad asks of the khan, however, removes all suspicions of his being the author and publisher of X. M. M.—he asks if I am a Ferenghi and whither I am going; Kron would have asked me for tabulated statistics of my tour through Persia.

A couple of hours' rest in the Eliaute camp, and we bid adieu to this queer little oasis of human life within the barbarous boundary-line of the Dasht-i-na-oomid, and proceed on our way. One of the Eliautes accompanies us some little distance to guide us through a belt of badly broken country immediately surrounding their camp. The country continues to be a regular jumble of odds and ends of physical geography all the afternoon, and several times the horses of the sowars, without preliminary warning, break through the thin upper crust of some treacherous boggy spot and sink suddenly to their bellies. During the afternoon the mirza is pitched headlong over his horse's head once, and the khan and the mudbake twice. In one tumble the khan's loosely sheathed sword slips from its scabbard, and he well nigh falls a victim to the accident a la King Saul. While traversing this treacherous belt of territory I make the sowars lead the way and perform the office of pathfinder for myself and wheel. Whenever one of them gets stuck in boggy ground, and his horse flounders wildly about, to the imminent risk of unseating its rider, his two hopeful comrades bubble over with merriment at his expense; his own sincere exclamations of "Allah!" being answered by unsympathetic jeers and sarcastic remarks. A few minutes later, perchance one of the hilarious twain finds himself unexpectedly in the same predicament; it then becomes his turn to look scared and importune Allah for protection, and also his turn to be the target for the wild hilarity of the others.

And so this lively and eventful afternoon passes away, and about five o'clock we round the base of a conglomerate hill that has been shutting out the prospect ahead, cross a small spring freshet, and emerge upon an extensive gravelly plain stretching away eastward to the horizon. It is the central plain of the Dasht-i-na-oomid, the heart of the desert, of which the wild, heterogeneous territory traversed since morning forms the setting. So far as the utility of the bicycle and the horses is concerned, the change is decidedly for the better, even more so for the former than for the latter. The gravelly plain presents very good wheeling surface, and I forge ahead of my escort, following a trail so faint that it is barely distinguishable from the general surface. Shortly after leaving the mountainous country the three sowars hip their horses into a smart canter to overtake the bicycle. As they come clattering up, the khan shouts loudly for me to stop, and the mirza and mudbake supplement his vocal exertions by gesticulating to the same purpose. Dismounting, and allowing them to approach, in reply to my query of "Chi mi khoi?" the khan's knavish countenance becomes overspread with a ridiculously thin and transparent assumption of seriousness and importance, and pointing to an imaginary boundary-line at his horse's feet he says: "Bur-raa (brother), Afghanistan." "Khylie koob, Afghanistan inja-koob, hoob, sowari." (Very good, I understand, we are entering Afghanistan; all right, ride on.) "Sowari neis," replies the khan; and he tries hard to impress upon me that our crossing the Afghan frontier is a momentous occasion, and not to be lightly regarded. Several times during the day has my delectable escort endeavored to fathom the extent of my courage by impressing upon me the danger to be apprehended in Afghanistan by a Ferenghi. Not less than half a dozen times have they indulged in the grim pantomime of cutting their own throats, and telling me that this is the tragic fate that would await me in Afghanistan without their valuable protection. And now, as we stand on the boundary line, their bronzed and bared throats are again subjected to this highly expressive treatment; and transfixing me with a penetrating stare, as though eager to read in my face some responsive sign of fear or apprehension, the khan repeats with emphasis: "Bur-raa-ther, Afghanistan." Seeing me still inclined to make light of the matter, he turns to his comrades for confirmation. "O, bur-raa-ther, Afghanistan," assents the mirza; and the mudbake chimes in with the same words. "Well, yes, I understand; Afghanistan—what of it?" I inquire, amused at this theatrical display of their childish knavery.

For answer they start to loading up their guns and pistols, which up to now they have neglected to do; and they examine, with a ludicrous show of importance, the edges of their swords and the points of their daggers, staring the while at me to see what kind of an impression all this is making. Their scrutiny of my countenance brings them small satisfaction, methinks, for so ludicrous seems the scene, and so transparent the motives of this warlike movement, that no room is there for aught but a genuine expression of amusement.

Having loaded up their imposing array of firearms, the khan gives the word to advance, with as much show of solemnity as though leading a forlorn hope on some desperate undertaking, and he impresses upon me the importance of keeping as close to then as possible, instead of riding ahead. All around us is the unto-habited plain; not a living thing or sign of human being anywhere; but when I point this out, and picking up a stone, ask the khan if it is these that are dangerous, he replies, as before: "Bur-raa-ther, Afghanistan," and significantly taps his weapons. As we advance the level plain becomes covered with a growth of wild thyme and camel-thorn, the former permeating the desert air with its agreeable perfume. The evening air is soft and balmy I as we halt in the dusk of the evening to camp alongside the trail; each sowar has a large leathern water-bottle swinging from his stirrup-strap filled at the little freshet above mentioned, and for food we have bread and the remains of the cold kid. The horses are fastened to stout shrubs, and a fire is kindled with dried camel-thorn collected by the mudbake. Not a sound breaks the stillness of the evening as we squat around the fire and eat our frugal supper—all about us is the oppressive silence and solitude of the desert Away off in the dim distance to the northeast can be seen a single speck of light—the camp-fire of some wandering Afghan tribe.

"What is the fire yonder?" I ask of the khan. The khan looks at it, says something to his comrades, and then looks at me and draws his finger yet again across his throat; the mirza and the mudbake follow suit. The ridiculous frequency of this tragic demonstration causes me to laugh outright, in spite of an effort to control my risibilities. The khan replies to this by explaining, "Afghani Noorzais-dasht-adam," and then goes on to explain that the Noorzais are very bad Afghans, who would like nothing better than to murder a Ferenghi. From the beginning of our acquaintance I have allowed my escort to think my understanding of the conversation going on among themselves is extremely limited. By this means have they been thrown somewhat off their guard, and frequently committed themselves within my hearing. It is their laudable purpose, I have discovered, to steal money from me if an opportunity presents without the chance of being detected. Besides being inquisitive about the probable amount in my possession, there has evolved from their collective brain during the day, a deep-laid scheme to find out something about the amount of backsheesh they may expect me to bestow upon them at the end of our journey. This deep-laid scheme is for the khan to pretend that he is sending the mirza and the mudbake back to Beerjand from this point, and for these two hopeful accomplices to present themselves before me as about ready to depart, and so demand backsheesh. This little farce is duly played shortly after our arrival; it is a genuine piece of light comedy, acted on the strangely realistic stage of the lonely desert, to which the full round moon just rising above the eastern horizon. These advances are met on my part by broad intimations that if they continue to act as ridiculously during the remainder of the journey as they have to-day they will surely get well bastinadoed, instead of backsheeshed, when we reach Ghalakua. The actors retire from the stage with visible discomfiture and squat themselves around the fire. Long after I have stretched my somewhat weary frame upon a narrow strip of saddle-blanket for the night, my three "protectors" squat around the smouldering embers of the camel-thorn fire, discussing the all-absorbing topic of my money. Little do they suspect that concealed in a leathern money-belt beneath my clothes are one hundred Russian gold Imperials, the money obtained in Teheran for the journey through Turkestan and Siberia to the Pacific. Though sleeping with the traditional one eye open and my Smith & Wesson where it can be readily used, there is little apprehension of being robbed, owing to their obligation to take back the receipt for my safe delivery to Heshmet-i-Molk.

It is the weather-changeful period of the full moon, and about midnight a clap of thunder rolls over the desert, and a smart shower descends from a small dark cloud, that sails slowly across the sky, obscuring for a brief period the moist-looking countenance of the moon, and then disappears. A couple of hours later a rush of wind is heard careering across the desert toward us, accompanied by a wildly scudding cloud. The cloud peppers us with hailstones in the most lively manner, and the wind strikes us almost with the force of a tornado, knocking over the bicycle, which I have leaned against a clump of shrubs at my head, and favoring us with a blinding fusilade of sand and gravel.

It rains and hails enough to make us wet and uncomfortable, and the mudbake gets up and kindles another fire. In a short time the squally midnight weather has given place to a dead calm; the clouds have dispersed; the moon shines all the brighter from having had its face washed; the stars twinkle themselves out one by one as the gray dawn gradually makes itself manifest. It is a most lovely morning; the bruising hailstones and the moistening rain have proved themselves stimulants in the laboratory of the wild-thyme shrubs, setting free and disseminating a new supply of aroma; and while until now the voice of animate nature has been conspicuous by its absence, the morning vespers of song-birds seed almost to be issuing, like flowers, from the ground. There is an indescribable charm about this morning's experience on the desert; dawn appears, the moon hangs low-suspended in the heavens, the birds carol merrily, and every inspiration one takes is a tonic to stimulate the system. Half an hour later the sun has risen, the song-birds have one and all lapsed into silence, the desert is itself again, stern, silent, uncompromising, and apparently destitute of life.

Total depravity, it appears, has not yet claimed my worthy escort for its own entirely, for while saddling up their horses during this brief display of nature's kindlier mood they call my attention to the singing of the birds and the grateful perfumery in the air. The germ of goodness still lingers within their semi-civilized conception of things about them; they are the children of Nature, and are profoundly impressed by their mother's varying moods. Their prostrations toward Mecca and their matutinal prayers to Allah seem to gain something of sincerity from the accompanying worship of the birds and the sympathetic essence of the awakening day. Eastward from our camping-ground the trail is oftentimes indistinguishable; but a few loose stones have been tossed together at intervals of several hundred yards, to guide wayfarers across the desert. A surface of mingled sand and gravel characterizes the way; sometimes it is unridably heavy, and sometimes the wheeling is excellent for a mile or two at a stretch, enabling me to leave the ambling yahoos of the sowars far behind. Beautiful mirages sometimes appear in the distance —lakes of water, waving groves of palms, and lovely castles; and often, when far enough ahead, I can look back, and see the grotesque figures of the khan, the mirza, and the mudbake apparently riding through the air.

Perhaps twenty miles are covered, when we arrive at a pile of dead brush that has been erected for a landmark, and find a dilapidated well containing water. The water is forty feet below the surface, and contains a miscellaneous assortment of dead lizards, the carcasses of various small mammalia, and sundry other unfortunate representatives of animated nature that have fallen in. Beyond this well the country assumes the character of a broad sink or mud-basin, the shiny surface of its mud glistening in the sun like a sheet of muddy water. Sloughs innumerable meander through it, fringed with rank rushes and shrubs. A far heavier down-pour than we were favored with on the plain has drenched a region of stony hills adjacent, and the drainage therefrom has, for the time being, filled and overflowed the winding sloughs.

A dozen or more of these are successfully forded, though not without some difficulty; but we finally arrive at the parent slough, of which the others are but tributaries. This proves too deep for the sowars' horses to ford, and after surveying the yellow flood some minutes and searching up and down, the khan declares ruefully that we shall have to return to Beerjand. As I remonstrate with him upon his lack of enterprise in turning from so trifling a difficulty, the khan finally orders the mudbake to strip off his purple and fine linen and try the depth. The mudbake proceeds to obey his superior, with many apprehensive glances at the muddy freshet, and wades gingerly in, muttering prayers to Allah the while. Deeper and deeper the yellow waters creep up his shivering form, and when nearly up to his neck, a sudden deepening causes him to bob unexpectedly down almost over his head. Hurriedly retreating, spluttering and whining, he scrambles hastily ashore, where his two companions, lolling lazily on their horses, watching his attempt, are convulsed with merriment over his little misadventure and his fright.

The shivering mudbake, clad chiefly in goose-pimples, now eagerly supplements the khan's proposition for us all to return to Beerjand, and the mirza with equal eagerness murmurs his approval of the same course of action. Making light of their craven determination, I prepare to cross the freshet without their assistance, and announce my intention of proceeding alone. The stream, though deep, is not over thirty yards wide, and a very few minutes suffices for me to swim across with my clothes, my packages, and the saddle of the bicycle; the small, strong rope I have carried from Constantinople is then attached to the bicycle, and, swimming across with the end, the wheel is pulled safely through the water. Neither of the sowars can swim, and they regard the prospect of being left behind with no little consternation. Their guileful souls seem to turn naturally to Allah in their perplexity; and they all prostrate themselves toward Mecca, and pray with the apparent earnestness of deep sincerity. Having duly strengthened and fortified themselves with these devotional exercises, they bravely prepare to resign themselves to kismet and follow my instructions about crossing the stream.

The khan's iron-gray being the best horse of the three, and the khan himself of a more sanguine and hopeful disposition, I make him tie all his clothes and damageable things into a bundle and fasten them on his saddle; the rope is then tied to the bridle and the horse pulled across, his gallant rider clinging to his tail, according to my orders, and praying aloud to Allah on his own account. The gray swims the unfordable middle portion nobly, and the khan comes through with no worse damage than a mouthful or two of muddy water. As the dripping charger scrambles up the bank, the khan allows himself to be hauled up high and dry by its tail; he then looks back at his comrades and favors them with a brief but highly exaggerated account of his sensations.

The mirza and the mudbake deliver themselves of particularly deep-chested acclamations of "Allah, Allah!" at the prospect of undergoing similar sensations to those described by the khan, whereupon that unsympathetic individual vents his hilarity in a gleeful, heartless peal of laughter, and tells them, with a diabolical chuckle of delight, that they will most likely fare ten times worse than himself on account of the inferiority of their horses compared with the gray. Much threatening, bantering, and persuasion is necessary to induce them to follow the leadership of the khan; but, trusting to kismet, they finally venture, and both come through without noteworthy misadventure. The khan's wild hilarity and ribaldish jeers at the expense of his two subordinates, as he stands on the solid foundation of a feat happily already accomplished and surveys their trepidation, and hears their prayers as they are pulled like human dinghies through the water, is in such ludicrous contrast to his own prayerful utterances under the same circumstances a minute before that my own risibilities are not to be wholly controlled.

This little episode makes a profound impression upon the minds of my escort; they now regard me as a very dare-devil and determined individual, a person entirely without fear, and their deference during the remainder of the afternoon is in marked contrast to their previous attempts to work upon my presumed apprehensions of the dangers of Afghanistan.

Following the guidance of a few rude landmarks of piled brush, we discover, a few miles off to the left, and on the eastern environ of the slough-veined basin, a considerable body of tents and a herd of grazing camels. The sowars pronounce them to be a certain camp of Einiucks that they have been expecting to find somewhere in this vicinity, and with whose chief the khan says he is acquainted.

Wending our way thither we find a large camp of about fifty tents occupying a level stretch of clean gravelly ground, slightly elevated above the mud-flats. The tents are of brownish-black goat-hair, similar in material to the tents of Koords and Eliautes; in size and structure they are larger and finer than those of the Eliautes, but inferior to the splendid tent-palaces of Koordistan. A couple of hundred yards from the tents is a small spring of water, enclosed within a rude wall of loosely-piled stone; the water is allowed to trickle through this wall and accumulate in a basin outside. Here, as we ride up, are several women filling goat-skin vessels to carry to the tents.

The tent of the chief stands out conspicuously from the others, and the khan, desirous of giving his "bur-raa-ther," as he now terms the Eimuck chieftain, a surprise, suggests that I ride ahead of the horsemen and dismount before his tent. This capital little arrangement is somewhat interfered with by the fact that a goodly proportion of the male population present have already become cognizant of our presence, and are standing in white-robed groups about their tents trying with hand-shaded eyes to penetrate the secret of my strange appearance. Nevertheless, I ride ahead and alight at the entrance to the chief's tent. The chief is a middle-aged man of medium height and inclined to obesity. He and all the men are arrayed in garments of coarse white cotton stuff throughout, loose pantaloons, bound at the ankles, and an over-garment of a pattern very much like a night-shirt; on their heads are the regulation Afghan turbans, with long, dangling ends, and their feet are incased in rude moccasins with upturned toes. As I dismount, and the chief fully realizes that I am a Ferenghi, his face turns red with embarrassment. Instead of the smiles or the grave kindliness of a

Koordish sheikh, or the simple, childlike greeting of an Eliaute, the Eimuck chief motions me into his tent in a brusque, offish manner, his countenance all aglow with the redness of what almost looks like a guilty conscience.

With the intuition that comes of long and changeful association with strange peoples, the changing countenance of the Afghan chief impresses me at once as the fiery signal of inbred Mussulman fanaticism, lighting up spontaneously at the unexpected and unannounced arrival of a lone Ferenghi in his presence. It savors somewhat of bearding a dangerous lion in his own den. He certainly betrays deep embarrassment at my appearance; which, however, may partly result from not yet knowing the character of my companions, or the wherefore of this strange visitation. When my escort rides up his whole demeanor instantly undergoes a change; the cloud of embarrassment lifts from his face, he and the khan recognize and greet each other cordially as "bur-raa-ther," and kiss each-other's hands; some of his men standing by exchange similar brotherly greetings with the mirza and the mudbake.

After duly refreshing and invigorating ourselves with sundry bowls of doke, the inevitable tomasha is given, and the chief asks the khan to get me to ride up before one row of tents and down the other for the edification of the women and children, curious groups of whom are gathered at every door. The ground between the two long, even rows of tents resembles a macadam boulevard for width and smoothness, and I give the wild Eimuck tribes-people a ten minutes' exhibition of circling, speeding, and riding with hands off handles. A strange and novel experience, surely, this latest triumph of high Western civilization, invading the isolated nomad camp on the Dasht-i-na-oomid and disporting for the amusement of the women and children. Some of the women are attired in quite fanciful colors; Turkish pantaloons of bright blue and jackets of equally bright red render them highly picturesque, and they wear a profusion of bead necklaces and the multifarious gewgaws of semi-civilization. The younger girls wear nose-rings of silver in the left nostril, with a cluster of tiny beads or stones decorating the side of the nose. The wrists of most of the men are adorned with bracelets of plain copper wire about the size of ordinary telegraph wire; they average large and well-proportioned, and seem intellectually superior to the Eliautes. A very striking peculiarity of the people in this particular camp is a sort of lisping, hissing accent to their speech. When first addressed by the chief, I fancied it simply an individual case of lisping; but every person in the camp does likewise. Another peculiarity of expression, that, while not peculiar to this particular camp, is made striking by reason of its novelty to me at this time, the use of the expression "O" as a term of assent, in lieu of the Persian "balli." The sowars, from their proximity to the frontier, have sometimes used this expression, but here, in the Eimuck camp, I come suddenly upon a people who use it to the total exclusion of the Persian word. The change from the "balli sahib" of the Tabbas villagers to the "O, O, O" of the Afghan nomads is novel and entertaining in the extreme, and I sit and listen with no small interest to the edifying conversation of the khan, the mirza, and the mudbake on the one side, and the Eimuck chieftain and prominent members of the tribe on the other.

Standing behind the chief, who sits cross-legged on a Persian nummud, is a handsome, intelligent-looking man, who seems to be the most pleasant-faced and entertaining conversationalist of the nomads. The kahn grows particularly talkative and communicative, the evening hours flow on, and while addressing his remarks and queries directly to the chief, he gazes about him to observe the effects of his words on the general assembly gathered inside and crowded about the tent-entrance. The pleasant-faced man does far more talking in reply than does the chief himself. In reply to the khan's innumerable queries he replies, in the peculiar, hissing shibboleth of the camp, "O, O, O-O bus-s-s-orah, b-s-s-s-orah." Sometimes the khan delivers himself of quite a lengthy disquisition, and as his remarks are followed by the assembled nomads with the eager interest of people who seldom hear anything but the music of their own voices, the interesting individual above referred to sprinkles his assenting "O, O, O" thickly along the line of the khan's presumably edifying narrative; now and then the chief himself chimes in with a quiet "b-s-s-s-orah." Here also, in this camp of surprises and innovations, do I first hear the word "India" used in lieu of "Hindostan" among Asiatics.

The fatigue of the day's journey, and the imperfect rest of the two preceding nights, cause me to be overcome with drowsiness, early in the evening, and I stretch oat alongside the bicycle and fall into a deep sleep. An hour or two later I am awakened for the evening meal. Flat, pancake-like sheets of unleavened bread, inferior to the bread of Persia, and partaking somewhat of the character of the chupalties of India, boiled goat, and the broth preserved from the same, together with the regulation mast and doke, constitute the Eimuek supper. A liberal bowl of the broth, an abundance of meat, bread, mast and doke are placed before me on a separate wooden tray, while my escort, the chief, and several of his men gather around a communal spread of the same variety of edibles. A crowd of curious people occupy the remainder of the space inside, and stand at the door. As I rise and prepare to eat, all eyes are turned upon me as though anticipating some surprising exhibition of the strange manners of a Ferenghi at his meals. Surveying the broth, I motion the khan to try and obtain a spoon. The chief looks inquiringly at the khan, and the khan with the gladsome expression of a person conscious of having on hand a rare piece of information for his friends, explains that a Ferenghi eats soup with a spoon. The chief and his men smile incredibly, but the khan emphasizes his position by appealing to the mirza and the mudbake for confirmation. "Eat soup with a spoon?" queries the chief in Persian; and he casts about him a look of unutterable astonishment.

Recovering somewhat from his incredulity, however, he orders an attendant to fetch one, which shortly results in the triumphant production of a rude wooden ladle. These uncivilized children of the desert watch me drink broth from the ladle with most intense curiosity. In their own case, an attendant tears several of the sheets of bread into pieces and puts them in the broth; each person then helps himself to the broth-soaked bread with his fingers. What broth remains at the bottom of the bowl is drunk by them from the vessel itself in turns. After consuming several generous chunks of "gusht" bread and mast and broth, and supplementing this with a bowl of doke, I stretch myself out again and at once become wrapped in sound, refreshing slumbers that last till morning.

It is a glorious morning as, after breakfasting off the cold remains of the meat left over from the evening meal, we bid farewell to the hospitable Eimuek camp and resume our journey. As we leave, I offer to shake hands with the chief to see if he understands our mode of greeting; he seizes my hand between his two palms and kisses it. For the first few miles the country is gravelly and undulating, after which it changes to a sort of basin, partially covered by dense patches of tall, rank weeds. On either side are rocky hills, almost rising to the dignity of mountains; the rain and melting snow evidently convert this basin into a swamp at certain periods, but it is now dry. A mile or so off to the right we catch a glimpse, of some wild animal chasing a small herd of antelope. From its size and motion, I judge it to be a leopard or cheetah; the sowars regard it, bounding along after the fleet-footed antelope, with lively interest; they call it a "baab" (tiger), and say there are many in the reeds. It looks quite a likely spot for tigers, and it is not at all unlikely that it may have been one, for, while not plentiful hereabout, Tigris Asiaticus occasionally makes his presence known in the patches of reed and jungle in Southern Afghanistan and Seistan.

All three of the sowars are frisky as kittens this morning, the result, it is surmised, of the generous hospitality of the Eimuek chief —gusht galore and rich broth cause their animal spirits to run riot. Like overfed horses they "feel their oats" as they sniff the fresh and invigorating morning air, and they point toward the shadowy form of the racing baab a mile away, and pretend to take aim at it with their guns. They sing and shout and swoop down on one another about the basin, flourishing their swords and aiming with their guns, and they whip their poor, long-suffering yahoos into wild, sweeping gallops as they swoop down on some imaginary enemy. This wild hilarity and mimic warfare of the desert is kept up until the ragged edge of their exuberance is worn away, and their horses are well-nigh fagged out; we then halt for an hour to allow the horses to recuperate by nibbling at a patch of reeds.

About ten miles from the Eimuek camp, the country develops into a wilderness of deep, loose sand and bowlders. Across this sandy region stretches a range of dark volcanic hills; the bases of the hills terminate in billows of whitish-yellow sand; the higher waves of the sandy sea stretch well up the sides like giant ocean breakers driven by the gale up the side of the rocky cliffs. It is a tough piece of country even for the sowars' horses, and dragging a bicycle through the mingled sand and bowlders is abominable in the extreme. The heat becomes oppressive as we penetrate deeper into the belt of sand-hills, and after five miles of desperate tugging I become tired and distressed. The sowars lolling lazily in their saddles, well-nigh sleeping, while I am struggling and perspiring, form another chapter of experience entirely novel in the field of European travel in Asia. Usually it is the natives who have to sweat and toil and administer to the comfort of the traveller.

Revolving these things over in my mind, and becoming really wearied, I suggest to the khan that he change places for a brief spell and give me a chance to rest. The idea of himself trundling the asp-i-awhan appeals to the khan as decidedly novel, and he bites at the bait quite readily. Mounting his vacated saddle, I join the mirza and the mudbake in watching him struggle along through the sand with it for some two hundred yards. Along that brief course he topples over with it not less than half a dozen times. The novel spectacle of the khan trundling the asp-i-awhan arouses his two comrades from the warmth-inspired semi-torpidity of their condition, and whenever the khan topples over, they favor him with jeers and laughter. At the end of two hundred, yards the khan declares himself exhausted and orders the mudbake to dismount and try it; this, however, the mudbake bluntly refuses to do. After a little persuasion the inirza is induced to try the experiment of a trundle; it is but an experiment, however, for, being less active than the khan, the first time he tumbles the bicycle over finds him sprawling on top of it, and, fearful lest he should snap some spokes, I take it in hand again myself.

Another couple of miles and the eastern edge of the sandy area I is reached, after which a compensational proportion of smooth gravel abounds. Shortly after noon another small camp of nomads I is reached, some half-dozen inferior tents, pitched on the shelterless edge of an exposed gravelly slope. The afternoon is oppressively hot, and the men are comfortably snoozing in all sorts of outlandish places among the scrubby camel-thorn. Only the I women and children are visible as we approach the tents; but youngsters are despatched forthwith, and, lo! several tall white-robed figures seem to rise up literally out of the ground at different spots round about; they were burrowed away under the low, bushy shrubbery like rabbits. The women and children among these nomads always seem industriously engaged, the former with domestic duties about the tents, and the latter tending the flocks; but the men put in most of their unprofitable lives loafing, sleeping, and gossiping.

We are not invited into the tents, but bread and mast is provided, and, while we eat, four men hold the corners of an ample blue turban sheet over us to shelter us from the sun. Spread out on sheets and on the roofs of the tents are bushels of curds drying in the sun; the curds are compressed into round balls the size of an apple, and when dried into hard balls are excellent things to put in the pocket and nibble along the road. Here we learn that the Harood is only one farsakh distant, and a couple of stalwart young nomads accompany us to assist us across. At Beerjand the Harood was "deep as a house;" at our last night's camp we were told that it was fordable with camels; here we learn, that, though very swift, it is really fordable for men and horses. First we come to a branch less than waist-deep. My nether garments are handed to the khan; in the pocket of my pantaloons is a purse containing a few kerans. While engaged in fording this branch the khan ferrets out the purse and extracts something from it, which he deftly slips into the folds of his kammerbund. All this I silently observe from the corners of my eyes, but say nothing.

Emerging from the stream, the wily khan points across the intervening three hundred yards or thereabout to the main stream, and motions for me to go ahead. The discovery of the purse and the purloined kerans has aroused all the latent cupidity of his soul, and he wants me to ride ahead, so that he can straggle along in the rear and investigate the contents of the purse at his leisure. While winking at the amusing little act of petty larceny already detected, I do not propose to give his kleptomaniac tendencies full swing, and so I meet his proposal to sowar and go ahead by peremptorily ordering him to take the lead.

Arriving at the bank of the Harood, I retire behind a clump of reeds, and fold my money-belt, full of gold, up in the middle of my clothes, making a compact bundle, with my gossamer rubber wrapped around the outside. The river is about a hundred and fifty yards wide at the ford, with a sand-bar about mid-stream, and is not above shoulder-deep along the ridge that renders it fordable; the current, however, is frightfully strong. Like the Indians of the West, the Afghan nomads are accustomed from infancy to battling with the elements, and are comparatively fearless in regard to rivers and deserts and storms, etc.

Such, at least, is the impression created by the conduct of the two young men who have come to assist us across. The bicycle, my clothes, and all the effects of the sowars are carried across on their heads, the rushing waters threatening to sweep them off their feet at every step; but nothing is allowed to get wet. When they are carrying across the last bundle, the khan, solicitous for my safety, wants me to hang on to a short rope tied around the waist of the strongest of the nomads. Naturally disdaining any such arrangement as this, however, I declare my intention of crossing without assistance, and wade in forthwith. Ere I have progressed thirty yards, the current fairly sweeps me off my feet and I have to swim for it. Fancying that I am overcome and in a fair way of being drowned, the sowars set up a wild howl of apprehension, and shout excitedly to the nomads to rescue me from a watery grave. The Afghans are not so excited, however, over the outlook; they see that I am swimming all right, and they confine themselves to motioning the direction for me to take. The current carries me some little distance down stream, when I find footing on the lower extremity of the sand-bar, and on it, wade up; stream again with some difficulty against swiftly rushing water four feet deep. The khan thinks I have had the narrowest possible escape, and in tones of desperation he shouts out and begs me not to attempt to cross the other channel without assistance. "The receipt!" he shouts, "the receipt! Allah preserve us! the receipt; Hesh met-i-Molk." The worthy khan is afflicted with a keen consciousness of coming punishment awaiting him at Beerjand, should I happen to come to grief while under his protection, and he, no doubt, suffers an agony of apprehension during the fifteen minutes I am battling with the rapid current of the Harood.

The second channel is found less swift and comparatively easy to ford. The sturdy nomads, having transported all of my escort's damageable effects, those three now stark-naked worthies mount with fear and trembling their equally stark-naked steeds-naked all, save for the turbans of the men and the bridles of their horses. Whatever of intrepidity the khan possesses is of a quantity scarcely visible to the naked eye, and it is, therefore, scarcely surprising to find him trying to persuade, first the mudbake and then the mirza, to take the initiative. His efforts prove wholly ineffectual, however, to bring the feebly flowing tide of their courage up to the high-water level of assuming the duties of leadership, and so in the absence of any alternative, he finally screws up his own courage and leads the way. The others allow their horses to follow closely behind. The horses seem to regard the rushing volume of yellow water about them with far less apprehension than do their riders. While dressing myself on the eastern bank, the frightened mutterings of "Allah" from these gallant horsemen come floating across the water, and, as they reach the sand-bar in the middle of the stream, I can hear their muttered importunities for

Providential protection change, like the passing shadow-whims of Nature's children that they are, into gleeful chuckles at their escape.

When the khan emerges from the water, the ruling passion within his avaricious nature asserts itself with ridiculous promptness. With the water dripping from his dangling feet, he rides hastily to where I am dressing and whispers, "Pool neis; Afghani dasht-adam, pool neis." By this he desires me to understand that the men who have been so industrious and ready in helping us across, being Afghan nomads, will not expect any backsheesh for their trouble. The above-mentioned ruling passion is wonderfully strong in the rude breast of the khan, and in view of his own secret machinations against my money he, no doubt, entertains objections to leakages in other directions. So far as presenting these hospitable souls of the desert with money for their services is concerned, the khan's advice probably contains a good deal more wisdom than would appear from a superficial view of the case merely. Assisting travellers across streams and through difficult places evidently appeals to these people as the most natural thing in the world for them to do. It is a part of the un-written code of the hospitality of their uncivilized country, and is, in all probability, undertaken without so much as a mercenary thought. Presenting them with a money-consideration for their services certainly has a tendency to awaken the latent spirit of cupidity, generally resulting in their transformation from simple and unsophisticated children, hospitable both by nature and tradition, into wretched mercenaries, who regard the chance traveller solely from a backsheesh-giving stand-point. The baneful result of this is today glaringly apparent along every tourist route in the East; and, among the pool-loving subjects of the Shah of Persia, travellers do not have to appear very frequently to keep alive and foster a wild yearning for backsheesh that effectually suppresses all loftier considerations.

These Afghans, however, seem to be people of an altogether different mould; the ubiquitous Western traveller has not yet become a palpable factor in their experiences. The hidden charms of backsheesh will not become apparent to the wild Afghans until their fierce Mussulman fanaticism has cooled sufficiently to allow the Ferenghi tourist to wander through their territory without being in danger of his life.

The danger of corruption in the present instance is exceedingly small, considering that I am the only representative of the Occident that has ever happened along this way, and the probability that none other will follow for many a year after; therefore I ignore the khan's wholly disinterested advice and make the two worthy nomads a small present. They accept the proffered kerans with a look of bewilderment, as though quite unable to comprehend why I should tender them money, and they lay it carelessly down on the sand while they assist the sowars to resaddle their horses. To see the indifference with which the magnificent Afghan nomads toss the silver pieces on the sand, and the eager, covetous expression that the sight of the same coins lying there inspires in the three Persians is, of itself, an instructive lesson on the difference between the two peoples. The sowars become inspired, as if touched by the magic wand of alchemy, to the discussion of their favorite theme; but the Afghans pay no more heed to their remarks about money than if they were talking in an unknown tongue. They really act as though they regarded the subject of money as something altogether beyond their comprehension.

CHAPTER IX

AFGHANISTAN

A few miles across a stretch of gravelly river-bottom, interspersed with scattering patches of cultivation, brings us to a hamlet of some twenty mud dwellings. The houses are small, circular structures, unattached, and each one removed some dozen paces from its neighbor; they are built of mud with the roof flat, as in Asia Minor. The sun is setting as we reach this little Harood hamlet, and, as Ghalakua is some three farsakhs distant, we decide to remain here for the night. We pitch our camp on a smooth threshing-floor in the centre of the village, and the headman brings pieces of carpet for me to recline on, together with a sort of a carpet bolster for a pillow.

The khan impresses upon these simple-minded, out-of-the-world people a due sense of my importance as the guest of his master, the Ameer of Seistan, and they skirmish around in the liveliest manner to provide what creature comforts their meagre resources are equal to. The best they can provide in the way of eatables is bread and eggs, and muscal, but they make full amends for the absence of variety by bestowing upon us a superabundance of what they have, and no slaves of Oriental despot ever displayed more eager haste to anticipate their ruler's wants than do these, my first acquaintances among the Afghan tillers of the soil, to wait upon us. All the evening long no female ventures anywhere near our alfresco quarters; the rigid exclusion of the female sex in this conservative Mohammedan territory forbids them making any visible show of interest in the affairs of men whatsoever. When the hour arrives for the preparation of the evening meal, closely shrouded figures flit hastily through the dusk from house to house, bearing camel-thorn torches. They are women who have been to their neighbors to obtain a light for their own fire. From the number of these it is plainly evident that the housewives of the entire village light their fires from one original kindling. The shrouds of the women are red and black plaid; the men wear overshirts of coarse white; material that reach to their knees, pointed shoes that turn up at the toes, white Turkish trousers, and the regulation Afghan turban. The night is most lovely, and frogs innumerable are in the lowlands round about us, croaking their appreciation of the mellow moonlight, the balmy air, and the overflowing waters of the river. For hours they favor us with a musical melange, embracing everything between the hoarse bass croak of the full-blown bull-frog, to the tuneful "p-r" of the little green tree-frogs ensconced in the clumps of dwarf-willow hard by. Soothed by the music of the frogs I spend a restful night beneath the blue, calm dome of the Afghan sky, though awakened once or twice by the sowars' horses breaking loose and fighting.

There are no geldings to speak of in Central Asia, and unless eternal vigilance is maintained and the horses picketed very carefully, a fight or two is sure to occur among them during the night. As it seems impossible for semi-civilized people to exercise forethought in small matters of this kind, a night without being disturbed by a horse-fight is a very rare occurrence, when several are travelling together.

The morning opens as lovely as the close of evening yesterday; a sturdy villager carries me and the bicycle through a small tributary of the Harood. He shakes his head when I offer him a present. How strange that an imaginary boundary-line between two countries should make so much difference in the people! One thinks of next to nothing but money, the other refuses to take it when offered.

The sowars are in high glee at having escaped what seems to me the imaginary terrors of the passage across the Dasht-i-na-oomid, and as we ride along toward Ghalakua their exuberant animal spirits find expression in song. Few things are more harrowing and depressing to the unappreciative Ferenghi ear than Persian sowars singing, and three most unmelodious specimens of their kind at it all at once are something horrible.

The country hereabouts is a level plain, extending eastward to the Furrah Rood; within the first few miles adjacent to the Harood are seen the crenellated walls of several villages and the crumbling ruins of as many more. Clumps of palm-trees and fields of alfalfa and green young wheat environ the villages, and help to render the dull gray ruins picturesque. The atmosphere seems phenomenally transparent, and the trees and ruins and crenellated walls, rising above the level plain, are outlined clear and distinct against the sky.

In the distance, at all points of the compass, rocky mountains rise sheer from the dead level of the plain, looking singularly like giant cliffs rising abruptly from the bed of some inland sea. One of these may be thirty miles away, yet the wondrous clearness of the air renders apparent distances so deceptive that it looks not more than one-third the distance. It is a strikingly interesting country, and its inhabitants are a no less strikingly interesting people.

A farsakh from our Harood-side camping-place, we halt to obtain refreshments at a few rude tents pitched beneath the walls of a little village. The owners of the tents are busy milking their flocks of goats. It is an animated scene. No amount of handling, nor years of human association, seems capable of curbing the refractory and restless spirit of a goat. The matronly dams that are being subjected to the milking process this morning have, no doubt, been milked regularly for years; yet they have to be caught and held firmly by the horns by one person, while another robs them of what they seem reluctant enough to give up.

The sun grows uncomfortably warm, and myriads of flies buzz hungrily about our morning repast. Before we resume our journey a little damsel, in flaming red skirt and big silver nose-ring, enters the garden and plucks several roses, which she brings to me on a pewter salver. These people are Eliautes, and the women are less fearful of showing themselves than at the village where we passed the night. Several of them apply to me for medical assistance. The chief trouble is chronic ophthalmia; nearly all the children are afflicted with this disease, and at the eyes of each poor helpless babe are a mass of hungry flies. The wonder is, not that ophthalmia runs amuck among these people, but rather, that any of the children escape total blindness.

Several villages are passed through en route to Ghalakua; the people turn out en masse and indulge in uproarious demonstrations at the advent of the Ferenghi and the bicycle. These people seem as incapable of controlling their emotions and their voices as so many wild animals; they shout and gesticulate excitedly, and run about like people bereft of their senses. The uncivilization crops out of these obscure Harood villagers far plainer than it does in the tents of the wandering tribes. They are noisier and more boisterous than the nomads, who, as a matter of fact, are sober-sided and sedate in their deportment.

No women appear among the crowd on the street, but a carefully covered head is occasionally caught peeping furtively from behind a chimney on the roof of a house, or around some corner. A glance from me, and the head is withdrawn as rapidly as if one were taking hostile aim at it with a rifle.

Fine large irrigating ditches traverse this partially cultivable area, and in them are an abundance of fish. In one ditch I catch sight of a splendid specimen of the speckled trout, that must have been three feet long. Travelling leisurely next morning, we arrive at Ghalakua in the middle of the forenoon; quarters are assigned us by Aminulah Khan, the Chief of the Ghalakua villages and tributary territory. In appearance he is a typical Oriental official, his fluffy, sensuous countenance bearing traces of such excesses as voluptuous Easterns are wont to indulge in, and this morning he is suffering with an attack of "tab" (fever). Wrapped in a heavy fur-lined over-coat, he is found seated on the front platform of a inenzil beneath the arched village gateway, smoking cigarettes; in his hand is a bouquet of roses, and numerous others are scattered about his feet. Dancing attendance upon him is a smart-looking little fellow in a sheepskin busby almost as bulky in proportion as his whole body, and which renders his appearance grotesque in the extreme. His keen black eyes sparkle brightly through the long wool of his remarkable headgear, the ends of which dangle over his eyes like an overgrown and wayward bang. The bravery of his attire is measurably enhanced by a cavalry sword, long enough and heavy enough for a six-foot dragoon, a green kammerbund, and top-boots of red leather. This person stands by the side of Aminulah Khan, watches keenly everything that is being said and done, receives orders from his master, and transmits them to the various subordinates lounging about. He looks the soul of honesty and watchfullness, his appearance and demeanor naturally conjuring up reflections of faithful servitors about the persons of knights and nobles of old; he is apparently the Khan of Ghalakua's confidential retainer and general supervisor of affairs about his person and headquarters.

Our quarters are in the bala-khana of a small half-ruined konak outside the village, and shortly after retiring thither the khan's sprightly little retainer brings in tea and fried eggs, besides pomegranates and roses for myself. A new departure makes its appearance in the shape of sugar sprinkled over the eggs. While we are discussing these refreshments our attendant stands in the doorway and addresses the sowars at some length in Persian. He is apparently delivering instructions received from his master; whatever it is all about, he delivers it with the air of an orator addressing an audience, and he supplements his remarks with gestures that would do credit to a professional elocutionist. He is as agreeable as he is picturesque; he and I seem to fall en rapport at once, as against the untrustworthiness of the remainder of our company. As his keen, honest eyes scrutinize the countenances of the sowars, and then seek my own face, I feel instinctively that he has sized my escort up correctly, and that their innate rascality is as well revealed to him as if he had accompanied us across the desert.

Several visitors drop in to pay their respects; they salaam respectfully to me, and greet the sowars as "bur-raa-thers," and kiss, their hands. One simple, unsophisticated mortal, who in his isolated life has never had the opportunity of discriminating between a Mussulman and a Ferenghi, addresses me also as "bur-raa-ther," and favors my palm with the regulation osculatory greeting. The Afghans present view this extraordinary proceeding with dignified silence, and if moved in any manner by the spectacle, manage to conceal their emotions beneath a stolid exterior. The risibilities of the sowars, however, are stirred to their deepest depths, and they nearly choke themselves in desperate efforts to keep from laughing outright.

Offerings of roses are brought into our quarters by the various visitors, and boys and men toss others in through door and windows, until our room is gratefully perfumed and roses are literally carpeting the floor. One might well imagine the place to be Gulistan itself; every person is carrying bunches of roses in his hands, smelling of them, and wearing them in his turban and kammerbund. The people seem to be fairly revelling in the delights of these choicest gems from Flora's evidently overflowing storehouse. The men average tall and handsome; they look like veritable warrior-priests in their flowing white costumes, and they make a strange picture of mingled barbarism and aestheticism as they loaf in lazy magnificence about the tumble-down ruins of the konak, toying with their roses in silence. They seem contented and happy in their isolation from the great busy outer world, and, impressed by their universal appreciation of a flower, it occurs to me, on the impulse of ocular evidence, that it would be the greatest pity to disturb and corrupt these people by attempting to thrust upon them our Western civilization—they seem far happier than a civilized community.

The khan obtains his receipt for my delivery, and by and by Aminulah Khan sends his man to request the favor of a tomasha. Leaving my other effects behind in charge of the sowars, I take the bicycle and favor him with a few turns in front of the village gate. Among the various contents of my leathern case is a bag of kerans; but, although the case is not locked, it is provided with a peculiar fastening which I fondly imagine to be beyond the ingenuity of the khan to open. So that, while well enough aware of that guileful individual's uncontrollable avarice in general, and his deep, dark designs on my money in particular, I think little of leaving it with him for the few minutes I expect to be absent. It strikes me as a trifle suspicious, however, upon discovering that while everybody else comes to see the tomasha, all three of the sowars remain behind.

Instinctively I arrive at the conclusion that with these three worthy kleptomaniacs left alone in a room with some other person's portable property, something is pretty sure to happen to the property; so, excusing myself as quickly as courtesy will permit, I hasten back to our quarters. The mudbake is found posted at the outer gate of the konak. He is keeping watch while his delectable comrades search the package in which they sagaciously locate the silver lucre they so much covet. Seeing me approaching, he makes a trumpet of his hands and sings out warningly to his accomplices that I am coming back. Taking no more notice of him than usual, I pass inside and repair at once to the bala-khana, to find that the khan and the mirza have disappeared. The mudbake follows me in to watch my movements. In the simplicity of his semi-civilized understanding he is wondering within himself whether or no I entertain suspicions of anything being wrong, and he is watching me closely to find out. In his dense ignorance he imagines the khan and the mirza artful almost beyond human comprehension, and in thinking this he no doubt merely supplements the sentiments of these two wily individuals themselves. Time and again on the journey from Tabbas has he joined them in chuckling with ghoulish glee over some self-laudatory exposition of their own deep, deep, cunning. They well know themselves to be unfathomably cute beside the simple-hearted and honest ryots and nomads with whom they are wont to compare themselves, and from these standards they confidently judge the world at large. The mudbake colors up like a guilty school-boy upon seeing me proceed without delay to examine the leathern case. The erstwhile orderly arranged contents are found tumbled about in dire confusion. My bag of about one hundred kerans have dwindled nearly half that number as the result of being in their custody ten minutes.

"Some of you pedar sags have stolen my money; who is it? where's the khan?" I inquire, addressing the guilty-looking mud-bake. He is now shivering visibly with fright, but makes a ludicrous effort to put a bold face on the matter, and brazenly asks, "Chand pool" (How much is missing?). "Khylie! where is the khan and the inirza? I will take you all to Aminulah Khan and have you bastinadoed!" The poor mudbake turns pale at the bare suggestion of the bastinado, and stoutly maintains his own innocence. He would no doubt as stoutly proclaim the guilt of his comrades if by so doing he could escape punishment himself. Nor is this so surprising, when one reflects that either of these worthies would, without a moment's hesitation, perform the same office for him or for each other.

Without wasting time in bandying arguments with the mudbake, I sally forth in search of the others, and meet them just outside the gate; they are returning from hiding the money in the ruins. The crimson flood of guilt overspreads their faces as I raise my finger and shake it at them by way of admonition. With them following behind with all the meekness of discovered guilt, I lead the way back up into the bala-khana. Arriving there, both of them wilt so utterly and completely, and proceed to plead for mercy with such ludicrous promptness, that my sense of the ridiculous outweighs all other considerations, and I regard their demonstrations of remorse with a broad smile of amusement. It is anything but a laughing matter from their own standpoint, however; the mudbake warns them forthwith that I have threatened to have them bastinadoed, and they fairly writhe and groan in an agony of apprehension. The khan, owing to his more sanguine temperament, and a lively conception that the heaviest burden of guilt and accompanying punishment would naturally fall on his own shoulders as the chief of my escort, removes his turban and then lies down on the floor and grovels at my feet.

All the hair he possesses is a little tuft or two left on his otherwise smoothly shaven pate, by which he confidently expects at his demise to be tenderly lifted up into Paradise by the Prophet Mohammed. After kissing most of the dust off my geivehs, and banging his head violently against the floor, he signifies his willingness to relinquish all anticipations of eternal happiness, black-eyed houris and the like, by attempting to yank out even this Celestial hand-hold, hoping that the woeful depth of his anguish and the sincerity of his repentance may prove the means of escaping present punishment. His eyes roll wildly about in their sockets, and in a voice choking with emotion he begs me pathetically to keep the matter a secret from the Khan of Ghalakua. "O Sahib, Sahib! Hoikim no, hoikim no!" he pleads, and the anguish-stricken khan accompanies these pleadings with a look of unutterable agony, and furthermore indulges in the pantomime of sawing off his ears and his hands with his forefinger. This latter tragic demonstration is to let me know that the result of exposure would be to have the former, and perhaps the latter, of these useful members cut off, after the cruel and summary justice of this country. The mirza and mudbake cluster around and supplement their superior's pathetic pleadings with deep-drawn groans of "Allah, Allah!" and sundry prostrations toward Mecca.

It is a ludicrous and yet a strangely touching spectacle to see these three poor devils grovelling and pleading before me, and at the same time praying to Allah for protection in the little bala-khana, hoping thereby to save themselves from cruel mutilation and lifelong disgrace. A watchful eye is kept outside by the mirza, who does his groaning and praying near the door, and the sight of an Afghan approaching is the signal for a mute appeal for mercy from all three, and a transformation to ordinary attitudes and vocations, the completeness of which would do credit to professional comedians.

When a favorable opportunity presents, with much peering about to make sure of being unobserved, his comrades lower the khan down over the rear wall of the bala-khana, and a minute later they hoist him up again with the same show of caution.

Producing from his kammerbund a red handkerchief containing the stolen kerans, he advances and humbly lays it at my feet, at the same time kneeling down and implanting yet another osculatory favor on my geivehs. Joyful at seeing my readiness to second them in keeping the matter hidden from stray Afghans that come dropping in, the guilty sowars are still fearful lest they have not yet secured my complete forgiveness. Consequently, the khan repeatedly appeals to me as "bur-raa-ther," lays his forefingers together, and enlarges upon the fact that we have passed through the dangers and difficulties of the Dasht-i-na-oomid together. The dread spectre of possible mutilation and disgrace as the consequence of their misdeeds pursues these guileful, grown-up children even in their dreams. All through the night they are moaning and muttering uneasily in their sleep, and tossing restlessly about; and long before daybreak are they up, prostrating themselves and filling the room with rapidly muttered prayers, The khan comes over to my corner and peers anxiously down into my face. Finding me awake, he renews his plea for mercy and forgiveness, calling me "bur-raa-ther" and pleading earnestly "Hoikim no, hoikim no!"

The sharp-eyed wearer of the big busby, the cavalry sword, and red jackboots turns up early next morning. He dropped in once or twice yesterday, and being possessed of more brains than the three sowars put together, he gathered from appearances, and his general estimation of their character, that all is not right. These suspicions he promptly communicated to his master. Aminulah Khan is only too well acquainted with the weakest side of the Persian character, and at once jumps to the conclusion that the sowars have stolen my money. Sending for me and summoning the sowars to his presence, without preliminary palaver he accuses them of robbing me of "pool." Addressing himself to me, he inquires: "Sahib, Parses namifami?" (Do you understand Persian?) "Kam Kam" (a little), I reply. "Sowari pool f pool koob; rupee-rupee Jcoob?" "O, O, pool koob; rupee koob; sowari neis, sowari khylie koob adam." In this brief interchange of disconnected Persian the khan has asked me whether the sowars have stolen money from me, and I have answered that they have not, but that, on the contrary, they are most excellent men, both "trustie and true." May the recording angel enter my answer down with a recommendation for mercy! During this examination the little busby-wearer stands and closely scrutinizes the changeful countenances of the accused. He thoroughly understands that I am mercifully shielding them from what he considers their just deserts, and he chips in a word occasionally to Aminulah Khan, aside, like a sharp lawyer watching the progress of a cross-examination. The chief himself, though ostensibly accepting my statement, has his own suspicions to the same purpose, and before dismissing them he shakes his finger menacingly at the sowars and significantly touches the hilt of his sword. The three culprits look guilty enough to satisfy the most merciful of judges, but, relying on my operation to shield them, they stoutly maintain their innocence.

Some little delay occurs about starting for Furrah, my next objective point on the road to India; the khan explains that all of his sowars have been sent off to help garrison Herat; that the best he can provide in the form of a mounted escort is an elderly little man whom he points out, with an evident doubt as to my probable appreciation.

The man looks more like a Persian than an Afghan, which he probably is, as the population of these borderland districts is much mixed. Nothing would have pleased me better than to have had Aminulah Khan bid me go ahead without any escort whatever, but next to nobody at all, the most satisfactory arrangement is the harmless-looking old fellow in the Persian lamb's-wool hat. Telling him that he has done well in sending his sowars to Herat, and that the old fellow will answer very well as guide, I prepare to take my departure. My guide disappears, and shortly returns mounted on a powerful and spirited gray. Aminulah Khan gives him a letter, and after mutual salaams, and "good ahfis," the old sowar leads the way at a pace which shows him to be filled with exaggerated ideas about my speediness.

Irrigating ditches and fields characterize the way for some few miles, after which we emerge upon a level desert whose hard gravel surface is ridable in any direction without regard to beaten trails. Numerous lizards of a peculiar spotted variety are observed scuttling about on this gravelly plain as we ride along. The sun grows hot, but the way is level and smooth, and about ten o'clock we arrive at the oasis of Mahmoudabad, five farsakhs from Ghalakua. Mahmoudabad consists of a few mud dwellings surrounded by a strong wall, and a number of tents. Water is brought in a ditch from some distant source, and my faculty of astonishment is once again assailed by the sight of flourishing little patches of "Windsor beans." This is the first growth of these particular legumes that have come beneath my notice in Asia; dropping on them in the little oasis of Mahmoudabad is something of a surprise, to say the least.

The men of Mahmoudabad wear bracelets and ankle-ornaments of thick copper wire, and necklaces of beads. Nothing whatever is seen of the women; so far as ocular evidence is concerned, Mahmoudabad might be a community of men and boys exclusively. The plain continues level and gravelly, and pretty soon it becomes thinly covered with green young camel-thorn. The widely scattered shrubs fail to cover up much of the desert's nakedness at close quarters, but a wider view gives a pleasant green plain, out of which the dark, massive mountains rise abrupt with striking effect.

Late in the afternoon the hard surface of the desert gives place to the loose adobe soil of the Furi-ah Eooi bottom-lands. For some distance this is so loose and soft that one sinks in shoe-top deep at every step, and the path becomes a mere trail through dense thickets of reeds that wave high above one's head. Beyond this is a narrow area of cultivation and several walled villages, most of which are distinguished by one or two palms. Arriving at one of these villages, an hour before sunset, the old guide advocates remaining for the night. In obedience to his orders the headman brings out a carpet and spreads it beneath the shadow of the wall, and pointing to it, says, "Sahib, bismillah!" Taking the proffered seat, I inquire of him the distance to Furrah. Ho says it is across the Furrah Rood, and distant one farsakh. "Kishtee ass?" "O, Idshtee" Turning to the guide, I suggest: "Bismillah Furrah." The old fellow looks disappointed at the idea of going on, but he replies, "Bismillah." The carpet is taken away again, and the village headman sends a younger man to guide us through the fields and gardens to the river.

The Furrah Rood is broader and swifter here than the Harood, and when at sunset we reach the ferry, it is to find that the boat is on the other side and the ferrymen gone to their homes for the night. Several hundred yards back from the river the city of Furrah reveals itself in the shape of a sombre-looking high mud wall, forming a solid parallelogram, I should judge a third of a mile long and of slightly less width. The walls are crenellated, and strengthened by numerous buttresses. It occupies slightly rising ground, and nothing is visible from without but the walls. The old guide shouts lustily at a couple of men visible on the opposite bank; but he only gets shouted back at for his pains.

Darkness is rapidly settling down upon us, and I begin to realize my mistake in not abiding by the guide's judgment and stopping at the village. Another village is seen a couple of miles across the reedy lowland to our rear, and thitherward we shape our course. The intervening space is found to consist largely of tall reeds, swampy or overflowed areas, and irrigating ditches. Many of the latter are too deep to ford, and darkness overtakes us long before the village is reached. Finding it impossible to do anything with the bicycle, I remove my packages and lay the naked wheel on top of a conspicuous place on the bank of a ditch, where it may be readily found in the morning.

For some reason unintelligible to me accommodation is refused us at the village. The old guide addresses the people in tones loud and authoritative, but all to no purpose—they refuse to let us remain. While hesitating about what course to pursue, one of the men comes out and volunteers to guide us to a camp of nomads not far away. Following his guidance, a camp of a dozen tents is shortly reached, and in their hospitable midst we spend the night on a piece of carpet beneath the sky. The usual simple refreshments are provided, as also quilts for covering. Upon waking in the morning I am surprised to find the bicycle lying close to my head. The hospitable nomads, having heard the story of its abandonment from the guide, have been out in the night and found it and brought it in.

The same friendly person who brought us to the camp turns up at daybreak and voluntarily guides us through the area of ditches and impenetrable reed-patches to the river. Several people are squatting on the bank watching a crew of half-naked men tugging a rude but strong ferryboat up-stream toward them. The boat is built of heavy hewn timber, and capable of ferrying fifty passengers.

The Furrah Rood, at the ferry, is about two hundred yards wide, and with a current of perhaps five miles an hour. A dozen stalwart men with rude, heavy sweeps propel the boat across; but at every passage the swift current takes it down-stream twice as far as the river's width. After disembarking the passengers, the boatmen have to tow it this distance up-stream again before making the next crossing. The boatmen wear a single garment of blue cotton that in shape resembles a plain loose shirt. When nearing the shore, three or four of them deftly slip their arms out of the sleeves, bunch the whole garment up around their necks, and spring overboard. Swimming to shallow water with a rope, they brace themselves to stay the down-stream career of the boat.

A small gathering of wild-looking men are collected at the landing-place, and my astonishment is awakened by the familiar figure of a Celestial among the crowd. He is a veritable John Chinaman—beardless face, queue, almond eyes, and everything complete. The superior thriftiness of the Chinaman over the Afghans needs no further demonstration than the ocular evidence that among them all he wears by far the best and the tidiest clothes. In this, not less than in the strong Mongolian type of face, is he a striking figure among the people.

John Chinaman is a very familiar figure to me, and I regard this strange specimen with almost as great interest as if I had thus unexpectedly met a European. His grotesque figure and dress, representing, so it seems to me at the moment, a speck of civilization among the barbarousness of my surroundings, is quite a relief to the senses. A closer investigation, however, on the bank, while waiting for the guide's horse, reveals the fact that he is far from being the John Chinaman of Chinatown, San Francisco. Instead of hailing from the rice-fields of Quangtung, this fellow is a native of Kashgaria, a country almost as wild as Afghanistan. A moment's scrutiny of his face removes him as far from the civilized seaboard Celestials of our acquaintance as is the Zulu warrior from the plantation-darky of the South. Except for the above-mentioned comparative neatness of appearance, it is very evident that the Mongolian is every bit as wild as the Afghans about him.

The people regard me with a deep and peculiar interest; very few remarks are made among themselves, and no one puts a single question to me or ventures upon any remarks. All this is in strange contrast to the everlasting gabble and the noisy and persistent importunities of the Persians. The Afghans are plainly full of speculations concerning my mission, who I am, and what I am doing in their country; although they regard the bicycle with great curiosity, the machine is evidently a matter of secondary importance. Like the Eimuck chieftain on the Dasht-i several of these men change countenance when I favor them with a glance. Whether this peculiar reddening of the face among the Afghans comes of embarrassment, or what it is, it always impresses me as much like the "perturbation of a wild animal at finding himself suddenly confronted with a human being."

Hiding part way to the city gate, I send the guide ahead to notify the governor of my arrival, and to present the letter from Aininulah Khan. He is absent what appears to me an unnecessarily long time, and I determine to follow him in and take my chances on the tide of circumstances, as in the cities of Persia. It is not without certain lively apprehensions of possible adventure, however, that I approach the little arched gateway of this gray-walled Afghan city, conscious of its being filled with the most fanatical population in the world. In addition to this knowledge is the disquieting reflection of being a trespasser on forbidden territory, and therefore outside the pale of governmental sympathy should I get into trouble.

The fascination of penetrating the strange little world within those high walls, however, ill brooks these retrospective reflections, or thoughts of unpleasant consequences, and I make no hesitation about riding up to the gate. A sharp, short turn and abrupt rise in the road occurs at the gate, necessitating a dismount and a trundle of about thirty yards, when I suddenly find myself confronting a couple of sentries beneath the archway of the gate. The sensation of surprise seems quite in order of late, and these sentries furnish yet another sensation, for they are wearing the red jackets of British infantrymen and the natty peaked caps of the Royal Artillery. The same crimson flush of embarrassment—or whatever it may be—that was observed in the countenance of the Eimuck chief, overspreads their faces, and they seem overcome with confusion and astonishment; but they both salute mechanically as I pass in. Fifty yards of open waste ground enables me to mount and ride into the entrance of the principal street. I have precious little time to look about me, and no opportunity to discover what the result of my temerity would be after the people had recovered from their amazement, for hardly have I gotten fairly into the street when I am met by my old guide, conducting a guard of twelve soldiers who have been sent to bring me in.

CHAPTER X

ARRESTED AT FURRAH

Perhaps no stranger occurrence in the field of personal adventure in Central Asia has happened for many a year than my entrance into Furrah on a bicycle. Only those who know Afghanistan and the Afghans can fully realize the ticklish character of this little piece of adventure.

My soldier-escort are fine-looking fellows, wearing the well-known red jackets of the British Army, evidently the uniform of some sepoy regiment. Forming around me, they conduct me through the gate of an inner enclosure near by, and usher me into a small compound where Mahmoud Yusuph Khan, the commander-in-chief of the garrison, is engaged in holding a morning reception of his subordinate chiefs and officers. The spectacle that greets my astonished eyes is a revelation indeed; the whole compound is filled with soldiers wearing the regimentals of the Anglo-Indian army. As I enter the compound and trundle the bicycle between long files of soldiers toward Mahmoud Yusuph Khan and his officers, five hundred pairs of eyes are fixed on me with intense curiosity. These are Cabooli soldiers sent here to garrison Furrah, where they will be handy to march to the relief of Herat, in case of demonstrations against that city by the Russians. The tension over the Penjdeh incident has not yet (April, 1886) wholly relaxed, and I feel instinctively that I am suspected of being a Russian spy.

In the centre of the compound is a large bungalow, surrounded by a slightly raised porch. Seated on a mat at one end of this is Mahmoud Yusuph Khan, and ranged in two long rows down the porch are his chiefs and officers. They are all seated cross-legged on a strip of carpet, and attendants are serving them with tea in little porcelain cups. They are the most martial-looking assembly of humans I ever set eyes on. They are fairly bristling with quite serviceable looking weapons, besides many of the highly ornamented, but less dangerous, "gewgaws of war" dear to the heart of the brave but conservative warriors of Islam. Prominent among the peculiarities observed are strips of chain mail attached to portions of their clothing as guards against sword-cuts, noticeably on the sleeves. Some are wearing steel helmets, some huge turbans, and others the regular Afghan military hat, this latter a rakish-looking head-piece something like the hat of a Chinese Tartar general.

Mahmoud Yusupli Khan himself is wearing one of these hats, and is attired in a tight-fitting suit of buckram, pipe-clayed from head to foot; in his hat glitters a handsome rosette of nine diamonds, which I have an opportunity of counting while seated beside him. He is a stoutish person, full-faced, slightly above middle age, less striking in appearance than many of his subordinates. When I have walked up between the two rows of seated chieftains and gained his side, he forthwith displays his knowledge of the English mode of greeting by shaking hands. He orders an attendant to fetch a couple of camp chairs, and setting one for me, he rises from the carpet and occupies the other one himself. Tea is brought in small cups instead of glasses, and is highly sweetened after the manner of the Persians; sweetmeats are handed round at the same time. After ascertaining that I understand something of Persian, he expresses his astonishment at my appearance in Furrah. At first it is painfully evident that he suspects me of being a Russian spy; but after several minutes of questions and answers, he is apparently satisfied that I am not a Muscovite, and he explains to his officers that I am an "Ingilis nockshi" (correspondent). He is greatly astonished to hear of the route by which I entered the country, as no traveller ever entered Afghanistan across the Dasht-i-na-oomid before. I tell him that I am going to Kandahar and Quetta, and suggest that he send a sowar with me to guide the way. He smiles amusedly at this suggestion, and shaking his head vigorously, he says, "Kandahar neis; Afghanistan's bad; khylie bad;" and he furthermore explains that I would be sure to get killed. "Kliylie koob; I don't want any sowar, I will go alone; if I get killed, then nobody will be blamable but myself." "Kandahar neis," he replies, shaking his finger and head, and looking very serious; "Kandahar neis; beest (20) sowars couldn't see you safely through to Kandahar; Afghanistan's bad; a Ferenghi would be sure to get killed before reaching Kandahar." Pretending to be greatly amused at this, I reply, "koob; if I get killed, all right; I don't want any sowars; I will go alone." At hearing this, he grows still more serious, and enters into quite an eloquent and lengthy explanation, to dissuade me from the idea of going. He explains that the Ameer has little control over the fanatical tribes in Zemindavar, and that although the Boundary Commission had a whole regiment of sepoys, the Ameer couldn't guarantee their safety if they came to Furrah. He furthermore expresses his surprise that I wasn't killed before getting this far. The officer of the guard who brought me in, and who is standing against the porch close by, speaks up at this stage of the interview and tells with much animation of how I was riding down the street, and of the people all speechless with astonishment.

Mahmoud Yusuph Khan repeats this to his officers, with comments of his own, and they look at one another and smile and shake their heads, evidently deeply impressed at what they consider the dare-devil recklessness of a Ferenghi in venturing alone into the streets of Furrah. The warlike

Afghans have great admiration for personal courage, and they evidently regard my arrival here without escort as a proof that I am possessed of a commendable share of that desirable quality. As the commander-in-chief and a few grim old warriors squatting near us exchange comments on the subject of my appearance here, and my willingness to proceed alone to Kandahar, notwithstanding the known probability of being murdered, their glances of mingled amusement and admiration are agreeably convincing that I have touched a chord of sympathy in their rude, martial breasts.

Half an hour is passed in drinking tea and asking questions. Mahmoud Yusuph Khan proves himself not wholly ignorant of English and British-Indian politics. "General Roberts Sahib, Cabool to Kandahar?" he queries first. The Afghans regard General Roberts' famous march as a wonderful performance, and consequently hold that distinguished officer's name in high repute. He asks about Sir Peter Lumsden and Colonel Sir West Ridgeway; and speaks of the Governor-General of India. By way of testing the extent of his knowledge, I refer to Lord Ripon as the present Governor-General of India, when he at once corrects me with, "No; Lord Dufferin Sahib." He speaks of London, and wants to know about Mr. Gladstone and Lord Salisbury—which is now Prime Minister? I explain by pantomime that the election is not decided; he acknowledges his understanding of my meaning by a nod. He then grows inquisitive about the respective merits of the two candidates. "Gladstone koob or Salisbury koob?" he queries. "Gladstone koob, England, ryot, nune, gusht, kishrnish, pool-Salisbury koob, India, Afghanistan, Ameer, Russia soldier, officer," is the reply. To the average reader this latter reads like so much unintelligible shibboleth; but it is a fair sample of the disjointed language by which I manage to convey my meaning plainly to the Afghan chieftain. He understands by these few disconnected nouns that I consider Gladstone to be the better statesman of the two for England's domestic affairs, and Salisbury the better for the foreign policy of the Empire.

All this time the troops are being put through their exercises, marching about the compound in companies and drilling with their muskets. Some are uniformed in the picturesque Anglo-Oriental regimentals of the Indian sepoy, and others in neat red jackets, peaked caps, and white trousers with red stripes. The buttons, belts, bandoleers, and buckles are all wanderers from the ranks of the British army. The men themselves—many of them, at least—might quite as readily be credited to that high standard of military prowess which characterizes the British army as the clothes and accoutrements they are wearing, judging from outward appearances. Not only do their faces bear the stamp of both fearlessness and intelligence, but some of them are possessed of the distinctively combative physiognomy of the born pugilist. The captain of the Governor's guard has a particularly plucky and aggressive expression; he is a man whose face will always remain pictured on my memory. The interesting expression this officer habitually wears is that of a prize-ring champion, with a determined bull-dog phiz, watching eagerly to pounce on some imaginary antagonist. Seeing that his attention is keenly centred upon me the whole time I am sitting by the side of his chief, he becomes an object of more than passing interest. He watches me with the keen earnestness of a bull-dog expectantly awaiting the order to attack.

Mahmoud Yusuph Khan now attempts to explain at length sundry reasons why it is necessary to place me, for the time being, under guard. He seems very anxious to convey this unpleasant piece of information in the flowery langue diplomatique of the Orient, or in other words, to coat the bitter pill of my detention with a sugary coating of Eastern politeness.

His own linguistic abilities being unequal to the occasion, he sends off somewhere for a dusky Hindostani, who shortly arrives and, in obedience to orders, forthwith begins jabbering at me in his own tongue. Of this I, of course, know literally nothing, and, ever swayed by suspicion, it is easily perceivable that their first impression of my being a Russian spy is in a measure revived by my ignorance of Hindostani. They seem to think it inconsistent that one could be an Englishman and not understand the language of a native of India. After the interview the twelve red-jackets that appear to constitute the Governor's bodyguard are detailed to conduct me to a walled garden—outside the city. Before departing, however, I give the strange assembly of Afghan warriors an exhibition of riding around the compound. The guard, under the leadership of the officer with the bull-dog phiz, fix bayonets and form into a file on either side of me as I trundle back through the same street traversed upon my arrival. Accompanying us is a man on a gray horse whom everybody addresses respectfully as "Kiftan Sahib" (Captain), and another individual afoot in a bottle-green roundabout, a broad leathern belt, a striped turban, white baggy pantalettes, and pointed red shoes. Kiftan Sahib looks more like an English game-keeper than an Afghan captain; he wears a soiled Derby hat, a brown cut-away coat, striped pantaloons, and Northampton-made shoes without socks; his arms are a cavalry sabre and a revolver.

Outside the gate, at the suggestion of the young man in the bottle-green roundabout, I mount and ride, wheeling slowly along between the little files of soldiers. The soldiers are delighted at the novelty of their duty, and they swing briskly along as I pedal a little faster. They smile at the exertion necessary to keep up, and falling in with their spirit of amusement, I gradually increase my speed, and finally shoot ahead of them entirely. Kiftan Sahib comes galloping after me on the gray, and with good-humored anxiety motions for me to stop and let the soldiers catch up. He it is upon whom the commander-in-chief has saddled the responsibility for my safe-keeping, and this little display of levity and my ability to so easily outdistance the soldiers, awakens in him the spirit of apprehension at once. One can see that he breathes easier as soon as we are safely inside the garden gate.

A couple of little whitewashed bungalows are the only buildings in the garden, and one of these is assigned to me for my quarters. Kiftan Sahib and the young man in the bottle-green roundabout give orders about the preparation of refreshments, and then squat themselves down near me to gladden their eyes with a prolonged examination of my face. The red-jackets separate into three reliefs of four each; one relief immediately commences pacing back and forth along the four sides of the bungalow, one soldier on each side, while the remainder seek the shade of a pomegranate grove that occupies one side of the garden. By-and-by servitors appear bearing trays of sweetmeats and more substantial fare. The variety and abundance of eatables comprising the meal, are such as to thoroughly delight the heart of a person who has grown thin and gaunt and wolfish from semi-starvation and prolonged physical exertion. The two long skewers of smoking kabobs and the fried eggs are most excellent eating, the pillau is delicious, and among other luxuries is a sort of pomegranate jam, some very good butter (called muscal), a big bowl of sherbet, and dishes of nuts, sweetmeats, and salted melon seeds. After dinner the young man in bottle-green, who seems anxious to cultivate my good opinion, smiles significantly at me and takes his departure; he turns up again in a few minutes bearing triumphantly an old Phillips' Atlas, which he deferentially places at my feet. Opening it, I find that the chief countries and cities of the world are indicated in written Hindostani characters. In this manner some English officer has probably been the undesigning medium of giving these Afghans a peep into the configuration of the earth they live on, and their first lesson in geography.

I reward the young man by asking him whether he too is a "kiftan." He acknowledges the compliment by a broad grin and two salaams made in rapid succession.

After noon a messenger arrives from Mahmoud Yusuph Khan bringing salaams and a pair of stout English walking-boots to replace my old worn-out geivehs; and a cake of toilet soap, also of English make. Both shoes and soap, as may be easily imagined, are highly acceptable articles. The advent of the former likewise answers the purpose of enlightening me a trifle in regard to matters philological; the Afghans call their foot-gear "boots" (the Chinese call their foot-wear "shoes," and their gloves "tung-shoes," or hand-shoes).

About four o'clock I am visited by a fatherly old khan in a sky-blue gown, and an interesting Cabooli cavalry colonel, with pieces of chain mail distributed about his uniform, and a fierce-looking moustache that stands straight out from his upper lip. Sweetmeats enough to start a small candy shop have been sent me during the afternoon, and setting them out before my guests, we are soon on the most familiar terms. The colonel shows me his weapons in return for a squint down the shining rifled barrel of my Smith & Wesson, and he explains the merits and demerits of both his own firearms and mine. The 38-calibre S. & W. he thinks a perfect weapon in its way, but altogether too small for Afghanistan. With expressive pantomime he explains that, while my 38 bullet would kill a person as well as a larger one, it requires a heavier missile to crash into a man who is making for you with a knife or sword, and stop him. His favorite weapon for close quarters is a murderous-looking piece, half blunderbuss, half pistol, that he carries thrust in his kammerbund, so that the muzzle points behind him. This weapon has a small single-hand musket stock, and the bell-mouthed barrel is filled nearly to the muzzle with powder and round bullets the size of buckshot. This formidable firearm is for hand-to-hand fighting on horseback, and at ten paces might easily be warranted to blow a man's head into smithereens.

The colonel is an amiable old warrior, and kindly points this interesting weapon at my head for me to peer down the barrel and satisfy myself that it is really loaded almost to the top! Like Injun-slaying youngsters in America, the doughty Afghan warriors seem to delight in having their weapons loaded, their sidearms sharp, and their bayonets fixed, and seem anxious to impress the beholder with the fact that they are real warriors, and not mere make-believe soldiers. The colonel wears a dark-brown uniform profusely trimmed with braid, a Kashgarian military hat, and English army shoes. In matters pertaining to his wardrobe it is very evident that he has profited to no small extent by Afghanistan being adjacent territory to British India; but his semi-civilized ambition has not yet soared into the aesthetic realm of socks; doubtless he considers Northampton-made shoes sufficiently luxurious without the addition of socks.

The mission of these two officers is apparently to prepare me gradually for the intelligence that I am to be taken back to Herat. So skillfully and diplomatically does the old khan in the cerulean gown acquit himself of this mission, that I thoroughly understand what is to be my disposition, although Herat is never mentioned. He talks volubly about the Ameer, the Wali, the Padishah, the dowleh, Cabool, Allah, and a host of other subjects, out of which I readily evolve my fate; but, as yet, he breathes nothing but diplomatic hints, and these are clothed in the most pleasant and reassuring smiles, and given in tones of paternal solicitude. The colonel sits and listens intently, and now and then chimes in with a word of soothing assent by way of emphasizing the subject, when the khan is explaining about the Ameer, or Allah, or kismet. Mahmoud Tusuph Khan himself comes to the garden in the cool of the evening, and for half an hour occupies bungalow No. 2. He betrays a spark of Oriental vanity by having an attendant follow behind, bearing a huge and wonderful sun-shade, into the make-up of which peacock feathers and other gorgeous material largely enters. Noticing this, I make a determined assault upon his bump of Asiatic self-esteem, by asking him if he is brother to the Ameer. He smiles and says he is a brother of Shere Ali, the ex-Ameer deposed in favor of Abdur Bahman. His remarks during our second interview are largely composed of furtive queries, intended to penetrate what he evidently, even as yet, suspects to be the secret object of my mysterious appearance in the heart of the country. The Afghan official is nothing if not suspicious, and although he professed his own conviction, in the morning, of my being an English "nokshi," his constitutionally suspicious nature forbids him accepting this impression as final.

During this interview two more natives of India are produced and ordered to assail my long-suffering ears with the battery of their vernacular. They are an interesting pair, and they evince the liveliest imaginable interest in finding a Sahib alone in the hands of the Afghans. They are vivacious and intelligent, and try hard to make themselves understood. From their own vocal and pantomimic efforts and the Persian of the Afghans, I learn that they are sepoys in charge of three prisoners from the Boundary Commission camp, whom they are taking through to Quetta.

They seem very anxious to do something in my behalf, and want Mahmoud Yusuph Khan to let them take me with them to Quetta. I lose no time in signifying my approval of this suggestion; but the Governor shakes his head and orders them away, as though fearful even to have such a proposition entertained. All the time the sepoys are endeavoring to make themselves understood, every Afghan present regards my face with the keenest scrutiny; so glaringly evident are their suspicions that the situation becomes too much for my gravity. The sepoys grin broadly in response, whereupon the pugilistic-faced captain of the Governor's guard remonstrates with them for their levity, by roughly making them stand in a more respectful attitude. I dislike very much to see them ordered off, for they are evidently anxious to champion my cause; moreover, it would have been interesting to have accompanied them through to Quetta. Understanding thoroughly by this time that I am not to be allowed to go through by way of Girishk and Kandahar, and dreading the probability of being taken back into Persia, I ask permission to travel south to Jowain and the frontier of Beloochistan. The Afghan-Beloochi boundary is not more than fifty or sixty miles south of Furrah, and while it would be difficult to say what advantage would be gained by reaching there, it would at all events be some consolation to find myself at liberty.

The interview ends, however, without much additional light being shed on their intentions; but the advent of more sweetmeats shortly after the Governor's departure, and the unexpected luxury of a bottle of Shiraz wine, heightens the conviction that my own wishes in the matter are to be politely ignored. The red-jackets patrol my bungalow till dark, when they are relieved by soldiers in dark-blue kilts, loose Turkish pantalettes, and big turbans. I sit on the threshold during the evening, watching their soldierly bearing with much interest; on their part they comport themselves as though proudly conscious of making a good impression. I judge they have been especially ordered to acquit themselves well in my presence, and so impress me, whether I am English or Russian, with a sense of their military proficiency. All about the garden red-coated guards are seen prostrating themselves toward Mecca in the prosecution of their evening devotions. Full of reflections on the exciting events of the day and the strange turn affairs have taken, I stretch myself on a Turkoman rug and doze off to sleep. The last sound heard ere reaching the realms of unconsciousness is the steady tramp of the sentinels pacing to and fro. Scarcely have I fallen asleep—so at least it seems to me —when I am awakened by my four guards singing out, one after another, "Kujawpuk! Ki-i-puk!!" This appears to be their answer to the challenge of the officer going his rounds, and they shout it out in tones clear and distinct, in succession. This programme is repeated several times during the night, and, notwithstanding the sleep-inducing fatigues of the last few days, my slumbers are light enough to hear the reliefs of the guard and their strange cry of "Kujawpuk, ki-i-puk" every time it is repeated.

As the sun peeps over the wall of the garden my red-jackets reappear at their post; roses are stuck in their caps' and their buttonholes, and fastened to their guns. A big bouquet of the same fragrant "guls" is presented to me, and a dozen gholams are busy gathering all that are abloom in the garden. These are probably gathered every morning in the rose season, and used for making rose-water by the officers' wives. During the forenoon the blue-gowned old khan and his major-domo, the mail-clad colonel, again present themselves at my bungalow. They are gracious and friendly to a painful degree, and sugar would scarcely melt in the mouth of the paternal old khan as he delivers the "Wall's salaams to the Sahib." Tea and sweetmeats are handed around, and Kiftan Sahib and Bottle Green join our company.

Nothing but the formal salaams has yet been said; but intuition is a faithful forerunner, and ere another word is spoken, I know well enough that the khan and the colonel have been sent to break the disagreeable news that I am to be taken to Herat, and that Kiftan Sahib and Bottle Green have dropped in out of curiosity to see how I take it.

The kindly old khan finds his task of awakening the spirit of disappointment anything but congenial, and he seems very loath to deliver the message. When he finally unburdens himself, it is with averted eyes and roundabout language. He commences by a rambling disquisition on the dangers of the road to Kandahar, apologizing profusely for the Ameer's inability to guarantee the good behavior of the wandering tribes, and the consequent necessity of forbidding travellers to enter the country.

He dwells piously and at considerable length upon our obligations to submit to the will of Allah, not forgetting a liberal use of the Oriental fatalist's favorite expression: "kismet." For the sake of argument, rather than with any hope of influencing things in my favor, I reply:" All right, I don't ask the Ameer's protection; I will go to Kandahar and Quetta alone, on my own responsibility; then if I get murdered by the Ghilzais, nobody but myself will be to blame." "The Wali has his orders from the Padishah, the Ameer Abdur Eahman Khan, that no Ferenghi is to come in the country." "Tell the Wali that Afghanistan is Allah's country first and Abdur Eahman's country second. Inshallah, Allah gives everybody the road." The old khan is evidently at a loss how to meet so logical an argument, and the colonel, Kiftan Sahib, and Bottle Green are deeply impressed at what they consider my unanswerable wisdom. They look at one another and shake their heads and smile.

The chief concern of the khan is apparently to convince me that it is only out of consideration for my own safety that I am forbidden to go through, and, after a brief consultation with the others, he again addresses his flowery eloquence to me. He comes and squats beside me, and, with much soothing patting of my shoulder, he says: "The Wali is only taking you to Herat to obtain Ridgeway Sahib's and Faramorz Khan's permission for you to go through. Inshallah, after you have seen Herat, if it is the will of Allah, and your kismet to go to Kandahar, the Ameer will let you go." To this comforting assurance I deem it but justice to the well-meaning old chieftain to signify my submission to the inevitable. Before departing, he requests the humble present of a pencil-sketch of the bicycle as a souvenir of my visit to Furrah. During the day I get on quite intimate terms with my guard, and among other things compete with them in the feat of holding a musket out at arm's length, gripping the extreme end of the barrel. Tall, strapping fellows some of them are, but they are not muscular in comparison; out of a round dozen competitors I am the only one capable of fairly accomplishing this feat.

Many of the soldiers carry young pheasants about with them in cages, and seem to derive a good deal of pleasure in feeding them and attending to their wants. The cages are merely pieces of white muslin, or mosquito-netting, about the size of a pocket-handkerchief, enclosing a four-inch disk of wood for the inmate to stand on. The crape is gathered and loosely tied at the corners. It is carried as one would carry anything suspended in a handkerchief, and is hung on the limb of a tree in the same manner.

Late in the afternoon of the second clay my scarlet guard marshal themselves in front of the bungalow, and Kiftan Sahib and Bottle Green bid me prepare for departure to Herat. The old khan and the colonel, and several other horsemen, appear at the gate; the soldiers form themselves into two files, and between them I trundle from my circumscribed quarters. The rude ferry-boat is awaiting our coming, and in a few minutes the khan and the colonel bid me quite an affectionate farewell on the river-bank, gazing eagerly into my face as though regretful at the necessity of parting so soon. My escort favor me with the, same lingering gaze. These people are evidently fascinated by the strange and mysterious manner of my coming among them; who am I, what am I, and wherefore my marvellous manner of travelling, are questions that appeal strongly to their Asiatic imagination, and they are intensely loath to see me disappear again without having seen more of me and my wonderful iron horse, and learned more about it.

Several horsemen have already crossed and are awaiting us on the opposite shore. Kiftan Sahib and another officer with a henna-tinted beard are in charge of the party taking me back. Besides myself and these two, the party consists of eleven horsemen; with sundry modifications, their general appearance, arms, and dress resemble the make-up of a Persian sowar rather than the regular Afghan soldier. The sun is just setting behind those western mountains I passed three days ago as we reach the western shore, the boatmen are unloading the saddles and accoutrements of our party, and I sit down on the bank and survey the strange scene just across the river. The steep bluff opposite is occupied by people who accompanied us to the river. Many of them are seizing this opportune moment to prostrate themselves toward the Holy City, the geographical position of which is happily indicated by the setting sun.

Prominent among the worshippers are seen side by side the cerulean figure of the khan, and the colonel in all the bravery of his military trappings, his chain armor glistening brightly in the waning sunlight. A little removed from the crowd, the twelve red-coats are ranged in a row, performing the same pious ceremony; as their bared heads bob up and down one after another, the scarlet figures outlined in a row against the eastern sky are strangely suggestive of a small flock of flamingoes engaged in fishing.

CHAPTER XI

UNDER ESCORT TO HERAT

Our party camps near a village not far from the river, but it takes us till after dark to reach the place, owing to ditches and overflow. A few miles of winding trails and intricate paths through the reedy river-bottom next morning, and we emerge upon a flinty upland plain. At first a horseman is required to ride immediately ahead of the bicycle, my untutored escort being evidently suspicious lest I might suddenly forge ahead, and with the swiftness of a bird disappear from their midst.

As this leader, in his ignorance, occasionally stops right in the narrow path, and considers himself in duty bound to limit my speed to that of the walking horses, this arrangement quickly becomes very monotonous. Appealing to Kiftan Sahib, I point out the annoyance of having a horse just in front, and promise not to go too far ahead. He points appealingly to a little leathern pouch attached to his belt. The pouch contains a letter to the Governor of Herat, and he it is whom Mahmoud Yusuph Khan expects to take back a receipt. The chief responsibility for my safe delivery rests upon his shoulders, and he is disposed to be abnormally apprehensive and suspicious.

Reassuring him of my sincerity, he permits the horseman to follow along behind. When the condition of the road admits of my pushing ahead a little, this sowar canters along immediately behind, while the remainder of the party follow more leisurely.

One of the party carries a skin of water, and as the morning grows fearfully hot, frequent halts are made to wait for him and get a drink, otherwise we two are usually some distance ahead. These water-vessels are merely goat-skins, taken off with as little mutilation of the hide as possible; one of the legs serves as a faucet, and the tying or untying of a piece of string opens or closes the "tap." It is the handiest imaginable contrivance for carrying liquids on horseback, the tough, pliant goat-skin resisting any amount of hard usage and accommodating itself readily to the contour of the pack-saddle, or itself forming a soft enough seat to the rider.

Near noon we reach the ruins of Suleimanabad, entirely deserted save by hideous gray lizards a foot long, numbers of which scuttle off into their hiding places at our approach. In the distance ahead are visible the black tents of a nomad camp. The glowing, reflected heat of the stony desert

- 157 -

produces an unquenchable thirst, and the generous bowls of cool, acidulous doke obtained in the tents are quaffed most eagerly by the entire party.

The solicitude of Kiftaii Sahib as displayed on my behalf is quite amusing, not to say affecting; while the others are attending to their horses he squats down before me underneath the little goat-hair tent and gazes at me with an attention so close that one might imagine him afraid lest I should mysteriously change into some impalpable spirit and float away.

The nomads themselves appear to be amiably disposed, intent chiefly on supplying our wants and fulfilling the traditions of tented hospitality. They look wild enough, but, withal, pleasant and intelligent. Kiftan Sahib, however, watches every movement of the stalwart nomads with keen interest; and small power of penetration is required to see that apprehension, if not positive suspicion, enters very largely into his thoughts concerning them and myself.

A howling wind and dust-storm comes careering across the plain, creating a wild scene, and black cloud-banks gather and pile up ominously in the west. The threatened rain-storm, however, passes off with a pyrotechnic display of great brilliancy, and the evening air lowers to a refreshing temperature as we stretch ourselves out on nummuds, fifty yards away from the tents. Kiftan Sahib spreads his own couch on the right side of mine and the red-whiskered chief of the sowars occupies the left.

Waking up during the night, I am somewhat taken by surprise at finding one of my escort standing guard over me with fixed bayonet. This extraordinary precaution appears to me at the time as being altogether superfluous; while recognizing these nomads as lawless and fanatical, I should nevertheless have no hesitation in venturing alone among them.

The morning star is just soaring above the eastern horizon, and the feeble rays of Luna's half-averted face are imparting a ghostly glimmer of light, when I am awakened from a sound sleep. The horses have all been saddled and packed, and everybody is ready to start. Daylight comes on apace and, finding the trail hard and reasonably smooth, I am happily able to "sowari," and not only able to ride but to forge right ahead of the party. The country is level and open, and uninhabited, so that Kiftan Sahib is far less apprehensive than he was yesterday.

I am perhaps a couple of miles ahead when I come to a splendid, large, irrigating canal, evidently conveying water from the Harood down across the desert to the low cultivable lands near the Furrah Rood. The water is three feet deep, and I revel in the luxury of a cooling and refreshing bath until overtaken by the escort.

The plain, heretofore hard, now changes into loose sand and gravel, and the trail becomes quite obliterated. In addition to these undesirable changes, the wind commences blowing furiously from the north, making it absolutely impossible to ride. Rounding the base of an abutting mountain, we emerge upon the grassy lowlands of the Harood in the vicinity of Subzowar. Subzowar is a sort of way-station between Furrah and Herat, the only inhabited place, except tents, on the whole journey. It is on the west side of the Harood and the broad, swift stream is full to overflowing, a turgid torrent rushing along at a dangerous pace.

After much shouting and firing of guns, a score of villagers appear on the opposite bank, and several of them come wading and swimming across. They seem veritable amphibians, capable of stemming the tide that well-nigh sweeps strong horses off their feet. The river is fordable by following a zigzag course well known to the local watermen. One of them carries the bicycle safely across on his head, and others lead the sowars' horses by the bridle.

When all the Afghans but Kiftan Sahib have been assisted over, the strongest horse of the party is brought back for my own passage. A dozen natives are made to form a close cordon about me to rescue me in case of misadventure, while one leads the horse by his bridle and another steadies him by holding on to his tail. Kiftan Sahib himself brings up the rear, and, as the rushing waters deepen around us, he abjures me to keep a steady seat and, in a voice that almost degenerates into an apprehensive whine, he mutters: "The receipt, Sahib, the receipt."

A ripple of excitement occurs in the middle of the river by one the men being swept off his feet and carried down stream; and, although he swims like a duck, the treacherous undercurrent sucks him under several times. It looks as though he would be drowned; a number of his comrades race down the bank and plunge in to swim to his rescue, but he finally secures footing on a submerged sand-bank, and after resting a few minutes swims ashore.

The remainder of the day, and the night, are passed in tents near Subzowar, it being very evidently against Afghan social etiquette for strangers to take shelter within the confines of the village itself.

Whether from their knowledge of the unsuitableness of the country ahead, or from a new spasm of apprehension concerning their responsibility, does not appear; but in the morning Kiftan Sahib and the chief of the sowars insist upon me mounting a horse and handing the bicycle over to the tender mercies of the person in charge of the nummud pack-horse. They point in the direction of Herat, and deliver themselves of a marvellous quantity of deprecatory pantomime. My own impression is that, having recrossed the Harood, the only great obstacle in the path of a wheelman between Furrah and Herat, their abnormally suspicious minds imagine that there is now nothing to prevent me taking wings and outdistancing them to the latter place.

Finding them determined, and, moreover, nothing loath to try a horse for a change, on the back-stretch, I take the wheel apart and distribute fork, backbone, and large wheel among the sowars. The only fit place for the latter is on the top of the nummuds and blankets on the spare pack-horse, and, before starting, I see to fastening it securely on top of the load. This pack-horse is a powerful black stallion that puts in a good share of his time trying to attack the other horses. Owing to this uncontrollable pugnacity, he is habitually led along at some considerable distance from the party, generally to the rear.

The person in charge of him is a young negro as black, and proportionately powerful, as himself. Wild and ferocious as is the stallion, he is a civilized and mild-mannered animal compared with his manager. In the matter of facial expression and intellectual development this uncivilized descendant of Ham is first cousin to a wild gorilla, and it is not without certain misgivings that I leave the web-like bicycle-wheel in his charge. He has been a very interesting study of uncivilization all along, and his bump of destructiveness is as large as an orange. The military Afghans, one and all, impress me as being especially created to destroy the fruits of other people's industry and thrift, whether it be in wearing out clothes and shoes made in England, or devouring the substance of the peaceful villagers of their own territory; and this untamed darkey fairly bristles with the evidence of his capacity as a destroyer.

Everything about him is in a dilapidated condition; the leathern scabbard of his sword is split half way up, revealing a badly notched and rusted blade. An orang-outang, fresh from the jungles of Sumatra, could scarcely display less intelligence concerning human handicraft than he; he bubbles over with laughter at seeing anything upset or broken, growls sullenly at receiving uncongenial orders, calls on Allah, and roars threateningly at the stallion, all in the same breath. No wonder I ride ahead, feeling somewhat apprehensive; and yet the wheel looks snug and safe enough on top of the big pile of soft nummuds.

The day's march is long and dreary, through a country of desert wastes and stony hills. The only human habitation seen is a small cluster of tents near some wells of water. The people seem overjoyed at the sight of travellers, and come running to the road with their kammerbunds full of little hard balls of sun-dried mast. We fill our pockets with these and nibble and chew them as we ride along. They are pleasantly sour, containing great thirst-quemhing properties, as well as being very nourishing.

The sun goes down and dusk settles over our trail, and still the chief of the sowars and Kiftan Sahib lead the way. Many of the horses are pretty badly fagged, they have had nothing to eat all day and next to nothing to drink, and the party are straggling along the trail for a couple of miles back. At length lights are observed twinkling in the darkness ahead. Half an hour later we dismount in a nomad camp, and one after another the remainder of the party come straggling in, some of them leading their horses. Both men and animals are well-nigh overcome with fatigue.

The shrill neighing of the ferocious and spirited black stallion is heard as he approaches and realizes that he is coming into camp; he is a glorious specimen of a horse, neither hunger nor thirst can curb his spirit. He is carrying far the heaviest load of the party, yet he comes into camp at ten o'clock, after hustling along over stones and sand since before daylight, without food or water; neighing loudly and ready to fight all the horses within reach. The chief of the sowars goes out to superintend the unloading of the black stallion; and soon I hear him addressing the negro in angry tones, supplementing his reproachful words with several resounding blows of his riding-whip. The wild darkey's disapproval of these proceedings finds expression in a roar of pain and fear that would do justice to a yearling bull being dragged into the shambles.

The cause of this turmoil shortly turns up in the shape of my wheel, with no less than eleven spokes broken, and the rim considerably twisted out of shape. Kiftan Sahib surveys 'the damaged wheel a moment, draws his own rawhide from his kammerbund, and rises to his feet. With a hoarse cry of alarm the negro vanishes into the surrounding gloom; the next moment is heard his eager chuckling laugh, the spontaneous result of his lucky escape from Kiftan Sahib's vengeful rawhide. Kiftan Sahib keeps a desultory lookout for him all the evening, but the wary negro is more eagerly watchful than he, and during supper-time he hovers perpetually about the encircling wall of darkness, ready to vanish into its impenetrable depths at the first aggressive demonstration.

The explanation of the negro is that the black horse laid down with his load. The wheel presents a well-nigh ruined appearance, and I retire to my couch in a most unenviable frame of mind; lying awake for hours, pondering over the probability of being able to fix it up again at Herat.

One of our party of stragglers has failed to come in, and a couple of nomads start out about 2 a.m. to try and find him; but neither absentee nor searchers turn up at daybreak, and so we pull out without him.

The wind blows raw and chilly from the north as we depart at early dawn, and the men muffle themselves up in whatever wraps they happen to have. Unwilling to trust the wheel further in the charge of the negro, I carry it myself, resting it on one stirrup, and securing it with a rope over my shoulder. It is a most awkward thing to carry on horseback; but, unhandy though it be, I regret not having so carried it the whole way from Subzowar.

Our route leads through a dreary country, much the same character as yesterday, but we pass a pool of very good water about mid-day, and meet three men driving laden pack-horses from Herat. They are halted and questioned at great length concerning the contents of their packages, whither they are bound and whence they come; and their firearms are examined and commented upon. The members of our party appear to address them with a very domineering spirit, as though wantonly revelling in the sense of their own numerical superiority. On the other hand, the three honest travellers comport themselves with what looks like an altogether unnecessary amount of humility during the interview, and they seem very thankful and relieved when permitted to take their departure. The significance of all this, I imagine, is that my escort were sorely tempted to overhaul the effects of the weaker party, and see if they had any toothsome eatables from the bazaars of Herat; and the latter, justly apprehensive of these designs on their late purchases, consider themselves fortunate in escaping without being ruthlessly looted.

Toward evening we pass a comparatively new cemetery on a knoll; no signs of human habitation are about, and Kiftan Sahib, in response to my inquiries, explains that it is the graveyard of a battle-field.

Several times during the afternoon we lose the trail; we seem to be going across an almost trailless country, and more than once have to call a halt while men are sent to the summit of some neighboring hill to survey the surrounding country for landmarks.

At dark we pitch our camp in a grassy hollow, where the horses are made happy with heaps of pulled bottom-grass. Neither trees nor houses are anywhere in sight; but the chief of the sowars and another man ride away over the hills, and late at night return with two men carrying bread and mast and fresh goat-milk enough to feed the whole hungry party.

We make a leisurely start next morning, the reason of the dalliance being that we are but a few farsakhs from Herat. The country develops into undulating, grassy upland prairie, the greensward being thickly spangled with yellow flowers. A two flours' ride brings us to a camp of probably not less than one hundred tents. Large herds of camels are peacefully browsing over the prairie, numbers of them being females rejoicing in the possession of woolly youngsters, whose uncouth but tender proportions are swathed in old quilts and nummuds to protect them from the fierce rays of the sun.

Sheep are being sheared and goats milked by men and boys; some of the women are baking bread, some are jerking skin churns, suspended on tripods, vigorously back and forth, and others are preparing balls of mast for drying in the sun. The whole camp presents a scene of picturesque animation.

From the busy nomad camp, the trail seems to make a gradual ascent until, on the morning of April 30th, we arrive at the bluff-like termination of a rolling upland country, and behold! spread out below is the famous valley of Herat. Like a panorama suddenly opened up before me is the charmed stretch of country that has time and again created such a stir in the political and military circles of England and Russia, the famous "gate to India" about which the two greatest empires of the world have sometimes almost come to blows. Several populous villages are scattered about the valley within easy range of human vision; the Heri Rood, now bursting its natural boundaries under the stimulus of the spring floods, glistens broadly at intervals like a chain of small lakes. The fortress of Herat is dimly discernible in the distance beyond the river, probably about twenty miles from our position; it is rendered distinguishable from other masses of mud-brown habitations by a cluster of tall minarets, reminding one of a group of factory chimneys. The whole scene, as viewed from the commanding view of our ridge, embraces perhaps four hundred square miles of territory; about one-tenth of this appears to be under cultivation, the remainder being of the same stony, desert-like character as the average camel-thorn dasht.

Doubtless a good share of this latter might be reclaimed and rendered productive by an extensive system of irrigating canals, but at present no incentive exists for enterprise of this character. In its present state of cultivation the valley provides an abundance of food for the consumption of its inhabitants, and as yet the demand for exportation is limited to the simple requirements of a few thousand tributary nomads. The orchards and green areas about the villages render the whole scene, as usual, beautiful in comparison with the surrounding barrenness, but that is all. Compared with our own green hills and smiling valleys, the Valley of Herat would scarcely seem worth all the noise that has been made about it. There has been a great amount of sentiment wasted in eulogizing its alleged beauty. Of its wealth and commercial importance in the abstract, I should say much exaggeration has been indulged in. Still, there is no gainsaying that it is a most valuable strategical position, which, if held by either England or Russia, would exercise great influence on Central Asian and Indian affairs.

Such are my first impressions of the Herat Valley, and a sojourn of some ten days in one of its villages leaves my conjectures about the same.

A few miles along a stony and gradually descending trail, and we are making our way across the usual chequered area of desert, patches, abandoned fields, and old irrigating ditches that so often tell the tale of decay and retrogression in the East. These outlying evidences of decay, however, soon merge into green fields of wheat and barley, poppy gardens, and orchards, and flowing ditches; and two hours after obtaining the first view of Herat finds us camped in a walled apricot garden in the important village of Rosebagh (?).

Overtopping our camping ground are a pair of dilapidated brick minarets, attached to what Kiftan Sahib calls the Jami Mesjid, and which he furthermore volunteers was erected by Ghengis Khan. The minarets are of circular form, and one is broken off fifteen feet shorter than its neighbor. In the days of their glory they were mosaicked with blue, green and yellow glazed tiles; but nothing now remains but a few mournful-looking patches of blue, surviving the ravages of time and decay. Pigeons have from time to time deposited grains of barley on the dome, and finding sustenance from the gathered dirt and the falling rains, they have sprouted and grown, and dotted the grand old mosque with patches of green vegetation.

One corner of the orchard is occupied by a stable, to the flat roof of which I betake myself shortly after our arrival to try and ascertain my bearings, and see something of the village. High walls rise up between the roofs of the houses and divide one garden from another, so that precious little opportunity exists for observation immediately around, and from here not even the tall minarets of Herat are visible.

The adjacent houses are mostly bee-hive roofed, and within the little gardens attached the soil is evidently rich and productive. Pomegranate, almond, and apricot trees abound, and produce a charming contrast to the prevailing crenellated mud walls. A very conspicuous feature of the village is a cluster of some half-dozen venerable cedars.

The stable roof provides sleeping accommodation for the chief of the sowars, Kiftan Sahib, and myself, the remainder of the party curl themselves up beneath the apricot-trees below. During the night one of the sowars, an old fellow whose morose and sulky disposition has had the effect of rendering him socially objectionable to his comrades on the march from Furrah, comes scrambling on the roof, and in loud tones of complaint addresses himself to Kiftan Sahib's peacefully snoozing proportions. His midnight eruption consists of some grievance against his fellows; perhaps some such wanton act of injustice as appropriating his blanket or stealing his "timbakoo" (tobacco).

The only satisfaction he obtains from his superior takes the form of angry upbraidings for daring to disturb our slumbers; and, continuing his complaints, Kiftan. Sahib springs up from beneath his red blanket and administers several resounding cuffs.

Having meted out this summary interpretation of Afghan petty justice, Kiftan Sahib resumes his blanket, and the old sowar comes and squats alongside my own rude couch, and endeavors to heal his wounded spirit by muttering appeals to Allah. His savage groanings render it impossible for me to go to sleep, and several times I motion him away; but he affects not to take any notice.

Determined to drive him away, I rise up hastily as though about to attack him,—a piece of strategy that causes him to scramble off the roof far quicker than he climbed on. His fit of rage lasts through the night, finding vent in mutterings that are heard long after his hurried departure from my vicinity, and in the morning he is seen perched in a corner of the wall by himself, still angry and unappeased.

The rising sun ushers in May-day with unmistakable indications of his growing powers, and when he glares fiercely over the walls of our little orchard retreat, we find it profitable to crouch in the shade. It is already evident that I am not to be permitted to enter Herat proper, or see or learn any more of my surroundings than my keepers can help.

Letters are forwarded to the city immediately upon our arrival, and on the following morning an officer and several soldiers make their appearance, to receive me from Kiftan Sahib and duly receipt for my transfer. The officer announces himself as having once been to Bombay, and proceeds to question me in a mixture of Persian and Hindostani.

Finding me ignorant of the latter language, he openly accuses me of being a Russian, raising his finger and wagging his head in a deprecatory manner. He is a simple-minded individual, however, and open to easy conviction, and moreover inclined to be amiable and courteous. He tells me that Faramorz Khan is "Wall of the soldiers" and Niab Alookimah Khan the "dowleh" (civil governor), and after listening to my explanation of being English and not Russian, he takes upon himself to deliver salaams from them both.

"Merg Sahib," the political agent of the Boundary Commission, he says is at Murghab, and "Ridgeway Sahib" at Maimene. Learning that a courier is to be sent at once to them with letters in regard to myself, I quickly embrace the opportunity of sending a letter to each by the same messenger, explaining the situation, and asking Colonel Ridgeway to try and render me some assistance in getting through to India.

By request of the officer I send the governor of Herat a sketch of the bicycle, to enlighten him somewhat concerning its character and appearance. No doubt, it would be a stretching of his Asiatic dignity as the governor of an important city, to come to Rosebagh on purpose to see it for himself, and on no circumstances can I, an unauthorized Ferenghi invading the country against orders, be permitted to visit Herat.

The transfer having been duly made, I am conducted, a mile or so, to the garden of a gentleman named Mohammed Ahziin Khan, my quarters there being an open bungalow just large enough to stretch out in. Here is provided everything necessary for the rude personal comfort of the country, and such additional luxuries as raisins and pomegranates are at once brought. Here, also, I very promptly make the acquaintance of Moore's famous bul-buls, the "sweet nightingales" of Lalla Eookh. The garden is full of fruit-trees and grape-vines, and here several pairs of bul-buls make their home. They are great pets with the Afghans, and when Mohammed Ahzim Khan calls "bul-bul, bul-bul," they come and alight on the bushes close by the bungalow and perk their heads knowingly, evidently expecting to be favored with tid-bits. They are almost tame enough to take raisins out of the hand, and hesitate not to venture after them when placed close to our feet. It is the first time I have had the opportunity of a close examination of the bul-bul. They are almost the counterpart of the English starling as regards size and shape, but their bodies are of a mousey hue; the head and throat are black, with little white patches on either "cheek;" the tail feathers are black, tipped with white, and on the lower part of the body is a patch of yellow; the feathers of the head form a crest that almost rises to the dignity of a tassel.

While the bul-bul is a companionable little fellow and possessed of a cheery voice, his warble in no respects resembles the charming singing of the nightingale, and why he should be mentioned in connection with the sweet midnight songster of the English woodlands is something of a mystery. His song is a mere "clickety click" repeated rapidly several times. His popularity comes chiefly from his boldness and his companionable associations with mankind. The bul-bul is as much of a favorite in the Herat Valley as is robin red-breast in rural England, or the bobolink in America.

The second day in the garden is remembered as the anniversary of my start from Liverpool, and I have plenty of time for retrospection. It is unnecessary to say that the year has been crowded with strange experiences. Not the least strange of all, perhaps, is my present predicament as a prisoner in the Herat Valley.

In the afternoon there arrives from Herat a Peshawari gentleman named Mirza Gholam Ahmed, who is stationed here in the capacity of native agent for the Indian government. He is an individual possessed of considerable Asiatic astuteness, and his particular mission is very plainly to discover for the governor of Herat whether I am English or Russian. He is a somewhat fleshy, well-favored person, and withal of prepossessing manners. He introduces himself by shaking hands and telling me his name, and forthwith indulges in a pinch of snuff preparatory to his task of interrogation. Accompanying him is the officer who received me from Kiftan Sahib in the apricot garden, and whose suspicions of my being a Russian spy are anything but allayed.

During the interview he squats down on the threshold of the little bungalow, and concentrates his curiosity and suspicion into a protracted penetrating stare, focused steadily at my devoted countenance. Mohammed Ahzim Khan imitates him to perfection, except that his stare contains more curiosity and less suspicion.

Mirza Gholam Ahmed proceeds upon his mission of fathoming the secret of my nationality with extreme wariness, as becomes an Oriental official engaged in a task of significant import, and at first confines himself to the use of Persian and Hindostani. It does not take me long, however, to satisfy the trustworthy old Peshawari that I am not a Muscov, and fifteen minutes after his preliminary pinch of snuff, he is unbosoming himself to me to the extent of letting me know that he served with General Pollock on the Seistan Boundary Commission, that he went with General Pollock to London, and moreover rejoices in the titular distinction of C. I. E. (Companion Indian Empire), bestowed upon him for long and faithful civil and political services. The C. I. E. he designates, with a pardonable smile of self-approval, as "backsheesh" given him, without solicitation, by the government of India; a circumstance that probably appeals to his Oriental conception as a most extraordinary feature in his favor. Bribery, favoritism, and personal influence enter so largely into the preferments and rewards of Oriental governments, that anything obtained on purely meritorious grounds may well be valued highly.

He understands English sufficiently well to comprehend the meaning of my remarks and queries, and even knows a few words himself. From him I learn that I will not be permitted to visit Herat, and that I am to be kept under guard until Faramorz Khan's courier returns from the Boundary Commission Camp with Colonel Ridgeway's answer. He tells me that the fame of the bicycle has long ago been brought to Herat by pilgrims returning from Meshed, and the marvellous stories of my accomplishments are current in the bazaars. Fourteen farsakhs (fifty-six miles) an hour, and nothing said about the condition of the roads, is the average Herati's understanding of it; and many a grave, turbaned merchant in the bazaar, and wild warrior on the ramparts, indulges in day-dreams of an iron horse little less miraculous in its deeds than the winged steed of the air we read of in the Arabian Nights.

The direct results of Mirza Gholam Ahmed's visit and favorable report to the Governor of Herat, are made manifest on the following day by the appearance of his companion of yesterday in charge of two attendants, bringing me boxes of sweetmeats, almonds, raisins, and salted nuts, together with a package of tea and a fifteen-pound cone of loaf-sugar; all backsheesh from the Governor of Herat. Mirza Gholam Ahmed himself contributes a cake of toilet soap, a few envelopes and sheets of paper, and Huntley & Palmer's Beading biscuits. Upon stumbling upon these latter acceptable articles, one naturally falls to wondering whether this world-famed firm of biscuit-makers suspect that their wares sometimes penetrate even inside the battlemented walls of Herat. With them come also three gunsmiths, charged with the duty of assisting in the reparation of the bicycle, badly damaged by the horse, it is remembered, on the way from Furrah.

Their implements consist of a pair of peculiar goat-skin bellows, provided with wooden nozzles tipped with iron. A catgut bowstring drills for boring holes, and screw-drills for cutting threads, hammers, and an anvil. A rude but ingenious forge is constructed out of a few handfuls of stiff mud, and, building a charcoal fire, they spend the evening in sharpening and tempering drills for tomorrow's operations.

Everybody seems more attentive and anxious to contribute to my pleasure, the result, evidently, of orders from Herat. The officer, who but two days ago openly accused me of being a Russian, is to-day obsequious beyond measure, and his efforts to atone for Ma openly assured suspicions are really quite painful and embarrassing; even going the length of begging me to take him with me to London. The supper provided to-day consists of more courses and is better cooked and better served; Mohammed Ahzim Khan himself squats before me, diligently engaged in picking hairs out of the butter, pointing out what he considers the choicest morsels, and otherwise betrays great anxiety to do the agreeable.

The whole of the fifth and sixth days are consumed in the task of repairing the damages to the bicycle, the result being highly satisfactory, considering everything. Six new spokes that I have with me have been inserted, and sundry others stretched and the ends newly threaded. The gunsmiths are quite expert workmen, considering the tools they have to work with, and when they happen to drill a hole a trifle crooked, they are full of apologies, and remind me that this is Afghanistan and not Frangistan. They know and appreciate good material when they see it, and during the process of heating and stretching the spokes, loud and profuse are the praises bestowed upon the quality of the iron. "Koob awhan," they say, "Khylie koob awhan; Ferenghi awhan koob." As artisans, interested in mechanical affairs, the ball-bearings of the pedals, one of which I take apart to show them, excites their profound admiration as evidence of the marvellous skill of the Ferenghis. Much careful work is required to spring the rim of the wheel back into a true circle, every spoke having to be loosened and the whole wheel newly adjusted. Except for the handy little spoke-vice which I very fortunately brought with me, this work of adjustment would have been impossible. As there is probably nothing obtainable in Herat that would have answered the purpose, no alternative would have been left but to have carried the bicycle out of the country on horseback. After the coterie of gunsmiths have exhausted their ingenuity and my own resources have been expended, three spokes are missing entirely, two others are stretched and weakened, and of the six new ones some are forced into holes partially spoiled in the unskillful boring out of broken ends. Yet, with all these defects, so thoroughly has it stood the severest tests of the roads, that I apprehend little or no trouble about breakages.

Day after day passes wearily along; wearily, notwithstanding the kindly efforts of my guardians to make things pleasant and comfortable. From an Asiatic's standpoint, nothing could be more desirable than my present circumstances; with nothing to do but lay around and be waited on, generous meals three times daily, sweetmeats to nibble and tea to drink the whole livelong day; conscious of requiring rest and generous diet—all this, however, is anything but satisfactory in view of the reflection that the fine spring weather is rapidly passing away, and that every day ought to see me forty or fifty miles nearer the Pacific Coast.

Time hangs heavily in the absence of occupation, and I endeavor to relieve the tedium of slowly creeping time by cultivating the friendship of our new-found acquaintances, the bul-buls. My bountiful supply of raisins provides the elements of a genuine bond of sympathy between us, and places us on the most friendly terms imaginable from the beginning. During the day my bungalow is infested with swarms of huge robber ants, that make a most determined onslaught on the raisins and sweetmeats, invading the boxes and lugging them off to their haunts among the grape-vines. A favorite occupation of the bul-buls is sitting on a twig just outside the bungalow and watching for the appearance of these ants dragging away raisins. The bul-bul hops to the ground, seizes the raisin, shakes the ant loose, flies back up in his tree, and swallows the captured raisin, and immediately perks his head in search of another prize.

Among other ideas intended to contribute to my enjoyment, a loud-voiced pee-wit imprisoned in a crape cage is brought and hung up outside the bungalow. At intervals that seem almost as regular as the striking of a clock, this interesting pet stretches itself up at full length and gives utterance to a succession of rasping cries, strangely loud for so small a creature. A horse is likewise brought into the garden, for the pleasure it will presumably afford me to watch it munch bunches of pulled grass, and switch horseflies away with his tail. The horse is tied up about twenty yards from my quarters, but in his laudable zeal to cater to my amusement Mohammed Ahzim Khan volunteers to station it close by if more agreeable.

All these trifling occurrences serve to illustrate the Asiatic's idea of personal enjoyment.

Every day a subordinate called Abdur Rahman Khan rides into Herat to report to the Governor, and Mohammed Ahzim Khan himself keeps watch and ward over my person with faithful vigil. Sometimes I wander about the little garden for exercise, and either he or one of his assistants follows close behind, faithful in their attendance as a shadow. Occasionally I grow careless and indifferent about possible danger, and leave my revolver hanging up in the bungalow; noticing its absence, he bids me buckle it around me, saying warningly, "Afghanistan; Afghanistan;" he also watches me retire at night to make sure that I put it under my pillow.

One day, a visitor appears upon the scene, carrying a walking-cane. Mohammed Ahzim Khan pounces upon him instantly and I grabbing the stick, examines it closely, evidently suspicious lest it should be a sword-stick. He is the most persistent "gazer" I have yet met in Asia; hour after hour he squats on his hams at my feet and stares intently into my face, as though trying hard to read my inmost thoughts. Oriental-like, he is fascinated by the mystery of my appearance here, and there is no such thing as shaking off his silent, wondering gaze for a minute. He is on hand promptly in the morning to watch my rude matinual toilet, and he always watches me retire for the night. Even when I betake myself to a retired part of the garden in the dusk of evening to take a sluice-bath with a bucket of water, his white-robed figure is always loitering near.

Four men are stationed about my bungalow at night; their respective armaments vary from a Martini-Henry rifle attached to a picturesque Asiatic stock, owned by Abdur Rahman Khan, to an immense knobbed cudgel wielded by a titleless youth named Osman.

Osman's sole wardrobe consists of a coarse night-shirt style of garment, that in the early part of its career was probably white, but which is now neither white nor equal to the task of protecting him from the penetrating rays of the summer sun. His occupation appears to be that of all-round utility man for whomsoever cares to order him about. Osman has to bring water and pour it on my hands whenever I want to wash, hie him away to the bazaar to search for dates or anything my epicurean taste demands in addition to what is provided, feed the horse, change the position of the pee-wit to keep it in the shade, sweep out my bungalow, and perform all sorts of menial offices. Every noble loafer about my person seems anxious to have Osman continually employed in contributing to my comfort; Mohammed Ahzim Khan even deprecates the independence displayed in lacing up my own shoes. "Osman," he says, "let Osman do it."

Osman's chief characteristic is a reckless disregard for the conventionalities of social life and religion; he never seems to bother himself about either washing his person or saying his prayers. Somewhere, not far away, every evening the faithful are summoned to prayer by a muezzin with the most musical and pathetic voice I have heard in all Islam. The voice of this muezzin calling "Allah-il-A-l-l-a-h," as it comes floating over the houses and gardens in the calm silence of the summer evenings, is wonderfully impressive. From the pulpits of all Christendom I have yet to hear an utterance so full of pathos and supplication, or that carries with it the impressions of such deep sincerity as the "Allah-il-A-l-l-a-h" of this Afghan muezzin in the Herat Valley. It is a supplication to the throne of grace that rings in my ears even as I write, months after, and it touches the hearts of every Afghan within hearing and taps the fountain of their piety like magic. It calls forth responsive prayers and pious sighings from everybody around my bungalow—everybody except Osman. Osman can scarcely be called imperturbable, for he has his daily and hourly moods, and is of varying temper; but he carries himself always as though conscious of being an outcast, whom nothing can either elevate or defile. When his fellow Mussulmans are piously prostrating themselves and uttering religious sighs sincere as fanaticism can make them, Osman is either curled up beneath a pomegranate bush asleep, feeding the horse, or attending to the pee-wit.

Observing this, I often wonder whether he is considered, or considers himself, too small a potato in this world to hope for any attention from the Prophet in the next. The paradise of the Mohammedans, its shady groves, marble fountains, walled gardens, and cool retreats, its kara ghuz kiz and wealth of material pleasures, no doubt seem to poor Osman, with his one tattered garment and unhappy servility, far beyond the aspirations of such as he. Like the gutter-snipe of London or New York who gazes into the brilliant shop windows, he feels privileged to feast his imagination, perchance, but that is all.

Big bouquets of roses are gathered for me every morning, and when the store in our own little garden is exhausted they are procured from somewhere else. The efforts of those about me to render my forced detention as pleasant as possible is very gratifying, and all the time I am buoyed up by the hope that the Boundary Commissioners will be able to do something to help me get through to India.

The Boundary Commission camp is stationed over two hundred miles from Herat; eight days roll wearily by and my movements are still carefully confined to the little garden, and my person attended by guards day and night. Every day I amuse myself with giving raisins to the robber ants, for the sake of seeing the ever-watchful bul-buls pounce upon them and rob them. Morning and evening the imprisoned pee-wit awakens the echoes with his ratchetty call, and every sunset is commemorated by the sincerely plaintive utterances of the muezzin mentioned above.

Thus the days of my detention pass away, until the ninth day after my arrival here. On the evening of May 8th, the officer who first interviewed me in the apricot orchard comes to my bungalow, and brings salaams from Faramorz Khan. He and Mohammed Ahzim Khan, after a brief discussion between themselves, commence telling me, in the same roundabout manner as the blue-gowned Khan at Furrah, that the Ameer at Cabool has no control over the fanatical nomads of Zemindavar. Mohammed Ahzim Khan draws his finger across his throat, and the officer repeats "Afghan badmash, badmash, b-a-d-m-a-s-h." (desperado).

This parrot-like repetition is uttered in accents so pleaful, and is, withal, accompanied by such a searching stare into my face, that its comicality for the minute overcomes any sense of disappointment at the fall of my hopes. For my experience at Furrah teaches me that this is really the object of their visit.

Another ingenious argument of these polite and, after a certain childish fashion, astute Asiatics, is a direct appeal to my magnaminity. "We know you are brave, and to accomplish your object would even allow the Ghilzais to cut your throat; but the Wali begs you to sacrifice yourself for the reputation of his country, by keeping out of danger," they plead. "If you get killed, Afghanistan will get a bad name."

They are in dead earnest about converting me by argument and pleadings to their view of the case. I point out that, so far as the reputation of Afghanistan is concerned, there can be little difference between forbidding travellers to go through for fear of their getting murdered, and their actual killing. I remind them, too, that I am a "nokshi," and can let the people of Frangistan understand this if I am turned back.

These arguments, of course, avail me nothing; the upshot of instructions received from the Boundary Commission camp, is that I am to be conducted at once back into Persia.

Horses have to be shod, and all sorts of preparations made next morning, and it is near about noon before we are ready to start. Our destination is the Persian frontier village of Karize, about one hundred miles to the west. Everything is finally ready; when it transpires that Mohammed Ahzim Khan's orders are to put me on a horse and carry the bicycle on another. This programme I utterly refuse to sanction, knowing only too well what the result is likely to be to the bicycle. In defence of the arrangement, Mohammed Ahzim Khan argues that, as the bicycle goes fourteen farsakhs an hour, the horses will not be able to keep up; and strict orders are issued from Herat that I am not to separate myself from my escort while on Afghan territory.

Off posts Abdur Kahman Khan, hot haste to Herat, to report the difficulty to the Governor, while we return to the garden. It being too late in the day when he returns, our departure is postponed till morning, and Osman, with his knobbed stick, performs the office of nocturnal guard yet once again.

During the evening Mohammed Ahzim Khan unearths from somewhere a couple of photographs of English ladies. These, he tells me, came into his possession from one of Ayoob Khan's fugitive warriors after their dispersion in the Herat Valley, on their flight before General Roberts' command at Kandahar. They were among the effects gathered up by Ayoob Khan's plundering crew from the disastrous field of Maiwand.

CHAPTER XII
TAKEN BACK TO PERSIA

The Governor of Herat sends "khylie salaams" and permission for me to ride the bicycle, stipulating that I keep near the escort. So, with many an injunction to me about dasht-adam, kooh, dagh, etc., by way of warning me against venturing too far ahead, we bid farewell to the garden, with its strange associations, in the early morning. Beside Mohammed Ahzim Khan and myself are three sowars, mounted on splendid horses.

The morning is bright and cheerful, and shortly after starting the animal spirits of the sowars find vent in song. I have been laboring under the impression that, for soul-harrowing vocal effort, the wild-eyed sowars of Khorassan, as exemplified in my escort from Beerjand, were entitled to the worst execrations of a discriminating Ferenghi, but the Afghans can go them one better. If it is possible to imagine anything in the whole world of sound more jarring and discordant than the united efforts of these Afghan sowars, I have never yet discovered it. Out of pure consideration and courtesy, I endure it for some little time; but they finally reach a high-searching key that is positively unendurable, and I am compelled in sheer self-protection to beg the khan to suppress their exuberance. "These men are not bul-buls; then why do they sing?" is all that is necessary for me to say. They all laugh heartily at the remark, and the khan orders them to sing no more. Over a country that consists chiefly of trailless hills and intervening strips of desert, we wend our weary way, the bicycle often proving more of a drag than a benefit. The weather gets insufferably hot; in places the rocks fairly shimmer with heat, and are so hot that one can scarce hold the hand to them. We camp for the first night at a village, and on the second at an umbar that suggests our approach to Persia, and in the morning we make an early start with the object of reaching Karize before evening.

The day grows warm apace, and, at ten miles, the khan calls a halt for the discussion of what simple refreshments we have with us. Our larder embraces dry bread and cold goat-meat and a few handfuls of raisins. It ought also to include water in the leathern bottle swinging from the stirrup of one of the sowars; but when we halt, it is to discover that this worthy has forgotten to fill his bottle. The way has been heavy for a bicycle, trundling wearily through sand mainly, with no riding to speak of; and young as is the day, I am well-nigh overcome with thirst and weariness. I am too thirsty to eat, and, miserably tired and disgusted, one gets an instructive lesson in the control of the mind over the body. Much of my fatigue comes of low spirits, born of disappointment at being conducted back into Persia.

One of the sowars is despatched ahead to fill his bottle with water at a well known to be some five miles farther ahead, and to meet us with it on the way. On through the sand and heat we plod wearily, myself almost sick with thirst, fatigue, and disgust. Mohammed Ahzim Khan, observing my wretched condition, insists upon me letting one of the sowars try his hand at trundling the wheel, while I rest myself by riding his horse. Both the sowars bravely try their best to relieve me, but they cut ridiculous figures, toppling over every little while. At length one of them upsets the bicycle into a little gully, and falling on it, snaps asunder two spokes. The khan gives him a good tongue-lashing for his carelessness; but one can hardly blame the fellow, and I take it under my own protection again, before it goes farther and fares worse.

About 2 p.m. the sowar sent forward meets us with water; but it is almost undrinkable. Far better luck awaits us, however, farther along. Sighting an Eimuck camel-rider in the distance, one of the sowars gives chase and halts him until we can come up. Slung across his camel he has a skin of doke, the most welcome thing one can wish for under the circumstances. Everybody helps himself liberally of the refreshing beverage, shrinking the Eimuck's supply very perceptibly. The Eimuck joins heartily with our party in laughing at the altered contour of the pliant skin, as pointed out jocularly by Mohammed Ahzim Khan, bids us "salaam aleykum," and pursues his way across country.

During the afternoon we cross several well-worn trails; though evidently but little used of late, they have seen much travel. My escort explains that they are daman trails, in other words the trails worn by Turkoman raiders passing back and forth on their man-stealing expeditions, before their subjugation by the Russians.

By and by we emerge from a belt of low hills, and descend into a broad, level plain. A few miles off to the right can be seen the Heri Rood, its sinuous course plainly outlined by a dark fringe of jungle. Some miles ahead the village-fortress of Kafir Kaleh is visible. A horseman comes galloping across the plain to intercept us. Mohammed Ahzim Khan produces his written orders concerning my delivery at Karize and reads it to the new arrival. Thereupon ensues a long explanation, which ends in, our turning about and following the new-comer across the trailless plain toward the Heri Rood.

"What's up now?" I wonder; but the only intelligible reply I get in reply to queries is that we are going to camp in the jungle. Misgivings as to possible foul play mingle with speculations regarding this person's mission, as I follow in the wake of the Afghans.

We camp on a plot of rising ground that elevates us above the overflow, and shortly after our arrival we are visited by a band of nomads who are hunting through the jungle with greyhounds, Mohammed Ahzim Khan informs me that both baabs, and palangs (panthers) are to be found along the Heri Rood.

Luxuriant beds of the green stuff known in the United States as lamb's-quarter, abound, and I put one of the sowars to gathering some with the idea of cooking it for supper. None of our party know anything about its being good to eat, and Mohammed Ahzim Khan shakes his head vigorously in token of disapproval. A nomad visitor, however, corroborates my statement about its edibleness, and fills our chief with wonderment that I should know something in common with an Afghan nomad, that he, a resident of the country, knows nothing about. By way of stimulating his wonderment still further, I proceed to call off the names of the various nomad tribes inhabiting Afghanistan, together with their locations.

"Where did you learn all this." he queries, evidently suspicious that I have been picking up altogether too much information.

"London," I reply.

"London!" he says; "Mashallah! they know everything at London."

The horseman who intercepted us rode away when we camped for the night. Nothing more was seen of him, and at a late hour I turn in for the night —if one can be said to turn in, when the process takes the form of stretching one's self out on the open ground. No explanation of our detention here has been given me during the evening, and as I lay down to sleep all sorts of speculations are indulged in, varying from having my throat cut before morning, to a reconsideration by the authorities of the orders sending me back to Persia.

Some time in the night I am awakened. A strange horseman has arrived in camp with a letter for me. He wears the uniform of a military courier. The sowars make a blaze of brushwood for me to read by. It is a letter from Mr. Merk, the political agent of the Boundary Commission. It is a long letter, full of considerate language, but no instructions affecting the orders of my escort. Mr. Merk explains why Mahmoud Yusuph Khan could not take the responsibility of allowing me to proceed to Kandahar. The population of Zemindavar, he points out, are particularly fanatical and turbulent, and I should very probably have been murdered; etc.

The march toward Karize is resumed in good season in the morning. "What was that? a cuckoo?" At first I can scarcely believe my own senses, the idea of cuckoos calling in the jungles of Afghanistan being about the last thing I should have expected to hear, never having read of travellers hearing them anywhere in Central Asia, nor yet having heard them myself before. But there is no mistake; for ere we pass Kafir Kaleh, I hear the familiar notes again and again.

The road is a decided improvement over anything we have struck since leaving Herat, and by noon we arrive at Karize. For some inexplicable reason the Sooltan of Karize receives our party with very ill grace. He looks sick, and is probably suffering from fever, which may account for the evident sourness of his disposition.

Mohammed Ahzim Khan is anything but pleased at our reception, and as soon as he receives the receipt for my delivery makes his preparations to return. I don't think the Sooltan even tendered my escort a feed of grain for their horses, a piece of inhospitality wholly out of place in this wild country.

As for myself, he simply orders a villager to supply me with food and quarters, and charge me for it. Mohammed Ahzim Khan comes to my quarters to bid me good-by, and he takes the opportunity to explain "this is Iran, not Afghanistan. Iran, pool; Afghanistan, pool neis." There is no need of explanation, however; the people rubbing their fingers eagerly together and crying, "pool, pool," when I ask for something to eat, tells me plainer than any explanations that I am back again among our pool-loving friends, the subjects of the Shah. As I bid Mohammed Ahzim Khan farewell, I feel almost like parting—from a friend; he is a good fellow, and with nine-tenths of his inquisitiveness suppressed, would make a very agreeable companion.

And so, here I am within a hundred and sixty miles of Meshed again. More than a month has flown past since I last looked back upon its golden dome; it has been an eventful month. My experiences have been exceptional and instructive, but I ought now to be enjoying the comforts of the English camp at Quetta, instead of halting overnight in the mud huts of the surly Sooltan of Karize.

The female portion of Karize society make no pretence of covering up their faces, which impresses me the more as I have seen precious little of female faces since entering Afghanistan. All the women of Karize are ugly; a fact that I attribute to the handsomest specimens being carried off to Bokhara, for decades past, by the Turkomans. The people that assemble to gaze upon me are the same sore-eyed crowd that characterizes most Persian villages; and among them is one man totally blind. The loss of sight has not dimmed his inquisitiveness any, however; nothing could do that, and he gets someone to lead him into my room, where he makes an exhaustive examination of the bicycle with his hands.

A village luti entertains me during the evening with a dancing deer; a comical affair of wood, made to dance on a table by jerking a string. The luti plays a sort of "whangadoodle" tune on a guitar, and manipulates the string so as to make the deer keep time to the tune. He tells me he obtained it from Hindostan.

Among the wiseacres gathered around me plying questions, is one who asks, "Chand menzils inja to London?" He wants to know how many marches, or stopping-places, there are between Karize and London. This is a fair illustration of what these people think the world is like. His idea of a journey from here to London is that of stages across a desert country like Persia from one caravanserai to another; beyond that conception these people know nothing. London, they think, would be some such place as Herat or Meshed.

At the hour of my departure from Karize, on the following morning, a little old man presents himself, and wants me to employ him as an escort. The old fellow is a shrivelled-up little bit of a man, whom I could well-nigh hold out at arm's length and lift up with one hand. Not feeling the need of either guide or guard particularly, I decline the old fellow's services "with thanks," and push on; happy, in fact, to find myself once more untrammelled by native company.

Small towers of refuge, dotting the plain thickly about Karize, tell of past depredations by the Turkomans. An outlying village like Karize must, indeed, have had a hard struggle for existence; right in the heart of the daman country, too. For miles the plain is found to be grassy as the Western prairies; an innovation from the dreary gray of the camel-thorn dasht that is quite refreshing. A stream or two has to be forded, and many Afghans are met returning from pilgrimage to Meshed.

The village of Torbet-i-Sheikh Jahm is reached at noon, a pleasant town containing many shade-trees. Here, I find, resides Ab-durrahzaak Khan, a sub-agent of Mirza Abbas Khan, and consequently a servant of the Indian Government. He is one of the frontier agents, whose duty it is to keep track of events in a certain section of country and report periodically to headquarters. He, of course, receives me hospitably, does the agreeable with tea and kalians, and provides substantial refreshments. The soothing Shirazi tobacco provided with his kalians, and the excellent quality of his tea, provoke me to make comparison between them and the wretched productions of Afghanistan. Abdurrahzaak laughs good-humoredly at my remark, and replies, "Mashallah! there is nothing good in Afghanistan." He isn't far from right; and the English officer who named the products of Afghanistan as "stones and fighting men" came equally near the truth.

Fair roads prevail for some distance after leaving Torbet-i-Sheikh Jahm; a halt is made at an Eliaute camp to refresh myself with a bowl of doke. A picturesque dervish emerges from one of the tents and presents his alms-receiver, with "huk yah huk." Both man and voice seem familiar, and after a moment I recognize him as a familiar figure upon the streets of Teheran last winter. He says he is going to Cabool and Kandahar. A unique feature of his makeup is a staff with a bayonet fixed on the end, in place of the usual club or battle-axe.

The night is spent in an Eliaute camp; nummuds seem scarce articles with them, and I spend a cold and uncomfortable night, scarcely sleeping a wink. The camp is not far from the village of Mahmoudabad, and a rowdy gang of ryots come over to camp in the middle of the night, having heard of my arrival.

From Mahmoudabad the road follows up a narrow valley with a range of hills running parallel on either hand. The southern range are quite respectable mountains, with lingering patches of snow, and—can it be possible!—even a few scattering pines. Pines, and, for that matter, trees of any kind, are so scarce in this country that one can hardly believe the evidence of his own eyes when he sees them.

On past the village of Karizeno my road leads, passing through a hard, gravelly country, the surface generally affording fair riding except for a narrow belt of sand-hills. At Karizeno, a glimpse is obtained of our old acquaintances the Elburz Mountains, near Shah-riffabad. They are observed to be somewhat snow-crowned still, though to a measurably less extent than they were when we last viewed them on the road to Torbeti.

The approach of evening brings my day's ride to a close at Furriman, a village of considerable size, partially protected by a wall and moat, Stared at by the assembled population, and enduring their eager gabble all the evening, and then a nummud on the roof of a villager's house till morning. The night is cold, and sleeplessness, with shivering body, again rewards me for a long, hard day's journey. But now it is but about six farsakhs to Meshed, where, "Inshallah," a good bed and all kindred comforts await me beneath Mr. Gray's hospitable roof. Ere the forenoon is passed the familiar gold dome once again appears as a glowing yellow beacon, beckoning me across the Meshed plain.

A camel runs away and unseats his rider in deference to his timidity at my strange appearance as I bowl briskly across the Meshed plain at noon. By one o'clock I am circling around the moat of the city, and by two am snugly ensconced in my old quarters, relating the adventures of the last five weeks to Gray, and receiving from him in exchange the latest scraps of European news. I have made the one hundred and sixty miles from Karize in two days and a half—not a bad showing with a bicycle that has been tinkered up by Herati gunsmiths.

Among other interesting items of news, it is learned that a hopeful Meshedi blacksmith has been inspired to try his "prentice hand" at making a bicycle. One would like to have seen that bicycle, but somehow I didn't get an opportunity. Friendly telegrams reach me from Teheran, and also another order from the British Legation, instructing me not to attempt Afghanistan again.

Since my departure from Meshed, southward bound, another wandering correspondent has invaded the Holy City. Mr. E———, "special" of a great London daily paper, whom I had the pleasure of meeting once or twice in Teheran, has come eastward in an effort to enter Afghanistan. He has been halted by peremptory orders at Meshed. Disgusted with his ill-luck at not being permitted to carry out his plans, he is on the eve of returning to Constantinople. As I am heading for the same point myself, we arrange to travel there in company. Being somewhat under the weather from a recent attack of fever, he has contracted for a Russian fourgon to carry him as far as Shahrood, the farthest point on our route to which vehicular conveyance is practicable. Our purpose is to reach the Caspian port of Bunder Guz, thence embark on a Russian steamer to Baku, over the Caucasus Railway to Batoum, thence by Black Sea steamer to Constantinople.

On the afternoon of May 18th, R———makes a start with the fourgon. It is a custom (unalterable as the laws of, etc.) with all Persians starting on a journey of any length to go a short distance only for the first stage. The object of this is probably to find out by actual experience on the road whether anything has been forgotten or overlooked, before they get too far away to return and rectify the mistake. Semi-civilized peoples are wedded very strongly to the customs in vogue among them, and the European traveller finds himself compelled, more or less, to submit to them. My intention is to overtake the fourgon the following day at Shahriffabad.

Accordingly, soon after sunrise on the morrow, the road around the outer moat of Meshed is circled once again. A middle-aged descendant of the Prophet, riding a graceful dapple-gray mare, spurs his steed into a swinging gallop for about five miles across the level plain in an effort to bear me company. Three miles farther, and for miles over the steep and unridable gradients of the Shah-riffabad hills, I may anticipate the delights of having his horse's nose at my shoulder, and my heels in constant jeopardy. To avoid this, I spurt ahead, and ere long have the satisfaction of seeing him give it up.

In the foothills I encounter, for the first time, one of those characteristics of Mohammedan countries, and more especially of Persia, a caravan of the dead. Thousands of bodies are carried every year, on horseback or on camels, from various parts of Persia, to be buried in holy ground at Meshed, Kerbella, or Mecca. The corpses are bound about with canvas, and slung, like bales of merchandise, one on either side of the horse. The stench from one of these corpse-caravans is something fearful, nothing more nor less than the horrible stench of putrid human bodies. And yet the drivers seem to mind it very little indeed. One stout horse in the party I meet this morning carries two corpses; and in the saddle between them rides a woman. "Mashallah." perchance those very bodies, between which she sits perched so indifferently, are the remains of small-pox victims. But, what cares the woman?—is she not a Mohammedan, and a female one at that?—and does she not believe in kismet. What cares she for Ferenghi "sanitary fads?"—if it is her kismet to take the small-pox, she will take it; if it is her kismet not to, she won't. One would think, however, that common sense and common prudence would instruct these people to imitate the excellent example of the Chinese, in taking measures to dispose of the flesh before transporting the bones to distant burial-places. Many of the epidemics of disease that decimate the populations of Eastern countries, and sometimes travel into the West, originate from these abominable caravans of the dead and kindred irrationalities of the illogical and childlike Oriental.

As the golden dome of Imam Riza's sanctuary glimmers upon my retreating figure yet a fourth time as I reach the summit of the hill whence we first beheld it, I breathe a silent hope that I may never set eyes on it again. The fourgon is overtaken, as agreed upon, at Shahriffabad, and after an hour's halt we conclude to continue on to the caravanserai, where, it will be remembered, my friend the hadji and Mazanderan dervish and myself found shelter from the blizzard.

B___'s Turkish servant, Abdul, a handy fellow, speaking three or four languages, and numbering, among other accomplishments, the knack of always having on hand plenty of cold chicken and mutton, is a vast improvement upon obtaining food direct from the villagers. Resting here till 2 a.m., we make a moonlight march to Gadamgah, arriving there for breakfast. The trail is a revelation of smoothness, in comparison to my expectations, based upon its condition a few weeks ago. The moon is about full, and gives a light as it only does in Persia, and one can see to ride the parallel camel-paths very successfully.

Persians are very much given to night-travelling, and as I ride well ahead of the fourgon, the strange, weird object, gliding noiselessly along through the moonlight, fills many a superstitious pilgrim with misgivings that he has caught a glimpse of Sheitan. I can hear them rapidly muttering "Allah." as they edge off the road and hurry along on their way.

Many Arabs from the Lower Euphrates valley are now mingled with the pilgrim throngs en route to Meshed. They are evil-looking customers, black as negroes almost; they look capable of any atrocity under the sun. These Arab pilgrims are hadjis almost to a man, coming, as they do, from much nearer Mecca than the Persians; but their holiness does not prevent them bearing the unenviable reputation of being the most persistent thieves. Abdul knows them well, and when any of them are about, keeps a sharp lookout to see that none of them approach our things.

On the following evening, at a caravanserai near Nishapoor, we meet and spend the night with a French scientific party of three sent out by the Paris Geographical Society to make geographical and geological researches in Turkestan. The three Frenchmen are excellent company; they entertain us with European news, their views on the political aspect, and of incidents on their fourgon journey from Tiflis. Among their charvadars is a man who saw me last autumn at Ovahjik.

Much good riding surface prevails, and we pass the night of the 21st at Lafaram. The crowds that everywhere gather about us are very annoying to K———, whose fever and consequent weakness is hardly calculated to sweeten his temper under trying circumstances. A whole swarm of women gather to stare at us at Lafaram. "I'll soon scatter them, anyway," says R————; and he reaches for a pair of binoculars hanging up in the fourgon. Adjusting them to his eyes, he levels them at the bunch of females, expecting to see them scatter like a flock of partridges. Scattering is evidently about the last thing the women are thinking of doing, however; they merely turn their attention to the binoculars and concentrate their comments upon them instead of on other of our effects, for the moment, but that is all.

In the vicinity of Subzowar we find the people engaged in harvesting the crop of opium. The way they do it is to go through the fields of poppy every morning and scarify the green heads with a knife-blade notched for the purpose, like a saw. During the day the milky juice oozes out and solidifies. In the evening the harvesters pass through the fields again, scrape off the exuded opium, and collect it in vessels. This, after the watery substance has been worked out with frequent kneadings and drying, is the opium of commerce. The chief opium emporium of Persia is Shiraz, where buyers ship it by camel-caravan to Bushire for export. Persian opium commands the topmost prices in foreign markets.

Here every idler about the villages seems to be amusing himself by working a ball of opium about in his hands, much as a boy delights in handling a chunk of putty. Lumps as large as the fist are freely offered me by friendly people, as they would hand one a piece of bread or a pomegranate; I might collect pounds of the stuff by simply taking what is offered me without the asking.

In the caravanserai at Miandasht, Abdul's failure to appreciate our whilom and egotistical friend, the la-de-da telegraph-jee, at his own valuation comes near resulting in a serious fracas. One of Abdul's most valued services is keeping at a respectful distance the crowds of villagers that invariably swarm about us when we halt. In doing this he sometimes flogs about him pretty lively with the whip. As a general thing the natives take this sort of thing in the greatest good humor; in fact, rather enjoy it than otherwise.

At Miandasht, however, Abdul's whip happens to fall rather heavily upon the shoulders of the telegraph-jee's farrash, who is in the crowd. This individual, reflecting something of his master's self-esteem, takes exceptions to this, and complains, with the customary Persian elaboration, no doubt, to the consequential head of the place. The consequence is that a gang of villagers, headed by the telegraph-jee himself, gather around, and suddenly attack poor Abdul with clubs. Except for the prompt assistance of R——— —and myself, he would have been mauled pretty severely. As it is, he gets bruised up rather badly; though he inflicts almost as much damage as he receives, with a hatchet hastily grabbed from the fourgon. The fact of his being a Turk, whom the Persians consider far less holy than themselves, Abdul explains, accounts for the attack on him as much as anything else.

A new surprise awaits us at Mijamid, something that we are totally unprepared for. As we reach the chapar-khana there, a voice from the roof greets us with "Sprechen sie Deutsch." Looking up in astonishment, we behold Colonel G———, a German officer in the Shah's army, whom both of us are familiarly acquainted with by sight, from seeing him so often at the morning reviews in the military maiden at Teheran. But this is not all, for with him are his wife and daughter. This is the first time European ladies have traversed the Meshed-Teheran road, Teheran being the farthest point eastward in Persia that lady travellers have heretofore penetrated to. Colonel G has been appointed to the staff of the new Governor-General of Khorassan, and is on his way to Meshed. The appearance of Ferenghi ladies in the Holy City will be an innovation that will fairly eclipse the introduction of the bicycle. All Meshed will be wild with curiosity, and the poor ladies will never be able to venture into the streets without disguise.

There is furor enough over them in Mijamid; the whole population is assembled en masse before the chapar-khana. The combination of the bicycle, three Ferenghis, and, above all, two Ferenghi ladies, is an event that will form a red-letter mark in the history of Mijamid for generations of unborn Persian ryots to talk about and wonder over.

The colonel produces a bottle of excellent Shiraz wine and a box of Russian cigarettes. The ladies have become sufficiently Orientalized to number among their accomplishments the smoking of cigarettes. They are delighted at meeting us, and are already acquainted with the main circumstances of my misadventure in Afghanistan. Camp-stools are brought out, and we spend a most pleasant hour together, before continuing on our opposite courses. The wondering natives are almost speechless with astonishment at the spectacle of the two ladies sitting out there, faces all uncovered, smoking cigarettes, sipping claret, and chatting freely with the men. It is a regular circus-day for these poor, unenlightened mortals. The ladies are charming, and the charm of female society loses nothing, the reader may be sure, from one's having been deprived of it for a matter of months.

The colonel's lingual preference is German, Mrs. G————'s, French, and the daughter's, English; so that we are quite cosmopolitan in the matter of speech. All of us know enough Persian to express ourselves in that language too. In commenting upon my detention by the Afghans, the colonel characterizes them as "pedar sheitans," Madame as "le diable Afghans," and Miss G————as well, "le diable" in plain yet charmingly broken English.

The next day, soon after noon, we roll into Shahrood, where B———— discharges his fourgon and we engage mules to transport us over the Tash Pass, a breakneck bridle-trail over the Elburz range to the Asterabad Plain and the Caspian.

A half-day search by Abdul results in the employment of an outfit comprising three charvadars, with three mules, a couple of donkeys, and riding horses for ourselves. A liberal use of the whip by R on the charvadars' shoulders, awful threats, and sundry other persuasive arguments, assist very materially in getting started at a decent hour on the morning following our arrival. The bicycle is taken apart and placed on top of the mule-packs, where, in remembrance of its former fate under somewhat similar conditions, I keep it pretty strictly under surveillance.

The Asterabad trail is a steady ascent from the beginning; and before many miles are covered, scattering dwarf pines on the, mountains indicate a change from the utter barrenness that characterizes their southern aspect. One lone tree of quite respectable dimensions, standing a mile or so off to our left, suggests a special point of demarcation between utter barrenness and where a new order of things begins.

Our way leads up fearful rocky paths, where the horses have to be led, and at times assisted; up, up, until our elevation is nearly ten thousand feet, and we are among a chaotic wilderness of precipitous rocks and scrub pines. A false step in some places, and our horses would roll down among the craggy rocks for hundreds of feet. It is a toilsome march, but we cross the Tash Pass, camp for the night in a little inter-mountain valley, beside a stream at the foot of a pine-covered mountain. The change from the interior plains is already novel and refreshing. Grass abounds abundance, and the prospect is the greenest I have seen for nine months. We camp out in the open, and are put to some discomfort by passing showers in the night.

A march of a dozen miles from this valley over a tortuous mountain trail brings us into a country the existence of which one could never, by any stretch of the imagination, dream of in connection with Persia, as one sees it in its desert-like character south of the mountains. The transformation is from one extreme of vegetable nature to the other. We camp for lunch on velvety greensward beneath a grove of oak and cherry trees. Cuckoos are heard calling round about, singing birds make melody, and among them we both recognize the cheery clickety-click of my raisin-loving Herati friends, the bul-buls. Flowers, too, are here at our feet in abundance, forget-me-nots and other familiar varieties.

The view from our position is remarkably fine, reminding me forcibly of the Balkans south of Nisch, and of the Californian slopes of the Sierra Nevadas, where they overlook the Sacramento Valley. The Asterabad Plain is spread out below us like a vast map.

We can trace the windings and twistings of the various streams, the tracts of unreclaimed forest, and the cultivated fields. Asterabad and numerous villages dot the plain, and by taking R———'s binoculars we can make out, through the vaporous atmosphere, the shimmering surface of the Caspian Sea. It is one of the most remarkable views I ever saw, and the novelty and grandeur of it appeals the more forcibly to one's imagination, no doubt, because of its striking contrast to what the eyes have from long usage become accustomed to. From dreary, barren dasht, and stony wastes, to densely wooded mountains, jungle-covered plains, tall, luxurious tiger-grass, and beyond all this the shimmering background of the sea is a big change to find but little more than a day's march apart. We are both captivated by the change, and agree that the Caspian slope is the only part of Persia fit to look at.

The descent of the northern slope is even steeper than the other side; but instead of rocks, it is the rich soil of virgin forests. Open parks are occasionally crossed, and on one of these we find a large camp of Turcomans, numbering not less than a hundred tents. Mountaineers are always picturesquely dressed, and so, too, are nomads. When, therefore, one finds mountaineer nomads, it seems superfluous almost to describe them as being arrayed chiefly in gewgaws and bright-colored clothes. Camped here amid the dark, luxurious vegetation, they and their tents make a charming picture—a scene of life and of contrast in colors which if faithfully transferred to canvas would be worth a king's ransom.

Down paths of break-neck steepness and slipperiness, our way descends into a dark region where vegetation runs riot in the shape of fine tall timber, of a semi-tropical variety. Many of the trees present a fantastic appearance, by reason of great quantities of hanging moss, that in some instances fairly load down the weaker branches. Banks of beautiful ferns, and mossy rocks join with the splendid trees in making our march through these northern foothills of the Elburz Mountains an experience long to be remembered.

A curious and interesting comparison that comes under our observation is that, on the gray plains and rocky mountains of the interior the lizards are invariably of a dull and uninteresting color, quite in keeping with their surroundings. No sooner, however, do we find ourselves in a district where nature's deft hand has painted the whole canvas of the country a bright green, than the lizards which we see scuttling through the ferns and moss-beds are also the greenest of all the green things. These scaly little reptiles shine and glisten like supple shapes of emerald, as one sees them gliding across the path. This is but another link in the chain of evidence that seems to prove that animals derive much of their distinctive character and appearance from the nature of their surroundings. In Northern China are a species of small monkey with a quite heavy coat of fur. They are understood to be the descendants of a comparatively hairless variety which found its way there from the warm jungles of the South, the change from a warm climate to a cold one being responsible for the coat of fur. In the same way, after noting the complete change that has come over the lizards, we conclude that, if a colony of the gray species from the other side of the mountains were brought and turned loose among the green foot-hills here, their descendants, a few generations hence, would be found with coats as green as those of the natives. This conviction gathers force from the fact that no gray lizards whatever are encountered here; all the lizards we see are green.

Emerging from the foot-hills, we find ourselves in a country the general appearance of which reminds me of a section of Missouri more than anything I have seen in Asia. Fields and pastures are fenced in with the same rude corduroy-fences one sees in the Missouri Valley, some well kept and others neglected. The pastures are blue grass and white clover; bees are humming and buzzing from flower to flower, and, to make the similitude complete, one hears the homely tinkle of cow-bells here and there. It is difficult to realize that all this is in Persia, and that one has not been transported in some miraculous manner back to the United States. A little farther out from the base of the mountains, however, and we come upon wild figs, pomegranates, and other indigenous evidences of Eastern soil; and by and by our path almost becomes a tunnel, burrowing through a wealth of tiger-grass twenty feet high. The fields and little clearings which, a few miles back, were devoted to the cultivation of wheat and rye, now become rice-fields overflowed from irrigating ditches, and in which bare-legged men and women are paddling about, over their knees in mud and water.

Early in the evening we reach the city of Asterabad, which we find totally different from the sombre, mud-built cities of the interior. The wall surrounding it is topped with red tiles, and the outer moat is choked with rank vegetation. The houses are gabled, and roofed with tiles or heavy thatch, presenting an appearance very suggestive of the picturesque towns and villages about Strasburg. The streets are narrow and ill-paved, and neglect and decay everywhere abound. The cemeteries are a chaotic mass of tumbledown tombstones and vagrant vegetation. Pools of water covered with green scum, and heaps of filth everywhere, fill the reeking atmosphere with malaria and breed big clouds of mosquitoes. The people have a yellowish, waxy complexion that tells its own story of the unhealthiness of the place, without instituting special inquiry. One can fairly sniff fever and ague in the streets.

Much taste is displayed in architectural matters by the wealthier residents. The walls surrounding the little compounds are sometimes adorned with house-leeks or cactus, tastefully set out along the top; and, in other cases, with ornamental tiles. The walls of the houses are decorated with paintings depicting, in bright colors, scenes of the chase, birds, animals, and mythological subjects.

The charvadars lead the way to a big caravanserai in the heart of the city. The place is found to be filled with a miscellaneous crowd of caravan people, travellers, merchants, and dervishes. The serai also appears to be a custom-house and emporium for wool, cotton, and other products of the tributary country. Horses, camels, and merchandise crowd the central court, and rising fifty feet above all this confusion and babel is a wooden tower known as a tullar. This is a dilapidated framework of poles that sways visibly in the wind, the uses of which at first sight it is not easy to determine. Some of the natives motion for us to take possession of it, however; and we subsequently learn that the little eyrie-like platform is used as a sleeping-place by travellers of distinction. The elevation and airiness are supposed to be a safeguard against the fever and a refuge from the terrible mosquitoes, of which Asterabad is over-full.

An hour after our arrival, Abdul goes out and discovers a Persian gentleman named Mahmoud Turki Aghi, who presents himself in the capacity of British agent here. As we were in ignorance of the presence of any such official being in Asterabad, he comes as a pleasant surprise, and still more pleasant comes an invitation to accept his hospitality.

From him we learn that the steamer we expect to take at Bunder Guz, the port of Asterabad, eight farsakhs distant, will not sail until six days later. Mindful of the fever, from which he is still a sufferer to an uncomfortable extent, E———looks a trifle glum at this announcement, and, after our traps are unpacked at Mahmoud Turki Aghi's, he ferrets out a book of travels that I had often heard him refer to as an authority on sundry subjects. Turning over the leaves, he finds a reference to Bunder Guz, and reads out the story of a certain "gimlet-tailed fly" that makes life a burden to the unwary traveller who elects to linger there on the Caspian shore. Between this gimlet-tailed pest, however, and the mosquitoes of Asterabad we decide that there can be very little to choose, and so make up our minds to accept our host's hospitality for a day and then push on.

During the day we call on the Russian consul to get our passports vised. As between English and Russian prestige, the latter are decidedly to the fore in Asterabad. The bear has his big paw firmly planted on this fruitful province—it is more Russian than Persian now; before long it will be Russian altogether. Nothing is plainer to us than this, as we reach the Russian Consulate and are introduced by Mahmoud Turki Aghi to the consul. He is no "native agent." On the contrary, he is one of the biggest "personages" I have seen anywhere. He is the sort of man that the Russian Government invariably picks out for its representation at such important points in Asia as Asterabad.

A six-footer of magnificent physique, with a smooth and polished address, all smiles and politeness, the Russian consul wears a leonine mustache that could easily be tied in a knot at the back of his head. Although he is the only European resident of Asterabad save a few Cossack attendants, he wears fashionable Parisian clothes, a wealth of watch-chain, rings, and flash jewellery, patent-leather shoes, and all the accompaniments of an ostentatious show of wealth and personal magnificence. His rooms are equally gorgeous, and contain large colored portraits of the Czar and Czarina.

The intent and purpose of all this display is to fill the minds of the natives, and particularly the native officials, with an overwhelming sense of Russian grandeur and power. No Persian can enter the presence of this Russian consul in his rooms without experiencing a certain measure of awe and admiration. They regard with covetous eyes the rich and comfortable appointments of the rooms, and the big gold watch-chains and rings on the consul's person. They too would like to be in the Russian service if its rewards are on such a magnificent scale. Of patriotism to the Shah they know nothing—self-interest is the only master they willingly serve.

No one knows this better than the Russian consul; and in the case of influential officials and other useful persons, he sees to it that gold watches and such-like tokens of the Czar's esteem are not lacking. The result is that Asterabad, both city and province, is even now more Russian than Persian, and when the proper time arrives will drop into the bear's capacious maw like a ripe plum.

At daybreak on the morning of departure the charvadars wake us up by pounding on the outer gate and shouting "hadji" to Abdul Abdul lets them in, and the next hour passes in violent and wordy disputation among them as they load up their horses.

All three have purchased new Asterabad hats, big black busbies much prized by Persians from beyond the mountains. The acquisition of these imposing head-dresses has had the effect of increasing their self-esteem wonderfully. They regard each other with considerable hauteur, and quarrel almost continually for the first few miles. E puts up with their angry shouting and quarrelling for awhile, and then chases them around a little with the long hunting whip he carries. This brings them to their senses again, and secures a degree of peace; but the inflating effect of the new hats crops out at intervals all day.

Our road from Asterabad leads through jungle nearly the whole distance to Bunder Guz. In the woods are clearings consisting of rice-fields, orchards, and villages. The villages are picturesque clusters of wattle houses with peaked thatch roofs that descend to within a few feet of the ground. Groves of English walnut-trees abound, and plenty of these trees are also scattered through the jungle.

During the day we encounter a gang of professional native hunters hunting wild boars, of which these woods contain plenty, as well as tigers and panthers. They are a wild-looking crowd, with long hair, and sleeves rolled up to their elbows. Big knives are bristling in their kammerbunds, besides which they are armed with spears and flint-lock muskets. They make a great deal of noise, shouting and hallooing one to another; one can tell when they are on a hot trail by the amount of noise they make, just as you can with a pack of hounds.

We reach our destination by the middle of the afternoon, and find the place a wretched village, right on the shore of the Caspian. We repair to the caravanserai, but find the rooms so evil-smelling that we decide upon camping out and risking the fever rather than court acquaintance with possible cholera, providing no better place can be found elsewhere. This serai is a curious place, anyway. All sorts of people, some of them so peculiarly dressed that none of our party are able to make out their character or nationality. A dervish is exhorting a crowd of interested listeners at one end of the court-yard, and a strolling band of lutis are entertaining an audience at the other end. There are six of these lutis; while two are performing, four are circulating among the crowd collecting money. In any other country but Persia, five would have been playing and one passing the hat.

E———and Abdul go ahead to try and secure better quarters, and shortly the latter returns, and announces that they have been successful. So I, and the charvadars, with the horses, follow him through a crooked street of thatched houses, at the end of which we find R———seated beneath the veranda of a rude hotel kept by an Armenian Jew. As we approach I observe that my companion looks happier than I have seen him look for days. He is pretty thoroughly disgusted with Persia and everything in it, and this, together with his fever, has kept him in anything but an amiable frame of mind. But now his face is actually illumined with a smile.

On the little table before him stand a half-dozen black bottles, imperial pints, bearing labels inscribed with outlandish Russian words.

"This is civilization, my boy—civilization reached at last," says E———, as he sees me coming.

"What, this wretched tumble-down hole." I exclaim, waving my hand at the village.

"No, not that," replies E———; "this—this is civilization," and he holds up to the light a glass of amber Russian beer.

Apart from Russians, we are the first European travellers that have touched at Bunder Guz since McGregor was here in 1875. We keep a loose eye out for the gimlet-tailed flies, but are not harassed by them half so much as by fleas and the omnipresent mosquito. These two latter insects have dwindled somewhat from the majestic proportions described by McGregor; they are large enough and enterprising enough as it is; but

McGregor found one species the size of "cats," and the other "as large as camels." Bunder Guz is simply a landing and shipping point for Asterabad and adjacent territory. A good deal of Russian bar iron, petroleum, iron kettles, etc., are piled up under rude sheds; and wool from the interior is being baled by Persian Jews, naked to the waist, by means of hand-presses. Cotton and wool are the chief exports. Of course, the whole of the trade is in the hands of the Russians, who have driven the Persians quite off the sea. The Caspian is now nothing more nor less than a Russian salt-water lake.

The harbor of Bunder Guz is so shallow that one may ride horseback into the sea for nearly a mile. The steamers have to load and unload at a floating dock a mile and a half from shore. Very pleasant, in spite of the wretched hole we are in, is it to find one's self on the seashore —to see the smoke of a steamer, and the little smacks riding at anchor.

The day after our arrival, a man comes round and tells Abdul that he has three fine young Mazanderan tigers he would like to sell the Sahibs. We send Abdul to investigate, and he returns with the report that a party of Asterabad tiger-hunters have killed a female tiger and brought in three cubs. The man comes back with him and impresses upon us the assertion that they are khylie koob baabs (very splendid tigers), and would be dirt cheap at three hundred kerans apiece, the price he pretends to want for them. From this we know that the tigers could be bought very cheap, and since Mazanderan tigers are very rare in European menageries, we determine to go and look at them anyway. They are found to be the merest kittens, not yet old enough to see. They are savage little brutes, and spend their whole time in dashing recklessly against the bars of the coop in which they are confined. They refuse to eat or drink, and although the Persians declare that they would soon learn to feed, we conclude that they would be altogether too much trouble, even if it were possible to keep them from dying of starvation.

On the evening of June 3d we put off, together with a number of native passengers, in a lighter, for the vessel which is loading up with bales of cotton at the floating dock. Most of the night is spent in sitting on deck and watching the Persian roustabouts carry the cargo aboard, for the shouting, the inevitable noisy squabbling, and the thud of bales dumped into the hold render sleep out of the question.

The steamer starts at sunrise, and the captain comes round to pay his respects. He is more of a German than a Russian, and seems pleased to welcome aboard his ship the first English or American passengers he has had for years. He makes himself agreeable, and takes a good deal of interest in explaining anything about the burning of petroleum residue on the

Caspian steamers, instead of coal. He takes us down below and shows us the furnaces, and explains the modus operandi. We are delighted at the evident superiority of this fuel over coal, and the economy and ease of supplying the furnaces. Seven copecks the forty pounds, the captain says, is the cost of the fuel, and two and a half roubles the expense of running the vessel at full speed an hour. There is not an ounce of coal aboard, the boiler-house is as clean and neat as a parlor, and no cinders fall upon the deck or awnings. In place of huge coal-bunkers, taking up half the vessel's carrying space, compact tanks above the furnaces hold all the liquid fuel. Pipes convey it automatically, much or little, as easily as regulating a water-tap, to the fire-boxes. Jets of steam scatter it broadcast throughout the box in the form of spray, and insures its spontaneous combustion into flame. A peep in these furnaces displays a mass of flame filling an iron box in which no fuel is to be seen. A slight twist of a brass cock increases or diminishes this flame at once. A couple of men in clean linen uniforms manage the whole business. We both concluded that it was far superior to coal.

Many windings and tackings are necessary to get outside Ashdurada Bay; sometimes we are steaming bow on for Bunder Guz, apparently returning to port; at other times we are going due south, when our destination is nearly north. This, the captain explains, is due to the intricacy of the channel, which is little more than a deeper stream, so to speak, meandering crookedly through the shallows and sand-bars of the bay. Buoys and sirens mark the steamer's course to the Russian naval station of Ashdurada. Here we cross a bar so shallow that no vessel of more than twelve feet draught can enter or leave the bay. Our own ship is a light-draught steamer of five hundred tons burden.

A little steam-launch puts out from Ashdurada, bringing the mails and several naval officers bound for Krasnovodsk and Baku. The scenery of the Mazanderan coast is magnificent. The bold mountains seem to slope quite down to the shore, and from summit to surf-waves they present one dark-green mass of forest.

The menu of these Caspian steamers is very good, based on the French school of cookery rather than English. No early breakfast is provided, however; breakfast at eleven and dinner at six are the only refreshments provided by the ship's regular service—anything else has to be paid for as extras. At eleven o'clock we descend to the dining saloon, where we find the table spread with caviare, cheese, little raw salt fishes, pickles, vodka, and the unapproachable bread of Russia. The captain and passengers are congregated about this table, some sitting, others standing, and all reaching here and there, everybody helping himself and eating with his fingers. Now and then each one tosses off a little tumbler of vodka. We proceed to the table and do our best to imitate the Russians in their apparent determination to clean off the table. The edibles before us comprise the elements of a first-class cold luncheon, and we sit down prepared to do it ample justice. By and by the Russians leave this table one by one, and betake themselves to another, on the opposite side of the saloon. As they sit down, waiters come in bearing smoking hot roasts and vegetables, wine and dessert.

A gleam of intelligence dawns upon my companion as he realizes that we are making a mistake, and pausing in the act of transferring bread and caviare to his mouth, he says to me, impressively: "This is only sukuski, you know, on this table." "Why, of course. Didn't you know that. Your ignorance surprises me; I thought you knew.". And then we follow the example of everybody else and pass over to the other side.

The sukuski is taken before the regular meal in Russia. The tidbits and the vodka are partaken of to prepare and stimulate the appetite for the regular meal. Not yet, however, are we fully initiated into the mysteries of the Caspian steamer's service. Wine is flowing freely, and as we seat ourselves the captain passes down his bottle. Presently I hold my glass to be refilled by a spectacled naval officer sitting opposite. With a polite bow he fills it to the brim. The next moment, I happen to catch the captain's eye, it contains a meaning twinkle of amusement. Heavens! this is not a French steamer, even if the cookery is somewhat Frenchy; neither is it a table-d'hote with claret flowing ad libitum. The ridiculous mistake has been made of taking the captain's polite hospitality and the liberal display of bottles for the free wine of the French table-d'hote. The officer with the eyeglasses lands at Tchislikar in the afternoon, for which I am not sorry.

At Tchislikar we are met by a lighter with several Turcoman passengers. The sea is pretty rough, and the united efforts of several boatmen are required to hoist aboard each long-gowned Turcoman, each woman and child. They are Turcoman traders going to Baku and Tiflis with bales of the famous kibitka hangings and carpets. Tchislikar is the port whence a few years ago the Russian expedition set out on their campaign against the Tekke Turcomans. Three hundred miles inland is the famous fortress of Geoke Tepe, where disaster overtook the Russians, and where, in a subsequent campaign, occurred that massacre of women and children which caused the Western world to wonder anew at the barbarism of the Russian soldiery.

Still steaming north, our little craft ploughs her way toward Krasnovodsk, an important military station on the eastern coast.

At night the surface of the sea becomes smooth and glassy, the sun sets, rotund and red, in a haze suggestive of Indian summer in the West. The cabins are small and stuffy, so I sleep up on the hurricane-deck, wrapping a

Persian sheepskin overcoat about me. An awning covers this deck completely, but this does not prevent everything beneath getting drenched with dew. Never did I see such a fall of dew. It streams off the big awning like a shower of rain, and soaks through it and drips, drips on to my recumbent form and everything on the hurricane-deck.

Early in the morning we moor our ship to the dock at Krasnovodsk, and load and unload merchandise till noon. Here is where railway material for the Transcaspian railway to Merv is landed, the terminus being at Michaelovich, near by. We go ashore for a couple of hours and look about. The inmates of a military convalescent hospital are passing from the doctor's office to their barracks. They are wearing long dressing-gowns of gray stuff, with hoods that make them look wonderfully like a lot of monks arrayed in cowls. A company of infantry are target-practising at the foot of rocky buttes just outside the town. Not a tree nor a green thing is visible in the place nor on all the hills around—nothing but the blue waters of the Caspian and the dull prospect of rude rock buildings and gray hills.

Except for the sea, and the raggedness and abject servility of the poor class of people, one might imagine Krasnovodsk some Far Western fort. Scarcely a female is seen on the streets, soldiers are everywhere, and in the commercial quarter every other place is a vodka-shop. We visit one of these and find men in red shirts and cowhide boots playing billiards and drinking, others drinking and playing cards. Rough and sturdy men they look—frontiersmen; but there is no spirit, no independence, in their expression; they look like curs that have been chastised and bullied until the spirit is completely broken. This peculiar humbled and resigned expression is observable on the faces of the common people from one end of Russia to the other. It is quite extraordinary for a common Russian to look one in the eye. Nor is this at all deceptive; a social superior might step up and strike one of these men brutally in the face without the slightest provocation, and, though the victim of the outrage might be strong as an ox, no remonstrance whatever would be made. It is difficult for us to comprehend How human beings can possibly become so abjectly servile and spiritless as the lower-class Russians. But the terrors of the knout and Siberia are ever present before them. Cheap chromolithographs of Gregorian saints hang on the walls of the saloon, and with them are mingled fancy pictures of Tiflis and Baku cafe-chantant belles. Long rows of vodka-bottles are the chief stock-in-trade of the place, but "peevo" (beer) can be obtained from the cellar.

Quite a number of army officers, with their wives, come aboard at Krasnovodsk. They seem good fellows, nearly all, and inclined to cultivate our acquaintance. Individually, the better-class Russian and the Englishman have many attributes in common that make them like each other. Except for imperial matters, Russian and English officers would be the best of friends, I think. The ladies all smoke cigarettes incessantly. There is not a handsome woman aboard, and they show the lingering traces of Russian barbarism by wearing beads and gewgaws.

The most interesting of our passengers is a Persian dealer in precious stones. He is a well-educated individual, quite a linguist, and a polished gentleman withal. He is taking diamonds and turquoises that he has collected in Persia, to Vienna and Paris.

Another night of drenching dew, and by six o'clock next morning we are drawing near to the great petroleum port of Baku. From Krasnovodsk we have crossed the Caspian from east to west right on the line of latitude 40 deg.

CHAPTER XIII

ROUNDABOUT TO INDIA

Baku looks the inartistic, business-like place it is, occupying the base of brown, verdureless hills. Scarcely a green thing is visible to relieve the dull, drab aspect roundabout, and only the scant vegetation of a few gardens relieves the city a trifle itself. To the left of the city the slopes of one hill are dotted with neatly kept Christian cemeteries, and the slopes of another display the disorderly multitude of tombstones characteristic of the graveyards of Islam. On the right are seen numbers of big iron petroleum-tanks similar to those in the oil regions of Pennsylvania. Numbers of petroleum-schooners are riding at anchor in the harbor, and two or three small steamers are moored to the dock.

Our steamer moves up alongside a stout wooden wharf, the gang-plank is ran out, and the passengers permitted to file ashore. A cordon of police prevents them passing down the wharf, while custom-house officers examine their baggage. We are, of course, merely in transit through the country; more than that, the Russian authorities seem anxious, for some reason, to make a very favorable impression upon us two Central Asian travellers; so a special officer comes aboard, takes our passports, and with an excessive show of politeness refuses to take more than a mere formal glance at our traps. A horde of ragamuffin porters struggle desperately for the privilege of carrying the passengers' baggage. Poor, half-starved wretches they seem, reminding me, in their rags and struggles, of desperate curs quarrelling savagely over a bone. American porter's strive for passengers' baggage for the sake of making money; with these Russians, it seems more like a fierce resolve to obtain the wherewithal to keep away starvation. Burly policemen, armed with swords, like the gendarmerie of France, and in blue uniforms, assail the wretched porters and strike them brutally in the face, or kick them in the stomach, showing no more consideration than if they were maltreating the merest curs. Such brutality on the one hand, and abject servility and human degradation on the other is to be seen only in the land of the Czar. Servility, it is true exists everywhere in Asia, but only in Russia does one find the other extreme of coarse brutality constantly gloating over it and abusing it.

Our stay in Baku is limited to a few hours. We are to take the train for Tiflis the same afternoon, as we land at two o'clock so can spare no time to see much of the city or of the oil-refineries.

Summoning one of the swarm of drosky-drivers that beset the exit from the wharf, we are soon tearing over the Belgian blocks to the Hotel de l'Europe. The Russian drosky-driver, whether in Baku or in Moscow, seems incapable of driving at a moderate pace. Over rough streets or smooth he plies the cruel whip, shouts vile epithets at his half-wild steed, and rattles along at a furious pace.

Baku is the first Europeanized city either R———or I have been in for many months; the rows of shops, the saloons, drug-stores, barber-shops, and, above all, the hotels—how we appreciate it all after the bazaars and wretched serais of Persia!

We patronize a barber-shop, and find the tonsorial accommodations equal in every respect to those of America. One of the chairs is occupied by a Cossack officer. He is the biggest dandy in the way of a Cossack we have yet seen. Scarce had we thought it possible that one of these hardy warriors of the Caucasus could blossom forth in the make-up that bursts upon our astonished vision in this Baku barber-chair. The top-boots he wears are the shiniest of patent leather from knee to toe; lemon-colored silk or satin is the material of the long, gown-like coat that distinguishes the Cossack from all others. His hair is parted in the middle to a hair, and smoothed carefully with perfumed pomade; his mustache is twirled and waxed, his face powdered, and eyebrows pencilled. A silver-jointed belt, richly chased, encircles his waist, and the regulation row of cartridge-pockets across his breast are of the same material. He wears a short sword, the hilt and scabbard of which display the elaborate wealth of ornament affected by the Circassians. During the forenoon we take a stroll about the city afoot, but the wind is high, and clouds of dust sweep down the streets. A Persian in gown and turban steps quietly up behind us in a quiet street, and asks if we are mollahs. We know his little game, however, and gruffly order him off. The houses of Baku are mostly of rock and severely simple in architecture; they look like prisons and warehouses mostly—massive and gloomy.

Everywhere, everywhere, hovers the shadow of the police. One seems to breathe dark suspicion and mistrust in the very air. The people in the civil walks of life all look like whipped curs. They wear the expression of people brooding over some deep sorrow. The crape of dead liberty seems to be hanging on every door-knob. Nobody seems capable of smiling; one would think the shadow of some great calamity is hanging gloomily over the city. Nihilism and discontent run riot in the cities of the Caucasus; government spies and secret police are everywhere, and the people on the streets betray their knowledge of the fact by talking little and always in guarded tones.

Our stay at the hotel is but a few hours, but eleven domestics range themselves in a row to wait upon our departure and to smirk and extend their palms for tips as we prepare to go. No country under the sun save the Caucasus could thus muster eleven expectant menials on the strength of one meal served and but three hours actual occupation of our rooms.

Another wild Jehu drives us to the station of the Tiflis & Baku Railway, and he loses a wheel and upsets us into the street on the way. The station is a stone building, strong enough almost for a fort. Military uniforms adorn every employee, from the supercilious station-master to the ill-paid wretch that handles our baggage. Mine is the first bicycle the Tiflis & Baku Railroad has ever carried. Having no precedent to govern themselves by, and, withal, ever eager to fleece and overcharge, the railway officials charge double rates for it; that is, twice as much as an ordinary package of the same weight. No baggage is carried free on the Tiflis & Baku Railroad except what one takes with him in the passenger coach.

The cars are a compromise between the American style and those of England. They are divided into several compartments, but the partitions have openings that enable one to pass from end to end of the car. The doors are in the end compartments, but lead out of the side, there being no platform outside, nor communication between the cars. The seats are upholstered in gray plush and are provided with sliding extensions for sleeping at night. Overhead a second tier of berths unfolds for sleeping. No curtains are employed; the arrangements are only intended for stretching one's self out without undressing. The engines employed on the Tiflis & Baku Railway are without coal-tenders. They burn the residue of petroleum, which is fed to the flames in the form of spray by an atomizer. A small tank above the furnace holds the liquid, and a pipe feeds it automatically to the fire-box. The result of this excellent arrangement is spontaneous conversion into flame, a uniformly hot fire, cleanliness aboard the engine, a total absence of cinders, and almost an absence of smoke. The absence of a tender gives the engine a peculiar, bob-tailed appearance to the unaccustomed eye.

The speed of our train is about twenty miles an hour, and it starts from Baku an hour behind the advertised time. For the first few miles unfenced fields of ripe wheat characterize the landscape, and a total absence of trees gives the country a dreary aspect. The day is Sunday, but peasants, ragged and more wretched-looking than any seen in Persia, are harvesting grain. The carts they use are most peculiar vehicles, with wheels eight or ten feet in diameter. The tremendous size of the wheels is understood to materially lighten their draught. After a dozen miles the country develops into barren wastes, as dreary and verdureless as the deserts of Seistan. At intervals of a mile the train whirls past a solitary stone hut occupied by the family of the watchman or section-hand. Sometimes a man stands out and waves a little flag, and sometimes a woman. Whether male or female, the flag-signaller is invariably an uncouth bundle of rags. The telegraph-poles consist of lengths of worn-out rail, with an upper section of wood on which to fasten the insulators. These make substantial poles enough, but have a make-shift look, and convey the impression of financial weakness to the road. The stations are often quite handsome structures of mingled stone and brickwork. The names are conspicuously exposed in Russian and Persian and Circassian. Beer, wine, and eatables are exposed for sale at a lunch-counter, and pedlers vend boiled lobsters, fish, and fruit about the platforms. On the platform of every station hangs a bell with a string attached to the tongue. When almost ready for the train to start, an individual, invested with the dignity of a military cap with a red stripe, jerks this string slowly and solemnly thrice. Half a minute later another man in a full military uniform blows a shrill whistle; yet a third warning, in the shape of a smart toot from the engine itself, and the train pulls out. Full half the crowd about the stations appear to be in military uniform; the remainder are a heterogeneous company, embracing the modern Russian dandy, who affects the latest Parisian fashions, the Circassians and Georgians in picturesque attire, and the ever-present ragamuffin moujik. At one station we pass an institution peculiarly Russian—a railway prison-car conveying convicts eastward. It resembles an ordinary box-car, with iron grating toward the top. We can see the poor wretches peeping through the bars, and the handcuffs on their wrists. Outside at either end is a narrow platform, where stands, with loaded guns and fixed bayonets, a guard of four soldiers.

Once or twice before dark the train stops to replenish the engine's supply of fuel. Elevated iron tanks containing a supply of the liquid fuel take the place of the coal-sheds familiar to ourselves. The petroleum is supplied to the smaller tank on the engine through a pipe, as is water to the reservoir.

Such villages as we pass are the most unlovely clusters of mud hovels imaginable. Only the people are interesting, and the life of the railway itself. The Circassian peasantry are picturesque in bright colors, and the thin veneering of Western civilization spread over the semi-barbarity of the Russian officials and first-class passengers is an interesting study in itself.

We have been promising ourselves a day in Tiflis, the old Georgian capital, and now the head-quarters of the Russian army of the Caucasus, which our friends of the French scientific party said we would find interesting.

We find it both pleasant and interesting, for here are all modern improvements of hotel and street, as well as English telegraph officers, one a former acquaintance at Teheran. Tiflis now claims about one hundred and sixty thousand inhabitants, and is situated quite picturesquely in the narrow valley of the Kur. The old Georgian quarters still retain their Oriental appearance—gabled houses, narrow, crooked streets, and filth. The modernized, or European, portion of the city contains broad streets, rows of shops in which is displayed everything that could be found in any city in Europe, and street-railways.

These latter were introduced in 1882, and at first met with fierce antagonism from the drosky-drivers, who swarm here as in every city in Russia. These wild Jehus of the Caucasus expected the tram-cars to turn out the same as any other vehicle. Four people were killed by collisions the first day. Severe punishment had to be resorted to in order to stop the hostility of the drosky-drivers against the strange innovation.

The day is spent in seeing the city and visiting the hot sulphur baths and in the evening we attend a big bal masque in a suburban garden. A regimental band of fifty pieces plays "Around the World," by order of Prince Nicholas F, who exerts himself to make things pleasant for us in the garden. The famed beauties of Georgia, Circassia, and Mingrelia, masked and costumed, promenade and waltz with Russian officers, and sometimes join Circassian officers in a charming native dance.

We spend our promised clay in Tiflis, enjoy it thoroughly, and then proceed to Batoum. The Tiflis railway-station is a splendid building, with fountains and broad nights of stone terrace leading up to it from the street behind. Our drosky-driver rattles up to the foot of these terraced approaches at 8 a.m., and draws up a steed with an abruptness peculiar to the half-wild Jehus of the Caucasus. The same employee of the Hotel de Londres who had mysteriously hailed us by name from the platform as our train glided in from Baku the morning before, accompanies us to the depot now. All English travellers in Russia are supposed to be millionaires; all Americans, possessed of unlimited wealth. Bearing this in mind, our Russian-Armenian henchman has from first to last been most assiduous in his attentions, paying out of his own pocket the few odd copecks to porters carrying our luggage up from drosky to depot, in order to save us bother.

The station is crowded with people going away themselves or seeing friends off. As usual, the military overshadows and predominates everything. Between civilians and the wearers of military uniforms one plainly observes in a Russian Caucasus crowd that no love is lost. The strained relationship between the native population and the military aliens from the north is generally made the more conspicuous by the comparative sociability of the Georgians among themselves and kindred people of the Caucasus. Circassian officers in their picturesque uniforms and beautifully chased swords and pistols mingle sociably with the civilians, and are evidently great favorites; but that the blue-coated, white-capped Russians are hated with a bitter, sullen hatred requires no penetrating eye to see. The military brutality that crushed the brave and warlike people of Georgia, Circassia, and Mingrelia, and well-nigh depopulated the country, has left sore wounds that will take the wine and oil of time many a generation to heal completely up.

With an inner consciousness of duty well done and services faithfully rendered, our friend from the hotel flicks off our seats in the car with the tail of his long linen duster. Not that they need dusting; but as a gentle reminder of the extraordinary care he has bestowed upon us, in little things as well as in bigger, during our brief acquaintance with him, he dusts them off. That last attentive flick of his coat-tail is the finishing touch of an elaborate retrospective panorama we are expected to conjure up of the valuable services he has rendered us, and for which he is now justly entitled to his reward.

The customary three bells are struck, the inevitable military-looking official blows shrilly on his little whistle, and still the train lingers; lastly, the engine toots, however, and we pull slowly out of Tiflis. The town lies below us to the left, the River Kur follows us around a bend, the train speeds through deep gravel cuttings, and when we emerge from them the Georgian capital is no longer visible.

Between Baku and Tiflis, the Caucasus Railway runs for the most part through a flat, uninteresting country. Wastes as dreary and desolate as the steppes of Central Russia or the deserts of Turkestan sometimes stretched away to the horizon on either side of the track. At other points were gray, verdureless slopes and rocky buttes, or saline mud-flats that looked like the old bed of some ancient sea. Occasional oases of life appeared here and there, a few wheat-fields and a wretched mud-built village, or a picturesque scene of smoke-browned tents, gayly dressed nomads, and grazing flocks and herds. At night we had passed through a grassy steppe, a facsimile of the rolling prairies of the West. Though but the 6th of June, the country was parched, and the grass dried, as it stood, into hay by the heat and drought. We saw at one point a wide sweep of flame that set the darkening sky aglow and caused the railway-rails ahead to gleam. It was the steppe on fire—another reproduction of a Far Western prairie scene.

All this had changed as we woke up an hour before reaching Tiflis. The country became green, lovely, and populous in comparison. The people seemed less 'ragged, poverty-stricken, and wretched; the native women wore garments of brightest red and blue; the men put on more style, with their long Circassian coats and ornamental daggers, than I had yet observed. East of Tiflis, the Caucasus Hallway may, roughly speaking, be said to traverse the dreary wastes of an Asiatic country; west of it to wind around among the green hills and forest-clad heights of Europe's southeastern extremity. Lovelier and more beautifully green grows the country, and more interesting, too, grow the people and the towns, as our train speeds westward toward Batoum and the Black Sea coast. Everything about the railway, also, seems to be more prosperous, and better equipped. The improvised telegraph poles of worn-out lengths of rail seen east of Tiflis give place to something more becoming. Sometimes we speed for miles past ordinary cedar poles, procured, no doubt, from the mountain forests near at hand. Occasionally are stretches of iron poles imported from England, and then poles composed of two iron railway-rails clamped together. For much of the way we see the splendidly equipped Indo-European Telegraph Company's line, the finest telegraph line in the world. Equipped with substantial iron poles throughout, and with every insulator covered with an iron cap in countries where the half-civilized natives are wont to do them damage, this line runs through the various countries of Europe and Asia to Teheran, Persia, where it joins hands with the British Government line to India.

Following along the valley of the River Kur, our train is sometimes rattling along up a wild gorge between rugged heights whose sides are bristling with dark coniferous growth, or more precipitous, with huge jagged rocks and the variegated vegetation of the Caucasus strewn in wild confusion. Again, we emerge upon a peaceful grassy valley, lovely enough to have been the Happy Valley of Rasselas, and walled in almost completely with forest-clad mountains. Through it, perhaps, there winds a mountain stream, fed by welling springs and hidden rivulets, and on the stream is sure to be a town or village. An old Georgian town it would be, picturesque but dirty, built, too, with an eye to security from attack. One town is particularly noteworthy—not a very large town, but more important, doubtless, in times past than now. Out of the valley there rises a rocky butte, abrupt almost as though it were some monstrous vegetable growth. On the summit of this natural fortress some old Georgian chief had, in the good old days of independence, built a massive castle, and nestling beneath its protecting shadow around the base of the butte is the town, a picturesque town of adobe and wattle walls and quaint red tiles. So intensely verdant is the valley, so thickly wooded the dark surrounding mountains, so brown the walls, so red the tiles, and so picturesque the elevated castle, that even K goes into raptures, and calls the picture beautiful.

The improvement in the Russian telegraph line, perhaps, owes something to its brief association with the invading stranger from England; and now among the sublime loveliness of this Caucasian Switzerland one finds the station-houses built with far more pretence to the picturesque than on the barren steppes toward Baku and the Caspian. Here is the Caucasia of our youthful dreams, and the mystic hills and vales whence Mingrelian princes issued forth to deeds of valor in old romantic tales. Urchins, small mountaineers, more picturesquely clad than anything seen in Alpine Italy, even, now offer us little baskets of wild strawberries at ten copecks a basket-strawberries they and their little brothers and sisters have gathered this very morning at the foot of the hills. The cuisine at the lunch-counters embraces fresh trout from neighboring mountain streams, caught by vagrant Mingrelian Isaac Waltons, who bring them in on strings of plaited grass to sell.

Humorous scenes sometimes enliven our stops at the stations. The Russian warnings for travellers to seek the train before it is everlastingly too late cover fully a minute of time. First come three raps of a bell suspended on the platform, afterward a station employe blows a little whistle, and lastly comes a toot from the engine itself, by way of an ultimatum. Once this afternoon a woman leaves the train to enter the waiting-room for something. Just as she is entering, the station-man rings the bell. The woman, evidently unaccustomed to railway travel, rushes hastily back to the train. Everybody greets her performance with good-natured merriment. Finding the train not pulling out, and encouraged by some of the passengers, the woman ventures to try it again. As she reaches the waiting-room door, the station-man blows a shrill blast on his whistle. The woman rushes back, as before. Again the people laugh, and again words of encouragement tempt her to venture back again. This time it is the toot of the engine that brings that poor female scurrying back across the platform amid the unsympathetic laughter of her fellow-passengers, and this time the train really starts. From this it would appear that too many signals are quite as objectionable at railway-stations as not signals enough. Every stoppage at a lunch-counter station, or where venders of things edible come on the platform, gives us opportunity to turn our minds judicially upon the civilization of our fellow first-class passengers. They present a curious combination of French fashion and polite address, on the one hand, and want of taste and ignorance of civilization's usages on the other. Gentlemen and ladies, dressed in the latest Parisian fashions, stand out on the platform and devour German sausage or dig their teeth into big chunks of yellow cheese with the gusto of half-starved barbarians.

We double our engines—our compact, tenderless, petroleum-burning engines—at the foot of the Suran Pass. At its base, a stream disappears in an arched cave at the foot of a towering rocky cliff, and I have bethought me since of whether, like Allan Quatermain's subterranean stream, it would, if followed, reveal things heretofore unseen. And so we climb the lovely

Suran Pass, rattle down the western slope upon the Black Sea coast, and reach Batoum at 11 p.m.

As the chief mercantile port of the Caucasus, Batoum is an important shipping point. By the famous Berlin treaty it was made a free port; but nothing is likely to remain free any length of time upon which the Russian bear has managed to lay his greedy paw. Consequently, Batoum is now afflicted with all sorts of commercial taxes and restrictions, peculiar to a protective and autocratic semi-Oriental government. Notwithstanding this, however, ships from various European ports crowd its harbor, for not only is it the shipping point of Baku petroleum, but also the port of entry for much of the Persian and Central Asian importations from Europe. An oil-pipe line is seriously contemplated from Baku to replace the iron-tank cars now run on the railroad.

Big fortifications are under headway to protect the harbor; its strategic importance as the terminus of the Caucasus Railway and the shipping point for troops and war material making Batoum a place of special solicitation on the part of the Russian military authorities. R———and I walk around and take a look at the fortification works, as well as one can do this; but no strangers are allowed very near, and we are conscious of close surveillance the whole time we are walking out near the scene of operations.

A pleasant day in Batoum, and we take passage aboard a Messageries Maritimes steamer for Constantinople. Late at night we depart, amid the glare and music of a violent thunder-storm, and in the morning wake up in the roadstead of Trebizond.

To fully realize the difference between mock-civilization and the genuine article, one cannot do better than to transfer from a Russian Caspian steamer to a Messageries Maritimes. The Russians affect French methods and manners in pretty much everything; but the thinness and transparency of the varnish becomes very striking in contrast aboard the steamers.

The scenery along the Anatolian coast is striking and lovely in the extreme as we steam along in full view of it all next day. It is mountainous the whole distance, but the prospect is charmingly variable. Sometimes the mountains are heavily wooded down to the water's edge, and sometimes the slopes are prettily chequered with clearings and cultivation.

More and more lovely it grows next day, as we pass Samsoon, celebrated throughout the East for chibouque tobacco; Sinope, memorable as the place where the first blow of the Crimean War was delivered; and, on the morning of the third day, Ineboli, the "town of wines."

On the evening of the third day we lay off the entrance to the Bosphorus till morning, when we steam down that charming strait to

Constantinople. It is almost a year since I took, in company with our friend Shelton Bey, a pleasure trip up the Bosphorus and gazed for the first time on its wondrous beauties. I have seen considerable since, but the Bosphorus looks as fresh and lovely as ever.

While yielding as full a measure of praise to the Bosphorus as any of its most ardent admirers, I would, however, at the same time, recommend those in search of lovely coast scenery to take a coasting voyage along the southern shore of the Black Sea in June. I have no hesitation in saying that the traveller who goes into raptures over the beauties of the Bosphorus would, if he saw it, include the whole Anatolian coast to Batoum.

Several very pleasant days are spent in Constantinople, talking over my Central Asian adventures with former acquaintances and seeing the city. But as these were pretty thoroughly described in Volume I., there is no need of repetition here. With many regrets I part company with R, who has proved a very pleasant companion indeed, and set sail for India.

The steamers of the Khedivial Line, plying between Constaninople and Alexandria, have their mooring buoys near the Stamboul side of the Golden Horn, between Seraglio Point and the Galata bridge. During the forenoon, Shelton Bey, R—, and I had taken a caique and sought out from among the crowd of shipping in the harbor the steamship Behera, of the above-mentioned line, on which I have engaged my passage to Alexandria, so that we should have no difficulty in finding it in the afternoon. In the afternoon the Behera is found surrounded by a swarm of caiques, bringing passengers and friends who have come aboard to see them off. These slender-built craft are paddling about the black hull of the steamer in busy confusion. A fussy and authoritative little police boat seems to take a wanton delight in increasing the confusion by making sallies in among them to see that newly arriving passengers have provided themselves with the necessary passports, and that their baggage has been duly examined at the custom-house. All is bustle and confusion aboard the Behera, and in two hours after the advertised time (pretty prompt for an Egyptian-owned boat) a tug-boat assists her from her moorings, paddles glibly to one side, and in ten minutes Seraglio Point is rounded, and we are steaming down the Marmora with the domes and minarets of the Ottoman capital gradually vanishing to the rear.

People whose experience of steamship travel is confined to voyages in western waters, and the orderliness and neatness aboard an Atlantic steamer, can form little idea of the appearance aboard an Oriental passenger boat. The small foredeck is reserved for the use of first and second-class passengers; the remainder of the deck-room is pretty well crowded with the most motley and picturesque gathering imaginable. Arabs and Egyptians returning from a visit to Stamboul, pilgrims going to Mecca via Egypt,

Greeks, Levantines, and Armenians, all more or less fantastically attired and occupying themselves in their own peculiar way. The nomadic instinct of the Arabs asserts itself even on the deck of the steamer; ere she is an hour from Stamboul they may be seen squatting in little circles around small pans of charcoal, cooking their evening meal in precisely the same manner in which they are wont to cook it in the desert, leaving out, of course, the difference between camel chips and charcoal.

The soothing "bubble bubble" of the narghileh is heard issuing from all sorts of quiet corners, where dreamy-looking Turks are perched cross-legged, happy and contented in the enjoyment of their beloved water-pipe and in the silent contemplation of the moving scenes about them. As we ply our way at a ten-knot speed through the blue waves of the Marmora, and the sun sinks with a golden glow below the horizon, the spirit moves one of the Mecca pilgrims to climb on top of a chicken coop and shout "Allah-il!" for several minutes; the dangling ends of his turban flutter in the fresh evening breeze, streaming out behind him as he faces the east, and flapping in his swarthy face as he turns round facing to the opposite point of the compass. His supplications seem to be addressed to the dancing, white-capped waves, but the old Osmanlis mutter "Allah, Allah," in response between meditative whiffs of the narghileh, and the Arab and his fellow Mecca pilgrims swell the chorus with deep-fetched sighs of "Allah, Ali Akbar!"

A narrow space is walled off with canvas for the exclusive use of the female deck passengers, and in this enclosure scores of women and children of the above-named nationalities are huddled together indiscriminately for the night, packed, I should say, closer than sardines in a tin box. Male sleepers and family groups are sprawled about the deck in every conceivable position, and in walking from the foredeck to the after-cabins by the ghostly glimmer of the ship's lanterns, one has to pick his way cautiously among them. Woe to the person who attempts this difficult feat without the aid of a good pair of sea-legs; he is sure to be pitched head foremost by the motion of the vessel into the bosom of some family peacefully snoozing in a promiscuous heap, or to step on the slim, dusky figure of an Arab.

The ubiquitous Urasian who can speak "a leetle Inglis" soon betrays his presence aboard by singling me out and proceeding to make himself sociable. I am sitting on the foredeck perusing a late copy of a magazine which I had obtained in Constantinople, when that inevitable individual introduces himself by peeping at the corner of the magazine, and, with a winning smile, deliberately spells out its name; and soon we are engaged in as animated a discussion of the magazine as his limited knowledge of English permits. After listening with much interest to the various subjects of which it treats, he parades his profuse knowledge of Anglo-Saxon athletics by asking: "Does it also speak of ballfoot?"

The cuisine in both first and second-class cabins aboard the Egyptian liners is excellent, being served after the French style, with several courses and wine ad libitum. At our table is one solitary female, a Greek lady with an interesting habit of talking and gesticulating during meal-times, and of promenading the fore-deck in a profoundly pensive mood between meals. I have good reason to remember her former peculiarity, as she accidentally knocks a bottle of wine over into my soup-plate while gesticulating to a couple of Levantines across the table. She is a curious woman in more respects than one: she always commences to pick her teeth at the beginning of the meal, and between courses she sticks the little wooden toothpick, pen-fashion, behind her ear. Being Greek, of course she smokes cigarettes, and being Greek, of course she is also arrayed in one of those queer-looking garments that resemble an inverted cloth balloon, with the feet protruding from holes in the bottom. She sometimes absent-mindedly keeps the toothpick behind her ear while promenading the deck, and I have humbly thought that a woman promenading pensively back and forth in the national Greek costume, smoking a cigarette, and with a wooden toothpick behind her starboard ear, was deserving of passing mention.

The chief engineer of the ship is an Englishman with a large experience in the East; he has served with the late lamented General Gordon in the suppression of the slave trade in the Red Sea, and was anchored in Alexandria harbor during the last bombardment of the forts by the English ships. "The best thing about the whole bombardment," he says, "was to see the enthusiasm aboard the Yankee ships; the rigging swarmed with men, waving hats and cheering the English gunners, and whenever a more telling shot than usual struck the forts, wild hurrahs of approval from the American sailors would make the welkin ring again."

"There was no holding the Yankee sailors back when the English were preparing to go ashore," the old engineer continues, a gleam of enthusiasm lighting up his face, "and it was arranged that they should go ashore to protect the American Consulate—only to protect the American Consulate, you know," and the engineer winks profoundly, and thinking I might not comprehend the meaning of a profound wink, he winks knowingly as he repeats, "only to protect the American Consulate, you know." The engineer winds up by remarking: "That little affair in Alexandria harbor taught me more about the true feeling between the English and Americans than all the newspaper gabble on the subject put together." We touch at Smyrna and the Piraeus, and at the latter place a number of recently disbanded Greek soldiers come aboard; some are Albanian Greeks whose costume is sufficiently fantastic to merit description. Beginning at the feet, these extremities are incased in moccasins of red leather, with pointed toes that turn upward and inward and terminate in a black worsted ball. The legs look comfortable and active in tights of coarse gray cloth, but the piece de resistance of the costume is the kilt. This extends from the hips to the middle of the thighs, and instead of being a simple plaited cloth, like the kilt of the Scotch Highlanders, it consists of many folds of airy white material that protrude in the fanciful manner of the stage costume of a coryphee. A jacket of the same material as the tights covers the body, and is embellished with black braid; this jacket is provided with open sleeves that usually dangle behind like immature wings, but which can be buttoned around the wrists so as to cover the back of the arm. The head-gear is a red fez, something like the national Turkish head-dress, but with a huge black tassel that hangs half-way down the back, and which seems ever on the point of pulling the fez off the wearer's head with its weight. At noon of the fifth day out we arrive in Alexandria Harbor, to find the shipping gayly decorated with flags and the cannon booming in honor of the anniversary of Her Majesty Queen Victoria's coronation.

Alexandria is the most flourishing and Europeanized city I have thus far seen in the East. That portion of the city destroyed by the incendiary torches of Arabi Pasha is either built up again or in process of rebuilding. Like all large city fires, the burning would almost seem to have been more of a benefit than otherwise, in the long-run, for imposing blocks of substantial stone buildings, many with magnificent marble fronts, have risen, Phoenix-like, from the ashes of the inferior structures destroyed by the fire. After seeing Constantinople, Teheran, or even Tiflis, one cannot but be surprised at Alexandria—surprised at finding its streets well paved with massive stone blocks, smoothly laid, and elevated in the middle, after the most approved methods; surprised at the long row of really splendid shops, in which is displayed everything that can be found in a European city; surprised at the swell turn-outs on the Khediveal Boulevard of an evening; surprised at the many evidences of wealth and European enterprise. In the yet unfinished quarters of the city, houses are going up everywhere, the large gangs of laborers, both men and women, engaged in their erection, create an impression of beehive-like activity, and everybody looks happy and contented. After so many surprises comes a feeling of regret that this commercial and industrial rose, that looks so bright and flourishing under the stimulating influence of the English occupation, should ever again be exposed to the blighting influence of an Oriental administration. Red-coated "Tommy Atkins," stalking in conscious superiority down the streets, or standing guard in front of the barracks, is no doubt chiefly responsible for much of this flourishing state of affairs in Alexandria, and the withdrawal of his peace—insuring presence could not fail to operate adversely to the city's good.

The many groves of date-palms, rising up tall and slender, vying in gracefulness with the tapering minarets of the mosques, and with their feathery foliage mingling with and overtopping the white stone buildings, lends a charm to Alexandria that is found wanting in Constantinople — albeit the Osmanli capital presents by far the more lovely appearance from the sea. Massive marble seats are ranged along the Khediveal Boulevard beneath the trees, and dusky statues, in the scant drapery of the Egyptian plebe, are either sitting on them or reclining at lazy length, an occasional movement of body alone betraying that they are not part and parcel of the tomb-like marble slabs.

The tall, slim figures of Soudanese and Arabs mingle with the cosmopolitan forms in the streets; Nubians black as ebony, their skins seemingly polished, and their bare legs thin almost as beanpoles, slouch lazily along, or perhaps they are bestriding a diminutive donkey, their long, bony feet dangling idly to the ground. All the donkeys of Alexandria are not diminutive, however. Some of the finest donkeys in the world are here, large, sleek-coated, well-fed-looking animals, that appear quite as intelligent as their riders, or as the native donkey-boys who follow behind and persuade them along. These donkeys are for hire on every street-corner, and all sorts and conditions of people, from an English soldier to a lean Arab, may be seen coming jollity-jolt along the streets on the hurricane-deck of a donkey, with a half-naked donkey-boy racing behind, belaboring him along. The population of Alexandria is essentially cosmopolitan, but, considering the English occupation, one is scarcely prepared to find so few English. The great majority of Europeans are Germans, French, and Italian, nearly all the shopkeepers being of these nationalities. But English language and Bullish money seem to be almost universally understood, and probably the Board of Trade returns would show that English commerce predominates, and that it is only the retail trade in which the foreign element looms so conspicuously to the fore. An English evening paper, the Egyptian Gazette, has taken root here, and the following rather humorous account of a series of camel races, copied from its pages, serves to show something of how the sporting proclivities of the English army of occupation enlist the services of even the awkward and ungainly ships of the desert:

5.15 p.m.-Camel race, for gentlemen riders. Once round and a distance. Sweepstakes, 10 shillings. Don Juan, a fine, long-maned, fast-looking dromedary, started first favorite, Commodore Goodridge, K. N., our popular naval transport officer, being as good a judge of the ship of the desert as he is of a man-of-war. There was some difficulty at the post to get the riders together, owing to the fractiousness of Don Juan, who, with Kobert the Devil (ridden by Surgeon Porke), did not seem quite agreed about the Professional Beauty (ridden by Surgeon Moir). At the start Shaitan (ridden by Mr. Airey, E. N.) shoved to the front, closely followed by Surgeon Robertson's Mother-in-law, who, with Lieutenant Shuckburg's Purely Patience, Mr. Dumreicher's First Love, and Surgeon Halle's Microbe, rather shut out Don Juan. They kept this order until rounding Tattenham Corner, when Mr. Dumreicher brought his camel to the front, proving to his backers that he meant business with his First Love, and won a splendid race by her neck, Don Juan making a good second, with Professional Beauty about a length behind.

6.15 p.m.-Camel race, for sailors and soldiers. Once round and a distance. First prize, 10s.; second, 5s.; third, 2s. 6d. Eleven competitors turned up for this race, which was very well contested, although one of the camels appeared to think it too much trouble to run, and quietly squatted down immediately after the start, and could not be induced to join his fellows. Abdel Hal Hassin of the Coast Guard came in first, with Wickers of the Royal Artillery second, and Simpson of the commissariat and transport corps third.

"Second camel race, for gentlemen riders. This was got up on the course by a sporting naval officer. Five camels started: G. O. M., Hartington, Goschen, Chamberlain, and Unionist. This looked a certainty for G. O. M., as all but Unionist were in the same stable. However, the jockeys seem to have been 'got at,' for although G. O. M. got away with a good start, yet rounding the second corner he was shut out by a combined effort of Hartington, Goschen, Chamberlain, and Unionist, the latter winning, amid thunders of applause, by 30 lengths."

Egypt is pre-eminently the land of backsheesh, and Alexandria, as the chief port of arrival and departure, naturally comes in for its share of this annoying attention. From ship to hotel, and from hotel to railway-station, the traveller has to run the gauntlet of people deeply versed in the subtle arts and wiles of backsheesh diplomacy. At any time, as you stroll down the street, some native will suddenly bob up like a sable ghost beside you, point out something you don't want to see, and brazenly demand backsheesh for showing it. Cook's tourists' office is but a few hundred yards from my hotel. I have passed it before, and know exactly where it is, but one of these dusky shadows glides silently behind me, until the office is nearly reached, when he slips ahead, points it out, and with consummate assurance demands backsheesh for guiding me to it. The worst of it is there is no such thing as getting rid of these pests; they are the most persevering and unscrupulous blackmailers in their own small way that could be imagined. People whom you could swear you never set eyes on before will boldly declare they have acted as guide or something, and dog your footsteps all over the city; most of them are as "umble" as Uriah Heep himself in their annoying importunities, but some will not even hesitate to create a scene to gain their object, and, as the easiest way to get rid of them, the harassed traveller generally gives them a coin.

In leaving by the train, after one has backsheeshed the hungry swarm of hotel servitors, backsheeshed the porter who has doggedly persisted in coming with you to the station, regardless of repeatedly telling him he wasn't wanted, backsheeshed the baggage man, and bolted almost like a hunted thing into the railway-carriage from a small host of people who want backsheesh—one because he happened to detect your wandering gaze in search of the station clock and eagerly pointed out its whereabouts, another because he has told you, without being asked, that the train starts in ten minutes, another because he pointed out your carriage, which for a brief transitory instant you failed to recognize, and others for equally trivial things, for which they all seem keenly on the alert—you shut yourself in with a feeling of relief that must be something akin to escaping from a gang of brigands. King Backsheesh evidently rules supreme in Egypt yet.

My route to India takes me along the Egyptian Railway to Suez, thence by steamer down the Red Sea to Aden and Karachi. A passenger train on this railway consists of carriages divided into classes as they are in England, the first and second class cars being modelled on the same lines as the English. The third-class cars, however, are mere boxes provided with seats, and with iron bars instead of windows. Nice airy vehicles these, where the conditions of climate render airiness desirable, but it must be extremely interesting to ride in one of them through an Egyptian sand-storm.

At the Alexandria station, an old wrinkle-faced native, bronzed and leathery almost as an Egyptian mummy, pulls a bell-rope three times, the conductor comes to the car-window for the second time and examines your ticket, the engine gives a cracked shriek and pulls out. As the train glides through the suburbs one's attention is arrested by well-kept carriage-drives, lined and overarched with feathery palm-tree groves, and other evidences of municipal thrift.

From the suburbs we plunge at once into a rich and populous agricultural country, the famed Nile Delta, of which a passing descriptive glimpse will not here be considered out of place. Cotton seems to be the most important crop as seen from the windows of my car, and for many a mile after leaving Alexandria we glide through luxuriant fields of that important Egyptian staple.

Interspersed among the darker green of the growing cotton are fields of young rice, sometimes showing bright and green in contrast to the darker shade of the cotton, and sometimes being represented by square areas of glistening water, beneath which the young rice is submerged.

The Nile Delta is a net-work of irrigating ditches from end to end. Large canals, big enough to float barges, and on which considerable commerce is carried, tap the Nile above the Delta, and traversing it in all directions, furnish water to systems of smaller ditches and canals, and these again to still smaller channels of distribution.

The water in these channels is all below the surface, and a goodly proportion of the whole teeming population of the delta is engaged between seed-time and harvest in pumping the life-giving water from these ditches into the small surface trenches that conduct it over their fields and gardens. The water-pumping fellahs, ranged along the net-work of canals, often at intervals of not more than one hundred yards, create an impression of marvellous industry pervading the whole scene, as the train speeds its way alongside the larger canals.

The pumping in most cases is done by men or buffaloes, and the clumsy-looking but effective Egyptian water-wheel, a rough wooden contrivance that as it revolves, raises the water from below and pours it from holes in the side into a wooden trough, from whence it flows over the field.

Small rude shelters are erected close by, beneath which the attendant fellah can squat in the shade and keep the meek and gentle, but lazy buffaloes up to their task, by constant threats and bellicose demonstrations. Most of these animals are blindfolded, a contrivance that, no doubt, inspires them to pace round and round their weary circle with becoming perseverance, inasmuch as it tends to keep them in perpetual fear of the dusky driver beneath the shade.

People too poor, or with holdings too small, to justify the employment of oxen in pumping water, raise it from the ditches themselves, with buckets at the end of long well-sweeps; in some localities one can cast his eye over the landscape and see scores of these rude sweeps continually rising and falling, rising and falling.

A few windmills are also used for pumping, but the wind is a fickle thing to depend on, and his utter dependence on the water supply makes the Egyptian agriculturist unwilling to run such risks. Steam-engines, both stationary and portable, are observed at frequent intervals. Both the engines and the coal for fuel have to be imported from England; but they evidently pump enough water to repay the outlay, otherwise there would not be so many of them in use. It must be a rich, productive soil that can afford the expensive luxury of importing steam-engines and coal from a distant market to supply it with water for irrigation.

The sediment from the Nile, which settles in the canals and ditches, is cleaned out at frequent intervals and spread over the fields, providing a new dressing of rich alluvial soil to annually stimulate the productive capacity of the soil.

In the larger cotton-fields the dusky sons and daughters of Egypt are seen strung out in long rows, wielding cumbersome hoes, reminding one of old plantation days in Dixie; or they are paddling about in the inundated rice-fields like amphibious things. Swarms of happy youngsters are splashing about in the canals and ditches; all about is teeming with life and animation.

Villages are populous and close together. They are, for the most part, mere jumbles of low, mud houses with curious domed roofs, and they rise above the dead level of the delta like mounds. Many of these villages have probably occupied the same site since the days of the Pharaohs, the debris and rubbish of centuries have accumulated and been built upon again and again as the unsubstantial mud dwellings have crumbled away, until they have gradually developed into mounds that rise like huge mole-hills above the plain, and on which the present houses are built. Near each village is a graveyard, also forming a mound-like excrescence on the dead level of the surrounding surface.

At intervals the train passes some stately white mansion, looking lovely and picturesque enough for anything, peeping from a grove of date-palms or other indigenous vegetation. The tall, slender palms with their beautiful feathery foliage, lend a charm to the sunny Egyptian landscape with its golden dawns and sunsets that is simply indescribable. There seems no reason why every village on the whole delta should not be hiding its ugliness beneath a grove of this charming vegetation. Further east, near Fantah, nearly every village is found thus embowered, and date-palm groves form a very conspicuous feature of the landscape. One need hardly add that here the fellaheen look more intelligent, more prosperous and happy.

At all the larger stations women come to the train with roast quails stuffed with rice, which they sell at six-pence apiece, and at every station along the line children bring water in the porous clay bottles of the country. This latter is badly needed, for the train rattles along most of the time in a stifling cloud of dust, that penetrates the car and settles over one in incredible quantities.

During the afternoon we pass the battle-field of Tel-el-Kebre, the train whisking right through the centre of Arabi Pasha's earthworks.

Near the battle-field is a little cemetery where the English soldiers killed in the battle were buried. The cemetery is kept green and tidy, and surrounded by a neat iron fence; amid the gray desert that begins at Tel-el-Kebre this little cemetery is the only bright spot immediately about. From Tel-el-Kebre to Suez the country is a sandy desert, where sand-fences, like the snow-fences of the Rocky Mountains, have been found necessary to protect the railway from the shifting sand. On this dreary waste are seen herds of camels, happy, no doubt, as clams at high tide, as they roam about and search for tough camel-thorn shrubs, that here and there protrude above the wavy ridges of white sand. Put a camel in a pasture of rich, succulent grass and he will roam about with a far-away, disconsolate look and an expression of disgust, but here, on the glaring white sands of the desert with nothing to browse upon but prickly dry shrubs he is in the seventh 'heaven of a camel's delight.

Very curious it looks as we approach Suez to see the spars and masts of big steamers moving along the ship-canal, close at hand, without seeing anything of the water. The high dumps, representing the excavations from the canal, conceal everything but the masts and the top of the funnels even when one is close by.

Several days are spent at Suez, waiting for the steamer which we will call the Mandarin, on which I am to take passage to Karachi. Suez is a wretched hole, although there is a passably good English hotel facing the water-front. It is the month of Bairam, however, and there is consequently a good deal of picturesque life in the native quarters.

Suez seems swarming with guides, and as I am, for the greater part of a week, the only guest at the hotel, they show me far more attention than a dozen people would know what to do with. Some want to take me to see the place where Moses struck the rock, others urge me to visit the spot where the Israelites crossed the Red Sea; both these places being suspiciously handy to Suez.

Donkey boys dog one's footsteps with their long-eared chargers, whenever one ventures outside the hotel. "I'm the Peninsular and Oriental Donkey Boy, sir, Jimmy Johnson; I have a good donkey, sir, when you want to ride, ask for Jimmy Johnson." To all this, sundry seductive offers are added, such as a short trial trip along the bund.

The Mandarin comes along on July 7th, and a decidedly stably smell is wafted over the waters toward us as we follow behind her with the little launch that is to put me aboard when the steamer condescends to ease up and allow us to approach. The Mandarin, owing to the quarantine, has kept me waiting several days at Suez, and when at last she steams out of the canal and we give chase with the little launch, and finally range alongside, the whole length of the deck is observed to be bristling with ears. Some particularly hopeful agent of the Indian Government has been sanguine enough to ship one hundred and forty mules from Italy to Karachi during the monsoon season, on the deck of a notoriously rolling ship, and with nothing but temporary plank fittings to confine the mules. The mules are ranged along either side of the deck, seventy mules on each side, heads facing inward, and with posts and a two-inch plank separating them from the remainder of the deck, and into stalls of six mules each. Cocoanut matting is provided for them to stand on, and a plank nailed along the deck for them to brace their feet against when the vessel rolls. Nothing could be more happily arranged than this, providing the mules were unanimously agreed about remaining inside the railed-off space, and providing the monsoons had agreed not to roll the Mandarin violently about. With unpardonable short-sightedness, however, it seems that neither of these important factors in the case has been seriously considered or consulted, and, as an additional insult to the mules, the plank in front of them is elevated but four feet six above the deck.

They are a choice lot of four-year-old mules, unbroken and wild, harum-skarum and skittish. Well-fed four-year-old mules are skin-full of deviltry under any circumstances, and ranged like so many red herrings in their boxes, with no exercise, and every motion of the ship jostling them against one another, they very quickly developed a capacity for simon-pure cussedness that caused the officers of the ship no little anxiety from day to day, and a good deal more anxiety when they reflected on the weather that would be encountered on the Indian Ocean.

The officers of the Mandarin are excellent seamen; they are perfectly at home and at their ease when it comes to managing a vessel, but their knowledge of mules is not so profound and exhaustive as of vessels; in short, their experience of mules has hitherto been confined to casually noticing meek and sober-sided specimens attached to the street cars of certain cities they have visited. Three Italian muleteers have been hired to assist and instruct the coolies in feeding and watering the mules, and to supervise their general welfare. The three muleteers is an excellent arrangement, providing there were but three mules, but unfortunately there are one hundred and forty, and before they had been aboard the

Mandarin two days it became apparent that they ought to have engaged an equal number of Italians to keep the mules out of devilment.

Uneasy in their minds at the wild restlessness and seemingly daredevil and inconsiderate pranks of their long-eared and unspeakable charges, the officers are naturally anxious to avail themselves of any stray grains of enlightenment concerning their management they might perchance drop on to by appealing to persons they come in contact with. Accordingly, one of them approaches me, the only passenger aboard, except some Hindoos returning home from a visit to the Colinderies, and asks me if I understand anything about mules. I modestly own up to having reared, broken, driven, and generally handled mules in the West, whereat the officer is much pleased, and proceeds to unburden his mind concerning the animals aboard the ship. "Fine young mules," he says they are, and in reply to a question of what the government of India is importing mules from Europe for, instead of raising them in India, he says he thinks they must be intended for breeding purposes.

Understanding well enough that all this is quite natural and excusable in a sea-faring man, I succeed in checking a rising smile, and gently, but firmly, convince the officer of the erroneousness of this conclusion. The officer is delighted to find a person possessing so complete a knowledge of mules, and I am henceforth regarded as the oracle on this particular subject, and the person to be consulted in regard to sundry things they don't quite understand.

Between the two-inch plank and the awning overhead is a space of about three feet; the mate says he is a trifle misty as to how a sixteen-hand mule can leap through this small space without touching either the plank or the awning; "and yet," he says, "there is hardly a mule on board that has not performed this seemingly miraculous feat over and over again, and a good many of them, make a practice of doing it every night." This jumping mania makes him feel uneasy every night, the mate goes on to explain, for fear some of the reckless and "light-heeled cusses" should make a mistake and jump over the bulwarks into the sea; the bulwarks are no higher than the plank, yet, while half the mules were found outside the plank every morning, none of them had happened to jump outside the bulwarks so far. Many of the mules, he says, were putting in most of their time bulldozing their fellows, and doing their best to make their life unbearable, and the downtrodden specimens seem so desperately scared of the bulldozers that he expects to see some of them jump overboard from sheer fright and desperation.

At this juncture we are joined by another officer, and the mate joyfully informs him that I am a man who knows more about mules than anybody he had ever talked mule with. His brother officer is delighted to hear this, as he has been uneasy about the mules' appetites; they would devour all the hay and coarse feed they could get hold of, but didn't seem to have that constant hankering after grain that he had always understood to be part and parcel of a horse's, and, consequently, a mule's, nature. He knows something about horses, he says, for his wife keeps a pony in Scotland, and the pony would leave hay at any time to eat oats and bran; consequently, he thinks there must be something radically wrong with the mules; and yet they seem lively enough—in fact, they seem d-d lively.

The two salts are also troubled somewhat in their minds at the marvellous kicking powers and propensities of the mules. One says he could understand an animal kicking to defend itself when attacked in the rear, or when anything tickled its heels, but the mules aboard the Mandarin had their heels in the air most of the time, and they battered away at one another, and pounded the iron bulwarks, without the slightest provocation. "Yes," chimes in the other officer, "and, more than that, I've seen 'em throw their heels clear over the bulwarks, kicking at a white-capped wave—if you'll believe me, sir, actually kicking at a white-capped wave—that happened to favor them with a trifle of spray." I say I have no doubt what the officer says is true, and not necessarily exaggerated, and the officer says: "No, there is no exaggeration about it. You'll see the same thing yourself before you've been aboard twelve hours. There'll be h-ll to pay aboard this ship when we strike the monsoons."

After explaining to the officers that there are not men enough, nor bulldozing and tyrannical mules enough, aboard the Mandarin to scare the timidest mule of the consignment into jumping over the bulwarks into the sea; that it is quite natural for mules to prefer hay to bran and oats, and that it is as natural and necessary for a four-year-old mule to kick as it is to breathe, they thank me and say they shall sleep sounder tonight than they have for a week. The heat, as we steam slowly down the Red Sea, is almost overpowering at this time of the year, July. A universal calm prevails; day after day we glide through waters smooth as a mirror, resort to various expedients to keep cool, and witness fiery red sunsets every evening. Every day the deck presents a scene of animation, from the pranks and vagaries of our long-eared cargo.

All goes well with them, however, as we glide along the placid bosom of the Red Sea; the oppressive heat has a wilting effect even on the riotous spirits of the young mules. They still exhibit their mulish contempt for the barriers reared so confidently around them, and develop new and startling traits of devilment every day; but it is not until we leave Aden, and the long swells come rolling up from the monsoon region, that the real fun begins. The Mandarin lurches and rolls awfully, making it extremely difficult at times for any of the mules to keep their feet; each mule seems to think his next neighbor responsible for the jostling and crowding, and the kicking and squealing is continuous along both lines. While battering away at each other, each mule seems to be at the same time keeping a loose eye behind him for the oncoming waves and swells that occasionally curl over the bulwarks and irrigate and irritate them in the rear. Most of the mules seem capable of kicking at their neighbors and at a wave at the same time; but it is when their undivided attention is centred upon the crested billow of a swell that sweeps alongside the ship and flings a white, foamy cataract at the business end of each mule as it advances, that their marvellous heel-flinging capacity becomes apparent. Each mule batters frantically away as the wave strikes him, and the rattle of nimble and indignant hoofs on the iron bulwarks follows the wave along from one end of the ship to the other.

One of the most arrogant and overbearing of the animals aboard is a ginger-colored mule stationed almost amidships on the starboard side. This mule soon develops the extraordinary capacity of casting its eye over the heaving waste of waters and distinguishing the particular wave that intends coming over the bulwarks long before it reaches the vessel. The historical arrogance of Canute's followers in thinking the waves would recede at his command, is nothing in comparison to the cheeky assumption of this ginger mule. This mule will fold back its ears, look wild, and raise its heels menacingly at a white-crested wave when the wave is yet a hundred yards away; and on the second day out from Aden its arrogance develops in such an alarming degree that it bristles up and lifts its heels at waves that its experience and never-flagging observation must have taught it wouldn't come half-way up the bulwarks!

Now and then a mule will be caught off his guard and be flung violently to the deck, but the look of astonishment dies away as it nimbly regains its feet, and gives place to angry attack on its neighbor and a half-reproachful, half-apprehensive look at the sea. So far, however, the mules seem to more than hold their own, and, all oblivious of what is before them, they are comparatively happy and mischievous. But on the night of the third day out from Aden, the full force of the monsoon swells strikes the Mandarin, and, true to her character, she responds by rolling and pitching about in the trough of the sea in a manner that fills the mules with consternation, and ends in their utter collapse and demoralization. Planks break and give way as the whole body of mules are flung violently and simultaneously forward, and before midnight the mules are piled up in promiscuous and struggling heaps, while tons of water come on deck and wash and tumble them about in all imaginable shapes and forms.

All hands are piped up and kept busy tying the mules' legs, to prevent them regaining their feet only to be flung violently down again in the midst of a struggling heap of their fellows. There is only one mule actually dead in the morning, but the others are the worst used up, discouraged lot of mules I ever saw. Mules that but the day before would nearly jump out of their skins if one attempted to pat their noses, now seem anxious to court human attention and to atone for past sins. Many of them are pretty badly skinned up and bruised, and a few of them are well-nigh flayed alive from being see-sawed back and forth about the deck. It is not a pleasant picture to dwell upon, and it would be much pleasanter to have to record that the mules proved too much for the monsoon, but truth will prevail, and before we reach Karachi the monsoon has scored fourteen mules dead and pretty much all the others more or less wounded. But this is no discredit to the mules; in fact, I have greater respect for the staying qualities of a mule than ever before, since the monsoon only secures ten per cent of them for the sharks after all.

A week from Aden, and fourteen days from Suez we reach Karachi. The tide happens to be out at the time, and so we have to lay to till the following morning, when the Mandarin crosses the bar and drops anchor preparatory to unloading the now badly demoralized mules into lighters.

Karachi bids fair to develop into a very prominent sea-port in the near future. The extension of the frontier into Beloochistan gives Karachi a strategic importance as the port of arrival of troops and war material from England. Not less is its importance from a purely commercial view; for down the Indus Valley Railway to Karachi for shipment, come the enormous and yearly increasing wheat exportations from the Punjab.

Thus far my precise plans have been held in abeyance until my arrival on Indian soil. Whether I would find it practicable to start on the wheel again from Karachi, or whether it would be necessary to proceed to the northeast, I had not yet been able to find out. At any rate, it is always best to leave these matters until one gets on the spot.

The result of my investigations at once proves the impossibility, even were it desirable, of starting from Karachi. The Indus River is at flood, inundating the country, which is also jungly and wild and without roads. The heat throughout Scinde in July is something terrific; and to endeavor to force a way through flooded jungle with a bicycle at such a time would be little short of madness.

Under these conditions I decide to proceed by rail to Lahore, the capital of the Punjab, whence, I am told, there will be a good road all the way to Calcutta. As the crow flies, Lahore is nearer to Furrah than Karachi is, so that my purpose of making a continuous trail will be better served from that point anyhow.

It is an interesting jaunt by rail up the Indus Valley; but one's first impression of India is sure to be one of disappointment by taking this route. It is a desert country, taken all in all, this historic Scinde; through which, however, the Indus Valley makes a narrow streak of agricultural richness.

The cars on the railroad are provided with kus-kus tatties to mollify the intense heat. They are fixed into the windows so that the passengers may turn them round from time to time to raise the water from the lower half to the top, whence it trickles back again and cools the heated air that percolates through.

The heat increases as we reach Rohri and Sukhar, where passengers are transferred by ferry across the Indus; the country seems a veritable furnace, cracking and blistering with heat. At Sukhar our train glides through some rich date-palms, the origin of which, legend says, were the date-stones thrown away by the soldiers of Alexander the Great. They seem to have taken root in congenial soil, anyway, for every tree is heavily laden with ripe and ripening dates. Reclining under the date-trees or wandering about are many dusky sons and daughters of Scinde, the latter in bright raiment and with children in no raiment whatever. The heat, the fruitful date-palms, and the lotus-eating natives combine to make up a truly tropical scene.

Much of the country population seems to be nomadic, or semi-nomadic, dwelling in tents with which they remove to the higher ground when the Indus becomes inundated, and return again to the valley to cultivate and harvest their crops. They seem a picturesque people mostly, sometimes strangely incongruous in the matter of apparel, as, for instance, one I saw wearing a white breech-cloth and a hussar coat. This was the whole extent of his wardrobe, for he had neither shoes, shirt, nor hat.

Water-buffaloes are wading and swimming about in the overflowed jungle, browsing off bulrushes and rank grass. Youngsters are sometimes seen perched on the buffaloes' backs, taking care of the herd.

About Mooltan the aspect of the country changes to level, barren plain, and this, as we gradually approach Lahore, gives place to a cultivated country of marvellous richness. Here one first sees the matchless kunkah roads, traversing the country from town to town, the first glimpse of which is very reassuring to me.

It is July 28th when I at length find myself in Lahore. The heat is not only well-nigh unbearable, but dangerous. Prickly heat has seized hold upon me with a promptness that is anything but agreeable; the thermometer in my room at Clarke's Hotel registers 108 deg. at midnight. A punkah-wallah is indispensable night and day.

A couple of days are spent in affixing a new set of tires to my wheel and seeing something of the lions of Lahore. The Shalamar Mango Gardens, a few miles east of the city, and Shah-Jehan's fort, museum, etc., are the regular things to visit.

In the museum is a rare collection of ancient Asiatic arms, some of which throw a new light on the origin of modern firearms. Here are revolving muskets that were no doubt used long before the revolving principle was ever applied to arms in the West. But our narrative must not linger amid the antiquities of Lahore, fascinating as they may, peradventure, be.

CHAPTER XIV

THROUGH INDIA

The heat is intense, being at the end of the heated term at the commencement of the earliest monsoons. It is certainly not less than 130 deg. Fahr., in the sun, when at 3 p.m. I mount and shape my course toward Amritza, some thirty-five miles down the Grand Trunk Road.

In such a temperature and beneath such a sun it behooves the discreet Caucasian to dress as carefully for protection against the heat as he would against the frost of an Arctic winter. The United States army helmet which I have constantly worn since obtaining it at Fort Sydney, Neb., has now to be discarded in favor of a huge pith solar topee an inch thick and but little smaller than an umbrella. This overshadowing head-dress imparts a cheerful, mushroom-like aspect to my person, and casts a shadow on the smooth whitish surface of the road, as I ride along, that well-nigh obliterates the shadow of the wheel and its rider.

Thus sheltered from the rays of the Indian sun, I wheel through the beautifully shaded suburban streets of Lahore, past dense thickets of fruitful plantains, across the broad switch-yard of the Scinde, Delhi & Punjab Railway, and out on to the smooth, level surface of the Grand Trunk Road. This road is, beyond a doubt, the finest highway in the whole world. It extends for nearly sixteen hundred miles, an unbroken highway of marvellous perfection, from Peshawur on the Afghan frontier to Calcutta. It is metalled for much of its length with a substance peculiar to the country, known as kunkah. Kunkah is obtained almost anywhere throughout the Land of the Five Rivers, underlying the surface soil. It is a sort of loose nodular limestone, which when wetted and rolled cements together and forms a road-surface smooth and compact as an asphaltum pavement, and of excellent wearing quality. It is a magnificent road to bicycle over; not only is it broad, level, and smooth, but for much of the way it is converted into a veritable avenue by spreading shade-trees on either side. Far and near the rich Indian vegetation, stimulated to wear its loveliest garb by the early monsoon rains, is intensely green and luxuriant; and through the richly verdant landscape stretches the wide, straight belt of the road, far as eye can reach, a whitish streak, glaring and quivering with reflected heat.

The natives of the Punjab, the most loyal, perhaps, of the Indian races, are beginning to regard the Christian Sabbath as a holiday, and happy crowds of people in holiday attire are gathered at the Shalamar Mango Gardens, a few miles out of Lahore. Beyond the gardens, I meet a native in a big red turban and white clothes, en route to Lahore on a bone-shaker. He is pedalling ambitiously along, with his umbrella under his left arm. As we approach each other his swarthy countenance lights up with a "glad, fraternal smile," and his hand touches his turban in recognition of the mystic brotherhood of the wheel. There is a mysterious bond of sympathy recognizable even between the old native-made bone-shaker and its Punjabi rider and the pale-faced Ferenghi Sahib mounted on his graceful triumph of Western ingenuity and mechanical skill. The free display of ivories as we approach, the expectation of fraternal recognition so plainly evident in his face, and the friendly and respectful, rather than obsequious, manner of saluting, tell something of that levelling tendency of the wheel we sometimes hear spoken of.

The park-like expanse of country on either hand continues as mile after mile is reeled off; the shady trees, the ruins, the villages, and the roadside kos-minars, with the perfect highway leading through it all—what more could wheelman ask than this. A wayside police-chowkee is now seen ahead, a snug little edifice of brick beneath the sacred branches of a spreading peepul. A six-foot Sikh, in the red-and-blue turban and neat blue uniform of the Punjab soldier-police, stands at the door and executes a stiff military salute as I wheel past. A row of conical white pillars and a grass-grown plot of ground containing a few bungalows and camping space for a regiment indicate a military reservation. These spaces are reserved at intervals of ten or twelve miles all down the Grand Trunk Road; the distance from each represents a day's march for Indian troops in time of peace.

A bend in the road, and the bicycle sweeps over a substantial brick bridge, spanning an irrigating canal large enough to float a three-masted schooner. The bridge and the ditch convey early evidence of English enterprise no less conspicuous than the road itself. Neatly trimmed banks and a tropical luxuriance of overhanging vegetation give the long straight reach of water the charming appearance of flowing through a leafy tunnel. Under the stimulus of the monsoon rains and the more than tropical heat, the soil seems bursting with fatness, and earth, air, and water are teeming with life. The roadway itself is swarming with pedestrians, trudging along in both directions; some there are with the inevitable umbrellas held above their heads, but more are carrying them under their arms, as though in lofty contempt of 130 deg. Fahr.

Vehicles jingle past by the hundred, filled with villagers who have been visiting or shopping at Lahore or Amritza. Their light bamboo carts are provided with numbers of little brass cymbals that clash together musically in response to the motion of the vehicle; the occupants are fairly loaded down with silver jewellery, and for color and picturesqueness generally it is safe to assume that "not even Solomon in all his glory was arrayed like one of these." The women particularly seem to literally revel in the exuberance of bright coloring adorning their dusky proportions, the profusion of jewellery, the merry jingle-jangle of the cymbals, the more than generous heat, and the seeming bountifulness of everything. These Sikh and Jatni merry-makers early impress me as being particularly happy and light-hearted people.

Splendid wheeling though it be, it soon becomes distressingly apparent that propelling a bicycle has now to be considered in connection with the overpowering heat. Half the distance to Amritza is hardly covered, and the riding time scarcely two hours, yet it finds me reclining beneath the shade of a roadside tree more used up than five times the distance would warrant in a less enervating climate. The greensward around me as I recline in the shade is teeming with busy insects, and the trees are swarming with the beautiful winged life of the tropical air. Flocks of paroquets with most gorgeous plumage—blue, red, green, gold, and every conceivable hue—flit hither and thither, or sweep past in whirring flight.

Some of the native pedestrians pause for a moment and cast a wondering look at the unaccustomed spectacle of a Sahib and a bicycle reclining alone beneath a wayside tree. All salaam deferentially as they pass by, but there is a refreshing absence of the spirit of obtrusion that sometimes made life a burden among the Turks and Persians. In his disgust at the aggressive curiosity of the Persians, Captain E, my companion from Meshed to Constantinople, had told me, "You'll find, when you get to India, that a Sahib there is a Sahib," and the strikingly deferential demeanor of the natives I have encountered on the road to-day forcibly reminds me of his remarks.

The myriads of soldier-ants crossing the road in solid phalanx or climbing the trees, the winged jewels of the air flitting silently here and there, the picturesque natives and their deferential salaams—all these only serve to wean one's thoughts from the oppressive heat for a moment. At times one fairly gasps for breath and looks involuntarily about in forlorn search of some place of escape, if only for a moment, from the stifling atmosphere. A feeling of utter lassitude and loss of ambition comes over one; the importance of accomplishing one's object diminishes, and the necessity of yielding to the pressure of the fearful heat and taking things easy becomes the all-absorbing theme of the imagination. A supreme and heroic effort of the will is necessary to arouse one from the inclination to remain in the shade indefinitely, regardless of everything else.

No sort of accommodation is to be obtained this side of Amritza, however, so, waiting until the dreadful power of the sun is tempered somewhat by his retirement beneath the trees, I resume my journey, making several brief halts in deference to an overwhelming sense of lassitude ere completing the thirty-five miles. Owing to these frequent halts, it is after dark when I arrive at Amritza—a thoroughly wilted individual, and suffering agonies from the prickly heat aggravated by the feverish temperature superinduced by the exertion of the afternoon ride. My karki suit and underclothes hold almost as much moisture as though I had just been fished out of the river, and my dry-drained corporeal system is clamorous for the wherewithal to quench the fires of its feverish heat as I alight in the suburbs of Amritza and inquire for the dak bungalow.

A willing native guides me to a hotel where a smooth-mannered Parsee Boniface accommodates Sahibs with supper, charpoy, and chota-hazari for the small sum of Rs4; punkah-wallahs, pahnee-wallahs, sweepers, etc., extra. A cooling douche with water kept at a low temperature in the celebrated porous bottles, a change of underclothing, and a punkah-wallah vigorously engaged in creating an artificial breeze, soon change things for the better. All these refreshing and renovating appliances, however, barely suffice to stimulate one's energy up to the duty of jotting down in one's diary a brief summary of the day's happenings.

The punkah of India is a long, narrow fan, suspended by cords from the ceiling; attached to it is another cord which finds its way outside through a convenient hole in the wall or window-frame. For the magnificent sum of three annas (six cents) the hopeful punkah-wallah sits outside and fills the room with soothing, sleep-inducing breezes for the space of a day or night, by a constant seesawing motion of the string. Few Europeans are able to sleep at night or exist during the day without the punkah-wallah's services, for at least nine months in the year. The slightest negligence on his part at night is sufficient to summon the sleeper instantly from the land of dreams to the stern reality that the dusky imp outside has himself dropped off to sleep. A pardonable imprecation, delivered in loud, threatening tones; or, in the case of a person vengefully inclined, or once too often made a victim, a stealthy visit to the open door, a well-aimed boot, and the pendulous punkah again swings to and fro, banishing the newly awakened prickly heat, and fanning the recumbent figure on the charpoy with grateful breezes that quickly send him off to sleep again.

A slight fall of rain during the night tempers somewhat the oppressive heat, and the zephyrs of the prevailing monsoons blow stiffly against me as I pedal southward in the early morning. The rain has improved rather than injured the kunkah road, and it is, moreover, something of a toss-up as to whether the adverse wind is advantageous or otherwise. On the one hand it exacts increased muscular effort to ride against it, but on the other, its beneficent services as a cooler are measurably apparent.

One needs only to traverse the Grand Trunk Road for a few days in order to obtain a comprehensive idea of India's teeming population. Vehicles and pedestrians throng the road again this morning, pouring into Amritza as though to attend some great festival. The impression of some festive occasion obtains additional color from parties of musicians who keep up a perpetual tom-tom-ing on their drums as they trudge along; the object of their noisiness is apparently to gratify their own love of the sounding rattle of the drums.

At the police-chowkee of Ghundeala, ten miles from Amritza, a halt is made for rest and a drink of water. To avoid trampling on the caste prejudices, or the sanctimonious religious feelings of the natives, everybody drinks from his hands, or from a cheap earthenware dish that may afterward be smashed. The Sikhs and Mohammedans of the Punjab are far more reasonable in this matter than are the Brahmans and other ultra-holy idolaters of the country farther south. Among the Hindoos, where caste prejudices exist throughout all the strata of society, to avoid the awful consequences of touching their lips to a vessel out of which some unworthy wretch a shade less holy has previously drunk, the fastidious worshipper of Krishna, Vishnu, or Kamadeva always drinks from his hands, unless possessed of a private drinking vessel of his own. The hands are held in position to form a trough leading to the mouth; while an assistant pours water in at one end, the recipient receives it at the other. No little skill and care is required to prevent the water running down one's sleeve: the average native seems to think the human throat a gutter down which the water will flow as fast as he can pour it into the hands.

The flowing yellow flood of Beas River, now at flood, and spreading itself over the width of a mile, makes an impassable break in my road soon after mid-day. A ferryboat usually plies across the stream, but by reason of the broad area of overflow, and the consequent difficulty of working it, it is moored up for the time being. Fortunately, the Scinde, Punjab & Delhi Railroad crosses the river on a fine bridge near by, with a regular ferry-train service in operation. Repairing thither, I find, in charge of the ferry-train, an old Anglo-Indian engineer, who prevails upon me to accept his hospitality for the night.

Hundreds of natives pass the night round about the railway-station, waiting to cross the bridge on the first morning train. Nowhere else in the world does a gathering of people present so picturesque and interesting a sight as in sunny Hindostan. These people gathered about the Beas River station look more like a company rigged out for the spectacular stage than ordinary, everyday mortals attending to the prosaic business of life. The nose-rings worn by many of the women are so massive and heavy that silken cords are attached and carried to some support on the head to relieve the nostril of the weight. The rims of the ears are likewise grievously overburdened with ornaments. These unoffending appendages are pierced with a number of holes all round the rim from lobe to top; each hole contains a massive ring almost large and heavy enough for a bracelet, the weight of which pulls the ear all out of shape. Simple yet gaudy costumes prevail-garments of red, yellow, blue, green, olive, and white, with gold tinsel, drape the graceful forms of the dusky Sikh or Jatni belles; and not a whit less picturesque and parti-colored are the costumes of their husbands, brothers, and fathers-fine fellows mostly, tall, straight, military-looking men, with handsome faces and fierce mustashios. Not a few thoroughbred Jats are mingled in the crowd—the "stout-built, thick-limbed Jats," the warlike race with the steel or silver discus surmounting their queer pyramidal headdress. Under the independent government of their people by the Gurus, or ruler-priests, of the last century, and particularly under the regulations of the celebrated Guru Govind, every Sikh was considered a warrior from his birth, and was always required to wear steel iri some form or other about his person. The Jats, being the most enterprising and warlike tribe of the territory acknowledging the rule of the Gurus and the religious teachings of the Adi Granth as their faith, take especial pride in commemorating the bravery and warlike qualities of their ancestors by still wearing the distinguishing steel quoits on their heads.

Seesum or banyan trees, shading twenty yards' width of luxuriant greensward on either side of the road, and each and every tree sheltering groups of natives, resting, idling, washing their clothes in some silent pool, or tending a few grazing buffaloes, form a truly Arcadian scene for mile after mile next day. These buffaloes are huge, unwieldy animals with black, hairless hides, strong and heavy almost as rhinoceroses. In striking contrast to them are the aristocratic little cream-colored Brahmani cows, with the curious big "camel-hump" on their withers. These latter animals are pampered and revered and made much of among the Brahmans; mythology has it that Brahma created cows and Brahmans at the same time, and the cow is therefore an object of worship and veneration.

Taken all in all, the worship of the Hindoos has something eminently rational about it; their worship is frequently bestowed upon some tangible object that contributes directly to their material enjoyment. It is very much like going back to the first principles of gratitude for direct blessings received to worship "Mother Ganga," the noble stream that brings down the moisture from the Himalayas to water their plains and quicken into life their needy crops, or to worship the gentle bovine that provides them daily with milk and cheese and ghee. Wonderful legends are told of the cow in Hindoo mythology. The Ramayana tells of a certain marvellous cow owned by a renowned hermit. The hermit being honored by a visit from the king, who had with him a numerous retinue, was sorely puzzled how to provide refreshments for his princely guests. The cow, however, proved herself equal to the emergency, and—"Obedient to her saintly lord, Viands to suit each taste outpoured. Honey she gave, and roasted grain, Mead, sweet with flowers, and sugar-cane. Each beverage of flavor rare, And food of every sort, were there. Hills of hot rice, and sweetened cakes, And curdled milk, and soup in lakes. Vast beakers flowing to the brim, With sugared drink prepared for him; And dainty sweetmeats, deftly made, Before the hermit's guest were laid."

In all Brahman communities are sacred bulls, allowed to roam at their own sweet will among the crops and help themselves.

Chowel and dood (rice-and-milk) is obtained at noon from a village eating-stall; the rice is dished up to all customers in basins improvised from a broad banyan-leaf, so that nobody's caste may be jeopardized by handling spoons or dishes that others have touched. Most of the natives manage to eat with their fingers, but they bring for the Sahib a stiff green leaf which is bent into the form of a scoop and made to answer the purpose of a spoon. The milk is served in valueless earthenware basins that are tossed into the street and broken after being once used. There is a regular caste of artisans in India whose hereditary profession is the manufacture of this cheap pottery; almost every village has its family of pottery-makers, who manufacture them for the use of the community. The people are curious about the bicycle, and the Sahib's peculiar manner of travelling without the usual native servant and eating rice at an ordinary village stall. They are, however, far from being in the least obtrusive or annoying; on the contrary, their respectfulness and conservatism is something to admire; although they gather about the bicycle in a compact ring, not a hand in all the company is meddlesome enough to touch it.

Through the smooth kunkah-laid bazaars of Jullundar, so different from the unridable bazaars we have heretofore been made familiar with, and I wheel past the Queen's Gardens and into the cantonment along lovely avenues and perfect roads. The detachment of Royal Artillery, whose quarters my road leads directly past, is composed largely of the gallant sons of Erin, and as I wheel into the cantonment, an artilleryman seated on a eharpoy beneath a spreading neem-tree, sings out to his comrades, "Be jabbers, bhoys; here's the Yankee phat's travellin' around the worruld wid a bicycle."

I have with me a letter of introduction to an officer stationed at Jullundar. Upon inquiry, however, I find that he is absent at Simla on leave. Desirous of seeing something of Tommy Atkins in his Indian quarters, I therefore accept an invitation to remain at the barracks of the Royal Artillery until ready to resume my journey in the morning. At this season of the year, an Indian cantonment presents the appearance of a magnificent park. The barracks are large, commodious structures, built with a view to securing the best results for the health and comfort of the troops.

No soldiers in the world are so well fed, housed, and clothed as the British soldiers in India, and none receive as much pay, except the soldiers of the United States army. That they are justly entitled to everything that can contribute to their happiness and welfare, goes without saying. For actual service rendered, and the importance of the responsibilities resting on their shoulders, it is little enough to say that the British soldiers in India are entitled to a greater measure of consideration than the soldiers of any other army in existence. This little army of fifty or sixty thousand men is practically responsible for the good behavior of one-sixth of the world's population, saying nothing of affairs without. And in addition to this is the wearisome round of existence in an Indian barrack, the enervating climate and the ennui, so poisonous to the active Anglo-Saxon temperament.

After all that is said for or against the Anglo-Indian army, the unprejudiced critic cannot fail to admit that they are the finest body of fighting men in existence, a force against which it would be impossible for an equal number of the soldiers of any other country to contend. That the old dominant spirit of the British soldier is yet rampant as ever may be seen, perhaps, plainer in the cantonments of India than anywhere else. The manifest superiority of Tommy Atkins as a fighter stands out in bold relief against the gentle populations of India, who regard him as the very incarnation of war and warlike attributes. His own confidence in his ability to whip all the multitudinous enemies of England put together, is as great to-day as it ever was, and nothing would suit him better than a campaign against the military colossus of the North in defence of the British interests in India he now so faithfully guards.

The interest in my appearance is deepened by my recent adventures in Afghanistan and letters partly descriptive of the same that have appeared in late issues of the Indian press. A mile or so from the Artillery barracks are the quarters of a detachment of the Connaught Rangers. A couple of non-commissioned officers in the Rangers, I am happy to discover, are wheelmen, and when the tidings of the Around the World rider's arrival reaches them, they wheel over and endeavor to have me become their guest. The Royal Artillery boys refuse to give their protege up, however, and the rivalry is compromised by my paying the Rangers a visit and then coming back to my first entertainers' quarters for the night.

The evening is spent pleasantly in telling stories of camp-life in India and Afghanistan. Some of the soldiers present have been recently stationed at Peshawur and other points near the northern frontier, and tell of the extraordinary precautions that had to be adopted to prevent their rifles being stolen at night from the very racks within the barrack-rooms where they were sleeping.

An officer at the cantonment claims to have cured himself of enlarged spleen, the bane of so many Anglo-Indian officers, by daily riding on a tricycle. He then disposed of it to advantage to a native gentleman who had noted the marvellous improvement it had wrought in his health, and who was also affected with the same disease. The native also cured himself, and now firmly believes the tricycle possessed of some magic properties.

Reliefs of punkah-wallahs are provided for the barracks, a number of punkahs being connected so that one coolie fans the occupants of a dozen or more charpoys. In talking about these useful and very necessary servants, some of the comments indulged in by the gentleman who first invited me into the barracks are well worth repeating: "Be jabbers, an' yeez have to kape wide awake all night to swear at the lazy divils, in orther to git a wink av shlape"—and—"The moment yeez dhrap ashlape, yeez are awake," are choice specimens, heard in reference to the punkah-wallahs' confirmed habit of dozing off in the silent watches of the night.

The two wheelmen of the Connaught Rangers, accompany me five miles to the Bane River ferry, in the cool of early morning. They would have escorted me as far as Umballa, they say, had they known of my coming in time to arrange leave' of absence. Twenty-five miles of continuously smooth and level kunkah, bring me to Phillour, a Mohammedan town of several thousand inhabitants. The fort of Phillour is a conspicuous object on the left of the road; it was formerly an important depot of military supplies, and in the time of Sikh independence was regarded by them as the key to the Punjab. Since the mutiny it has dwindled in importance as a military stronghold, but is held by a detachment of native infantry.

A mile or so from Phillour is a splendid girder railway bridge crossing the River Sutlej. The overflow of the river extends for miles, converting the depressions into lakes and the dry ditches into sloughs and creeks. Resting under the shade of a peepul-tree, I while away a passing hour watching native fishermen endeavoring to beguile the finny denizens of the overflow into their custody. Their tactics are to stir up the water and make it muddy for a space around, so that the fish cannot see them; they then toss a flat disk of wood so that it falls with an audible splash a few yards away. This manoeuvre is intended to deceive the fish into thinking something eatable has fallen into the water. Woe betide the guileless fish, however, whose innocent, confiding nature is thus imposed upon, for "swish" goes a circular drop-net over the spot, from the meshes of which the luckless captive tries in vain to struggle.

The River Sutlej has its source in the holy lake of Manas Saro-vara, in Thibet's most mountainous regions, and for several hundred miles its course leads through mighty canons, grand and rugged as the canons of the Colorado and the Gunnison. It is on the upper reaches of the Sutlej that the celebrated swing bridges called karorus are in operation. A karorus consists of a bagar-grass or yak-hair rope, stretched from bank to bank, across which passengers are pulled, suspended in a swinging chair or basket. The karorus is also largely patronized by the swarms of monkeys inhabiting the foot-hill jungles of the Himalayas; nothing could well be more congenial to these festive animals than the Blondin-like performance of crossing over some deep, roaring gorge along the swaying rope of a karorus.

Like other rivers of the level Punjab plains, the Sutlej has at various times meandered from its legitimate channel; eight miles south of its present bed the large and flourishing city of Ludhiana once stood on its bank. Ludhiana and its dak bungalow, provides refreshments and a three hours' siesta beneath the cooling and seductive punkah, besides an interesting and instructive tete-a-tete with a Eurasian civil officer spending the day here. Among other startling confidences, this olive-tinted gentleman declares that to him the punkah is unbearable, its pendulous, swinging motion invariably making him "sea-sick."

Through a country of alternate sandy downs and grazing areas my road leads at length through the territory of the Rajah of Sir-hind. Picturesque and impressive fortresses, and high, crenellated stone walls around the villages give the rajah's little dominion here a most decided mediaeval appearance, and dark, dense patches of sugar-cane attest the marvellous richness of the sandy soil, wherever water can be applied. Moreover, as if to complete the interesting picture of a native prince's rule, on the road is encountered a gayly dressed party in charge of some youthful big-wig on a monster elephant. A thick, striped mattress makes a soft platform on the elephant's broad back, and here the young voluptuary squats as naturally as on the floor of his room. Some of the attendants are dancing along before him, noisily knuckling tambourines and drums, while others trudge alongside or behind. The elephant regards the bicycle with symptoms of mild apprehension, and swerves slightly to one side.

The police-officer of Kermandalah chowkee, just off the Rajah of Sirhind's territory, voluntarily tenders me the shelter of his quarters, just as the sun is finishing his race for the day by painting the sky with fanciful tints and streaks. The long, straight avenue which I have wheeled down, for miles hereabout runs east and west. The sun, rotund and fiery, sets immediately in the perspective of the avenue; and at his disappearance there shoot from the same point iridescent javelins that spread, fan-like, over the whole heavens. A sight never to be forgotten is the long white road and the ribs of the glorious celestial fan meeting together in the vista-like distance; and—oh, for the brush and palette and genius of a Turner!—one of the rainbow-tinted javelins spits the crescent moon and holds it to toast before the glowing sunset fires, like a piece of green cheese.

The heat of the night is ominously suggestive of shed's popularly conceived temperature, and, in the absence of the customary punkah and nodding, see-sawing wallah, a villager is employed to sit beside my charpoy and agitate the air immediately about my head with a big palm-leaf fan. But sleep is next to impossible; the morning finds me feeling but little refreshed and with a decided yearning to remain all day long in the shade instead of taking to the road. Not a moment's respite is possible from the oppressive heat; an hour in the saddle develops a sensation of grogginess and an amphibian inclination for wallowing in some road-side tank.

South of Sirhind the country develops into low, flat jungle, with much of it partly overflowed. The road through these semi-submerged lowlands is an embankment, rising many feet above the general level, and provided with numerous culverts and bridges to prevent the damming of the waters and the danger of washing away the road. The jungle is full of busy life. The air is thick with the low, murmuring hum of busy insect-life, birds shriek, whistle, call, hoot, peep, chirp, and sing among the intertwining branches, and frogs croak hoarsely in the watery shallows beneath. Noises, too, are heard, that would puzzle, I venture to say, many a scholarly, book-wise and specimen-wise naturalist to define as coming from the articulatory organs of bird, beast, or fish. The slow, measured sweep of giant wings beating the air is heard above, and the next moment a huge bustard floats down through the trees and alights in a moist footing of jungle-grass and water.

A little Brahman village at the railway station of Rajpaira is reached in the middle of the afternoon; but it provides little or nothing in the way of accommodation for a European. The chow-keedar of the dak bungalow blandly declares his inability to provide anything eatable for a Sahib, and the Eurasian employes at the railway station are unaccommodating and indifferent, owing to the travel-stained and ordinary appearance of my apparel. The Eurasians, by the by, impress me far less favorably as a race than do the better-class full-blood natives. It seems to be the unfortunate fate of most mixed races to inherit the more undesirable qualities of both progenitors, and the better characteristics of neither. No less than the mongrel populations of certain West Indian islands, the Spanish-speaking republics, and the mulattoes of the Southern States, do the Eurasians of India present in their character eloquent argumentation against the error of miscegenation.

A little Brahman village is anything but, an encouraging place for a traveller to penetrate in search of eatables. A thin, yellow-skinned Brahman, with a calico fig-leaf suspended from a cocoa-nut-fibre waist-string, and the white-and-red tattooing of his holy caste on his forehead, presides over a big lump of goodakoo (a preparation of tobacco, rose-leaves, jaggeree, bananas, opium, and cardamom seed, used for hookah-smoking), and his double performs the same office for sickly, warm goats' milk and doughy, unleavened chup-patties. Uninviting as is the prospect, one is compelled, by the total absence of any alternative, to patronize the proprietor of the latter articles.

As I step inside his little shed-like establishment to see what he has, he holds up his hands in holy trepidation at the unhallowed intrusion, and begs me to be seated outside. My entrance causes as much consternation as the traditional bull in the china shop, the explanation of which is to be found in the fact that anything I might happen to touch becomes at once defiled beyond redemption for the consumption of native customers. With the weather wilting hot, doughy chuppaties and lukewarm, unstrained, strong-tasting goats' milk can scarcely be called an appetizing meal, and the latter is served in the usual cheap, earthenware platter, which is at once tossed out and broken.

The natives of India are probably less concerned about their stomachs than the people of any other country in the world. They seem to delight in fasting, and growing thin and emaciated; their ordinary meal is a handful of parched grain and a few swallows of milk or water. Among the aesthetic Brahmans are many specimens reduced by habitual fasting and general meagreness of diet to the condition of living skeletons; yet they seem to enjoy splendid health, and live to a shrivelled old age. The Brahman shop-keeper squats contentedly among his wares, passing the hours in dreamy meditation and in consoling pipes of goodakoo. Nothing seems to disturb his calm serenity, any more than the reposeful expression on the countenance of a marble Buddha could be affected—nothing but the approach of a Sahib toward his shop. It is interesting to observe the mingled play of politeness, apprehension, and alarm in the actions of a Brahman shopkeeper at the appearance of a blundering, but withal well-meaning Sahib, among his wares. Knowing, from long experience, that the Englishman would on no account wilfully injure his property or trample wantonly on his caste prejudices, he is at his wits' end to comport himself deferentially and at the same time prevent anything from being handled.

Money has to be placed where the Brahman can pick it up without incurring the awful danger of personal contact with an unhallowed kaffir.

The fifty miles, that from the splendid condition of the roads I have thought little enough for the average day's run, is duly reeled off as I ride into the splendid civil lines and cantonment of Um-balla at dusk. But my few days' experience on the roads of India have sufficed to convince me that fifty miles is entirely beyond the bounds of discretion. It is, in fact, beyond the bounds of discretion to be riding any distance in the present season here; fifty miles is overcome to-day only by the exercise of almost superhuman will-power.

The average native, when asked for the dak bungalow, is quite as likely to direct one to the post-office, the kutcherry, or any other government building, from a seeming inability to discriminate between them. At the entrance to Umballa one of these hopeful participants in the blessings of enlightened government informs me, with sundry obsequious salaams, that the dak bungalow is four miles farther. So thoroughly has my fifty-mile ride used up my energy that even this four miles, on a most perfect road, seems utterly impossible of accomplishment; besides which, experience has taught that following the directions given would very likely bring me to the post-office and farther away from the dak bungalow than ever.

Above the trees, not far away, is observed the weathercock of a chapel-spire, plainly indicating the location of the European quarter. Taking a branch road leading in that direction, I discover a party of English and native gentlemen playing a game of lawn-tennis. Arriving on the scene just as the game is breaking up, I am cordially invited to "come in and take a peg." To the uninitiated a "peg" is a rather ambiguous term, but to the Anglo-Indian its interpretation takes the seductive form of a big tumbler of brandy and soda, a "long drink," than which nothing could be more acceptable in my present fagged-out condition. No hesitation is therefore made in accepting; and, under the stimulating influence of the generous brandy and soda, exhausted nature is quickly recuperated. While not an advocate of indiscriminate indulgence in alcoholic stimulants, after an enervating ride through the wilting heat of an Indian day I am convinced that nothing is more beneficial than what Anglo-Indians laconically describe as a "peg."

This very opportune meeting results, naturally enough, in a pressing invitation to stay over and recruit up for a day, a programme to which I offer no objections, feeling rather overdone and in need of rest and recuperation. Mine hosts are police-commissioners, having supervision over the police-district of Uniballa. One of their number is on the eve of departure for his summer vacation in the Himalayas and, in honor of the event, several guests call round to partake of a champagne dinner, the sparkling Pommery Sec being quaffed ad libitum from pint tumblers. At the present time, no surer does water seek its level than the after-dinner conversation of Anglo-Indian officials turns into the discussion of the great depreciation of the silver rupee and its relation to the exchange at home. As the rate of exchange goes lower and lower, and no corresponding increase of salary takes place, the natural result is a great deal of hardship and dissatisfaction among those who, from various causes, have to send money to England. From the Anglo-Indians' daily association with Orientals and their peculiarly subtle understandings, it is perhaps not so surprising to find an occasional flight of fancy brought to bear upon the subject that would do credit to a professional romancer. One ingenious young civil officer present evolves a deep, deep scheme to get even with the government for present injustice that for far-reaching and persistent revenge speaks volumes for the young gentleman's determination to carry his point. His brilliant scheme is to retire on a pension at the proper time, live to the age of eighty years, and then marry a healthy girl of sixteen. As the pension of an Anglo-Indian government officer descends to his surviving widow, the ingenuity and depth of this person's reasoning powers becomes at once apparent. He proposes to take revenge for the present shortcomings of the government by saddling it with a pension for a hundred years or more after his retirement from active service.

Tusked and antlered trophies of the chase adorning the walls, and panther and tiger skins scattered about the floor, attest the police-commissioners' prowess with the rifle in the surrounding jungle. The height of every young Englishman's ambition when he comes to India is to kill a tiger; not until with his own rifle he has laid low a genuine Tigris Indicus, and handed its striped pelt over to the taxidermist, does he feel entitled to hold his chin at a becoming elevation and to indulge in the luxury of talking about the big game of the jungle on an equality with his fellows. Among the pets of the establishment are a youthful black bear that spends much of its time in climbing up and down a post on the lawn, a recently captured monkey that utters cries of alarm and looks badly frightened when approached by a white person, and a pair of spotted deer. These, together with several hunting dogs that delight in taking wanton liberties with the bear and deer, form quite a happy, though not altogether trustful family party in the grounds.

The day's rest does me a world of good, and upon resuming my journey the voice of my own experience is augmented by the advice of my entertainers, in warning me against overexertion and fatigue in so trying a climate as India. It has rained during the night, and the early morning is signalled by cooler weather than has yet been experienced from Lahore.

Companies of tall Sikhs, magnificent-looking fellows, in their trim karki uniforms and monster turbans, are drilling within the native-infantry lines as I wheel through the broad avenues of one of the finest cantonments in all India, and English officers and their wives are taking the morning air on horseback.

This splendid cantonment contains no less than seven thousand two hundred and twenty acres and might well be termed a magnificent park throughout.

It is in the hilly tracts of the Umballa district that the curious custom prevails of placing infants beneath little cascades of water so that the stream of water shall steadily descend on the head. The cool water of some mountain-rivulet is converted into a number of streams appropriate for the purpose, by means of bamboo ducts or spouts. The infants are brought thither in the morning by their mothers and placed in proper position on beds of grass; the trickling water, pouring on their heads, keeps the brain cool and is popularly supposed to be efficacious in the prevention of many infantile diseases peculiar to the country. Children not subjected to this curious hydropathic treatment are said to generally die young, or grow up weaklings in comparison with the others.

A sudden freshet in the ordinarily shallow and partially dry bed of the Donglee River tells of the heaviness of last night's rainstorm among the hills, and compels a halt of a couple of hours until the rapidly subsiding water gets low enough to admit of fording it with a native bullock gharri. A branch of the same stream is crossed in a similar manner, and yet a third river, a few miles farther, has to be crossed on a curious raft made of a number of buoyant earthenware jars fixed in a bamboo frame. A splendid bridge spans the swollen torrent of the more formidable Markunda, and the well-metalled highway now cuts a wide straight swath through inundated jungle. A big wild monkey, the first of his species thus far encountered on the road, utters a shrill squeak of apprehension at seeing the bicycle come bowling down the road, and in his fright he leaps from the branches of a road-side tree into the shallow water and escapes into the jungle with frantic leaps and bounds.

Travelling leisurely, and resting often, for thirty miles, the afternoon brings me to the small town of Peepli, where a dak bungalow provides food and shelter of a certain kind. The sleeping-accommodation of the dak bungalow may hardly be described as luxurious; ants and other insects swarm in myriads, and lizards drag their slimy length about the timber of the walls and ceiling. The wild jungle encroaches on the village, and the dak bungalow occupies an isolated position at one end. The jungle resounds with the strange noises of animals and birds, and a friendly native, who speaks a little English, confides the joyful information that the deadly cobra everywhere abounds.

For the first time it is cool enough to sleep without the services of the punkah-wallah, and not a soul remains about the dak bungalow after nightfall. The night is dark and cloudy, but not by any means silent, for the "noises of the night" are multitudinous and varied, ranging from the tuneful croaking of innumerable frogs to the yelping chorus of the jackals-the weird nocturnal concert of the Indian jungle, a musical melange far easier to imagine than describe. About ten o'clock, out from the gloomy depths of the jungle near by is suddenly heard the unmistakable caterwauling of a panther, followed by that cunning arch-dissembler's inimitable imitation of a child in distress. As though awed and paralyzed by this revelation of the panther's dread presence, the chirping and juggling and p-r-r-ring and yelping of inferior creatures cease as if by mutual impulse moved, and the pitter-patter of little feet are heard on the clay floor of my bungalow. The cry of the forest prowler is repeated, nearer than before to my quarters, and presently something hops up on the foot of the charpoy on which my recumbent form is stretched; and still continues the pattering of feet on the floor. It is pitchy dark within the bungalow, and, uncertain of the nature of my strange visitant, I kick and "qu-e-e-k" at him and scare him off; but, evidently terrorized by the appearance of the panther, the next minute he again invades my couch.

To have one's room turned nolens volens into a place of refuge for timid animals, hiding from a prowling panther which is not unlikely to follow them inside, is anything but a desirable experience in the dark. Should his panthership come nosing inside the bungalow, in his eagerness to secure something for supper he might not pause to discriminate between brute and human; and as his awe-inspiring voice is heard again, apparently quite near by, I deem it expedient to warn him off. So reaching my Smith & Wesson from under the pillow, I fire a shot up into the thatched roof. The little intruders, whatever they may be, scamper out of the bungalow, nor wait upon the order of their going, and a loud scream some distance away a moment later tells of the panther's rapid retreat into the depths of the jungle.

Soon a courageous bull-frog gives utterance to a subdued, hesitative croak; his excellent example is quickly followed by others; answering noises spring up in every direction, and ere long the midnight concert of the jungle is again in full melody.

A comparatively cooling breeze blows across flooded jungle and rice-field in the morning. The country around resembles a shallow lake from out of which the rank vegetation of the jungle rears its multiform foliage; much of the water is merely the temporary overflow of the Markunda, silently moving through the shady forest, but over the more permanently submerged areas is gathered a thick green scum. Not unlike a broad expanse of level meadow-land do some of these open spaces seem, and the yellow, fallen blossoms of the gum arabic trees, scattered thickly about, are the buttercups spangling and beautifying the meadows.

Forty-eight miles from Umballa the Grand Trunk road leads through the civil lines and past the towering walls of ancient Kurnaul. Formerly on the banks of the river Jumna, Kurnaul is now removed several miles from that stream, owing to the wayward trick of Indian rivers carving out for themselves new channels during seasons of extraordinary flood. The city is old beyond the records of history, its name and fame glimmering faintly in the dim and distant perspective of ancient Hindostani legend and mythical tales. Within the last few hundred years, Kurnaul has been taken and retaken, plundered and destroyed, by Sikh, Rajput, Mogul, and Mahratta freebooters, and was occupied in 1795 by the celebrated adventurer George Thomas, who figured so largely in the military history of India during the latter part of the last century. Here also was fought the great battle between Nadir Shah and Mohammed Shah, the Emperor of Delhi, that resulted in the defeat of the latter, the subsequent looting of Delhi, and the carrying off to Persia of the famous peacock throne. Splendid water-tanks, spreading banyans, feathery date-palms, and toddy-palms render the suburbs of Kurnaul particularly attractive, these days; but the place is unhealthy, being very low and the surrounding country subject to the overflow that induces fever.

A letter of introduction from Umballa to Mr. D, deputy commissioner at Kurnaul, insures me hospitable recognition and creature comforts upon reaching the latter place at 9 a.m. Spending the heat of mid-day in Mr. D's congenial society, recounting the incidents of my journey and learning in return much valuable information in regard to India, I continue on my journey again when the fiercest heat of the sun has subsided in favor of the slightly more tolerable evening. The country grows more and more interesting from various standpoints as my progression carries me southward. Not only does it become intensely interesting by reason of its historical associations in connection with the old Mogul Empire, but in its peculiar aspect of Indian life to-day. Monkeys are hopping about all over the place, moving leisurely about the roofs and walls of the villages, or complacently examining one another's phrenological peculiarities beneath the trees. About the streets, shops, and houses these mischievous anthropoids are seen in droves, moving hither and thither at their own sweet will, as much at home as the human occupants and owners of the houses themselves.

Monkeys, being held sacred by the Hindoos, are allowed to remain in the towns and villages unmolested, doing pretty much as they please. Sometimes they swarm in such numbers that eternal vigilance alone keeps them from devouring the fruit, grain, and other eatables displayed for sale in front of the shops. When they get to be an insufferable nuisance, although the pious Hindoos would suffer from their depredations even to ruin rather than do them injury, they offer no objections to being relieved of their charges by the government officials, so long as the measures taken are not of a sanguinary nature. Sometimes the monkeys are caught and shipped off in car-loads to some point miles away and turned loose in the jungle. The appearance of a car-load of these exiles, however, always excites the sympathies of the pious Hindoo, and instances have been known when they have been stealthily liberated while the train was waiting at some other town.

An effectual remedy has been recently discovered in cleaning out colonies of the smaller varieties of monkeys and inducing them to remove somewhere else, by introducing into their midst a certain warlike and aggressive variety from somewhere in the Himalaya foot-hills. This particular race of monkey, being a veritable anthropoidal Don Juan among his fellows, when turned loose in a village commences making violent love to the wives and sweethearts of the resident monkeys. The faithless fair, ever ready for coquetry and flirtation, flattered beyond measure by the attentions of the gallant stranger, forsake their first loves by the wholesale, and bask shamelessly in the sunshine of his favor. The result is that the outraged males, afraid to attack the warlike libertine so rudely introduced into their peaceful community, gather up their erring spouses, giddy daughters, and small children and betake themselves off forever.

Not far from Kurnaul I overtake an interesting party of gypsies, moving with their bag and baggage piled on the backs of diminutive cows led by strings. Numbers of the smaller children also bestride the gentle little bovines, but the rest of the party are afoot. The ruling passion of the Romany, the wide world over, asserts itself at my approach; brown-bodied youngsters with sparkling, coal-black eyes race after the bicycle, holding out their hands and begging, "pice, sahib, pice, pice."

Facsimile in cry and gesture almost, and in appearance, are these Hindostani gypsies of their relatives in distant Hungary, who, fifteen months before, raced alongside the bicycle, and begged for "kreuzer, kreuzer." Many ethnologists believe India to have been the original abiding place of the now widely scattered Romanies; certain it is that no country and no clime would be so well adapted to their shiftless habits and wandering tent-life as India. Their language, subjected to analysis, has been traced in a measure to Sanscrit roots, and although spread pretty much all over the surface of the globe, this strange, romantic people are said to recognize one another by a common language, even should the one hail from India and the other from the frozen North. Certain professors claim to have discovered a connecting link between the gypsies of the Occident and the Jats of the Punjab.

A boy tending a sacred cow undertakes to drive that worshipful animal out of my way as he sees me come bowling briskly down the road. The bovine, pampered and treated with the greatest deference and consideration from her earliest calfhood, resents this treatment by making a short but determined spurt after me as I sweep past. Whether the sacred cows of India are spoiled by generations of overindulgence, or whether the variety is constitutionally evil-tempered does not appear, but they one and all take pugnacious exception to the bicycle. Spurting away from a chasing Brahmani cow is an every-day experience.

Mr. D has kindly telegraphed from Kurnaul to Nawab Ali Ahmed Khan, a hospitable Mohammedan gentleman at Paniput, apprising him of my coming. More ancient even than Kurnaul, Paniput's vast antiquity is reputed to extend back to the period of the great Pandava War described in the Mahabharat, and supposed to have been fought nearly four thousand years ago. The city occupies a commanding position to the left of the road, and is rendered conspicuous by several white marble domes and minarets.

The nawab and another native gentleman, physician to the Paniput Hospital, are seated in a dog-cart watching for my appearance, at a fork in the road near one of the city gates. The nawab's place is a mile and a half off the main road, but the smooth, level kunkah leads right up to the fine, commodious bungalow, in which I am duly installed. A tepid bath, prepared in deference to the nawab's anticipation of my preference, is awaiting my pleasure, and from the moment of arrival I am the recipient of unstinted attention. A large reclining chair is placed immediately beneath the punkah, and a punkah-wallah, ambitious to please, causes the frilled hangings of this desirable and necessary piece of furniture to wave vigorously to and fro but a foot or eighteen inches above my head. A smiling servant kneels at my feet and proceeds to knead and "groom" the muscles of the legs. Judging from the attentions lavished upon my pedal extremities, one might well imagine me to be a race-horse that had just endeared himself to his groom and owner by winning the Derby.

An ample supper is followed by a most refreshing sleep, and in the morning, when ready to depart, my watchful attendants present themselves with broad smiles and sheets of paper. Each one wants a certificate showing that he has contributed to my comfort and entertainment, and lastly comes the nawab himself and his bosom friend, the hospital doctor, to bid me farewell and request the same favor. This certificate-foible is one of the greatest bores in India; almost every native who performs any service for a Sahib, whether in the capacity of a mere waiter at a native hotel, or as retainer of some wealthy nabob—and not infrequently the nabob himself, if a government official—wants a testimonial expressing one's approval of his services. An old servitor who has mingled much among Europeans must have whole reams of these useless articles stowed away. What in the world they want with them is something of a puzzler; though the idea is, probably, that they might come in useful to obtain a situation some time or other.

South of Paniput the trees alongside the road are literally swarming with monkeys; they file in long strings across the road, looking anxiously behind, evidently frightened at the strange appearance of the bicycle. Shinnying up the toddy-palms, they ensconce themselves among the foliage and peer curiously down at me as I wheel past, giving vent to their perturbation in excited cries. Twenty-five miles down the road, an hour is spent beneath a grove of shady peepuls, watching the amusing antics of a troop of monkeys in the branches. Their marvellous activity among the trees is here displayed to perfection, as they quarrel and chase one another from tree to tree. The old ones seem passively irritable and decidedly averse to being bothered by the antics and mischievous activity of the youngsters. Taking possession of some particular branch, they warn away all would-be intruders with threatening grimaces and feints. The youthful members of the party are skillful of pranks and didoes, carried on to the great annoyance of their more aged and sedate relatives, who, in revenge, put in no small portion of their time punishing or pursuing them with angry cries for their deeds of wanton annoyance. One monkey, that has very evidently been there many and many a time before on the same thievish errand, with an air of amusing secrecy and roguishness, slips quickly along a horizontal bough and thrusts its arm into a hole. Its eyes wander guiltily around, as though expectant of detection and attack—an apprehension that quickly justifies itself in the shape of a blue-plumaged bird that flutters angrily about the robber's head, causing it to beat a hasty retreat. Birds' eggs are the booty it expected to find, and, me-thinks, as I note the number and activity of the freebooters to whom birds' eggs would be most toothsome morsels, watchful indeed must be the parent-bird whose maternal ambition bears its legitimate fruit in this monkey-infested grove. In me the monkeys seem to recognize a possible enemy, and at my first appearance hasten to hide themselves among the thickest foliage; peering; cautiously down, they yield themselves up to excited chattering and broad grimaces.

Peacocks, too, are strutting majestically about the greensward beneath the trees, their gorgeous tails expanded, or, perched on some horizontal branch, they awake the screaming echoes in reply to others of their kindred calling in the jungle. In the same way that monkeys are regarded and worshipped as the representatives of the great mythological monkey-king Hanumiin, who assisted Kama, in his war with Havana for the possession of Sita, so is the peacock revered and held sacred as the bird upon which rode Kartikeya the god of war and commander-in-chief of the armies of the Puranic gods. Thus do both these denizens of the jungle obtain immunity from harm at the hands of the natives, by reason of mythological association. English sportsmen shoot them, however, except in certain specified districts where the government has made their killing prohibitory, in deference to the religious prejudices of the Hindoos. The Rajput warriors of Ulwar used to march to battle with a peacock's feather in their turbans; they believe that the reason why this fine-plumaged bird screams so loudly when it thunders is because it mistakes the noise for the roll of war-drums. Large, two-storied passenger-vans, drawn sometimes by one camel and sometimes two, are now frequently encountered; they are regular two-storied cages, with iron bars, like the animal-vans in a menagerie. The passengers squat on the floors, and when travelling at night, or through wild districts, are locked in between stages to guard against surprise and robbery.

CHAPTER XV

DELHI AND AGRA

From the police-thana of Rai, where the night is spent, to Delhi, the character of the road changes to a mixture of clay and rock, altogether inferior to kunkah. The twenty-one miles are covered, however, by 8.30 a.m., that hour finding me wheeling down the broad suburban road to the Lahore Gate amid throngs of country people carrying baskets of mangoes, plantains, pomegranates, and other indigenous products into the markets of the old Mogul capital. Massive archways, ruined forts and serais, placid water-tanks, lovely gardens, feathery toddy-palms, plantain-hedges, and throngs of picturesque people make the approach to historic Delhi a scene long to be remembered.

Entering the Lahore Gate, suitable accommodation is found at Northbrook Hotel, a comfortable hostelry under native management near the Moree Gate, and overlooking from its roof the scenes of the most memorable events connected with the siege of Delhi in 1857. Letters are found at the post-office apprising me of a bicycle-camera and paper negatives awaiting my orders at the American Consulate at Calcutta, and it behooves me to linger here for a few days until its arrival in reply to a telegram. No more charming spot could possibly be found to linger in than the old Mogul capital, with its wondrous wealth of historical associations, both remotely antique and comparatively modern, its glorious monuments of imperial Oriental splendor and its reminiscences of heroic deeds in battle.

A letter of introduction to an English gentleman, brought from Kurnaul, secures me friends and attention at once; in the cool of the evening we drive out together in his pony-phaeton along the historic granite ridge that formed the site of the British camp during the siege. The operations against the city were conducted mostly from this ridge and the intervening ground; on the ridge itself is erected a beautiful red granite monument memorial, bearing the names of prominent officers and the numbers of men killed, the names of the regiments, etc., engaged in the siege and assault. Here, also, is Hindoo Rao's house, and ancient obelisks.

East of the Moree Gate is the world-famed Cashmere Gate—world-famed in connection with the brilliant exploit of the little forlorn hope that, on the morning of September 14, 1857, succeeded, in the face of a deadly fusillade from the walls and the wicket gates, in carrying bags of gunpowder and blowing it up. Through the opening thus effected poured the eager troops that rescued the city from ten times their own number of mutineers and turned the beams of the scale in which the fate of the whole British Indian Empire was at the moment balanced. Perhaps in all the world's battles no more heroic achievement was ever attempted or carried out than the blowing up of the Cashmere Gate. "Salkeld laid his bags of powder, in the face of a deadly fire from the open wicket not ten feet distant; he was instantly shot through the arm and leg, and fell back on the bridge, handing the port-fire to Sergeant Burgess, bidding him light the fuse. Burgess was instantly shot dead in the attempt. Sergeant Carmichael then advanced, took up the port-fire, and succeeded in firing the fuse, but immediately fell, mortally wounded. Sergeant Smith, seeing him fall, advanced at a run, but finding that the fuse was already burning, flung himself into the ditch."

Difficult, indeed, would it be to crowd more heroism into the same number of words that I have here quoted from Colonel Medley, an eyewitness of the affair. Between the double archways of the gate is a red-sandstone memorial tablet, placed there by Lord Napier of Magdala, upon which is inscribed the names, rank, and regiment of those who took part in the forlorn hope. All is now peaceful and lovely enough, but the stone bastions and parapets still remain pretty much as when the British batteries ceased their plunging rain of shot and shell thirty years ago.

Not far from the Moree Gate is the tomb of General Nicholson, one of the most conspicuous and heroic characters of that trying period, and generally regarded as the saviour of Delhi. Enshrined in the hearts of the brave Sikhs no less than in the hearts of his own countrymen, his tomb has become a regular place of pilgrimage for the old Sikh warriors who fought side by side with the English against the mutineers.

It has been my good fortune, I find, to arrive at the old Mogul capital the day before the commencement of an annual merrymaking, picnicking, and general holiday at the celebrated Kootub Minar. The Kootub Minar is about eleven miles out of Delhi, situated amid the ruins of ancient Dilli (Delhi), the old Hindoo city from which the more modern city takes its name. It is conceded to be the most beautiful minar-monument in the world, and ranks with the Taj Mahal at Agra as one of the beautiful architectural triumphs peculiar to the splendid era of Mohammedan rule in India, and which are not to be matched elsewhere. The day following my arrival I conclude to take a spin out on my bicycle as far as the Kootub, and see something of it, the ruins amid which it stands, and the Hindoos in holiday attire. I choose the comparative coolness of early morning for the ride out; but early though it be, the road thither is already swarming with gayly dressed people bent on holiday-making. The road is a worthy offshoot of the Grand Trunk, not a whit less smooth of surface, nor less lovely in its wealth of sacred shade-trees. Moreover, it passes through a veritable wilderness of ruined cities, mosques, tombs, and forts the whole distance, and leads right through the magnificent remains of the ancient Hindoo city itself.

The Kootub Minar is found to be a beautifully fluted column, two hundred and forty feet high, and it soars grandly above the mournful ruins of old Dilli, its hoary wealth of crumbled idol temples, tombs, and forts. The minar is supposed to have been erected in the latter part of the twelfth century to celebrate the victory of the Mohammedans over the Hindoos of Dilli. The general effect of the tall, stately Mohammedan monument among the Hindoo ruins is that of a proud gladiator standing erect and triumphant amid fallen foes. At least, that is how it looks to me, as I view it in connection with the ruins at its base and ponder upon its history. A spiral stairway of three hundred and seventy-five steps leads to the summit. A group of natives are already up there, enjoying the cool breezes and the prospect below. In the comprehensive view from the summit one can read an instructive sermon of centuries of stirring Indian history in the gray stone-work of ruined mosques and tombs and fortresses and pagan temples that dot the valley of the Jumna hereabout almost as thickly as the trees.

Strange crowds have congregated on this rare old historic camping-ground in ages past. It was a strange crowd, gathered here for a strange purpose, on that traditional occasion, when Rajah Pithora, in the fourth century of the Christian era, had the celebrated iron shaft dug up to satisfy his curiosity as to whether it had transfixed the subterranean snake-god Vishay. There is a strange crowd gathered here to-day, too; I can hear their shouting and their tom-toming come floating up from among the ruins and the dark-green foliage as I look down from my beautiful eyrie on top of the Kootub upon their pygmy forms, thronging the walks and roads, brown and busy as swarms of ants.

It is a vast concourse of people, characteristic of teeming India; but they are not, on this occasion, congregated to witness pagan rites and ceremonies, nor to encourage iconoclastic Moolahs in smashing Hindoo gods and chipping offensive Hindoo carvings off their temples; they are a mixed crowd of Hindoos, Sikhs, and Mohammedans, who, having to some extent buried the hatchet of race and religious animosities under the just and tolerant rule of a Christian government, have gathered here amid the ruins and relics of their respective past histories to enjoy themselves in innocent recreation.

Descending from the Kootub Minar, I am resting beneath the shade of the dak bungalow hard by, when a gray-bearded Hindoo approaches, salaams, and hands me a paper. The paper is a certificate, certifying that the bearer, Chunee Lai, had performed before Captain Somebody of the Fusileers, and had afforded that officer excellent amusement. Before I have quite grasped the situation, or comprehended the purport of the tendered missive, several men and boys deposit a miscellaneous assortment of boxes and baskets before me and range themselves in a semicircle behind them. The old fellow with the certificate picks out a small box and raises the lid; a huge cobra thrusts out its hideous head and puffs its hooded neck to the size of a man's hand. It then dawns upon me that the gray-bearded Hindoo is a conjurer; and being curious to see something of Indian prestidigitation, I allow him to proceed.

Many of the tricks are quite commonplace and transparent even to a novice. For example, he mixes red, yellow, and white powders together in a tumbler of water and swallows the mixture, making, of course, a wry face, as though taking a dose of bitter medicine. He then calls a boy from among the by-standers and blows first red powder, then yellow, then white into the youngster's face. I judge he had small bags of dry powder stowed away in his cheek. He performs his tricks on the bare ground, without any such invaluable adjunct as the table of his European rival, and some of them, viewed in the light of this disadvantage, are indeed puzzling. For instance, he fills an ordinary tin pot nearly full of water, puts in a handful of yellow sand and a handful of red powder, and thoroughly stirs them up; he then thrusts his naked hand into the water and brings forth a handful of each kind, dry as when he put them in. A simple enough trick, no doubt, to the initiated; but the old conjurer's arm is bared, and the tin is, as far as I can discover, but an ordinary vessel, and the trick is performed without any cover, table, or cloth. After this he expectorates a number of glass marbles, and ends with a couple of solid iron jingal balls that he can scarce get out of his mouth. There is no mistake about their being of solid iron, and the old conjurer opens his mouth and lets me see them emerging from his throat. From what I see him do as the final act, and which there is no deception about, I am inclined to think the old fellow has actually acquired the power of swallowing these jingal balls and reproducing them at pleasure.

After a number of tricks too familiar to justify mentioning here he covers his head with a cloth for a minute, and then reappears with brass eyeballs, with a small hole bored in the centre of each to represent the pupils; and his mouth is rendered hideous with a set of teeth belonging to some animal. In this horrible make-up the old Hindoo tom-toms on a small oblong drum, while one of his assistants sings in broken English "Buffalo Gals." He then openly removes the false teeth, and taking out the brass eyeballs, he casts them jingling on the gravel at my feet. They are simply hemispheres of sheet-brass, and fitted closely over the eyeballs, beneath the lids. The conjurer's eyes water visibly after the brass covers are removed; and well enough they might; there is no sleight-of-hand about this—it is purely an act of self-torture.

In most of the conjuring tricks the conjurer would purposely make a partial failure in the first attempt; an assistant would then impart the necessary power by muttering cabalistic words over a monkey's skull.

A mongoose had been tethered to a stake at the beginning of the performance, and the little ferret-like enemy of the snake family kept tugging at his tether and sniffing suspiciously about whenever snakes appeared in the conjurer's manipulations. He had promised me a fight between the mongoose and a snake, and before presenting his little brass bowl for backsheesh he holds out a four-foot snake toward the eager little animal at the stake. The snake writhes and struggles to get away, evidently badly scared at the prospect of an encounter with the mongoose; but the man succeeds in depositing him within his adversary's reach. The mongoose nabs him by the neck in an instant, and would no doubt soon have finished him; but the assistants part them with wire crooks, putting the snake in a basket with several others and the mongoose in another.

While watching the interesting performances of the Hindoo, conjurers I have left the bicycle at a little dak bungalow near the old entrance-gate. From the commanding height of the Kootub-one could see that the Delhi road is a solid mass of vehicles and pedestrians (how the people in teeming India do swarm on these festive occasions!). It looks impossible to make one's way with a bicycle against that winding stream of human beings, and so, after wandering about a while among the striking and peculiar colonnades of the ancient pagan temples, paying the regulation tribute of curiosity to the enigmatic iron column, and doing the place in general, I return to the bungalow, thinking of starting back to Delhi, when I find that my "cycle of strange experiences" has attracted to itself a no less interesting gathering than a troupe of Nautch girls and their chaperone. The troupe numbers about a dozen girls, and they have come to the merry-making at the Kootub to gather honest shekels by giving exhibitions of their terpsichorean talents in the Nautch dance.

I had been wondering whether an opportunity to see this famous dance would occur during my trip through India; and so when four or five of the prettiest of these dusky damsels gather about me, smile at me winsomely ogle me with their big black eyes, smile again, smile separately, smile unanimously, smile all over their semi-mahogany but nevertheless not unhandsome faces, and every time displaying sets of pearly teeth, what could I do, what could anyone have done, but smile in return?

There is no language more eloquent or more easily understood than the language of facial expression. No verbal question or answer is necessary. I interpret the winsome smiles of the Nautchnees aright, and they interpret very quickly the permission to go ahead that reveals itself in the smile they force from me. Eight of the twelve are commonplace girls of from fourteen to eighteen, and the other four are "dark but comely"—quite handsome, as handsomeness goes among the Hindoos. Their arms are bare of everything save an abundance of bracelets, and the upper portion of the body is rather scantily draped, after the manner and custom of all Hindoo females; but an ample skirt of red calico reaches to the ankle. Rings are worn on every toe, and massive silver anklets with tiny bells attached make music when they walk of dance. They wear a profusion of bracelets, necklaces of rupees, head-ornaments, ear-rings, and pendent charms, and a massive gold or brass ring in the left nostril. The nostril is relieved of its burden by a string that descends from a head-ornament and takes up the weight.

The Nautch girls arrange themselves into a half-circle, their scarlet costumes forming a bright crescent, terminating in a mass of spectators, whose half-naked bodies, varying in color from pale olive to mahogany, are arrayed in costumes scarcely less showy than the dancers. The chaperone and eight outside girls tom-tom an appropriate Nautch accompaniment on drums with their fingers, the four prettiest girls advance, and favoring me with sundry smiles, and coquettish glances from their bright black eyes, they commence to dance.

An idea seems to prevail in many Occidental minds that the Nautch dance is a very naughty thing; but nothing is further from the truth. Of course it can be made naughty, and no doubt often is; but then so can many another form of innocent amusement. The Nautch dance is a decorous and artistic performance when properly danced; the graceful motions and elegant proportions of the human form, as revealed by lithe and graceful dancers, are to be viewed with an eye as purely artistic and critical as that with which one regards a Venus or other production of the sculptor's studio.

The four dancers take the lower hem of their red garment daintily between the thumb and finger of the right hand, spreading its ample folds into the figure of an opened fan, by bringing the outstretched arm almost on a level with the shoulder. A mantle of transparent muslin, fringed with silver spangles, is worn about the head and shoulders in the same indescribably graceful manner as the mantilla of the Spanish senorita. Raising a portion of this aloft in the left hand, and keeping the "fan" intact with the right, the dancers twirl around and change positions with one another, their supple figures meanwhile assuming a variety of graceful motions and postures from time to time. Now they imitate the spiral movement of a serpent climbing around and upward on an imaginary pole; again they assume an attitude of gracefulness, their dusky countenances half hidden in seeming coquetry behind the muslin mantle, the large red fan waving gently to and fro, the feet unmoving, but the undulating motions of the body and the tremor of the limbs sufficing to jingle the tiny ankle-bells. On the whole, the Nautch dance would be disappointing to most people witnessing it; its fame leads one to expect more than it really amounts to.

Before starting back to Delhi, I take a stroll through the adjacent village of Kootub, a place named after the minar, I suppose. The crooked main street of the village of Kootub itself presents to-day a scene of gayety and confusion that beggars description. Bunting floats gayly from every window and balcony, in honor of the festival, and is strung across the street from house to house. Thousands of globular colored lanterns are hanging about, ready to be lighted up at night. The streets are thronged with people in the gayest of costumes, and with vehicles the gilt and paint and glitter of which equal the glittering wagons and chariots of a circus parade at home.

The balconies above the shops are curtained with blue gauze, behind which are seen numbers of ladies, chatting, eating fruits and sweetmeats, and peeping down through the semi-transparent screens upon the animated scene in the streets. On the stalls, choice edibles are piled up by the bushel, and busy venders are hawking fruits, sweets, toddy, and all imaginable refreshments about among the crowds. Vacant lots are occupied by the tents of visiting peasants, and in out-of-the-way corners acrobatics, jugglery, and Nautch-dancing attract curious crowds.

The incoming tide of human life is at its flood as I start back to Delhi by the same road I came. Here one gets a glimpse of the real gorgeousness of India without seeking for it at the pageants of princes and rajahs. Small zemindars from outlying villages are bringing their wives and daughters to the festivities at the Kootub in circusy-looking bullock-chariots covered with gilt and carvings, and draped and twined with parti-colored ribbons. Some of these gaudy turn-outs are drawn by richly caparisoned, milk-white oxen, with gilded horns. Cymbals and sleigh-bells galore keep up a merry jingle, and tom-toming parties make their noisy presence known all along the line.

Still more gorgeous and interesting than the gilded ox-gharries of the ordinary zemindars are miniature chariots drawn by pairs of well-matched, undersized oxen covered with richly spangled trappings, and with horns curiously gilded and tipped with tiny bells. These are the vehicles of petted young nabobs in charge of attendants: tiny oxen with gorgeous trappings, tiny chariots richly gilded and carved and painted, tiny occupants richly dressed and jewelled. Troupes of Nautchnees add their picturesque appearance to the brilliant throngs, and here and there is encountered a holy fakir, unkempt and unwashed, having, perchance, registered a vow years ago never more to apply water to his skin, his only clothing a dirty waist-cloth and the yellow clay plastered on his body. Long strings of less pretentious bullock-gharries almost block the roadway, and people constantly dodging out from behind them in front of my wheel make it extremely difficult to ride.

Several days are passed at Delhi, waiting the arrival of a small bicycle-camera from Calcutta, which has been forwarded from America. Most of this time is spent in the pleasant occupation of reclining in an arm-chair beneath the punkah, the only comfortable situation in Delhi at this season of the year. Nevertheless, I manage to spin around the city mornings and evenings, and visit the famous fort and palace of Shah Jehan.

In the magnificent—magnificent even in the decline of its grandeur — fort-palace of the Mogul Emperor named, British soldiers now find comfortable quarters. This fort, together with modern Delhi (the real Indian name of Delhi is Shahjehanabad, after the emperor Shah Jehan, who had it built), is but about two hundred and fifty years old, the entire affair having been built to gratify the Mogul ambition for founding new capitals.

Although so modern compared with other cities near by, both city and palace have gone through strangely stirring and tragic experiences, and events have happened in the latter that, although sometimes trivial in themselves, have led to momentous results.

In this palace, in 1716, was given permission, by the Emperor Furrokh Seeur, to the Scotch physician, Gabriel Hamilton, the privileges that have gradually led up to the British conquest of the whole peninsula. As a reward for professional services rendered, permission to establish factories on the Hooghly was given; the Presidency of Fort William sprung therefrom, and at length the British Indian Empire. Twenty years after this, the terrible Nadir Shah, from Persia, occupied the palace, and held high jinks within while his army slaughtered over a hundred thousand of the inhabitants in the streets. When this red-handed marauder took his departure he carried away with him booty to the value of eighty millions sterling in the value of that time. Among the plunder was the famous Peacock Throne, alone reputed to be worth six million pounds. This remarkable piece of kingly furniture is said to be in the possession of the Shah of Persia at the present time. It is very probable, however, that only some unique portion of the throne is preserved, as it could hardly have been carried back to Persia by Nadir intact. This throne is thus described by a writer: "The throne was six feet long and four broad, composed of solid gold inlaid with precious stones. It was surmounted by a canopy of gold, supported on twelve pillars of the same material. Around the canopy hung a fringe of pearls; on each side of the throne stood two chattahs, or umbrellas, symbols of royalty, formed of crimson velvet richly embroidered with gold thread and pearls, and with handles of solid gold, eight feet long, studded with diamonds. The back of the throne was a representation of the expanded tail of a peacock, the natural colors of which were imitated by sapphires, rubies, emeralds, and other gems." This Peacock Throne was the envy and admiration of every contemporary monarch who heard of it, and was undoubtedly one of the chief elements in exciting the cupidity of the outer world that finally ended in the dissolution of the Mogul Empire.

Less than ten years after the departure of Nadir Shah, Ahmud Khan advanced with an army from Cabool, and took pretty much everything of value that the Khorassani freebooter had overlooked, besides committing more atrocities upon the population. At the end of another decade an army of Mahrattas took possession, and completed the spoilation by ripping the silver filigree-work off the ceiling of the Throne-room. Not long after this, yet another adventurer took a hand in the work of destruction, tortured the members of the imperial family, and put out the eyes of the helpless old emperor, Shah Alum. Here Lord Lake's cavalcade arrived, too, in 1803, and found the blinded chief of the royal house of Timour and his magnificent successors, who built Delhi and Agra, seated beneath the tattered remnants of a little canopy, a mockery of royalty, with every external appearance of misery and helplessness And lastly, here, in May, 1857, the last representative of the great Moguls, a not unwilling tool in the hands of the East India Company's mutinous soldiery, presided over the butchery of helpless English women and children.

It is difficult to realize that Delhi has been the theatre of such a stirring and eventful history, as nowadays one strolls down the Chandni Chouk and notes the air of peace and contentment that pervades the whole city. It seems quite true, as Edwin Arnold says in his "India Revisited," that Derby is now not more contentedly British than is Delhi. Whatever may be the faults of British rule in India, no impartial critic can say that the people are not in better hands than they have ever been before. One of the most interesting objects in the city is the Jama Mesjid, the largest mosque in India, and the second-largest in all Islam, ranking next to St. Sophia at Constantinople. Broad flights of red sandstone steps lead up to handsome gateways surmounted by rows of small milk-white marble domes or cupolas. Inside is a large quadrangular court, paved with broad slabs of sandstone; occupying the centre of this is a white marble reservoir of water. The mosque proper is situated on the west side of the quadrangle, an oblong structure two hundred feet long by half that many in width, ornamented and embellished by Arabic inscriptions and three shapely white marble domes. Very elegant indeed is the pattern and composition of the floor, each square slab of white marble having a narrow black border running round it, like the border of a mourning envelope. Very charming, also, are the two graceful minarets at either end, one hundred and thirty feet high, alternate strips of white marble and red sandstone producing a very pretty and striking effect.

In the northeastern corner of the quadrangle is a small cabinet containing the inevitable relics of the Prophet. Three separate guides have accumulated at my heels since entering the gate, and now a fourth, ancient and hopeful, appears to unravel, for the Sahib's benefit, the mysteries of the little cabinet. Unlocking the door, he steps out of his slippers into the entrance, stooping beneath an iron rail that further bars the entrance.

From an inner receptacle he first produces some ancient manuscript, which he explains was written by the same scribes who copied the Koran for Mohammed's grandson. Putting these carefully away, the Ancient and Hopeful then unwraps, very mysteriously, a handkerchief, and reveals a small oblong tin box with a glass face. The casket contains what upon casual observation appears to be a piece of bark curling up at the edges; this, I am informed, however, is nothing less than the sole of one of Mohammed's sandals. Putting away this venerable relic of the great founder of Islam, the old Mussulman assumes a look of profound importance and mystery. One would think, from his expression and manners, that he was about to reveal to the sacrilegious gaze of an infidel nothing less than the Prophet's fifth rib or the parings from his pet corn. Instead of these he exhibits a flat piece of rock bearing marks resembling the shape of a man's foot—the imprint of Mohammed's foot, miraculously made. To one whose soulful gaze has been enraptured with an imprint of the first Sultan's hand on the wall of St. Sophia, and the mosaic figure of the Virgin Mary persistently refusing to be painted out of sight on the dome of the same mosque, this piece of rock would scarcely seem to justify the vast display of reverence that is evidently expected of all visitors by the Ancient and Hopeful.

But perhaps it is on account of the place of honor it occupies immediately preceding what is undoubtedly a very precious relic indeed, a relic that fills the worthy custodian with mystery and importance. Or, perchance, mystery and importance have been found, during his long and varied experience with the unsophisticated tourist, excellent things to increase the volume of importance attached to the exhibited articles, and the volume of "pice" in his exchequer. At any rate, the Ancient and Hopeful assumes more mystery and importance than ever as he uncovers a second tin casket with a glass front. Glued to the glass, inside, is a single coarse yellow hair about two inches long; the precious relic, which has a suspicious resemblance to a bristle, is considered the gem of the collection, being nothing less than a hair from the Prophet's venerable mustache. Mohammedans swear by the beard of the Prophet, just as good Christians swear by "the great horned spoon," or by "great Caesar's ghost," so that the possession of even this one poor little hair, surrounded as it is by a blue halo of suspicion as to its authenticity, sheds a ray of glory upon the great Jama Mesjid scarcely surpassed by its importance as the second-largest mosque in the world. The two-inch yellow hair is considered the piece de resistance of the collection, and the Ancient and Hopeful stows it away with all due reverence, strokes his henna-stained beard with the air of a man who has got successfully through a very important task, steps into his slippers, and presents himself for "pice."

Pice is duly administered to him and his three salaaming associates, when, lo! a fifth candidate mysteriously appears, also smiling and salaaming expectantly. Although I haven't had the pleasure of a previous acquaintance with this gentleman, the easiest way to escape gracefully from the sacred edifice is to backsheesh him along with the others. These backsheesh considerations are, of course, small and immaterial matters, and one ought to feel extremely grateful to all concerned for the happy privilege of feasting one's soul with ever so brief a contemplation of the things in the cabinet, and more especially on the bristle-like yellow hair. These joy-inspiring objects, ramshackled from the storehouse of the musty past, fulfil the double mission of keeping alive the reverence of devout Mussulmans who visit the mosque, and keeping the Ancient and Hopeful well supplied with goodakoo.

My camera having duly arrived, together with a package of letters, which are always doubly welcome to a wanderer in distant lands, I prepare to resume my southward journey. The few days' rest has enabled me to recover from the wilting effects of riding in the terrific heat, and I have seen something of one of the most interesting points in all Asia. Delhi is sometimes called the "Home of Asia," which, it seems to me, is a very appropriate name to give it.

Neatly clad and modest-looking females, native converts to Christianity, are walking in orderly procession to church, testaments in hand, as I wheel through the streets of Delhi on Sunday morning toward the Agra road. Very interesting is it to see these dusky daughters of heathendom arrayed in modest white muslin gowns, their lithe and graceful forms freed from the barbarous jewellery that distinguishes the persons of their unconverted sisters. Very charming do they look in their Christianized simplicity and self-contained demeanor as they walk quietly, and at a becoming Sabbath-day pace, two by two, down the Chandni Chouk. They present an instructive comparison to the straggling groups of heathen damsels who watch them curiously as they walk past and then proceed to chant idolatrous songs, apparently in a spirit of wanton raillery at the Christian maidens and their simple, un-ornamented attire. The fair heathens of Delhi have a sort of naughty, Parisian reputation throughout the surrounding country, and so there is nothing surprising in this exhibition of wanton hilarity directed at these more strait-laced converts to the religion of the Ferenghis. The heathen damsels, arrayed in very worldly costumes, consisting of flaring red, yellow, and blue garments, the whole barbaric and ostentatious array of nose-rings, ear-rings, armlets, anklets, rupee necklaces, and pendents, and the multifarious gewgaws of Hindoo womankind, look surpassingly wicked and saucy in comparison with their converted sisters. The gentle converts try hard to regard their heathen songs with indifference, and to show by their very correct deportment the superiority of meekness, virtue, and Christianity over gaudy clothes, vulgar silver jewellery, and heathenism. The whole scene reminds one very forcibly of a gang of wicked street-boys at home, poking fun at a Sunday-school procession or a platoon of Salvation Army soldiers parading the streets.

Past the Queen's Gardens and the fort, down a long street of native shops, and out of the Delhi gate I wheel, past the grim battlements of Firozabad, along a rather flinty road that extends for ten miles, after which commences again the splendid kunkah. Villages are numerous, and the country populous; tombs and the ruins of cities dot the landscape, pahnee-chowkees, where yellow Brahmans dispense water to thirsty wayfarers, line the road, and at one point three splendid, massive archways, marking some place that has lost its former importance, span my road.

Hindoos are now the prevailing race, and their religion finds frequent expression in idol temples and shrines beneath little roadside groves. The night is spent on the porch of a dak bungalow just outside the walls of Pullwal, a typical Hindoo city, with all its curious display of hideous idols, idolatrous paintings, and beautiful carved temples with gilded spires. The groves about the bungalow are literally swarming with green parrots; in big flocks they sweep past near my charpoy, producing a great wh-r-r-ring commotion with their wings. A flock of parrots may be so far aloft as to be well-nigh beyond the range of human vision in the ethery depths, but the noise of their wings will be plainly audible.

A two hours' terrific downpour delays me at the village of Hodell next day, and affords an opportunity to inspect an ordinary little Hindoo village temple. The captain of the police-thana sends a tall Sikh policeman to show me in. The temple is only a small tapering marble edifice about thirty feet high, surmounted by a gilded crescent, and resting on a hollow plinth, the hollow of which provides quarters for the priest. One is expected to remove his foot-gear before going inside, the same as in a Mohammedan mosque. A taper is burning in a niche of the wall; mural paintings of snakes, many-handed gods, bulls, monsters, and mythical deities create a cheap and garish impression. In the centre of the floor is a marble linga, and grouped around it a miniature man, woman, and elephant; before these are laid offerings of flowers. The interior of the temple is not more than eight feet square, a mere cell in which the deities are housed; the worshippers mostly perform their prostrations on the plinth outside. The villagers gather in a crowd about the temple and watch every movement of my brief inspection; they seem pleased at the sight of a Sahib honoring their religion by removing his shoes and carefully respecting their feelings. When I descend from the plinth they fall back and greet me with smiles and salaams.

The rain clears up and I forge ahead, finding the kunkah road-bed none the worse for the drenching it has just received. Hour by hour one gets more surprised at the multitudes of pedestrians on the road; neither rain nor sun seems to affect their number. Some of the costumes observed are quite startling in their ingenuity and effect. One garment much affected by the Rajput women are yellowish shawls or mantles, phool-karis, in which, are set numerous small circular mirrors about the circumference of a silver half-dollar; the effect of these in the bright Indian sun, as the wearer trudges along in the distance, is as though she were all ablaze with gems. Whenever I wheel past a group of Rajput females, they either stand with averted faces or cover up their heads with their shawls.

The road-inspector's bungalow at Chattee affords me shelter, and an intelligent native gentleman, who speaks a misleading quality of English, supplies me with a supper of curried rice and fowl. Hard by is a Hindoo temple, whence at sunset issue the sweetest chimes imaginable from a peal of silver-toned bells. My charpoy is placed on the porch facing the east, and soon the rotund face of the rising moon floats above the trees, and the silvery tinkle of the bells is followed by a chorus of jackals paying their noisy compliments to its loveliness. My slumbers can hardly be said to be unbroken to-night, three pariah dogs have taken a fancy to my quarters; two of them sit on their haunches and howl dismally in response to the jackals, while number three reclines sociably beneath my charpoy and growls at the others as though constituting himself my protector. Some Indian Romeo is serenading his dusky Juliet in the neighboring town; flocks of roystering parrots go whirring past at all hours of the night, and a too liberal indulgence in red-hot curry keeps me on the verge of a nightmare almost till the silvery tinkle-tinkle of the Brahman bells announces the break of day.

Cynics have sometimes denounced Christians as worse than the heathens, in requiring loud church-bells to summon them to worship. Such, it appears, are putting the case rather thoughtlessly. Mohammedans have their muezzins, while both Christians and idolaters have their chiming bells. Neither Christians, nor Mohammedans, nor heathens need these agencies to summon them to their respective worldly enjoyments, so that, taken all in all, we are pretty much alike—cynics, notwithstanding, to the contrary, we are little or no worse than the heathens.

A loudly wailing woman with her head covered up, and supported between two companions who are vainly trying to console her, and a party conveying two cassowaries, a pair of white peacocks, and a kangaroo from Calcutta to some rajah's menagerie up country, are among the curiosities encountered on the road the following day. Spending the afternoon and night in the quarters of the Third Dragoon Guards at Muttra Cantonment, I resume my journey early in the morning, dodging from shelter to shelter to avoid frequent heavy showers.

It is but thirty-five miles from Muttra to Agra, and notwithstanding showers and heat, the distance is covered by half-past ten. Wheeling at this pace, however, is an indiscretion, and the completion of the stretch is signalized by a determination to seek shade and quiet for the remainder of the day. Once again the sociable officers of the garrison tender me the hospitality of their quarters, and the ensuing day is spent in visiting that wonder of the world, the Taj Mahal, Akbar's fort, and other wonderful monuments of the palmy days of the Mogul Empire.

Finer and more imposing in appearance even than the fort at Delhi, is that at Agra. Walls of red sandstone, seventy feet high, and a mile and a half in circuit, picturesquely crenellated, and with imposing gateways and a deep, broad moat, complete a work of stupendous dimensions. One is overcome with a sense of grandeur upon first beholding these Indian palace-forts, after seeing nothing more imposing than mud walls in Persia and Afghanistan; they are magnificent looking structures. The contrast, too, of the red sandstone walls and gates and ramparts, with the white marble buildings of the royal quarters, is very striking. The domes of the latter, seen at a distance, seem like snow-white bubbles resting ever so lightly and airily upon the darker mass; one almost expects to see them rise up and float away on the passing zephyrs like balloons.

Passing inside over a drawbridge and through the massive Delhi Gate, we proceed into the interior of the fort, traversing a broad ascent of sandstone pavement. Everything around us shows evidence of unstinted outlay in design, execution, and completion of detail in the carrying out of a stupendous undertaking. Everywhere the spirit of Akbar the Magnificent seems to hover amid his creations. One emerges from the covered gateway and the walled corrugated causeway, upon the parade ground. Crenellated walls, a park of artillery, and roomy English barracks greet the vision.

Sentinels—Sepoy sentinels in huge turbans, and English sentinels in white sun-helmets—are pacing their beats. But not on these does the gaze of the visitor rest. Straight ahead of him there rises, above the red sandstone walls and the bare parade ground, three marble domes, white as newly-fallen snow, and just beyond are seen the gilt pinnacles of Akbar's palace.

We wander among the beautiful marble creations, gaze in wonder at the snowy domes supported on marble pillars, mosaiced with jasper, agate, blood-stone, lapis-lazuli, and other rare stones. We stand on the white marble balustrades, carved so exquisitely as to resemble lace-work, and we look out upon the yellow waters of the Jumna, flowing sluggishly along seventy feet below. Here is where the Grand Mogul, Akbar, used to sit and watch elephant fights and boat races. There are none of these to be seen now; but that does not mean that the prospect is either tame or uninteresting. The banks of the Jumna are alive with hundreds of dusky natives engaged in washing clothes and spreading linen out in the sun to bleach. The prospect beyond is a revelation of vegetable luxuriance and wealth, and of historical reminiscence in the shape of ruins and tombs.

One's eyes, however, are drawn away from the contemplation of the picturesque life below, and from the prospect of grove and garden and crumbling tombs, by the mesmerism, of the crowning glory of all Indian architectural triumphs, the famous Taj. This matchless mausoleum rests on the right-hand bank of the Jumna, about a mile down stream. The Taj, with its marvellous beauty and snowy whiteness, seems to cast a spell over the beholder, from the first; one can no more keep his eyes off it, when it is within one's range of vision, than he can keep from breathing. It draws one's attention to itself as irresistibly as though its magnetism were a living and breathing force exerted directly to that end. It is the subtlety of its unapproachable loveliness, commanding homage from all beholders, whether they will or no.

We turn away from it awhile, however, and find ample scope for admiration close at hand. We tread the marble aisles of the Pearl Mosque, considered the most perfect gem of its kind in existence. One stands in its court-yard and finds himself in the chaste and exclusive companionship of snowy marble and blue sky. One feels almost ill at ease, as though conscious of being an imperfect thing, marring perfection by his presence. "Quiet as a nun, breathless with adoration," one enthusiastic visitor exclaims, in an effort to put his sentiments and impressions of the Moti Mesjid into words. Like this adoring traveller, the average visitor will rest content to be carried away by the contemplation of its chaste beauty, without prying around for possible defects in the details of the particular school of architecture it graces. He will have little patience with carping critics who point to the beautiful screens, of floriated marble tracery, and say: "Nuns should not wear collars of point lace."

From the Moti Mesjid, we visit the Shish Mahal, or mirrored bathrooms. The chambers and passages here remind me of the mirrored rooms of Persia; here, as there, thousands of tiny mirrors are used in working out various intricate designs. My three uniformed companions at once reflect not less than half a regiment of British soldiers therein.

From the fort we drive in a native gharri to the Taj, a mile-drive through suburban scenery, plantain-gardens, groves, and ruins. In approaching the garden of the Taj, one passes through a bazaar, where the skilful Hindoo artisans are busy making beautiful inlaid tables, inkstands, plates, and similar fancies, as well as models of the Taj, out of white Jeypore marble. These are the hereditary descendants and successors of the men who in the palmy days of the Mogul power spent their lives in decorating the royal palaces and tombs with mosaics and tracery. Nowadays their skill is expended on mere articles of virtue, to be sold to European tourists and English officers. Some of them are occasionally employed by the Indian Government to repair the work desecrated by vandals during the mutiny, and under the purely commercial government of the East India Company. One curious phase of this work is, that the men employed to replace with imitations the original stones that have been stolen receive several times higher pay than the men in Akbar's time, who did such splendid work that it is not to be approached, these days. Several months' imprisonment is now the penalty of prying out stones from the mosaic-work of the Taj.

This lovely structure has been described so often by travellers that one can scarce venture upon a description without seeming to repeat what has already been said by others. One of the best descriptions of its situation and surroundings is given by Bayard Taylor. He says: "The Taj stands on the bank of the Jumna, rather more than a mile to the eastward of the Fort of Agra. It is approached by a handsome road cut through the mounds left by the ruins of ancient palaces. It stands in a large garden, inclosed by a lofty wall of red sandstone, with arched galleries around the interior, and entered by a superb gateway of sandstone, inlaid with ornaments and inscriptions from the Koran in white marble. Outside this grand portal, however, is a spacious quadrangle of solid masonry, with an elegant structure, intended as a caravanserai, on the opposite side. Whatever may be the visitor's impatience, he cannot help pausing to notice the fine proportions of these structures, and the massive style of their construction. Passing under the open demi-vault, whose arch hangs high above you, an avenue of dark Italian cypress appears before you. Down its centre sparkles a long row of fountains, each casting up a single slender jet. On both sides, the palm, the banyan, and feathery bamboo mingle their foliage; the song of birds meets your ears, and the odor of roses and lemon-flowers sweetens the air. Down such a vista, and over such a foreground, rises the Taj."

Of the Taj itself, fault has been found with its proportions by severe critics, like the party who regards the Moti Mesjid "nun" as faulty because she wears a point-lace collar; but the ordinary visitor will find room for nothing but admiration and wonder. It is hard to believe that there is any defect, even in its proportions, for so perfect do these latter appear, that one is astonished to learn that it is a taller building than the Kootub Minar. One would never guess it to be anywhere near so tall as 243 feet. The building rests on a plinth of white marble, eighteen feet high and a hundred yards square. At each corner of the plinth stands a minaret, also of white marble, and 137 feet high. The mausoleum itself occupies the central space, measuring in depth and width 186 feet. The entire affair is of white Jeypore marble, resting upon a lower platform of sandstone: "A thing of perfect beauty and of absolute finish in every detail, it might pass for the work of a genii, who knew naught of the weaknesses and ills with which mankind are beset. It is not a great national temple erected by a free and united people, it owes its creation to the whim of an absolute ruler who was free to squander the resources of the State in commemorating his personal sorrows or his vanity."

Another distinguished visitor, commenting on the criticisms of those who profess to have discovered defects, says: "The Taj is like a lovely woman; abuse her as you please, but the moment you come into her presence, you submit to its fascination."

"If to her share some female errors fall, Look in her face, and you'll forget them all."

Passing beneath the vaulted gateway, we find a sign-board, telling that the best place from which to view the Taj is from the roof of the gateway. A flight of steps leads us to the designated vantage-point, when the tropic garden, the fountains, the twin mosques in the far corners, the river, the minarets, and, above all, the Taj itself lay spread out before us for our inspection. The scene might well conjure up a vision of Paradise itself. The glorious Taj: "So light it seems, so airy, and so like a fabric of mist and moonbeams, with its great dome soaring up, a silvery bubble," that it is difficult, even at a few hundred yards' distance, to believe it a creation of human hands. While gazing on the Taj, men let their cigars go out, and ladies drop their fans without noticing it.

Descending the steps again, we pass inside, and again pause to survey it from the end of the avenue. An element of the ridiculous here appears in the person and the appeals of an old Hindoo fruit-vender. This hopeful agent of Pomona squats beside a little tray, and, as we stand and feast our eyes on the sublimest object in the world of architecture, he persistently calls our attention to a dozen or two half-decayed mangoes and custard-apples that comprise his stock in trade.

We pass down the cypress aisle, and invade the plinth. Hundreds of natives, both male and female, are wandering about it. The dazzling whiteness of the promenade is in striking contrast to the color of their own bodies. As the groups of women walk about, their toe-rings and ankle-ornaments jingle against the marble, and their particolored raiment and barbarous gewgaws look curiously out of place here. The place seems more appropriate to vestal virgins, robed in white, than to dusky Hindoo females, arrayed in all the colors of the rainbow. Many of these people are pilgrims who have come hundreds of miles to see the Taj, and to pay tribute to the memory of Shah Jehan, and his faithful wife the Princess Arjumund, whose mausoleum is the Taj. Two young men we see, leading an aged female, probably their mother, down the steps to the vault, where, side by side, the remains of this royal pair repose. The old lady is going down there to deposit a rose or two upon Arjumund's tomb, a tender tribute paid to-day, by thousands, to her memory.

We climb the spiral stairs of one of the miuars, and sit out on the little pavilion at the top, watching the big ugly crocodiles float lazily on the surface of the Jumna at our feet. Before departing, we enter the Taj and examine the wonderful mosaics on the cenotaphs and the encircling screen-work. This inlaid flower-work is quite in keeping with the general magnificence of the mausoleum, many of the flowers containing not less than twenty-five different stones, assorted shades of agate, carnelian, jasper, blood-stone, lapis lazuli, and turquoise. Ere leaving we put to test the celebrated echo; that beautiful echoing, that—"floats and soars overhead in a long, delicious undulation, fading away so slowly that you hear it after it is silent, as you see, or seem to see, a lark you have been watching, after it is swallowed up in the blue vault of heaven."

We leave this garden of enchantment by way of one of the mosques. An Indian boy is licking up honey from the floor of the holy edifice with his tongue. We look up and perceive that enough rich honey-comb to fill a bushel measure is suspended on one of the beams, and so richly laden is it that the honey steadily drips down. The sanctity of the place, I suppose, prevents the people molesting the swarm of wild bees that have selected it for their storehouse, or from relieving them of their honey.

The Taj is said to have cost about two million pounds, even though most of the labor was performed without pay, other than rations of grain to keep the workmen from starving. Twenty thousand men were employed upon it for twenty-two years, and for its inlaid work "gems and precious stones came in camel-loads from various countries."

The next morning I bid farewell to Agra, more than satisfied with my visit to the Taj. It stands unique and distinct from anything else one sees the whole world round. Nothing one could say about it can give the satisfaction derived from a visit, and no word-painting can do it justice.

CHAPTER XVI

FROM AGRA TO SINGAPORE

A couple of miles from the cantonment, and the broad Jumna is crossed on a pontoon bridge, the buoys of which are tubular iron floats instead of boats. Crocodiles are observed floating, motionless as logs, their heads turned up-stream and their snouts protruding from the water. The road is undulating for a few miles and then perfectly level, as, indeed, it has been most of the way from Lahore.

Pilgrims carrying little red flags, and sometimes bits of red paper tied to sticks, are encountered by the hundred; mayhap they have come from distant points to gaze upon the beauties of the Taj Mahal, the fame of which resounds to the farthermost corners of India. They can now see it across the Jumna, resting on the opposite bank, looking more like a specimen of the architecture of the skies than anything produced by mere earthly agency.

A partly dilapidated Mohammedan mosque in the middle of a forty-acre walled reservoir, overgrown with water-lilies, forms a charming subject for the attention of my camera. The mosque is approached from an adjacent village by a viaduct of twenty arches; a propos of its peculiar surroundings, one might easily fancy the muezzin's call to prayer taking the appropriate form of, "Come where the water-lilies bloom," instead of the orthodox, "Allah-il-allah."

Villages are now rows of shops lining the road on either side, sometimes as much as half a mile in length. The entrance is usually marked by a shrine containing a hideous idol, painted red and finished off with cheap-looking patches of gold or silver tinsel. In the larger towns, evidences of English philanthropy loom conspicuously above the hut-like shops and inferior houses of the natives in the form of large and substantial brick buildings, prominently labelled "Ferozabad Hospital" or "Government Free Dispensary." A discouraging head-wind blows steadily all day, and it is near sunset when the thirty-seven miles to Sbikarabad is covered. A mile west of the town, I am told, is the Rohilcund Railway, the dak bungalow, and the bungalow of an English Sahib. Quite suitable for a one-mile race-track as regards surface is this little side-stretch, and a spin along its smooth length is rewarded by a most comfortable night at the bungalow of Mr. S, an engineer of the Ganges Canal, a magnificent irrigating enterprise, on the banks of which his bungalow stands. Several school-boys from Allahabad are here spending their vacation, shooting peafowls and fishing. Wild boars abound in the tall tiger-grass of the Shikobabad district and the silence of the gloaming is broken by the shouting of natives driving them out of their cane-patches, where, if not looked after pretty sharply, they do considerable damage in the night.

A curious illustration of native vanity and love of fame is pointed out here in the case of a wealthy gentleman who has spent some thousands of rupees in making and maintaining a beautiful flower-garden in the midst of a worthless piece of sandy land, close by the railway station. Close by is an abundance of excellent ground, where his garden might have been easily and inexpensively maintained. Asked the reason for this strange preference and seemingly foolish choice, he replied: "When people see this beautiful garden in the midst of the barren sand, they will ask, 'Whose garden is this?' and thus will my name become known among men. If, on the other hand, it were planted on good soil, nobody would see anything extraordinary in it, and nobody would trouble themselves to ask to whom it belongs."

Youthful Davids, perched on frail platforms that rise above the sugar-cane, indigo, or cotton crops, shout and wield slings with dexterous aim and vigor, to keep away vagrant crows, parrots, and wild pigs, all along the line of my next day's ride to Mainpuri. In many fields these young slingers and their platforms are but a couple of hundred yards apart, the range of their weapons covering the entire crop-area around. Sometimes I endeavor to secure one of these excellent subjects for my camera, but the youngsters invariably clamber down from their perch at seeing me dismount, and become invisible among the thick cane.

To the music of loud, rolling thunder, I speed swiftly over the last few miles, and dash beneath the porch of the post-office just in the nick of time to escape a tremendous downpour of rain. How it pours, sometimes, in India, converting the roads into streams and the surrounding country into a shallow lake in the space of a few minutes. Hundreds of youths, naked save for the redeeming breech-cloth, disport themselves in the great warm shower-bath, chasing one another sportively about and enjoying the downpour immensely.

The rain ceases, and, with water flinging from my wheel, I seek the civil lines and the dak bungalow three miles farther down the road. Very good meals are dished up by the chowkee-dar at this bungalow, who seems an intelligent and enterprising fellow; but the lean and slippered punkah-wallah is a far less satisfactory part of the accommodation. Twice during the night the punkah ceases to wave and the demon of prickly heat instantly wakes me up; and both times do I have to turn out and arouse him from the infolding arms of Morpheus. On the second occasion the old fellow actually growls at being disturbed. He is wide-awake and obsequious enough, however, at backsheesh-time in the morning.

The clock at the little English station-church chimes the hour of six as I resume my journey next morning along a glorious avenue of overarching shade-trees to Bhogan, where my road, which from Delhi has been a branch road, again merges into the Grand Trunk. Groves of tall toddy-palms are a distinguishing feature of Bhogan, and a very pretty little Hindoo temple marks the southern extremity of the town. A striking red and gilt shrine in a secluded grove of peepuls arrests my attention a few miles out of town, and, repairing thither, my rude intrusion fills with silent surprise a company of gentle Brahman youths and maidens paying their matutinal respects to the representation of Kamadeva, the Hindoo cupid and god of love. They seem overwhelmed with embarrassment at the appearance of a Sahib, but they say nothing. I explain that my object is merely a "tomasha" of the exquisitely carved shrine, and a young Brahman, with his smooth, handsome face fantastically streaked with yellow, follows silently behind as I walk around the building. His object is evidently to satisfy himself that nothing is touched by my unhallowed Christian hands.

Seven miles from Bhogan is the camping ground of Bheyo, where in December, 1869, an English soldier was assassinated in the night while standing sentry beneath a tree. His grave, beneath the gnarled mango where he fell, is marked by two wooden crosses, and the tree-trunk is all covered with memorial plates nailed there, from time to time, by the various troops who have camped here on their winter marches.

Twenty-eight miles are duly reeled off when, just outside a village, I seek the shade of a magnificent banyan. The kindly villagers, unaccustomed to seeing a Sahib without someone attending to his comfort, bring me a charpoy to recline on, and they inquire anxiously, "roti? pahni? doctor." (am I hungry, thirsty, or ill?). Nor are these people actuated by mercenary thoughts, for not a pice will they accept on my departure. "Nay, Sahib, nay," they reply, eagerly, smiling and shaking their heads, "pice, nay." The narrow-gauge Rohilcuud Railway now follows along the Grand Trunk road, being built on one edge of the broad road-bed. Miran Serai, a station on this road, is my destination for the day; there, however, no friendly dak bungalow awaits my coming and no hostelry of any kind is to be found.

The native station-master advises me to go to the superintendent of police across the way; the police-officer, in turn, suggests applying to the station-master. The police-thana here is a large establishment, and a number of petty prisoners are occupying railed-off enclosures beneath the arched entrance. They accost me through the bars of their temporary, cage-like prison with smiles, and "Sahib" spoken in coaxing tones, as though moved by the childish hope that I might perchance take pity on them and order the police to set them at liberty.

A small and pardonable display of "bounce" at the railway station finally secures me the quarters reserved for the accommodation of English officers of the road, and a Mohammedan employe about the station procures me a supply of curried rice and meat. The station-master himself is a high-caste Hindoo and can speak English; he politely explains the difficulty of his position, as an extra-holy person, in being unable to personally attend to the wants of a Sahib. Upon discovering that I have taken up my quarters in the station, the police-superintendent comes over and begs permission to send over my supper, as he is evidently anxious to cultivate my good opinion, or, at all events, to make sure of giving no offence in failing to accommodate me with sleeping quarters at the thana. He supplements the efforts of the Mohammedan employe, by sending over a dish of sweetened chuppaties.

On the street leading out of Miran Serai is a very handsome and elaborately ornamented temple. Passing by early in the morning, I pay it a brief, unceremonious visit of inspection, kneeling on the steps and thrusting my helmeted head in to look about, not caring to go to the trouble of removing my shoes. Inside is an ancient Brahman, engaged in sweeping out the floral offerings of the previous day; he favors me with the first indignant glance I have yet received in India. When I have satisfied my curiosity and withdrawn from the door-way, he comes out himself and shuts the beautifully chased brazen door with quite an angry slam. The day previous was the anniversary of Krishna's birth, and the blood of sacrificial goats and bullocks is smeared profusely about the altar. It is, probably, the enormity of an unhallowed unbeliever in one god, thrusting his infidel head inside the temple at this unseemly hour of the morning, while the blood of the mighty Krishna's sacrificial victims is scarcely dry on the walls, that arouses the righteous wrath of the old heathen priest—as well, indeed, it might.

Passing through a village abounding in toddy-palms, I avail myself of an opportunity to investigate the merits of a beverage that I have been somewhat curious about since reaching India, having heard it spoken of so often. The famous "palm-wine" is merely the sap of the toddy-palm, collected much as is the sap from the maple-sugar groves of America, although the palm-juice is generally, if not always, obtained from the upper part of the trunk. When fresh, its taste resembles sweetened water; in a day or two fermentation sets in, and it changes to a beverage that, except for slightly alcoholic properties, might readily be mistaken for vinegar and water.

Every little village or hamlet one passes through, south of Agra, seems laudably determined to own a god of some sort; those whose finances fail to justify them in sporting a nice, red-painted god with gilt trimmings, sometimes console themselves with a humble little two-dollar soapstone deity that looks as if he has been rudely chipped into shape by some unskilful prentice hand. God-making is a highly respectable and lucrative profession in India, but only those able to afford it can expect the luxury of a nice painted and varnished deity right to their hand every day. People cannot expect a first-class deity for a couple of rupees; although the best of everything is generally understood to be the cheapest in the end, it takes money to buy marble, red paint, and gold-leaf. A bowl of pulse porridge, sweet and gluey, is prepared and served up in a big banyan-leaf at noon by a villager. In the same village is one of those very old and shrivelled men peculiar to India. From appearances, he must be nearly a hundred years old; his skin resembles the epidermis of a mummy, and hangs in wrinkles about his attenuated frame. He spends most of his time smoking goodakoo from a neat little cocoa-nut hookah.

The evening hour brings me into Cawnpore, down a fine broad street divided in the centre by a canal, with flights of stone steps for banks and a double row of trees—a street far broader and finer than the Chandni Chouk—and into an hotel kept by a Parsee gentleman named Byramjee. Life at this hostelry is made of more than passing interest by the familiar manner in which frogs, lizards, and birds invade the privacy of one's apartments. Not one of these is harmful, but one naturally grows curious about whether a cobra or some other less desirable member of the reptile world is not likely at any time to join their interesting company. The lizards scale the walls and ceiling in search of flies, frogs hop sociably about the floor, and a sparrow now and then twitters in and out.

A two weeks' drought has filled the farmers of the Cawnpore district with grave apprehensions concerning their crops; but enough rain falls tonight to gladden all their hearts, and also to leak badly through the roof of my bedroom.

My punkah-wallah here is a regular automaton—he has acquired the valuable accomplishment of pulling the punkah-string back and forth in his sleep; he keeps it up some time after I have quitted the room in the morning, until a comrade comes round and wakes him up.

For three days the rains continue almost without interruption, raining as much as seven inches in one night. Slight breaks occur in the downpour, during which it is possible to get about and take a look at the Memorial Gardens and the native town. The Memorial Gardens and the well enclosed therein commemorate one of the most pathetic incidents of the mutiny—

the brutal massacre by Nana Sahib of about two hundred English women and children. This arch-fiend held supreme sway over Cawnpore from June 6, 1857, till July 15th, and in that brief period committed some of the most atrocious deeds of treachery and deviltry that have ever been, recorded. Backed by a horde of blood-thirsty mutineers, he committed deeds the memory of which causes tears of pity for his victims to come unbidden into the eyes of the English tourist thirty years after. Delicate ladies, who from infancy had been the recipients of tender care and consideration, were herded together in stifling rooms with the thermometer at 120 deg. in the shade, marched through the broiling sun for miles, subjected to heart-rending privations, and at length finally butchered, together with their helpless children. After the treacherous massacre of the few surviving Englishmen at the Suttee Chowra Ghaut, the remaining women and children were reserved for further cruelties, and the final act of Nana's fiendish vengeance. From the graphic account of this murderous period of Cawnpore's history contained in the "Tourists' Guide to Cawnpore" is quoted the following brief account of Nana's consummate deed of devilment.

But the Nana's reign of terror was now drawing to a close, though not to terminate without a stroke destined to make the civilized world shudder from end to end. He was now to put the finishing touch to his work of mischief. The councils of the wicked were being troubled. Danger was on its way. Stories were brought in by scouting Sepoys of terrible bronzed men coming up the Grand Trunk Road, before whose advance the rebel hosts were fleeing like chaff and dust before the fan of the threshing-floor, Futtehpore had fallen, and disaster had overtaken the rebel forces at Aoung. Reinforcements were despatched by Nana in rapid succession, but all was of no avail—on came Havelock and his handful of heroes, carrying everything before them in their determination to rescue the hapless women and children imprisoned at Cawnpore. About noon on July 15th a few troopers came in from the south and informed Nana that his last reinforcement had met the same fate as the others, and reported that the English were coming up the road like mad horses, caring for neither cannon nor musketry; nor did these appear to have any effect on them. The guilty Nana, with the blood of the recent treacherous massacre on his hands, grew desperate at the hopelessness of the situation, and called a council of war. What plans could they devise to keep out the English? what steps could they adopt to stay their advance. The conclusion arrived at in that council of human tigers could have found expression nowhere save in the brains of Asiatics, illogical, and diabolically cruel. "We will destroy the maims and baba logues," they said, "and inform the English force of it; they will then be disheartened, and go back, for they are only a handful in number!"

How the unfortunate innocents were butchered in cold blood in the beebeegurch where they were confined, by Sepoys who gloried in trying their skill at severing the ladies' heads from their bodies at one cut, in splitting little children in twain, and in smearing themselves with the blood of their helpless victims, is too harrowing a tale to dwell upon here. On the following morning "the mangled bodies of both dead and dying" were cast into the well over which now hovers the marble representation of the Pitying Angel. When the victorious relieving force scattered Nana's remaining forces and entered the city, two days later, instead of the living forms of those they had made such heroic efforts to save, they looked down the well and saw their ghastly remains.

In this lovely garden, where all is now so calm and peaceful, scarcely does it seem possible that beneath the marble figure of this Pitying Angel repose the dust of two hundred of England's gentle martyrs, whose murdered and mutilated forms, but thirty years ago, choked up the well into which they were tossed. While I stand and read the sorrowful inscription it rains a gentle, soft, unpattering shower. Are these gentle droppings the tender tribute of angels' tears. I wonder, and does it always rain so soft and noiselessly here as it does to-day?

No natives are permitted in this garden without special permission; and an English soldier keeps sentinel at the entrance-gate instead of the Sepoy usually found on such duty. The memory of this tragedy seems to hang over Cawnpore like a cloud even to this day, and to cause a feeling of bitterness in the minds of Englishmen, who everywhere else regard the natives about them with no other feelings than of the kindliest possible nature. Other monuments of the mutiny exist, notably the Memorial Church, a splendid Lombard-Gothic structure erected in memoriam of those who fell in the mutiny here. The church is full of tablets commemorating the death of distinguished people, and the stained-glass windows are covered with the names of the victims of Nana Sahib's treachery, and of those who fell in action.

Cawnpore is celebrated for the number and extensiveness of its manufactures, and might almost be called the Manchester of India; woollen, cotton, and jute mills abound, leather factories, and various kindred industries, giving employment to millions of capital and thousands of hands.

A stroll through the native quarter of any Indian city is interesting, and Cawnpore is no exception. One sees buildings and courts the decorations and general appearance of which leave the beholder in doubt as to whether they are theatre or temple. Music and tom-toming would seem rather to suggest the former, but upon entering one sees fakirs and Hindoo devotees, streaked with clay, fanciful paintings and hideous idols, and all the cheap pomp and pageantry of idolatrous worship. Strolling into one of these places, an attendant, noting my curious gazing, presents himself and points to a sign-board containing characters as meaningless to me as Aztec hieroglyphics.

In one narrow street a crowd of young men are struggling violently for position about a door, where an old man is flinging handfuls of yellow powder among the crowd. The struggling men are aspirants for the honor of having a portion of the powder alight on their persons. I inquire of a native by-stander what it all means; the explanation is politely given, but being in the vernacular of the country, it is wasted on the unprofitable soil of my own lingual ignorance.

Impatient to be getting along, I misinterpret a gleam of illusory sunshine at noon on the third day of the rain-storm and pull out, taking a cursory glance at the Memorial Church as I go. A drenching shower overtakes me in the native military lines, compelling me to seek shelter for an hour beneath the portico of their barracks. The road is perfectly level and smooth, and well rounded, so that the water drains off and leaves it better wheeling than ever; and with alternate showers and sunshine I have no difficulty in covering thirty-four miles before sunset. This brings me to a caravanserai, consisting of a quadrangular enclosure with long rows of cell-like rooms. The whole structure is much inferior to a Persian caravanserai, but there is probably no need of the big brick structures of Shah Abbas in a winterless country like India.

Interesting subjects are not wanting for my camera through the day; but the greatest difficulty is experienced about changing the negatives at night. A small lantern with a very feeble light, made still more feeble by interposing red paper, suffices for my own purpose; but the too attentive chowkee-dar, observing that my room is in darkness, and fancying that my light has gone out accidentally, comes flaring in with a torch, threatening the sensitive negatives with destruction.

The morning opens with a fine drizzle or extra-heavy mist that is penetrating and miserable, soaking freely into one's clothes, and threatening every minute to change into a regular rain. It is fourteen miles to Futtehpore, and thence two miles off the straight road to the railway-station, where I understand refreshments are to be obtained. The reward of my four-mile detour is a cup of sloppy tea and a few weevil-burrowed biscuits, as the best the refreshment-room can produce on short notice. The dense mist moves across the country in big banks, between which are patches of comparatively decent atmosphere. The country is perfectly flat, devoted chiefly to the cultivation of rice, and the depressions alongside the road are, of course, filled with water.

Timid youngsters, fleeing from the road at my approach, in their scrambling haste sometimes tumble "head-over-heels" in the water; but, beyond a little extra terror lest the dreadful object they see coming bowling along should overtake them, it doesn't matter—they haven't any clothes to spoil or soil. Neither rain nor heat nor dense, reeking, foggy atmosphere seems to diminish the swarms of people on the road, nor the groups bathing or washing clothes beneath the trees. Some of these latter make a very interesting picture. The reader has doubtless visited the Zoo and observed one monkey gravely absorbed in a "phrenological examination" of another's head. With equal gravity and indifference to the world at large, dusky humans are performing a similar office for one another beneath the roadside shade-trees.

Roasted ears of maize and a small muskmelon form my noontide repast, and during its consumption quite a comedy is enacted down the street between a fat, paunchy vender of goodakoo and the shiny-skinned proprietor of a dhal-shop. The scene opens with a wordy controversy about something; scene two shows the fat goodakoo merchant advanced midway between his own and his adversary's premises, capering about, gesticulating, and uttering dire threats; scene three finds him retreating and the valorous man of dhal held in check by his wife to prevent him following after with hostile intent. The men seem boiling over with rage and ready to chew each other up; but, judging from the supreme indifference of everybody else about, nobody expects anything serious, to happen. This is mentionable as being the first quarrel I have seen in India; as a general thing the people are gentleness personified.

Several tattooed Hindoo devotees are observed this afternoon paying solemn devotions to bel-trees streaked with red paint, near the road. Many of the trees also shelter rude earthenware animals, and hemispherical vessels, which are also objects of worship, as representing the linga. The bel-tree is sacred to Siva the Destroyer, and the third person in the Hindoo Triad, whom Brahma himself is said to have worshipped, although he is regarded as the Creator. In the absence of Siva himself, the worship of the bel-tree is supposed to be as efficacious as worshipping the idol direct.

Soon I overtake an individual doing penance for his sins by crawling on his stomach all the way to Benares, the Mecca of the Hindoo religion. In addition to crawling, he is dragging a truck containing his personal effects by a rope tied about his waist. Every fifty yards or so he stands up and stretches himself; then he lies prostrate again and worms his wearisome way along the road like a snake. Benares is still about a hundred miles distant, and not unlikely this determined devotee has already been crawling in this manner for weeks. This painful sort of penance was formerly indulged in by Hindoo fanatics very largely; but the English Government has now all but abolished the practice by mild methods of discouragement. The priests of the different idols in Benares annually send out thousands of missionaries to travel throughout the length and breadth of India to persuade people to make pilgrimages to that city. Each missionary proclaims the great benefits to be derived by going to worship the particular idol he represents; in this manner are the priests enriched by the offerings presented. Not long since one of these zealous pilgrim-hunters persuaded a wealthy rajah into journeying five hundred miles in the same manner as the poor wretch passed on the road to-day. The infatuated rajah completed the task, after months of torture, on all-fours, accompanied the whole distance by a crowd of servants and priests, all living on his bounty.

Many people now wear wooden sandals held on the feet by a spool-like attachment, gripped between the big and second toes. Having no straps, the solid sole of the sandal flaps up and mildly bastinadoes the wearer every step that is taken.

Another night in a caravanserai, where rival proprietors of rows of little chowkees contend for the privilege of supplying me char-poy, dood, and chowel, and where thousands of cawing rooks blacken the trees and alight in the quadrangular serai in noisy crowds, and I enter upon the homestretch to Allahabad.

In proof that the cycle is making its way in India it may be mentioned that at both Cawnpore and Allahabad the native postmen are mounted on strong, heavy bicycles, made and supplied from the post-office workshops at Allighur. They are rude machines, only a slight improvement upon the honored boneshaker; but their introduction is suggestive of what may be looked for in the future. As evidence, also, of the oft-repeated saying that "the world is small," I here have the good fortune to meet Mr. Wingrave, a wheelman whom I met at the Barnes Common tricycle parade when passing through London.

There is even a small cycle club in quasi existence at Allahabad; but it is afflicted with chronic lassitude, as a result of the enervating climate of the Indian plains. Young men who bring with them from England all the Englishman's love of athletics soon become averse to exercise, and prefer a quiet "peg" beneath the punkah to wheeling or cricket. During the brief respite from the hades-like temperature afforded by December and January, they sometimes take club runs down the Ganges and indulge in the pastime of shooting at alligators with small-bore rifles.

The walks in the beautiful public gardens and every other place about Allahabad are free to wheelmen, and afford most excellent riding.

Messrs. Wingrave and Gawke, the two most enterprising wheelmen, turn out at 6 a.m. to escort me four miles to the Ganges ferry. Some idea of the trying nature of the climate in August may be gathered from the fact that one of my companions arrives at the river fairly exhausted, and is compelled to seek the assistance of a native gharri to get back home. The exposure and exercise I am taking daily is positively dangerous, I am everywhere told, but thus far I have managed to keep free from actual sickness.

The sacred river is at its highest flood, and hereabout not less than a mile and half wide. The ferry service is rude and inefficient, being under the management of natives, who reck little of the flight of time or modern improvements. The superintendent will bestir himself, however, in behalf of the Sahib who is riding the Ferenghi gharri around the world: instead of putting me aboard the big slow ferry, he will man a smaller and swifter boat to ferry me over. The "small boat" is accordingly produced, and turns out to be a rude flat-boat sort of craft, capable of carrying fully twenty tons, and it is manned by eight oarsmen. Their oars are stout bamboo poles with bits of broad board nailed or tied on the end.

Much of the Ganges' present width is mere overflow, shallow enough for the men to wade and tow the boat. It is tugged a considerable distance up-stream, to take advantage of the swift current in crossing the main channel. The oars are plied vigorously to a weird refrain of "deelah, sahlah-deelah, sahlah!" the stroke oarsman shouting "deelah" and the others replying "sahlah" in chorus. Two hours are consumed in crossing the river, but once across the road is perfection itself, right from the river's brink.

Through the valley of the sacred river, the splendid kunkah road leads onward to Benares, the great centre of Hindoo idolatry, a city that is more to the Hindoo than is Mecca to the Mohammedans or Jerusalem to the early Christians. Shrines and idols multiply by the roadside, and tanks innumerable afford bathing and purifying facilities for the far-travelled pilgrims who swarm the road in thousands. As the heathen devotee approaches nearer and nearer to Benares he feels more and more devotionally inclined, and these tanks of the semi-sacred water of the Ganges Valley happily afford him opportunity to soften up the crust of his accumulated transgressions, preparatory to washing them away entirely by a plunge off the Kamnagar ghaut at Benares. Many of the people are trudging their way homeward again, happy in the possession of bottles of sacred water obtained from the river at the holy city. Precious liquid this, that they are carrying in earthenware bottles hundreds of weary miles to gladden the hearts of stay-at-home friends and relations.

At every tank scores of people are bathing, washing their clothes, or scouring out the brass drinking vessel almost everyone carries for pulling water up from the roadside wells. They are far less particular about the quality of the water itself than about the cleanliness of the vessel. Many wells for purely drinking purposes abound, and Brahmans serve out cool water from little pahnee-chowkees through window-like openings. Wealthy Hindoos, desirous of performing some meritorious act to perpetuate their memory when dead, frequently build a pahnee-chowkee by the roadside and endow it with sufficient land or money to employ a Brahman to serve out drinking-water to travellers.

Thirty miles from Allahabad, I pause at a wayside well to obtain a drink. It is high noon, and the well is on unshaded ground. For a brief moment my broad-brimmed helmet is removed so that a native can pour water into my hands while I hold them to my mouth. Momentary as is the experience, it is followed by an ominous throbbing and ringing in the ears—the voice of the sun's insinuating power. But a very short distance is covered when I am compelled to seek the shelter of a little road-overseer's chowkee, the symptoms of fever making their appearance with alarming severity.

The quinine that I provided myself with at Constantinople is brought into requisition for the first time; it is found to be ruined from not being kept in an air-tight vessel. A burning fever keeps me wide awake till 2 a.m., and in the absence of a punkah, prickly heat prevents my slumbering afterward. This wakeful night by the roadside enlightens me to the interesting fact that the road is teeming with people all night as well as all day, many preferring to sleep in the shade during the day and travel at night.

It is fifty miles from my chowkee to Benares, and the dread of being overtaken with serious illness away from medical assistance urges upon me the advisability of reaching there to-day, if possible. The morning is ushered in with a stiff head-wind, and the fever leaves me feeling anything but equal to pedalling against it when I mount my wheel at early daybreak. By sheer strength of will I reel off mile after mile, stopping to rest frequently at villages and under the trees.

A troop of big government elephants are having their hoofs trimmed at a village where a halt is made to obtain a bite of bread and milk. The elephants enter unmistakable objections to the process in the way of trumpeting, and act pretty much like youngsters objecting to soap and water. But a word and a gentle tap from the mahout's stick and the monster brutes roll over on their sides and submit to the inevitable with a shrill protesting trumpet.

Another diversion not less interesting than the elephants is a wrestling tournament at the police-thana, where twenty stalwart policemen, stripped as naked as the proprieties of a country where little clothing is worn anyhow will permit, are struggling for honor in the arena. Vigorous tom-toming encourages the combatants to do their best, and they flop one another over merrily, in the dampened clay, to the applause of a delighted crowd of lookers-on. The fifty miles are happily overcome by four o'clock, and with the fever heaping additional fuel on the already well-nigh unbearable heat, I arrive pretty thoroughly exhausted at Clarke's Hotel, in the European quarter of Benares.

Of all the cities of the East, Benares is perhaps the most interesting at the present day to the European tourist. Its fourteen hundred shivalas or idol temples, and two hundred and eighty mosques, its wonderful bathing ghauts swarming with pilgrims washing away their sins, the burning bodies, the sacred Ganges, the hideous idols at every corner of the streets, and its strange idolatrous population, make up a scene that awakens one to a keen appreciation of its novelty. One realizes fully that here the idolatry, the "bowing down before images" that in our Sunday-school days used to seem so unutterably wicked and perverse, so monstrous, and so far, far away, is a tangible fact. To keep up their outward appearance on a par with the holiness of their city, men streak their faces and women mark the parting in their hair with red. Sacred bulls are allowed to roam the streets at will, and the chief business of a large proportion of the population seems to be the keeping of religious observances and paying devotion to the multitudinous idols scattered about the city.

The presiding deity of Benares is the great Siva—"The Great God," "The Glorious," "The Three-Eyed," and lord of over one thousand similarly grandiloquent titles, and he is represented by the Bishesharnath ka shivala, a temple whose dome shines resplendent with gold-leaf, and which is known to Europeans as the Golden Temple. Siva is considered the king of all the Hindoo deities in the Benares Pauch-kos, and is consequently honored above all other idols in the number of devotees that pay homage to him daily. His income from offerings amounts to many thousands of rupees annually: there is a reservoir for the reception of offerings about three feet square by half that in depth. The Maharajah Ranjit Singh, Rajah of the Punjab, once filled this place with gold mohurs; many wealthy Hindoos have from time to time filled it with rupees.

The old guide whom I have employed to show me about then conducts me into the "Cow Temple," a filthy court containing a number of pampered-looking Brahman bulls, and several youthful bovines whose great privilege it is to roam about the court-yard and accept tid-bits from the hands of devotees. In the same court-yard-like shivala are several red idols, and the numerous comers and goers make the place as animated as a vegetable market at early morning. Priests, too, are here in numbers; seated on a central elevation they make red marks on the faces of the devotees, dipping in the mixture with their finger; in return they receive a small coin, or a pinch of rice or grain is thrown into a vessel placed there for the purpose.

In many stalls are big piles of flower-petals which devotees purchase to present as offerings. Men and women by the hundred are encountered in the narrow streets, passing briskly along with baskets containing a supply of these petals, a dish of rice, and a bowl of water; one would think, from their business-like manner, that they were going, or had been, marketing. They are going the morning round of their favorite gods, or the gods whose particular services they happen to stand in need of at the time; before these idols they pause for a moment, mutter their supplications, and sprinkle them with water and flower-petals, passing from one deity to another in a most business-like, matter-of-fact manner. Women unblessed with children throng to the idols of Sidheswari and Sankatadevi, bestowing offerings and making supplication for sons and daughters; pilgrims from afar are flocking to Sakhi-Banaik, whose office it is to testify in the next world of their pilgrimage in this. No matter how far a pilgrim has come, and how many offerings he has bestowed since his arrival, unless he repair to the shivala of Sakhi Banaik and duly report his appearance, his pilgrimage will have been performed in vain.

Everywhere, in niches of the walls, under trees, on pedestals at frequent corners, are idols, hideously ugly; red idols, idols with silver faces and stone bodies, some with mouths from ear to ear, big idols, little idols, the worst omnium gatherum imaginable. Sati, nothing visible but her curious silver face, beams over a black mother-hubbard sort of gown that conceals whatever she may possess in the way of a body; Jagaddatri, the Mother of the World, with four arms, seated on a lion; Brahma, with five eyes and four mouths, curiously made to supply quadruple faces. Karn-adeva, the handsome little God of Love (the Hindoo Cupid), whom the cruel Siva once slew with a beam from his third eye—all these and multitudinous others greet the curious sight-seer whichever way he turns. Hanuman, too, is not forgotten, the great Monkey King who aided Kama in his expedition to Ceylon; outside the city proper is the monkey temple, where thousands of the sacred anthropoids do congregate and consider themselves at home. Then there is the fakirs' temple, the most beautifully carved shivala in Benares; here priests distribute handfuls of soaked grain to all mendicants who present themselves. The grain is supplied by wealthy Hindoos, and both priests and patrons consider it a great sin to allow a religious mendicant to go away from the temple empty-handed.

Conspicuous above all other buildings in the city is the mosque of Aurungzebe, with its two shapely minarets towering high above everything else. The view from the summit of the minarets is comprehensive and magnificently lovely; the wonderful beauty of the trees and shivalas, the green foliage, and the gilt and red temples, so beautifully carved and gracefully tapering; the broad, flowing Ganges, the busy people, the moving boats, the rajahs' palaces along the water-front, make up a truly beautiful panorama of the Sacred City of the Hindoos. From here we take a native boat and traverse the water-front to see the celebrated bathing ghauts and the strange, animated scene of pilgrims bathing, bodies burning, and swarms of people ascending and descending the broad flights of steps. How intensely eager do these dusky believers in the efficacy of "Mother Ganga" as a purifier of sin dip themselves beneath the yellow water, rinse out their mouths, scrape their tongues, nib, duck, splash, and disport; they fairly revel in the sacred water; happy, thrice happy they look, as well indeed they might, for now are they certain of future happiness. What the "fountain filled with blood" is to the Christian, so is the precious water of dear Ganga to the sinful Hindoo: all sins, past, present, and future, are washed away.

Next to washing in the sacred stream during life, the Hindoo's ambition is to yield up the ghost on its bank, and then to be burned on the Burning Ghaut and have his ashes cast adrift on the waters. On the Manikarnika ghaut the Hindoos burn their dead. To the unbelieving Ferenghi tourist there seems to be a "nigger in the fence" about all these heathen ceremonies, and in the burning of the dead the wily priesthood has managed to obtain a valuable monopoly on firewood, by which they have accumulated immense wealth. No Hindoo, no matter how pious he has been through life, how many offerings he has made to the gods, or how thoroughly he has scoured his yellow hide in the Ganges, can ever hope to reach Baikunt (heaven) unless the wood employed at his funeral pyre come from a domra. Domras are the lowest and most despised caste in India, a caste which no Hindoo would, under any consideration, allow himself to touch during life, or administer food to him even if starving to death; but after his holier brethren have yielded up the ghost, then the despised domra has his innings. Then it is that the relatives of the deceased have to humble themselves before the domra to obtain firing to burn the body. Realizing that they now have the pull, the wily domras sometimes bleed their mournful patrons unmercifully. As many as a thousand rupees have been paid for a fire by wealthy rajahs. The domra who holds the monopoly at the Manikarnika ghaut is one of the richest men in Benares.

Two or three bodies swathed in white are observed waiting their turn to be burned, others are already burning, and in another spot is the corpse of some wealthier person wrapped in silver tinsel. Not the least interesting of the sights is that of men and boys here and there engaged in dipping up mud from the bottom and washing it in pans similar to the gold-pans of placer-miners; they make their livelihood by finding occasional coins and ornaments, accidentally lost by bathers. A very unique and beautifully carved edifice is the Nepaulese temple; but the carvings are unfit for popular inspection.

The whole river-front above the ghauts is occupied by temples and the palaces of rajahs, who spend a portion of their time here preparing themselves for happiness hereafter, by drinking Ganges water and propitiating the gods. On festival occasions, and particularly during an eclipse, as many as one hundred thousand people bathe in the Ganges at once; formerly many were drowned in the great crush to obtain the peculiar blessings of bathing during an eclipse, but now a large force of police is employed to regulate the movements of the people on such occasions. Formerly, also, fights were very frequent between the Mohammedans and Hindoos, owing to the clashing of their religious beliefs, but under the tolerant and conciliatory system of the British Government they now get along very well together.

A rest of two days and a few doses of quinine subdue the fever and put me in condition to resume my journey. Twelve miles from Benares, on the East Indian Kail way, is Mogul Serai, to which I deem it advisable to wheel in the evening, by way of getting started without over-exertion at first. Two English railroad engineers are stationed at Mogul Serai, and each of them is a wheelman. They, of course, are delighted to offer me the hospitality of their quarters for the night, and, moreover, put forth various inducements for a longer stay; but being anxious to reach Calcutta, I decide to pull out again next morning.

My entertainers accompany me for a few miles out. Mogul Serai is four hundred and twelve miles from Calcutta, and at the four hundred and fourth milestone my companions bid me hearty bon voyage and return. Splendid as are the roads round about Mogul Serai, this eight-mile stone is farther down the road than they have ever ridden before.

Twenty-five miles farther, and a sub-inspector of police begs my acceptance of curried chicken and rice. He is a five-named Mohammedan, and tells me a long story about his grandfather having been a reminder of a hundred and fifty villages, and an officer in the East India Company's army. On the pinions of his grandparents' virtues, his Oriental soul soars ambitiously after present promotion; on the strength of sundry eulogistic remarks contained in certificates already in his possession, he wants one from myself recommending him to the powers that be for their favorable consideration. He is the worst "certificate fiend" that I have met.

Near Sassaram I meet a most picturesque subject for my camera, a Rajput hill-man in all the glory of shield, spear, and gayly feathered helmet. He is leading a pack-pony laden with his travelling kit, and mechanically obeys when I motion for him to halt. He remains stationary, and regards my movements with much curiosity while I arrange the camera. When the tube is drawn out, however, and pointed at him, and I commence peeping through to arrange the focus, he gets uneasy, and when I am about ready to perpetuate the memory of his fantastic figure forever, he moves away. Nor will any amount of beckoning obtain for me another "sitting," nor the production and holding aloft of a rupee. Whether he fancied the camera in danger of going off, or dreaded the "evil eye," can only be surmised.

The famous fleet-footed mail-carriers of Bengal are now frequently encountered on the road; they are invariably going at a bounding trot of eight or ten miles an hour. The letter-bag is attached to the end of a stick carried over the shoulder, which is also provided with rings that jingle merrily in response to the motions of the runner. The day is not far distant when all these men will be mounted on bicycles, judging from the beginning already made at Allahabad and Cawnpore. The village women hereabouts wear massive brass ankle-ornaments, six inches broad, and which are apparently pounds in weight.

A deluge of rain during the night at Dilli converts the road into streams, and covers the low, flat land with a sheet of water. The ground is soaked full, like a wet sponge, and can absorb no more; rivers are overflowing, every weed, every blade of grass, and every tree-leaf is jewelled with glistening drops. The splendid kunkah is now gradually giving place to ordinary macadam, which is far less desirable, the heavy, pelting rain washing away the clay and leaving the surface rough.

Not less than four hours are consumed in crossing the River Sone at Dilli in a native punt, so swiftly runs the current and so broad is the overflow. The frequent drenching rains, the lowering clouds, and the persistent southern wind betoken the full vigor of the monsoons. One can only dodge from shelter to shelter between violent showers, and pedal vigorously against the stiff breeze. The prevailing weather is stormy, and inky clouds gather in massy banks at all points of the compass, culminating in violent outbursts of thunder and lightning, wind and rain. Occasionally, by some unaccountable freak of the elements, the monsoon veers completely around, and blowing a gale from the north, hustles me along over the cobbly surface at great speed.

Just before reaching Shergotti, on the evening of the third day from Benares, a glimpse is obtained of hills on the right. They are the first relief from the dead level of the landscape all the way from Lahore; their appearance signifies that I am approaching the Bengal Hills. From Mogul Serai my road has been through territory not yet invaded by the revolutionizing influence of the railway, and consequently the dak bungalows are still kept up in form to provide travellers with accommodation. Chowkeedar, punkah-wallah, and sweeper are in regular attendance, and one can usually obtain curried rice, chicken, dhal, and chuppatties. An official regulation of prices is posted conspicuously in the bungalow: For room and charpoy, Rs 1; dinner, Rs 1-8; chota-hazari, Rs 1, and so on through the scale. The prices are moderate enough, even when it is considered that a dinner consists of a crow-like chicken, curried rice, and unleavened chuppatties. The chowkeedar is usually an old Sepoy pensioner, who obtains, in addition to his pension, a percentage on the money charged for the rooms—a book is kept in which travellers are required to enter their names and the amount paid. The sweepers and punkah-wallahs are rewarded separately by the recipient of their attentions. Sometimes, if a Mohammedan, and not prohibited by caste obligations from performing these menial services, the old pensioner brings water for bathing and sweeps out one's own room himself, in which case he of course pockets the backsheesh appertaining to these duties also.

A few miles south of Shergotti the bridge spanning a tributary of the Sone is broken down, and no ferry is in operation. The stream, however, is fordable, and four stalwart Bengalis carry me across on a charpoy, hoisted on their shoulders; they stem the torrent bravely, and keep up their strength and courage by singing a refrain. From this point the road becomes undulating, and of indifferent surface; the macadam is badly washed by the soaking monsoon rains, and the low, level country is gradually merging into the jungle-covered hills of Bengal.

The character of the people has undergone a decided change since leaving Delhi and Agra, and the Bengalis impress one decidedly unfavorably in comparison with the more manly and warlike races of the Punjab. Abject servility marks the demeanor of many, and utter uselessness for any purpose whatsoever, characterizes one's intuitive opinion of a large percentage of the population of the villages. Except for the pressing nature of one's needs, the look of unutterable perplexity that comes over the face of a Bengali villager, to-day, when I ask him to obtain me something to eat, would be laughable in the extreme. "N-a-y, Sahib, n-a-y." he replies, with a show of mental distraction as great as though ordered to fetch me the moon. An appeal for rice, milk, dhal, chuppatties, at several stalls results in the same failure; everybody seems utterly bewildered at the appearance of a

Sahib among them searching for something to eat. The village policeman is on duty in the land of dreams, a not unusual circumstance, by the way; but a youth scuttles off and wakes him up, and notifies him of my arrival. Anxious to atone for his shortcomings in slumbering at his post, he bestirs himself to obtain the wherewithal to satisfy my hunger, his authoritative efforts culminating in the appearance of a big dish of dhal.

The country becomes hillier, and the wild, jungle-covered hills and dark ravines alongside the road are highly suggestive of royal Bengal tigers. The striped monsters infest these jungles in plenty; during the afternoon I pass through a village where a depredatory man-eater has been carrying off women and children within the last few days.

The chowkeedar at Burhee, my stopping-place for the night in the hill country, is a helpless old duffer, who replies "nay-hee, Sahib, nay-hee," with a decidedly woe-begone utterance in response to all queries about refreshments. A youth capable of understanding a little English turns up shortly, and improves the situation by agreeing to undertake the preparation of supper. Still more hopeful is the outlook when a Eurasian and a native school-master appear upon the scene, the former acting as interpreter to the genial pedagogue, who is desirous of contributing to my comfort by impressing upon my impromptu cook the importance of his duties. They become deeply interested in my tour of the world, which the scholarly pedagogue has learned of through the medium of the vernacular press. The Eurasian, not being a newspaper-reader, has not heard anything of the journey. But he has casually heard of the River Thames, and his first wondering question is as to "how I managed to cross the Thames!"

My saturated karki clothing has been duly wrung out and hung up inside the dak bungalow, the only place where it will not get wetter instead of dryer, and my cook is searching the town in quest of meat, when an English lady and gentleman drive up in a dog-cart and halt before the bungalow. Unaware of the presence of English people in the place, I am taken completely by surprise.

They are Mr. and Mrs. B, an internal revenue officer and his wife, who, having heard of my arrival, have come to invite me to dinner. Of course I am delighted, and they are equally pleased to entertain one about whose adventures they have recently been reading. Their ayah saw me ride in, and went and told her mistress of seeing a "wonderful Sahib on wheels," and already the report has spread that I have come down from Lahore in four days!

A very agreeable evening is spent at Mr. E 's house, talking about the incidents of my journey, Mr. E 's tiger-hunting exploits in the neighborhood, and kindred topics. Mr. R devotes a good deal of time in the winter season to hunting tigers in the jungle round about his station, and numerous fine trophies of his prowess adorn the rooms of his house. He knows of the man-eater's depredations in the village I passed to-day, and also of another one ahead which I shall go through to-morrow; he declares his intention of bagging them both next season.

Mrs. R arrived from Merrie England but eighteen months ago, a romantic girl whose knowledge of royal Bengal tigers was confined to the subdued habitues of sundry iron-barred cages in the Zoo. She is one of those dear confiding souls that we sometimes find out whose confidence in the omnipotent character of their husbands' ability is nothing if not charming and sublime. Upon her arrival in the wilds of Bengal she was fascinated with the loveliness of the country, and wanted her liege lord to take her into the depths of the jungle and show her a "real wild tiger." She had seen tigers in cages, but wanted to see how a real wild one looked in his native lair. One day they were out taking horseback exercise together, when, a short distance from the road, the horrible roar of a tiger awoke the echoes of the jungle and reverberated through the hills like rolling thunder. Now was the long-looked-for opportunity, and her husband playfully invited her to ride with him toward the spot whence came the roars. Mrs. R, however, had suddenly changed her mind.

Mrs. R was the first white lady the people of many of the outlying villages had ever seen on horseback, or perhaps had ever seen at all, and the timidest of them would invariably bolt into the jungle at her appearance. When her husband or any other Englishman went among them alone, the native women would only turn away their faces, but from the lady herself they would hastily run and hide. Here, also, I learn that the natives in this district are dying by the hundred with a malignant type of fever; that the present season is an exceptionally sickly one, all of which gives reason for congratulation at my own health being so good.

It is all but a sub-aqueous performance pedalling along the road next morning; the air is laden with a penetrating drizzle, the watery clouds fairly hover on the tree-tops and roll in dark masses among the hills, while the soaked and saturated earth reeks with steam. The road is macadamized with white granite, and after one of those tremendous downpourings that occur every hour or so the wheel-worn depressions on either side become narrow streams, divided by the white central ridge. Down the long, straight slopes these twin rivulets course right merrily, the whirling wheels of the bicycle flinging the water up higher than my head. The ravines are roaring, muddy torrents, but they are all well bridged, and although the road is lumpy, an unridable spot is very rarely encountered. For days I have not had a really dry thread of clothing, from the impossibility of drying anything by hanging it out. Under these trying conditions, a relapse of the fever is matter for daily and hourly apprehension.

The driving drizzle to-day is very uncomfortable, but less warm than usual; it is anything but acceptable to the natives; thousands are seen along the road, shivering behind their sheltering sun-shields, from which they dismally essay to extract a ray of comfort. These sun-shields are umbrella-like affairs made of thin strips of bamboo and broad leaves; they are without handles, and for protection against the sun or rain are balanced on the head like an inverted sieve. When carried in the hand they may readily be mistaken for shields. In addition to this, the men carry bamboo spears with iron points as a slipshod measure of defence against possible attacks from wild animals. When viewed from a respectable distance these articles invest the ultra-gentle Bengali with a suggestion of being on the war-path, a delusion that is really absurd in connection with the meek Bengali ryot.

The houses of the villages are now heavily thatched, and mostly enclosed with high bamboo fencing, prettily trailed with creepers; the bazaars are merely two rows of shed-like stalls between which runs the road. In lieu of the frequent painted idol, these jungle villagers bestow their devotional exercises upon rude and primitive representations of impossible men and animals made of twisted straw. These are sometimes set up in the open air on big horseshoe-shaped frames, and sometimes they are beneath a shed. In the privacy of their own dwellings the Bengali ryot bows the knee and solemnly worships a bowl of rice or a cup of arrack. The bland and childlike native of Hindostan falls down and worships almost everything that he recognizes as being essential to his happiness and welfare, embracing a wide range of subjects, from Brahma, who created all things, to the denkhi with which their women hull the rice. This denkhi is merely a log of wood fixed on a pivot and with a hammer-like head-piece. The women manipulate it by standing on the lever end and then stepping off, letting it fall of its own weight, the hammer striking into a stone bowl of rice. The denkhi is said to have been blessed by Brahma's son Narada, the god who is distinguished as having cursed his venerable and all-creating sire and changed him from an object of worship and adoration to a luster after forbidden things.

The country continues hilly, with the dense jungle fringing the road; all along the way are little covered platforms erected on easily climbed poles from twelve to twenty feet high. These are apparently places of refuge where benighted wayfarers can seek protection from wild animals. Occasionally are met the fleet-footed postmen, their rings jangling merrily as they bound briskly along; perhaps the little platforms are built expressly for their benefit, as they are not infrequently the victims of stealthy attack, the jingle of their rings attracting Mr. Tiger instead of repelling him.

Mount Parisnath, four thousand five hundred and thirty feet high, the highest peak of the Bengal hills, overlooks my dak bungalow at Doomree, and also a region of splendid tropical scenery, dark wooded ridges, deep ravines, and rolling masses of dark-green vegetation.

During the night the weather actually grows chilly, a raw wind laden with moisture driving me off the porch into the shelter of the bungalow. No portion of Parisnath is visible in the morning but the base, nine-tenths of its proportions being above the line of the cloud-masses that roll along just above the trees. Another day through the hilly country and, a hundred and fifty miles from Calcutta, the flourishing coal-mining district of Asansol brings me again to the East India Railway and semi-European society and accommodation. Instead of doughy chuppatties, throat-blistering curry, and octogenarian chicken, I this morning breakfast off a welcome bottle of Bass's ale, baker's bread, and American cheese.

My experience of hotels and hotel proprietors has certainly been somewhat wide and varied within the last two years; but it remains for Rannegunj to produce something entirely novel in the matter of tariff even to one of my experience. The cuisine and service of the hotel is excellent, and well worth the charges; but the tariff is arranged so that it costs more to stay part of a day than a whole one, and more to take two meals than to take three. If a person remains a whole day, including room and three meals, it is Rs 4, and he can, of course, suit himself about staying or going if he engages or pays in advance; but should he only take dinner, room, and chota-hazari, his bill reads: Dinner, Rs 2; room, Rs 1, 8 annas; chota-hazari, rupees 1; total, Rs 4, 8 annas, or 8 annas more than if he had remained and taken another square meal. The subtle-minded proprietor of this establishment should undoubtedly take out a patent on this very unique arrangement and issue licences throughout all Bonifacedom; there would be more "millions in it" than in anything Colonel Sellers ever dreamed of.

And now, beyond Rannegunj, comes again the glorious kunkah road, after nearly three hundred miles of variable surface. Level, smooth, and broad it continues the whole sixty-five miles to Burd-wan.

Notwithstanding an adverse wind, this is covered by three o'clock. The road leads through the marvellously fertile valley of the Dammoodah, an interesting region where groves of cocoa-nut palms, bamboo thickets, and thatched villages give the scenery a more decidedly tropical character than that north of the Bengal hills. Rice is still the prevailing crop, and the overflow of the Dammoodah is everywhere. Men and women are busily engaged among the pools, fishing for land-crabs, mussels, and other freshwater shell-fish, with triangular nets.

As my southward course brings me next day into the valley of the Hooghli River, the road partakes almost of the character of a tunnel burrowing through a mass of dense tropical vegetation. Cocoa-nut and toddy-palms mingle their feathery foliage with the dark-green of the mango, the wild pomolo, giant bamboo, and other vegetable exuberances characteristic of a hot and humid climate, and giant creepers swing from tree to tree and wind among the mass in inextricable confusion.

In this magnificent conservatory of nature big, black-faced monkeys, with tails four feet long, romp and revel through the trees, nimbly climb the creepers, and thoroughly enjoy the life amid the sylvan scenes about them. It is a curious sight to see these big anthropoids, almost as large as human beings, swing themselves deftly up among the festooned creepers at my approach—to see their queer, impish black faces peering cautiously out of their hiding-place, and to hear their peculiar squeak of surprise and apprehension as they note the strange character of my conveyance. Sometimes a gang of them will lope awkwardly along ahead of the bicycle, looking every inch like veritable imps of darkness pursuing their silent course through the chastened twilight of green-grown, subterranean passageways, their ridiculously long tails raised aloft, and their faces most of the time looking over their shoulders.

Youthful lotus-eaters, sauntering lazily about in the vicinity of some toddy-gatherer's hamlet, hidden behind the road's impenetrable environment of green, regard with supreme indifference the evil-looking apes, bigger far than themselves, romping past; but at seeing me they scurry off the road and disappear as suddenly as the burrow-like openings in the green banks will admit.

Women are sometimes met carrying baskets of plantains or mangoes to the village bazaars; sometimes I endeavor to purchase fruit of them, but they shake their heads in silence, and seem anxious to hurry away.

These women are fruit-gatherers and not fruit-sellers, consequently they cannot sell a retail quantity to me without violating their caste.

My experiences in India have been singularly free from snakes; nothing have I seen of the dreaded cobra, and about the only reminder of Eve's guileful tempter I encounter is on the road this morning. He is only a two-foot specimen of his species, and is basking in a streak of sunshine that penetrates the green arcade above. Remembering the judgment pronounced upon him in the Garden of Eden, I attempt to acquit myself of the duty of bruising his head, by riding over him. To avoid this indignity his snakeship performs the astonishing feat of leaping entirely clear of the ground, something quite extraordinary, I believe, for a snake. The popular belief is that a snake never lifts more than two-thirds of his length from the ground.

From the city of Hooghli southward, the road might with equal propriety be termed a street; it follows down the west side of the Hooghli River and links together a chain of populous towns and villages, the straggling streets of which sometimes fairly come together. Fruit-gardens, crowded with big golden pomolos, delicious custard, apples, and bananas abound; in the Hooghli villages the latter can be bought for two pice a dozen. Depots for the accumulation and shipment of cocoa-nuts, where tons and tons of freshly gathered nuts are stacked up like measured mounds of earth, are frequent along the river. Jute factories with thousands of whirring spindles and the clackety-clack of bobbins fill the morning air with the buzz and clatter of vigorous industrial life. Juggernaut cars, huge and gorgeous, occupy central places in many of the towns passed through. The stalls and bazaars display a variety of European beverages very gratifying from the stand-point of a hot and thirsty wayfarer, ranging from Dublin ginger ale to Pommery Sec. California Bartlett pears, with seductive and appetizing labels on their tin coverings, are seen in plenty, and shiny wrappers envelop oblong cakes of Limburger cheese.

For a few minutes my wheel turns through a district where the names of the streets are French, and where an atmosphere of sleepy Catholic respectability pervades the streets. This is Chandernagor, a wee bit of territory that the French have been permitted to retain here, a rosebud in the button-hole of la belle France's national vanity. Chanderuagor is a bite of two thousand acres out of the rich cake of the lower Hooghli Valley; but it is invested with all the dignity of a governor-general's court, and is gallantly defended by a standing army of ten men. The Governor-General of Chandernagor fully makes up in dignity what the place lacks in size and importance; when the East India Railway was being built he refused permission for it to pass through his territory. There is no doubt but that the land forces of Chandernagor would resist like bantams any wanton or arbitrary violation of its territorial prerogatives by any mercenary railroad company, or even by perfide Albion herself, if need be. The standing army of Chandernagor hovers over peaceful India, a perpetual menace to the free and liberal government established by England. Some day the military spirit of Chandernagor will break loose, and those ten soldiers will spread death and devastation in some peaceful neighboring meadow, or ruthlessly loot some happy, pastoral melon-garden. Let the Indian Government be warned in time and increase its army.

By nine o'clock the bicycle is threading its way among the moving throngs on the pontoon bridge that spans the Hooghli between Howrah and Calcutta, and half an hour later I am enjoying a refreshing bath in Cook's Adelphi Hotel.

I have no hesitation in saying that, except for the heat, my tour down the Grand Trunk Road of India has been the most enjoyable part of the whole journey, thus far. What a delightful trip a-wheel it would be, to be sure, were the temperature only milder!

My reception in Calcutta is very gratifying. A banquet by the Dalhousie Athletic Club is set on foot the moment my arrival is announced. With such enthusiasm do the members respond that the banquet takes place the very next day, and over forty applicants for cards have to be refused for want of room. For genuine, hearty hospitality, and thoroughness in carrying out the interpretation of the term as understood in its real home, the East, I unhesitatingly yield the palm to Anglo-Indians. Time and again, on my ride through India, have I experienced Anglo-Indian hospitality broad and generous as that of an Arab chief, enriched and rendered more acceptable by a feast of good-fellowship as well as creature considerations.

The City of Palaces is hardly to be seen at its best in September, for the Viceregal Court is now at Simla, and with it all the government officials and high life. Two months later and Calcutta is more brilliant, in at least one particular, than any city in the world. Every evening in "the season" there is a turn-out of splendid equipages on the bund road known as the Strand, the like of which is not to be seen elsewhere, East or West. It is the Rotten Row of Calcutta embellished with the gorgeousness of India. Wealthy natives display their luxuriousness in vying with one another and with the government officials in the splendor of their carriages, horses, and liveries.

Mr. P, a gentleman long resident in Calcutta, and a prominent member of the Dalhousie Club, drives me in his dog-cart to the famous Botanical Gardens, whose wealth of unique vegetation, gathered from all quarters of the world, would take volumes to do it justice should one attempt a description. Its magnificent banyan is justly entitled to be called one of the wonders of the world. Not less striking, however, in their way, are the avenues of palms; so straight, so symmetrical are these that they look like rows of matched columns rather than works of nature. Fort William, the original name of the city, and the foundation-stone of the British Indian Empire, is visited with Mr. B, the American Consul, a gentleman from Oregon. The glory of Calcutta, its magnificent Maidan, is overlooked by the American Consulate, and one of the most conspicuous objects in the daytime is the stars and stripes floating from the consulate flag-staff.

On the 18th sails the opium steamer Wing-sang to Hong-Kong, aboard which I have been intending to take passage, and whose date of departure has somewhat influenced my speed in coming toward Calcutta. To cross overland from India to China with a bicycle is not to be thought of. This I was not long in finding out after reaching India. Fearful as the task would be to reach the Chinese frontier, with at least nine chances out of ten against being able to reach it, the difficulties would then have only commenced.

The day before sailing, the bicycle branch of the Dalhousie Athletic Club turns out for a club run around the Maidan, to the number of seventeen. It is in the evening; the long rows of electric lamps stretching across the immense square shed a moon-like light over our ride, and the smooth, broad roads are well worthy the metropolitan terminus of the Grand Trunk.

My stay of five days in the City of Palaces has been very enjoyable, and it is with real regret that I bid farewell to those who come down to the shipping ghaut to see me off.

The voyage to the Andamans is characterized by fine weather enough; but from that onward we steam through a succession of heavy rain-storms; and down in the Strait of Malacca it can pour quite as heavily as on the Gangetic plains. At Penang it keeps up such an incessant downpour that the beauties of that lovely port are viewed only from beneath the ship's awning. But it is lovely enough even as seen through the drenching rain. Dense groves of cocoa-nut palms line the shores, seemingly hugging the very sands of the beach. Solid cliffs of vegetation they look, almost, so tall, dark, and straight, and withal so lovely, are these forests of palms. Cocoa-nut palms flourish best, I am told, close to the sea, a certain amount of salt being necessary for their healthful growth.

The weather is more propitious as we steam into Singapore, at which point we remain for half a day, on the tenth day out from Calcutta. Singapore is indeed a lovely port. Within a stone's-throw of where the Wing-sang ties up to discharge freight the dark-green mangrove bushes are bathing in the salt waves. Very seldom does one see green vegetation mingling familiarly with the blue water of the sea—there is usually a strip of sand or other verdureless shore—but one sees it at lovely Singapore.

A fellow-passenger and I spend an hour or two ashore, riding in the first jiniriksha that has come under my notice, from the wharf into town, about half a mile. We are impressed by the commercial activity of the city; as well as by the cosmopolitan character of its population. Chinese predominate, and thrifty, well-conditioned citizens these Celestials look, too, here in Singapore. "Wherever John Chinaman gets half a show, as under the liberal and honest government of the Straits Settlements or Hong-Kong, there you may be sure of finding him prosperous and happy."

Hindoos, Parsees, Armenians, Jews, Siamese, Klings, and all the various Eurasian types, with Europeans of all nationalities, make up the conglomerate population of Singapore. Here, on the streets, too, one sees the strange cosmopolitan police force of the English Eastern ports, made up of Chinese, Sikhs, and Englishmen.

CHAPTER XVII

THROUGH CHINA

Daily rains characterize our voyage from Singapore through the China Sea—rather unseasonable weather, the captain says; and for the second time in his long experience as a navigator of the China Sea, St. Elmo's lights impart a weird appearance to the spars and masts of his vessel. The rain changes into misty weather as we approach the Ladrone Islands, and, emerging completely from the wide track of the typhoon's moisture-laden winds on the following morning, we learn later, upon landing at Hong-kong, that they have been without rain there for several weeks.

It is my purpose to dwell chiefly on my own experiences, and not to write at length upon the sights of Kong-kong and Canton; hundreds of other travellers have described them, and to the average reader they are no longer unique. Several days' delay is experienced in obtaining a passport from the Viceroy of the two Quangs, and during the delay most of the sights of the city are visited. The five-storied pagoda, the temple of the five hundred genii, the water-clock, the criminal court—where several poor wretches are seen almost flayed alive with bamboos-flower-boats, silk, jade-stone, ivory-carving shops, temple of tortures, and a dozen other interesting places are visited under the pilotage of the genial guide and interpreter Ah Kum.

The strange boat population, numbering, according to some accounts, two hundred thousand people, is one of the most interesting features of Canton life. Wonderfully animated is the river scene as viewed from the balcony of the Canton Hotel, a hostelry kept by a Portuguese on the opposite bank of the river from Canton proper.

The consuls and others express grave doubts about the wisdom of my undertaking in journeying alone through China, and endeavor to dissuade me from making the attempt. Opinion, too, is freely expressed that the Viceroy will refuse his permission, or, at all events, place obstacles in my way. The passport is forthcoming on October 12th, however, and I lose no time in making a start.

Thirteen miles from Canton I reach the city of Fat-shan. Five minutes after entering the gate I am in the midst of a crowd of struggling, pushing natives, whose aggressive curiosity renders it extremely difficult for me to move either backward or forward, or to do aught but stand and endeavor to protect the bicycle from the crush. They seem a very good-natured crowd, on the whole, and withal inclined to be courteous, but the pressure of numbers, and the utter impossibility of doing anything, or prosecuting my search for the exit on the other side of the city, renders the good intentions of individuals wholly inoperative.

With perseverance I finally succeed in extricating myself and following in the wake of an intelligent-looking young man whom I fondly fancy I have enlightened to the fact that I am searching for the Sam-shue road. The crowd follow at our heels as we tread the labyrinthine alleyways, that seem as interminable as they are narrow and filthy. Every turn we make I am expecting the welcome sight of an open gate and the green rice-fields beyond, when, after dodging about the alleyways of what seems to be the toughest quarter of the city, my guide halts and points to the closed gates of a court.

It now becomes apparent that he has been mistaken from the beginning in regard to my wants: instead of taking me to the Sam-shue gate, he has brought me to some kind of a house. "Sam-shue, Sam-shue," I explain, making gestures of disapproval at the house. The young man regards me with a look of utter bewilderment, and forthwith betakes himself off to the outer edge of the crowd, henceforth contenting himself to join the general mass of open-eyed inquisitives. Another attempt to again enlist his services only results in alienating his sympathies still further: he has been grossly taken in by my assumption of intelligence. Having discovered in me a jackass incapable of the Fat-shan pronunciation of Sam-shue, he retires on his dignity from further interest in my affairs.

Female faces peer curiously through little barred apertures in the gate, and grin amusedly at the sight of a Fankwae, as I stand for a few minutes uncertain of what course to pursue. From sheer inability to conceive of anything else I seize upon a well-dressed youngster among the crowd, tender him a coin, and address him questioningly—"Sam-shue lo. Sam-shue lo." The youth regards me with monkeyish curiosity for a second, and then looks round at the crowd and giggles. Nothing is plainer than the evidence that nobody present has the slightest conception of what I want to do, or where I wish to go. Not that my pronunciation of Sam-shue is unintelligible (as I afterward discover), but they cannot conceive of a Fankwae in the streets of Fat-shan inquiring for Sam-shue; doubtless many have never heard of that city, and perhaps not one in the crowd has ever been there or knows anything of the road. As a matter of fact, there is no "road," and the best anyone could do would be to point out its direction in a general way. All this, however, comes with after-knowledge.

Imagine a lone Chinaman who desired to learn the road to Philadelphia surrounded by a dense crowd in the Bowery, New York, and uttering the one word "Phaladilfi," and the reader gains a feeble conception of my own predicament in Fat-shan, and the ludicrousness of the situation. Finally the people immediately about me motion for me to proceed down the street.

Like a drowning man, I am willing to clutch wildly even at a straw, in the absence of anything more satisfactory, and so follow their directions. Passing through squalid streets occupied by loathsome beggars, naked youngsters, slatternly women, matronly sows with litters of young pigs, and mangy pariahs, we emerge into the more respectable business thoroughfares again, traversing streets that I recognize as having passed through an hour ago. Having brought me here, the leaders in the latest movement seem to think they have accomplished their purpose, leaving me again to my own resources.

Yet again am I in the midst of a tightly wedged crowd, helpless to make myself understood, and equally helpless to find my own way. Three hours after entering the city I am following-the Fates only know whither—the leadership of an individual who fortunately "sabes" a word or so of pidgin English, and who really seems to have discovered my wants. First of all he takes me inside a temple-like building and gives me a drink of tea and a few minutes' respite from the annoying pressure of the crowds; he then conducts me along a street that looks somewhat familiar, leads me to the gate I first entered, and points triumphantly in the direction of Canton!

I now know as much about the road to Sam-shue as I did before reaching Fat-shan, and have learned a brief lesson of Chinese city experience that is anything but encouraging for the future. The feeling of relief at escaping from the narrow streets and the garrulous, filthy crowds, however, overshadows all sense of disappointment. The lesson of Fat-shan it is proposed to turn to good account by following the country paths in a general course indicated by my map from city to city rather than to rely on the directions given by the people, upon whom my words and gestures seem to be entirely thrown away.

For a couple of miles I retraverse the path by which I reached Fat-shan before encountering a divergent pathway, acceptable as, leading distinctly toward the northwest. The inevitable Celestial is right on hand, extracting no end of satisfaction from following, shadow-like, close behind and watching my movements. Pointing along the divergent northwest road, I ask him if this is the koon lo to Sam-shue; for answer he bestows upon me an expansive but wholly expressionless grin, and points silently toward Canton. These repeated failures to awaken the comprehension of intelligent-looking Chinamen, or, at all events, to obtain from them the slightest information in regard to my road, are somewhat bewildering, to say the least. So much of this kind of experience crowded into the first day, however, is very fortunate, as awakening me with healthy rudeness to a realizing sense of what I am to expect; it places me at once on my guard, and enables me to turn on the tap of self-reliance and determination to the proper notch.

Shaking my head at the almond-eyed informant who wants me to return to Canton, I strike off in a northwesterly course. The Chinaman grins and chuckles humorously at my departure, as though his risibilities were probed to their deepest depths at my perverseness in going contrary to his directions. As plainly as though spoken in the purest English, his chuckling laughter echoes the thought: "You'll catch it, Mr. Fankwae, before you have gone very far in that direction; you'll wish you had listened to me and gone back to 'Quang-tung.'"

The country is a marvellous field-garden of rice, vegetables, and sugar-cane for some miles. The villages, with their peculiar, characteristic Chinese architecture and groves of dark bamboo, are striking and pretty. The paths seem to wind about regardless of any special direction; the chief object of the road-makers would appear to have been to utilize every little strip of inferior soil for the public thoroughfare wherever it might be found. A scrupulous respect for individual rights and the economy of the soil has resulted in adding many a weary mile of pathway between one town and another. To avoid destroying the productive capacity of a dozen square yards of alluvial soil, hundreds of people are daily obliged to follow horseshoe bends around the edges of graveyards that after two hundred paces bring them almost to within jumping distance of their first divergence.

Occasionally the path winds its serpentine course between two tall patches of sugar-cane, forming an alleyway between the dark-green walls barely wide enough for two people to pass. Natives met in these confined passages, as isolated from the eyes of the world as though between two walls of brick, invariably recoil a moment with fright at the unexpected apparition of a Fankwae; then partially recovering themselves, they nimbly occupy as little space as possible on one side, and eye me with suspicion and apprehension as I pass.

Great quantities of sugar-cane are chewed in China, both by children and grown people, and these patches grown in the rich Choo-kiang Valley for the Fat-shan, Canton, and Hong-kong markets are worth the price of a day's journeying to see. So marvellously neat and thrifty are they, that one would almost believe every separate stalk had been the object of special care and supervision from day to day since its birth; every cane-garden is fenced with neat bamboo pickets, to prevent depredation at the hands of the thousands of sweet-toothed kleptomaniacs who file past and eye the toothsome stalks wistfully every day.

After a few miles the hitherto dead level of the valley is broken by low hills of reddish clay, and here the stone paths merge into well-beaten trails that on reasonably level soil afford excellent wheeling. The hillsides are crowded with graves, which, instead of the sugar-loaf "ant hillocks" of the paddy-fields, assume the traditional horseshoe shape of the Chinese ancestral grave. On the barren, gravelly hills, unfit for cultivation, the thrifty and economical Celestial inters the remains of his departed friends. Although in making this choice he is supposed to be chiefly interested in securing repose for his ancestors' souls, he at the same time secures the double advantage of a well-drained cemetery, and the preservation of his cultivable lands intact. Everything, indeed, would seem to be made subservient to this latter end; every foot of productive soil seems to be held as of paramount importance in the teeming delta of the Choo-kiang.

Beyond the first of these cemetery hills, peopled so thickly with the dead, rise the tall pawn-towers of the large village of Chun-Kong-hoi. The natural dirt-paths enable me to ride right up to the entrance-gate of the main street. Good-natured crowds follow me through the street; and outside the gate of departure I favor them with a few turns on the smooth flags of a rice-winnowing floor. The performance is hailed with shouts of surprise and delight, and they urge me to remain in Chun-Kong-hoi all night.

An official in big tortoise-shell spectacles examines my passport, reading it slowly and deliberately aloud in peculiar sing-song tones to the crowd, who listen with all-absorbing attention. He then orders the people to direct me to a certain inn. This inn blossoms forth upon my as yet unaccustomed vision as a peculiarly vile and dingy little hovel, smoke-blackened and untidy as a village smithy. Half a dozen rude benches covered with reed mats and provided with uncomfortable wooden pillows represent what sleeping accommodations the place affords. The place is so forbidding that I occupy a bench outside in preference to the evil-smelling atmosphere within.

As it grows dark the people wonder why I don't prefer the interior of the dimly lighted hittim. My preference for the outside bench is not unattended with hopes that, as they can no longer see my face, my greasy-looking, half-naked audience would give me a moment's peace and quiet. Nothing, however, is further from their thoughts; on the contrary, they gather closer and closer about me, sticking their yellow faces close to mine and examining my features as critically as though searching the face of an image. By and by it grows too dark even for this, and then some enterprising individual brings a couple of red wax tapers, placing one on either side of me on the bench.

By the dim religious light of these two candles, hundreds of people come and peer curiously into my face, and occasionally some ultra-inquisitive mortal picks up one of the tapers and by its aid makes a searching examination of my face, figure, and clothes. Mischievous youngsters, with irreligious abandon, attempt to make the scene comical by lighting joss-sticks and waving bits of burning paper.

The tapers on either side, and the youngsters' irreverent antics, with the evil-spirit-dispersing joss-sticks, make my situation so ridiculously suggestive of an idol that I am perforce compelled to smile. The crowd have been too deeply absorbed in the contemplation of my face to notice this side-show; but they quickly see the point, and follow my lead with a general round of merriment. About ten o'clock I retire inside; the irrepressible inquisitives come pouring in the door behind me, but the hittim-keeper angrily drives them out and bars the door.

Several other lodgers occupy the room in common with myself; some are smoking tobacco, and others are industriously "hitting the pipe." The combined fumes of opium and tobacco are well-nigh unbearable, but thera is no alternative. The next bench to mine is occupied by a peripatetic vender of drugs and medicines. Most of his time is consumed in smoking opium in dreamy oblivion to all else save the sensuous delights embodied in that operation itself. Occasionally, however, when preparing for another smoke, he addresses me at length in about one word of pidgin-English to a dozen of simon-pure Cantonese. In a spirit of friendliness he tenders me the freedom of his pipe and little box of opium, which is, of course, "declined with thanks."

Long into the midnight hours my garrulous companions sit around and talk, and smoke, and eat peanuts. Mosquitoes likewise contribute to the general inducement to keep awake; and after the others have finally lain down, my ancient next neighbor produces a small mortar and pestle and busies himself pounding drugs. For this operation he assumes a pair of large, round spectacles, that in the dimly lighted apartment and its nocturnal associations are highly suggestive of owls and owlish wisdom. The old quack works away at his mortar, regardless of the approach of daybreak, now and then pausing to adjust the wick in his little saucer of grease, or to indulge in the luxury of a peanut.

Such are the experiences of my first night at a Chinese village hittim; they will not soon be forgotten.

The proprietor of the hittim seems overjoyed at my liberality as I present him a ten-cent string of tsin for the night's lodging. Small as it sounds, this amount is probably three or four times more than he obtains from his Chinese guests.

The country beyond Chun-Kong-hoi is alternately level and hilly, the former highly cultivated, and the latter occupied mostly with graves. Peanut harvest is in progress, and men, women, and children are everywhere about the fields. The soil of a peanut-bed to the depth of several inches is dug up and all passed through a sieve, the meshes of which are of the proper size to retain the nuts. The last possible grain, nut, or particle of life-sustaining vegetable or insect life is extracted from the soil, ducks and chickens being cooped and herded on the fields and gardens after human ingenuity has reached its limit of research.

Big wooden pails of warm tea stand about the fields, from which everybody helps himself when thirsty. A party of peanut-harvesters are regaling themselves with stewed turnips and tough, underdone pieces of dried liver. They invite me to partake, handing me a pair of chopsticks and a bowl.

Gangs of coolies, strung in Indian file along the paths, are met, carrying lacquer-ware from some interior town to Fat-shau and Canton. Others are encountered with cages of kittens and puppies, which they are conveying to the same market. These are men whose business is collecting these table delicacies from outlying villages for the city markets, after the manner of egg and chicken buyers in America.

My course at length brings me to the town of Si-noun, on the south bank of the Choo-kiang. The river is here prevented from inundating the low country adjacent by strong levees; along these are well-tramped paths that afford much good wheeling, as well as providing a well-defined course toward Sam-shue. After following the river for some miles, however, I conclude that its course is altogether more southerly than there is any necessity for me to go; so, crossing the river at a village ferry, I strike a trail across-country in a north-westerly direction that must sooner or later bring me to the banks of the Pi-kiang. Sam-shue is at the junction of these two rivers, the one flowing from west to east and the other from north to south; by striking across-country, but one side of a triangle is traversed instead of the two formed by the rivers. My objective point for the night is Lo-pow, the first town of any size up the Pi-kiang.

A volunteer guide from one of the villages extricates me from a bewildering network of trails in the afternoon, and guides me across to the bottom-lands of the Pi-kiang. Receiving a reward, he eyes the piece of silver a moment wistfully, puts it away, and guides me half a mile farther. Pointing to the embankment of the Pi-kiang in the distance ahead, he presents himself for further reward. Receiving this, he thereupon conceives the brilliant idea of piloting me over successive short stages, with a view of obtaining tsin at the end of each stage.

John Chinaman is no more responsible, morally, for the "dark ways and vain tricks" accredited to him in the Western World than a crow is for the blackness of his plumage. The desperate struggle for existence in this crowded empire, that has no doubt been a normal condition of its society for ages, has developed traits of character in these later generations which are as unchangeable as the skin of the Ethiopian or the spots of the leopard. Either of these can be whitened over, but not readily changed; the same may be truthfully said of the moral leprosy of the average Celestial. Here is a simple peanut-farmer's son, who knows nothing of the outer world, yet no sooner does a stray opportunity present than he develops immediately financial trickery worthy of a Constantinople guide.

The paths across the Pi-kiang Valley are more walls than paths, often rising ten feet above the paddy-fields, and presenting a width of not more than two feet. Good riding, however, is happily found on the levees, and a few miles up-stream brings me to Lo-pow.

The hittim at Lo-pow is somewhat superior to that of yesterday; it is a two-storied building, and the proprietor hustles me up-stairs in short order, and locks me in. This is to prevent any possible hostility from the crowd that immediately swarms the place; for while I am in his house he is in a measure held responsible for my treatment. The bicycle is kept down-stairs, where it performs the office of a vent for the rampant curiosity of the thousands who besiege the proprietor for a peep at me.

A little cup and a teapot of hot tea is brought me at once, and my order taken for supper; the characters on ray limited written vocabulary proving invaluable as an aid toward making my g-astro-nomic preferences understood. A dish of boiled fish, pickled ginger, chicken entrees, young onions, together with rice enough to feed a pig, form the ingredients of a very good Chinese meal. Chop-sticks are, of course, provided; but, as yet, my dexterity in the manipulation of these articles is decidedly of the negative order, and so my pocket-knife performs the dual office of knife and fork; for the rice, one can use, after a manner, the little porcelain dipper provided for ladling an evil-smelling liquid over that staple. Bread, there is none in China; rice is the bread of both this country and Japan. During the night one gets a reminder of the bek-jees of Constantinople in the performances of a night policeman, who passes by at intervals loudly beating a drum. This, together with roystering mosquitoes, and a too liberal indulgence in strong tea, banishes sleep to-night almost as effectually as the pounding of the old drug-vender's pestle did at Chun-Kong-hoi.

The rooms below are full of sleeping coolies, cat-and-dog hucksters and travellers, when I descend at day-break to start. The first two hours are wasted in wandering along a levee that leads up a tributary stream, coming back again and getting ferried to the right embankment. The riding is variable, and the zigzagging of the levee often compels me to travel three miles for the gaining of one. My elevated path commands a good view of the traffic on the river, and of the agricultural operations on the adjacent lowlands.

The boating scenes on the river are animated, and peculiarly Chinese. The northern monsoons, called typhoons in China, are blowing strongly down stream, while the current itself is naturally strong; under the influence of wind and current combined, junks and sampans with butterfly sails all set are going down stream at racing speed. In striking contrast to these, are the up-stream boats, crawling along at scarcely perceptible pace against the current, in response to the rhythmical movements of a line of men, women, and children harnessed one behind another to a long tow-line.

The water in the river is low, and the larger boats have to be watched carefully to prevent grounding; sometimes, when the river is wide and the passable channel but a narrow place in the middle, the tow-people have to take to the water, often wading waist deep. Men and women are dressed pretty much alike, but in addition to the broad-legged pantaloons and blue blouse, the women are distinguished by a checked apron. Some of them wear broad bamboo hats, while others wear nothing but nature's covering, or perchance a handkerchief tied around their heads. The traffic on the river is something enormous, scores of boats dotting the river at every turn. It is no longer difficult to believe the oft-heard assertion, that the tonnage of China's inland fleet is equal to the ocean tonnage of all the world.

Below me on the right the scene is scarcely less animated; one would think the whole population of the country were engaged in pumping water over the rice-fields, by the number of tread-wheels on the go. One of the most curious sights in China is to see people working these irrigating machines all over the fields. Instead of the buffaloes of Egypt and India, everything here is accomplished by the labor of man. The tread-wheel is usually worked by two men or women, who steady themselves by holding to a cross-bar, while their weight revolves the tread-wheel and works a chain of water-pockets. The pockets dip water from a hole or ditch and empty it into troughs, whence it spreads over the field. The screeching of these wheels can be heard for miles, and the grotesque Chinese figures stepping up, up, up in pairs, yet never ascending, the women singing in shrill, falsetto voices, and the incessant gabble of conversation, makes a picture of industry the like of which is to be seen in no other part of the world.

Chin-yuen, my next halting-place, forma something of a crescent on the west shore of the river, and is distinguished by a seven-storied pagoda at the southern extremity of its curvature. As seen from the east bank, the city and its background of reddish hills, two peaks of which rise to the respectable height of, I should judge, two thousand feet, is not without certain pretensions to beauty. Many of the houses on the river front are built over the water on piles, and broad flights of stone steps lead down to the water.

The usual boat population occupy a swarm of sampans anchored before the city, while hundreds of others are moving hither and thither. The water is intensely blue, and the broad reaches of Band are dazzlingly white; on either bank are dark patches of feathery bamboo; the white, blue and green, the pagoda, the city with its towering pawn-houses, and the whole flanked by red clay hills, forms a picture that certainly is not wanting in life and color.

The quarters assigned me at the hittim, here, are again upstairs, and my room-companion is an attenuated opium smoker, who is apparently a permanent lodger. This apartment is gained by a ladder, and after submitting to much annoyance from the obtrusive crowds below invading our quarters, my companion drives them all out with the loud lash of his tongue, and then draws up the only avenue of communication. He is engaged in cooking his supper and in washing dirty dishes; when the crowd below gets too noisy and clamorous he steps to the opening and coolly treats them to a basin of dish-water. This he repeats a number of times during the evening, saving his dish-water for that special purpose.

The air is reeking with smoke and disagreeable odors from below, where cooking is going on, and pigs wallow in filth in a rear apartment. The back-room of a Chinese inn is nearly always a pigsty, and a noisome place on general principles. Later in the evening a few privileged characters are permitted to come up, and the room quickly changes into a regular opium-den. A tough day's journey and two previous nights of wakefulness, enable me to fall asleep, notwithstanding the evil smells, the presence of the opium-smoking visitors, and the grunting pigs and talkative humans down below.

During the day I have sprained my right knee, and it becomes painful in the night and wakes me up. In the morning my way is made through the waking city with a painful limp, that gives rise to much unsympathetic giggling among the crowd at my heels. Perhaps they think all Pankwaes thus hobble along; their giggling, however, is doubtless evidence of the well-known pitiless disposition of the Chinese. The sentiments of pity and consideration for the sufferings of others, are a well-nigh invisible quality of John Chinaman's character, and as I limp slowly along, I mentally picture myself with a broken leg or serious illness, alone among these people. A Fankwae with his leg broken! a Fankwae lying at the point of death! why, the whole city would want to witness such an extraordinary sight; there would be no keeping them out; one would be the centre of a tumultuous rabble day and night!

The river contains long reaches leading in a totally contrary direction to what I know my general course to be. My objective point is a little east of north, but for miles this morning I am headed considerably south of the rising sun. There is nothing for it, however, but to keep the foot-trail that now follows along the river bank, conforming to all its multifarious crooks and angles. Every mile or two the path is overhung by a big bamboo hedge, behind which is hidden a village.

The character of these little riverside villages varies from peaceful agricultural and fishing communities, to nests of river-pirates and hard characters generally, who covertly prey on the commerce of the Pi-kiang, and commit depredations in the surrounding country. A glimpse of me is generally caught by someone behind the hedge as I ride or trundle past; shouts of "the Fankwae, the Fankwae," and screams of laughter at the prospect of seeing one of those queer creatures, immediately follow the discovery. The gabble and laughter and hurrying from the houses to the hedge, the hasty scrambling through the little wicket gates, all occurs with a flutter and noisy squabble that suggest a flock of excited geese.

A few miles above Chin-yuen the river enters a rocky gorge, and the marvellous beauty of the scenery rivets me to the spot in wondering contemplation for an hour. It is the same picture of rocky mountains, blue water, junks, bridges, temples, and people, one sometimes sees on sets of chinaware. Never was water so intensely blue, or sand so dazzlingly white, as the Pi-kiang at the entrance to this gorge this sunny morning; on its sky-blue bosom float junks and sampans, their curious sails appearing and disappearing around a bend in the canon. The brown battlemented cliffs are relieved by scattering pines, and in the interstices by dense thickets of bamboo; temples, pagodas, and a village complete a scene that will be long remembered as one of the loveliest bits of scenery the whole world round. The scene is pre-eminently characteristic, and after seeing it, one no longer misunderstands the Chinaman who persists in thinking his country the great middle kingdom of landscape beauty and sunshine, compared to which all others are—"regions of mist and snow."

Across the creeks which occasionally join issue with the river, are erected frail and wabbly bamboo foot-rails; some of these are evidently private enterprises, as an ancient Celestial is usually on hand for the collection of tiny toll. Narrow bridges, rude steps cut in the face of the cliffs, trails along narrow ledges, over rocky ridges, down across gulches, and anon through loose shale on ticklishly sloping banks, characterize the passage through the canon. The sun is broiling hot, and my knee swollen and painful. It is barely possible to crawl along at a snail's pace by keeping my game leg stiff; bending the knee is attended with agony. Frequent rests are necessary, and an examination reveals my knee badly inflamed.

Hours are consumed in scrambling for three or four miles up and down steps, and over the most abominable course a bicycle was ever dragged, carried, up-ended and lugged over. At the end of that time I reach a temple occupying a romantic position in a rocky defile, and where a flight of steps leads down to the water's edge. All semblance of anything in the nature of a continuous path terminates at the temple, and hailing a sampan bound up stream, I obtain passage to the northern extremity of the canyon.

The sampan is towed by a team of seven coolies, harnessed to a small, strong rope made of bamboo splint. It is interesting, yet painful, to see these men clambering like goats about the rocky cliffs, sometimes as much as a hundred feet above the water; one of the number does nothing else but throw the rope over protuberant points of rock. One would naturally imagine that Chinese enterprise would be sufficient to construct something like a decent towpath through this caiion, considering the number of boats towed through it daily; but everything in China seems to be done by the main strength and awkwardness of individuals.

The boatmen seem honest-hearted fellows; at noon they invite me to participate in their frugal meal of rice and turnips. Passing sampans are greeted by the crew of our boat with the intelligence that a Fankwae is aboard; the news being invariably conveyed with a droll "ha-ha!" and received with the same. Indeed, the average Chinese river-man or agriculturist, the simple-hearted children of the water and the soil, seem to regard the Fankwae as a creature so remarkably comical, that the mere mention of him causes them to laugh.

Near the end of the canon the boat is moored at a village for the day, and my knee feeling much better from the rest, I pursue my course up the bank of the river. The bank is level in a general sense, but much cut up with small tributary creeks.

While I am resting on the bank of one of these creeks, partly hidden behind a clump of bamboo, a slave-woman carrying her mistress pick-a-back appears upon the scene. Catching sight of me, the golden lily utters a little cry of alarm and issues hurried orders to her maid. The latter wheels round and scuttles back along the path with her frightened burden, both maid and golden lily no doubt very thankful at finding themselves unpursued. A few minutes after their hasty flight, three men approach my resting-place with pitchforks. The frightened females have probably told them of the presence of some queer-looking object lurking behind the bushes, and like true heroes they have shouldered their pitchforks and sallied forth to investigate. A whoop and a feint from me would either put them to flight, or precipitate a conflict, as is readily seen from the extreme cautiousness of their advance. As I remained perfectly still, however, they approach by short stages, and with many stops for consultation, until near enough to satisfy themselves of my peaceful character. They loiter around until my departure, when they follow behind for a few hundred yards, watching me narrowly until I am past their own little cluster of houses.

It is almost dark when I arrive at the next village, prepared to seek such accommodations for the night as the place affords, if any. The people, however, seem decidedly inclined to give me the cold shoulder, eying me suspiciously from a respectful distance, instead of clustering, as usual, close about me. Being pretty tired and hungry, and knowing absolutely nothing of the distance to the next place, I endeavor to cultivate their friendship by smiles, and by addressing the nearest youngster in polite greetings of "chin-chin."

All this proves of no avail; they seem one and all to be laboring under the impression that my appearance is of evil portent to themselves. Perchance some social calamity they have just been visited with, is attributed in their superstitious minds to the fell influence of the foreign devil, who has so suddenly bobbed up in their midst just at this unhappy, inauspicious moment. Perad-venture some stray and highly exaggerated bit of news in regard to Fankwae aggression in Tonquin (the French Tonquin expedition) has happened to reach the little interior village this very day, and the excited people see in me an emissary of destruction, here for the diabolical purpose of spying out their country. A dozen reasons, however, might be here advanced, and all be far wide of the truth.

Whatever their hostility is all about is a mystery to me, the innocent object of sundry scowls and angry gestures. One individual contemplates me for a minute with unconcealed aversion, and then breaks out into a torrent of angry words and excited gestures. From all appearances, it behooves me to be clearing out, ere the pent-up feelings of the people find vent in some aggressive manner, as a result of this person's incitant eloquence. Greatly puzzled to account for this unpleasant reception, I quietly take myself off.

It is now getting pretty dark, and considering the unfortunate condition of my knee, the situation is, to say the least, annoying. It is not without apprehensions of being followed that I leave the village; and ere I am two hundred yards away, torches are observed moving rapidly about, and soon loud shouts of "Fankwae, Fankwae!" tell me that a number of men are in pursuit.

Darkness favors my retreat, and scrambling down the river bank, I shape my course across the sand and shallow side-channels to a small island, thickly covered with bamboo, the location of which is now barely outlined against the lingering streaks of daylight in the western sky. Half an hour is consumed in reaching this; but no small satisfaction is derived from seeing the flaming torches of my pursuers continue on up the bank. The dense bamboo thickets afford an excellent hiding-place, providing my divergence is not suspected. A little farther up-stream, on the bank, are the lights of another village; and as I crouch here in the darkness I can see the torches of the pursuing party entering this village, and can hear them making shouting inquiries of their neighbors about the foreign devil.

The thicket is alive with ravenous mosquitoes that issue immediately their peculiar policy of assurance against falling asleep. Unappeased hunger, mosquitoes, and the perilousness of the situation occupy my attention for some hours, when, seeing nothing further of the vengeful aspirants for my gore, I drag my weary way up-stream, through sand and shallow water. Keeping in the river-bed for several miles, I finally regain the bank, and, although my inflamed knee treats me to a twinge of agony at every step, I steadily persevere till morning.

An hour or two of morning light brings me to the town of Quang-shi, after an awful tugging through sand-hills, unbridged ravines and water. Hardly able to stand from fatigue and the pain of my knee, the desperate nature of the road, or, more correctly, the entire absence of anything of the kind, and the disquieting incident of the night, awaken me to a realizing sense of my helplessness should the people of Quang-shi prove to be hostile. Conscious of my inability to run or ride, savagely hungry, and desperately tired, I enter Quang-shi with the spirit of a hunted animal at bay. With revolver pulled round to the front ready to hand, and half expecting occasion to use it in defence of my life, I grimly speculate on the number of my cartridges and the probability of each one bagging a sore-eyed Celestial ere my own lonely and reluctant ghost is yielded up.

All this, fortunately, is found to be superfluous speculation, for the good people of Quang-shi prove, at least, passively friendly; a handful of tsin divided among the youngsters, and a general spendthrift scatterment of ten cents' worth of the same base currency among the stall-keepers for chow-chow heightens their friendly interest in me to an appreciable extent.

Chao-choo-foo is the next city marked on my itinerary, but as Quang-shi is not on my map I have no means of judging whether Chao-choo-foo is four li up-stream or forty. All attempts to obtain some idea of the distance from the natives result in the utter bewilderment of both questioned and querist. No amount of counting on fingers, or marking on paper, or interrogative arching of eyebrows, or repetition of "Chao-choo-foo li" sheds a glimmer of light on the mind of the most intelligent-looking shopkeeper in Quang-shi concerning my wants. Yet, withal, he courteously bears with my, to him, idiotic pantomime and barbarous pronunciation, and repeats parrot-like after me "Chao-choo-foo li; Chao-choo-foo li" with sundry beaming smiles and friendly smirks.

Far easier, however, is it to make them understand that I want to go to that city by boat. The loquacious owner of a twenty-foot sampan puts in his appearance as soon as my want is ascertained, and favors me with an unpunctuated speech of some five minutes' duration. For fear I shouldn't quite understand the tenor of his remarks, he insists on thrusting his yellow Mongolian phiz within an inch or two of mine own. At the end of five minutes I thrust my fingers in my ears out of sheer consideration for his vocal organs, and turn away; but the next moment he is fronting me again, and repeating himself with ever-increasing volubility. Finding my dulness quite impenetrable, he searches out another loquacious mortal, and by the aid of the tiny beam-scales every Chinaman carries for weighing broken silver, they finally make it understood that for six big rounds (dollars) he will convey me in his boat to Chao-choo-foo. Understanding this, I promptly engage his services.

Bundles of joss-sticks, rice, fish, pork, and a jar of samshoo (rice arrack) are taken aboard, and by ten o'clock we are underway. Two men, named respectively Ah Sum and Yung Po, a woman, and a baby of eighteen months comprise the company aboard. Ah Sum, being but an inconsequential wage-worker, at once assumes the onerous duties of towman; Yung Po, husband, father, and sole proprietor of the sampan, manipulates the rudder, which is in front, and occasionally assists Ah Sum by poling. The boat-wife stands at the stern and regulates the length of the tow-line; the baby puts in the first few hours in wondering contemplation of myself.

The strange river-life of China is all about us; small fishing-boats are everywhere plying their calling. They are constructed with a central chamber full of auger-holes for the free admittance of water, in which the fish are conveyed alive to market, or imprisoned during the owner's pleasure. Big freight sampans float past, propelled by oars if going downstream, and by the combined efforts of tow-line and poles if against the current. The propelling poles are fitted with neatly carved "crutch-trees" to fit the shoulder; the polers, sometimes numbering as many as a dozen, walk back and forth along side-planks and encourage themselves with cries of "ha-i, ha-i, ha-i." A peculiar and indescribable inflection would lead one, hearing and not seeing these boatmen, to fancy himself listening to a flight of brants in stormy weather. Yung Po, poling by himself, gives utterance to a prolonged cry of "Atta-atta-atta aaoo ii," every time he hustles along the side-plank.

Much of the scenery along the river is lovely in the extreme, and at dark we cast anchor in a smooth, silent reach of the river just within the frowning gateway of a rocky canon. Dark masses of rock tower skyward five hundred feet in a perpendicular wall, casting a dark shadow over the twilight shimmer of the water. In the north, the darksome prospect is invested with a lurid glow, apparently from some large fire; the canon immediately about our anchoring place is alive with moving torches, representing the restless population of the river, and on the banks clustering points of light here and there denote the locality of a village.

The last few miles has been severe work for poor Ah Sum, clambering among rocks fit only for the footsteps of a goat. He sticks to the tow-line manfully to the end, but wading out to the boat when over-heated, causes him to be seized with violent cramps all over; in his agony he rolls about the deck and implores Yung Po to put him out of his misery forthwith. His case is evidently urgent, and Yung Po and his wife proceed to administer the most heroic treatment. Hot samshoo is first poured down his throat and rubbed on his joints, then he is rolled over on his stomach; Yung Po then industriously flagellates him in the bend of the knees with a flat bamboo, and his wife scrapes him vigorously down the spine with the sharp edge of a porcelain bowl. Ah Sam groans and winces under this barbarous treatment, but with solicitous upbraidings they hold him down until they have scraped and pounded him black and blue, almost from head to foot. Then they turn him over on his back for a change of programme. A thick joint of bamboo, resembling a quart measure, is planted against his stomach; lighted paper is then inserted beneath, and the "cup" held firmly for a moment, when it adheres of its own accord.

This latter instrument is the Chinese equivalent of our cupping-glass; like many other inventions, it was probably in use among them ages before anything of the kind was known to us. Its application to the stomach for the relief of cramps would seem to indicate the possession of drawing powers; I take it to be a substitute for mustard plasters. While the wife attends to this, Yung Po pinches him severely all over the throat and breast, converting all that portion of his anatomy into little blue ridges. By the time they get through with him, his last estate seems a good deal worse than his first, but the change may have saved his life.

Before retiring for the night lighted joss-sticks are stuck in the bow of the sampan, and lighted paper is waved about to propitiate the spirit of the waters and of the night; small saucers of rice, boiled turnip, and peanut-oil are also solemnly presented to the tutelary gods, to enlist their active sympathies as an offset against the fell designs of mischievous spirits. Falling asleep under the soothing influence of these extraordinary precautions for our safety and a supper of rice, ginger, and fresh fish, I slumber peacefully until well under way next morning. Ah Sum is stiff and sore all over, but he bravely returns to his post, and under the combined efforts of pole and tow-line we speed along against a swift current at a pace that is almost visible to the naked eye.

This morning I purchase a splendid trout, weighing seven or eight pounds, for about twenty cents; off this we make a couple of quite excellent meals. Observing my awkward attempts to pick up pieces of fish with the chop-sticks, the good, thoughtful boat-wife takes a bone hair-pin out of her sleek, oily back hair, and offers it to me to use as a fork!

Before noon we emerge into a more open country; straight ahead can be seen an eight-storied pagoda. Reaching the pagoda, we pass, on the opposite shore, the town of Yang-tai (?). Fleets of big junks sail gayly down stream, laden with bales and packages of merchandise from Chao-choo-foo, Nam-hung, and other manufacturing points up the river. Others resemble floating hay-ricks, bearing huge cargoes of coarse hay and pine-needles down for the manufacture of paper.

Several war-junks are anchored before Yang-tai; unlike the peaceful (?) merchantmen on the Choo-kiang, they are armed with but a single cannon. They are, however, superior vessels compared with other craft on the river, and are manned with crews of twenty to thirty theatrical-looking characters; rows of muskets and boarding-pikes are observed, and conspicuous above all else are several large and handsome flags of the graceful triangular shape peculiar to China.

The crew of these warlike vessels are uniformed in the gayest of red, and in the middle of their backs and breasts are displayed white "bull's eyes" about twelve inches in diameter. The object of these big white circular patches appears to be the presentation of a suitable place for the conspicuous display of big characters, denoting the district or city to which they belong; or in other words labels. The wicked and sarcastic Fankwaes in the treaty ports, however, render a far different explanation. They say that a Chinese soldier always misses a bull's-eye when he shoots at it—under no circumstances does he score a bull's-eye. Observing this, the authorities concluded that Fankwae soldiers were tarred with the same unhappy feather. With true Asiatic astuteness, they therefore conceived and carried out the brilliant idea of decorating all Celestial warriors with bull's-eyes, front and rear, as a measure of protection against the bullets of the Fankwae soldiers in battle.

Ah Sum becomes sick and weary at noon and is taken aboard, Tung Po and his better half taking alternate turns at the line. Toward evening the river makes a big sweep to the southeast, bringing the prevailing north wind round to our advantage; if advantage it can be called, in blowing us pretty well south when our destination lies north. The sail is hoisted, and the crew confines itself to steering and poling the boat clear of bars.

Poor Ah Sum is subjected to further clinical maltreatment this evening as we lay at anchor before No-foo-gong; while we are eating rice and pork and listening to the sounds of revelry aboard the big passenger junks anchored near by, he is writhing and groaning with pain.

He is too stiff and sore and exhausted to do anything in the morning; the woman goes out to pull, and the babe makes Rome howl, with little intermission, till she comes back. The boat-woman seems an industrious, wifely soul; Yung Po probably paid as high as forty dollars for her; at that price I should say she is a decided bargain. Occasionally, when Yung Po cruelly orders her overboard to take a hand at the tow-line, or to help shove the sampan off a sand ridge, she enters a playful demurrer; but an angry look, an angry word, or a cheerful suggestion of "corporeal suasion," and she hops lightly into the water.

A few miles from No-foo-gong and a rocky precipice towers up on the west shore, something like a thousand feet high. The crackling of firecrackers innumerable and the report of larger and noisier explosions attract my attention as we gradually crawl up toward it; and coming nearer, flocks of pigeons are observed flying uneasily in and out of caves in the lower levels of the cliff.

In the course of time our sampan arrives opposite and reveals a curious two-storied cave temple, with many gayly dressed people, pleasure sampans, and bamboo rafts. This is the Kum-yam-ngan, a Chinese Buddhist temple dedicated to the Goddess of Mercy. It is the home of flocks of sacred pigeons, and the shrine to which many pilgrims yearly come; the pilgrims manage to keep their feathered friends in a chronic state of trepidation by the agency of fire-crackers and miniature bombs. Outside, under the shelter of the towering cliffs to the' right, are more temples or dwellings of the priests; they present a curious mixture of blue porcelain, rock, and brick which is intensely characteristic of China.

During the day we pass, on the same side of the river, yet another remarkable specimen of man's handiwork on the scene of one of nature's curious rockwork conceptions. Leading from base to summit of a sloping mountain are two perpendicular ridges of rock, looking very much like a couple of walls. Across the summit of the mountain, from wall to wall, some fanciful architect three hundred years ago built a massive battlement; in the middle he left a big round hole, which presents a very curious appearance, and materially heightens the delusion that the whole affair, from foot to summit, is the handiwork of man. This place is known as Tan-tsy-shan, or Bullet Mountain, and is the scene of a fight that occurred some time during the Ming dynasty. A legend is current among the people, that the robber Wong, a celebrated freebooter of that period, while firing on a pursuing party of soldiers, shot this moon—like hole through the mountain battlement with the huge musket he used to slaughter his enemies.

Many huge rafts of pine logs are now encountered floating down stream to the cities of the lower country; numbers of them are sometimes met, following close behind one another. Several huts are erected on each big raft, so that the sight not infrequently suggests a long straggling village floating with the tide. This suggestion is very much heightened by the score or more people engaged in poling, steering, al fresco cooking, etc., aboard each raft.

And anon there come along men, poling with surprising swiftness slender-built craft on which are perched several solemn and important-looking cormorants. These are the celebrated cormorant fishers of the Chinese rivers. Their craft is simply three or four stems of the giant bamboo turned up at the forward end; on this the naked fisherman stands and propels himself by means of a slender pole. His stock-in-trade consists of from four to eight cormorants that balance themselves and smooth their wet wings as the lightsome raft speeds along at the rate of six miles an hour from one fishing ground to another. Arriving at some likely spot the eager aspirant for finny prizes rests on his oars, and allows his aquatic confederates to take to the water in search of their natural prey, the fishes. A ring around the cormorants' necks prevents them swallowing their captives, and previous training teaches them to balance themselves on the propelling pole that the watchful fisherman inserts beneath them the moment they rise to the surface with a fish; captive and captor are then lifted aboard the raft, the cormorant robbed of his prey and hustled quickly off again to business. The sight of these nimble craft, skimming along with scarcely an effort, almost fills me with a resolve to obtain one of them myself and abandon Tung Po and his dreary lack of speed forever.

The third day of our voyage against the prevailing typhoons and the rapid current of the Pi-kiang, comes to an end, and finds us again anchored within the dark shadow of a towering cliff. Anchored alongside us is a big junk freighted with bags of rice and bales of paper; the hands aboard this boat indulge in a lively quarrel, during the evening chow-chow, and bang one another about in the liveliest manner. The peculiar indignation that finds expression in abusive language no doubt reaches its highest state of perfection in the Celestial mind. No other human being is capable of soaring to the height of the Chinaman's falsetto modulations, as he heaps reproaches and cuss-words on his enemy's queue-adorned head. A big boat's crew of naked Chinamen cursing and gesticulating excitedly, advancing and retreating, chasing one another about with billets of wood, knocking things over, and raising Cain generally, in the ghostly glimmer of fantastic paper lanterns, is a spectacle both weird and wild.

Another weird, but this time noiseless, affair is a long string of nocturnal cormorant fishers, each with a big, flaming torch attached to the prow of his raft, propelling themselves along close under the dark frowning cliff. The torches light up the black face of the precipice with a wild glare, and streak the shimmering water with moon-like reflections.

The country through which our watery, serpentine course winds all next day, is hilly rather than mountainous; grassy hills slope down to the water's blue ripples at certain places, but the absence of grazing animals is quite remarkable. Regions, which in other countries would be covered with flocks of sheep and herds of cows and horses, are without so much as a sign of herbivorous animals. Pigs are the prevailing meat-producing animals of Southern China; all the way up country I have not yet seen a single sheep, and but very few cattle; I have also yet to see the first horse. Instead of herbivorous quadrupeds peacefully browsing, are swarms of men, women, and children cutting, bundling, and stacking the grass for the manufacture of paper.

Among the fleeting curiosities of the day are a crowd of sampans flying black flags, evidently some military expedition; they are bound down stream, and it occurs to me that they are perhaps a reinforcement of these famous free-lances going to join the hordes of that denomination making things so uncomfortable for the French in Tonquin and Quang-tse. We also pass a district where the women enhance their physical charms by the aid of broad circular hats that resemble an inverted sieve. The edges, however, are not wood, but circular curtains of black calico; the roof of the hat is bleached bamboo chip.

Officers board us in the evening to search the vessel for dutiable goods; but they find nothing. The privilege of levying customs on salt and opium is farmed out by the government to people in various cities along the rivers. The tax on these articles from first to last of a long river voyage is very heavy, customs being levied at various points; it is scarcely necessary to add that under these arbitrary arrangements, the oily, conscienceless and tsin-loving Celestial boatman has reduced the noble art of smuggling to a science. Yung Po smiles blandly at the officer as he searches carefully every nook and corner of the sampan, even rooting about with a stick in the moderate amount of bilge-water collected between the ribs, and when he is through, dismisses him with an air of innocence and a wealth of politeness that is artfully calculated to secure less rigorous search next time.

The poling and towing is prolonged till nearly midnight, when we cast anchor among a lot of house-boats and miscellaneous craft before a city. Even at this unseemly hour we are visited by an owlish pedler, whose boat is fitted up with boxes containing various dishes toothsome to the heathen palates of the water-men. Yung Po and Ah Sum look wistfully over the ancient pastry-ped-ler's wares, and pick out tiny dishes of sweetened rice gruel; this they consume with the same unutterable satisfaction that hungry monkeys display when eating chestnuts, ending the performance by licking the platters. Although the price is nearly a farthing a dish, with wanton prodigality Yung Po orders dishes for the whole company, including even his passenger!

From various indications, it is surmised, as I seek my couch, that the city opposite is Chao-choo-foo. Inquiry to that effect, as usual, elicits nothing but a bland grin from Yung Po. When, however, he takes the unnecessary precaution of warning me not to venture outside the covered sleeping quarters during the night, intimating that I should probably get stabbed if I do, I am pretty well satisfied of our arrival. This cautious proceeding is to be explained by the fact that I am Yung Po's debtor for two days' diet of rice, turnips, and flabby pork, and he is suspicious that I might creep forth in the silence and darkness of the night and leave him in the lurch.

Yung Po now summons his entire pantomimic ability, to inform me that Chao-choo-foo is still some distance up the river, at all events that is my interpretation of his words and gestures. On this supposition I enter no objections when he bids me accompany him to the market and purchase a new supply of provisions for the remainder of the journey.

Impatient to proceed to Chao-choo-foo I now motion for them to make a start. Yung Po points to the frowning walls of the city we have just visited, and blandly says, "Chao-choo-foo." Having accomplished his purpose of bamboozling me into replenishing his larder, by making me believe our destination is yet farther upstream, he now turns round and tells me that we have already arrived. The neat little advantage he has just been taking of my ignorance with such brilliant results to the larder of the boat, has visibly stimulated his cupidity, and he now brazenly demands the payment of filthy lucre, making a circular hole with his thumb and finger to intimate big rounds in contradistinction to mere tsin.

The assumption of dense ignorance has not been without its advantages at various times on my journey around the world, and regarding Yung Po's gestures with a blankety blank stare, I order him to proceed up stream to Chao-choo-foo. The result of my refusal to be further bamboozled by the wily Yung Po, without knowing something of what I am doing, is that I am shortly threading the mazy alleyways of Chao-choo-foo with Ah Sum and Yung Po for escort. What the object of this visit may be I haven't the remotest idea, unless we are proceeding to the quarters of some official to have my passport seen to, or to try and enlighten my understanding in regard to Yung Po's claims for battered Mexican dollars.

Vague apprehensions arise that, peradventure, the six dollars paid at Quang-shi was only a small advance on the cost of my passage up, and that Yung Po is now piloting me to an official to establish his just claims upon pretty much all the money I have with me. Ignorant of the proper rate of boat-hire, disquieting visions of having to retreat to Canton for the lack of money to pay the expenses of the journey through to Kui-kiang are flitting through my mind as I follow the pendulous motions of Yung Po's pig-tail along the streets. The office that I have been conjuring up in my mind is reached at last, and found to be a neat room provided with forms and a pulpit like desk.

A pleasant-faced little Chinaman in a blue silk gown is examining a sheet of written characters through the medium of a pair of tortoise-shell spectacles. On the wall I am agreeably astonished to see a chromo of Her Majesty Queen Victoria, with an inscription in Chinese characters. The little man chin-chins (salaams) heartily, removes his spectacles and addresses me in a musical tone of voice. Yung Po explains obsequiously that my understanding Chinese is conspicuously unequal to the occasion, a fact that at once becomes apparent to the man in blue silk; whereupon he quickly substitutes written words for spoken ones and presents me the paper. Finding me equally foggy in regard to these, he excuses my ignorance with a courteous smile and bow, and summons a gray-queued underling to whom he gives certain directions. This person leads the way out and motions for me to follow. Yung Po and Ah Sum bring up behind, keeping in order such irrepressibles as endeavor to peer too obtrusively into my face.

Soon we arrive at a quarter with big monstrous dragons painted on the walls, and other indications of an official residence; palanquin-bearers in red jackets and hats with tassels of red horse-hair flit past at a fox-trot with a covered palanquin, preceded by noisy gong-beaters and a gayly comparisoned pony. This is evidently the yamen or mandarin's quarter, and here we halt before a door, while our guide enters another one, and disappears. The door before us is opened cautiously by a Celestial who looks out and bestows upon mo a friendly smile. A curly black dog emerges from between his legs and presents himself with much wagging of tail and other manifestations of canine delight.

All this occurs to me as very strange; but not for a moment does it prepare me for the agreeable surprise that now presents itself in the appearance of a young Englishman at the door. It would be difficult to say which of us is the most surprised at the other's appearance. Mutual explanations follow, and then I learn that, all unsuspected by me, two missionaries of the English Presbyterian mission are stationed at Chao-choo.

At Canton I was told that I wouldn't see a European face nor hear an English word between that city and Kui-kiang. On their part, they have read in English papers of my intended tour through China, but never expected to see me coming through Chao-choo-foo.

I am, of course, overjoyed at the opportunity presented by their knowledge of the language to arrange for the continuation of my journey in a manner to know something about what I am doing. They are starting down the river for Canton to-morrow, so that I am very fortunate in having arrived today. As their guest for the day I obtain an agreeable change of diet from the swashy preparations aboard the sampan, and learn much valuable information about the nature of the country ahead from their servants. They have never been higher up the river than Chao-choo-foo themselves, and rather surprise me by giving the distances to Canton as two hundred and eighty miles.

By their kind offices I am able to make arrangements for a couple of coolies to carry the bicycle over the Mae-ling Mountains as far as the city of Nam-ngan on the head waters of the Kan-kiang, whence, if necessary, I can descend into the Yang-tsi-kiangby river. The route leads through a mountainous country up to the Mae-ling Pass, thence down to the head waters of the Kan-kiang.

All is ready by eight o'clock on the morning of October 22d; the coolies have lashed the bicycle to parallel bamboo poles, as also a tin of lunch biscuits, a tin of salmon, and of corned beef, articles kindly presented by the missionaries.

Nam-ngan is said to be two hundred miles distant, but subsequent experience would lessen the distance by about fifty miles. Our way leads first through the cemeteries of Chao-choo-foo, and along little winding stone-ways through the fields leading, in a general sense, along the right bank of the Pi-kiang.

The villagers in the upper districts of Quang-tung are peculiarly wanting in facial attractiveness; in some of the villages on the Upper Pi-kiang the entire population, from puling infants to decrepit old stagers whose hoary cues are real pig-tails in respect to size, are hideously ugly. They seem to be simple, primitive people, bent on satisfying their curiosity; but in the pursuit of this they are, if anything, somewhat more considerate or more conservative than the Persians.

Mothers hurry home and fetch their babies to see the Fankwae, pointing me out to their notice, very much like pointing out a chimpanzee in the Zoological gardens. In these village inns the spirit of democracy embraces all living things; sore-eyed coolies, leprous hangers-on to the thread of life, matronly sows and mangy dogs, come, go, and freely mingle and associate in these filthy little kitchens. When cooking is in progress, nothing is set off the fire on to the ground but that a hungry pig stands and eyes it wistfully, but sundry burnings of their sensitive snouts during the days of their youthful inexperience have made them preternaturally cautious, so that they are not very meddlesome. The sleeping room is really a part of the pig-sty, nothing but an open railing separating pigs and people. A cobble-stone path now leads through a hilly country, divided up into little rice-fields, peanut gardens, pine copses, and cemeteries. Peanut stalls one encounters at short intervals, where ancient dames or wrinkled old men preside over little saucers of half-roasted nuts, peanut sweet cakes, peanut plain cakes, peanut crullers, peanut dough, peanut candy, peanuts sprinkled with sugar, peanuts sprinkled with salt, and peanuts fresh from the ground. The people seem to be well-nigh living on peanuts, which unhappy diet probably has something to do with their marvellous ugliness.

In a gathering of villagers standing about me are people with eyes that are pitched at the most peculiar angles, varying from long, narrow eyes that slope downward toward the cheek-bone, to others that seem almost perpendicular. No less astonishing is the contour of their mouths; ragged holes in their ugly faces are these for the most part, shapeless and uncouth as anything well could be. They are the most unprepossessing humans I have seen the whole world round.

As, on the evening of the third day from Chao-choo-foo, we approach Nam-hung, the people and the country undergo a great change for the better. The land is more level and better cultivated; villages are thicker and more populous, and the people are no longer conspicuously ill-favored. All evidence goes to prove that meagre diet and hard lines generally, continued from generation to generation, result in the production of an ill-conditioned and inferior race of people.

A three-storied pagoda on a prominent hill to the right marks the approach to Nam-hung, and another of nine stories marks the entrance. Swarms of people follow us through the streets, rushing with eager curiosity to obtain a glimpse of my face. Sometimes the surging masses of people, struggling and pushing and dodging, separate me from the coolies, and the din of the shouting and laughing is so great that my shouts to them to stop are unheard. A shout, or a wave of the hand results only in a quickening of the people's curiosity and an increase in the volume of their own noisiness. Thus hemmed in among a compact mass of apparently well-meaning, but highly inflammable Chinese, hooting, calling, laughing, and gesticulating, I follow the lead of Ching-We and Wong-Yup through a mile of streets to the hittim.

Rich native wares are displayed in great abundance, silks, satins, and fur-lined clothing so costly and luxurious, and in such numbers, that one wonders where they find purchasers for them all. Side by side with these are idol factories, where Joss may be seen in every stage of existence, from the unhewn log of his first estate to the proud pre-eminence of his highly finished condition, painted, gilded, and furbished. Coffin warehouses in which burial cases are displayed in tempting array are always conspicuous in a Chinese city. The coffins are made of curious slabs, jointed together in imitation of a solid log; some of these are varnished in a style calculated to make the eyes of a prospective corpse beam with joyous anticipation; others are plainly finished, destined for the abode of humbler and less pretentious remains.

At the hittim, with much angry expostulation and firmness of decision, the following mob are barred entrance to our room. They are not, by any means satisfied, however; they quickly smash in a little closed panel so they can look in, and every crack between the boards betrays a row of peering eyes. Ching-We is a hollow-eyed victim of the drug, and yearns for peace and quiet so that he can pass away the evening amid the seductive pleasures of the opium-smoker's heaven. The rattle and racket of the determined sight-seers outside, clamorously demanding to come in and see the Fankwae, annoy him to the verge of desperation under the circumstances.

He patiently endeavors to forget it all, however, and to banish the whole troublesome world from his thoughts, by producing his opium-pipe and lamp and attempting to smoke. But just as he is getting comfortably settled down to rolling the little knob of opium on the needle and has puckered his lips for a good pull, a decayed turnip comes sailing through the open panel and hits him on the back. The people looking in add insult to injury by indulging in an audible snicker, as Ching-We springs up and glares savagely into their faces. This indiscreet expression of their levity at once seals their doom, for Ching-We grabs a pole and hits the boards such a resounding whack, and advances upon them so savagely, that only a few undaunted youngsters remain at their post; the panel is repaired, and comparative peace and quiet restored for a short time. No sooner, however, has Ching-We mounted to the first story of heavenly beatitude from the effects of the first pipe of opium, than loud howls of "Fankwae. Fankwae!" are heard outside, and a shower of stones comes rattling against the boards. Ching-We goes to the partition door and indulges in an angry and reproachful attack upon the unoffending head of the establishment. The unoffending head of the establishment goes immediately to the other door and indulges in an angry and reproachful attack upon the shouters and stone-throwers outside. The Chinese are peculiar in many things, and in nothing, perhaps, more than their respect for words of reproach. Whether the long-suffering innkeeper hurled at their heads one of the moral maxims of Confucius, or an original production of his own brain, is outside the pale of my comprehension; but whatever it is, there is no more disturbance outside.

It must be about midnight when I am awakened from a deep sleep by the gabble of many people in the room. Transparent lanterns adorned with big red characters held close to my face cause me to blink like a cat upon opening my wondering eyes. These lanterns are held by yameni-runners in semi-military garb, to light up my features for the inspection of an officer wearing a rakish Tartar hat with a brass button and a red horse-hair tassel. The yameni-runners wear the same general style of head-dress, but with a loop instead of the brass button. The officer is possessed of a wonderfully soft, musical voice, and holds forth at great length concerning me, with Ching-We.

The officer takes my passport to the yamen, and ere leaving the room, pantomimically advises me to go to sleep again. In the morning Ching-We returns the two-foot square document with the Viceregal seal, and winks mysteriously to signify that everything is lovely, and that the goose of permission to go ahead to Nam-ngan hangs auspiciously high.

The morning opens up cool and cloudy, the pebble pathway is wider and better than yesterday, for it is now the thoroughfare along which thousands of coolies stagger daily with heavy loads of merchandise to the commencement of river navigation at Nam-hung. The district is populous and productive; bales of paper, bags of rice and peanuts, bales of tobacco, bamboo ware, and all sorts of things are conveyed by muscular coolies to Nam-hung to be sent down the river.

Gradually have we been ascending since leaving Nam-hung, and now is presented the astonishing spectacle of a broad flight of stone steps, certainly not less than a mile in length, leading up, up, up, to the summit of the Mae-ling Pass. Up and down this wonderful stairway hundreds of coolies are toiling with their burdens, scores of travellers in holiday attire and several palanquins bearing persons of wealth or official station. The stairway winds and zigzags up the narrow defile, averaging in width about twenty feet. Refreshment houses are perched here and there along the side, sometimes forming a bridge over the steps.

The stairway terminates at the summit in a broad stone archway of ancient build, over which are several rooms; this is evidently an office for the collection of revenue from the merchandise carried over the pass. Standing beneath this arch one obtains a comprehensive view of the country below to the north; a pretty picture is presented of gabled villages and temples, green hills, and pale-gold ripening rice-fields. The little silvery contributaries of the Kan-kiang ramify the picture like veins in the human palm, and the brown, cobbled pathways are seen leading from village to village, disappearing from view at short intervals beneath a cluster of tiled houses.

Steeper but somewhat shorter steps lead down from the pass, and the pathway follows along the bank of a tiny stream, leading through an almost continuous string of villages to the walls of Nam-ngan.

CHAPTER XVIII

DOWN THE KAN-KIANG VALLEY

The country is still nothing but river and mountains, and a sampan is engaged to float me down the Kan-kiang as far as Kan-tchou-foo, from whence I hope to be able to resume my journey a-wheel. The water is very low in the upper reaches of the river, and the sampan has to be abandoned a few miles from where it started. I then get two of the boatmen to carry the wheel, intending to employ them as far as Kan-tchou-foo.

From the stories current at Canton, the reputation of Kan-tchou-foo is rather calculated to inspire a lone Fankwae with sundry misgivings. Some time ago an English traveller, named Cameron, had in that city an unpleasantly narrow escape from being burned alive. The Celestials conceived the diabolical notion of wrapping him in cotton, saturating him with peanut-oil, and setting him on fire. The authorities rescued him not a moment too soon.

Ere traversing many miles of mountain-paths we emerge upon a partially cultivated country, where the travelling is somewhat better than in Quang-tung. The Mae-ling Pass was the boundary line between the provinces of Quang-tung and Kiang-se; my journey from Nam-ngan will lead me through the whole length of the latter great province, between three hundred and four hundred miles north and south.

The paths hereabout are of dirt mostly, and although wretched roads for a wheelman in the abstract, are nevertheless admirable in comparison with the stone-ways of Quang-tung. Gratified at the prospect of being able to proceed to Kui-kiang by land after all, I determine at once that, if the country gets no worse by to-morrow, I will dismiss the boatmen and pursue my way alone again on the bicycle. This resolve very quickly develops into an earnest determination to rid myself of the incubus of the snail-like movements of my new carriers, who are decidedly out of their element when walking, as I am very quickly brought to understand by the annoying frequency of their halts at way-side tea-houses to rest and smoke and eat.

Ere we are five miles from the sampan these festive mariners of the Kan-kiang have developed into shuffling, shirking gormandizers, who peer longingly into every eating-house we pass by and evince a decided tendency to convert their task into a picnic. Finding me uncomplaining in footing their respective "bills of lading" at the frequent places where they rest and indulge their appetites for tid-bits, they advance, in the brief space of four hours, from a simple diet of peanuts and bubbles of greasy pastry to such epicurean dishes as pickled duck, salted eggs, and fricasseed kitten!

Fricasseed kitten is all very well for people who have been reared in the lap of luxury, and tenderly nurtured; but neither of these half-clad Kankiang navigators was born with the traditional silver spoon. From infancy they have had to thrive the best way they could on rice, turnip-tops, peanuts, and delusive expectations of pork and fish; their assumption of the delicacies above mentioned betrays the possession of bumps of assurance bigger than goose-eggs. It is equivalent to a moneyless New York guttersnipe sailing airily into Delmonico's and ordering porter-house steak and terrapin, because some benevolent person volunteered to feed him for a day or two at his expense. Fearful lest their ambitious palates should soar into the extravagant and bankrupting realms of bird-nest soup, shark's fins, and deer-horn jelly, I firmly resolve to dispense with their services at the first favorable opportunity.

Many of the larger villages we pass through are walled with enormously massive brick walls, all bearing evidence of battering at the hands of the Tai-pings. Owing to the frequent restings of the carriers we are overtaken toward evening by a fellow boat-passenger, Oolong, who after our departure determined to follow our enterprising example and walk to Kantchou-foo. He comes trudging briskly along with a little white tea-pot swinging in his hand and an umbrella under his arm.

The day is disagreeably cold by reason of the chilly typhoons that blow steadily from the north. I have considerately encased the thinnest clad carrier in my gossamer rubbers to shield him from the wind, but Oolong is even thinner clad than he, and he has to hustle along briskly to keep his Celestial blood in circulation.

No sooner do we reach the hittim where it is proposed to remain over night than poor Oolong gets into trouble by appropriating to his own use the quilted garment of one of the employes of the place, which he finds lying around loose. The irate owner of the garment loudly accuses Oolong of wanting to steal it, and notwithstanding his vigorous protestations to the contrary he is denounced as a thief and summarily ejected from the premises.

The last I ever see of Oolong and his white tea-pot and umbrella is when he pauses for a moment to give his accusers a bit of his mind before vanishing into outer darkness.

The morning is quite wintry, and the people are clad in the seasonable costumes of the country. Huge quilted garments are put on one over another until their figures are almost of ball-like rotundity; the hands are drawn up entirely out of sight in the long, loosely flowing sleeves, while the head is half-hidden by being drawn, turtle-like, into their blue-quilted shells. Like the Persians, they seem nipped and miserable in the cold; looking at them, standing about with humped backs and pinched faces this morning, I wonder, with the Chinaman's happy nonchalance about committing suicide, why they don't all seek relief within the nice warm tombs at the end of the village. Surely it can be nothing but their rampant curiosity, urging them to live on and on in the hopes of seeing something new and novel, that keeps them from collapsing entirely in the winter.

My epicurean carriers indulge largely in chopped cayenne peppers this morning, which they mis liberally with their food.

The paths at least get no worse than they were yesterday, and to-day I meet the first passenger-wheelbarrow, with its big wheel in the centre, a bulky female with a baby on one side, and a bale of merchandise on the other. Sometimes our road brings us to the banks of the Kan-kiang, and most of the time, even when a mile or two away, we can see the queer, corrugated sails of the sampans.

Once to-day we happen upon a fleet of fourteen cormorant fishers at a moment when the excitement of their pursuit is at its height. About seventy or eighty cormorants are diving and chasing about among a shoal of fish in a big silent pool, while fourteen wildly excited Chinamen, clad in abbreviated breech-cloths, dart their bamboo rafts about hither and thither, urging each one his own cormorants to dive by tapping them smartly with their poles. The scene is animated in the extreme, a unique picture of Chinese river-life not to be easily forgotten.

About two o'clock in the afternoon we arrive at a city that I flatter myself is Kan-tchou-foo; all attempts to question the carriers or anybody else in regard to the matter results in the hopeless bewilderment of both them and myself. The carriers are not such ignoramuses in the art of pantomime, however, but that they are able to announce their intention of stopping here for the remainder of the day, and night.

The liberality of my purse for a short day and a half, with its concomitant luxurious living, has so thoroughly demoralized the unaccustomed river-men, that they encroach still further upon my bounty and forbearance by revelling all night in the sensuous delights of opium, at my expense, and turning up in the morning in anything but fit condition for the road. Putting this and that together, I conclude that we have not yet readied Kan-tchou-foo; but the carriers have developed into an insufferable nuisance, a hinderance to progress, rather than a help, so I determine to take them no farther.

I tell them nothing of my intentions until we reach a lonely spot a mile from the city. Here I tender them suitable payment for their services and the customary present, attach my loose effects to the bicycle and about my person, and motion them to return. As I anticipated, they make a clamorous demand for more money, even seizing hold of the bicycle and shouting angrily in my face. This I had easily foreseen, and wisely preferred to have their angry demonstrations all to myself, rather than in a crowded city where they could perhaps have excited the mob against me.

For the first time in China I have to appeal to my Smith & Wesson in the interests of peace; without its terrifying possession I should on this occasion undoubtedly have been under the necessity of "wiping up a small section of Kiang-se" with these two worthies in self defence. In the affairs of individuals, as of nations, it sometimes operates to the preservation of peace to be well prepared for war. How many times has this been the case with myself on this journey around the world!

The barometer of satisfaction at the prospect of reaching Kui-kiang before the appearance of old age rises from zero-level to a quite flattering height, as I find the pathways more than half ridable after delivering myself of the dead weight of native "assistance." Twelve miles farther and I am approaching the grim high walls of a large city that instinctively impresses me as being Kan-tchou-foo. The confused babel of noises within the teeming wall-encompassed city reaches my ears in the form of an "ominous buzz," highly suggestive of a hive of bees, into the interior of which it would be extremely ticklish work for a Fankwae to enter. "Half an hour hence," I mentally speculate, "the pitying angels may be weeping over the spectacle of my seal-brown roasted remains being dragged about the streets by the ribald and exultant rag, tag, and bobtail of Kan-tchou-foo."

Reflecting on the horrors of cotton, peanut-oil, and fire, I sit down for half an hour at a peanut-seller's stall, eat peanuts, and meditatively argue the situation of whether it would be better, if seized by a murderous mob, to take the desperate chances of being, like Cameron, rescued at the last minute from the horrors of incineration, or to take my own life. Fourteen cartridges and a 38 Smith & Wesson is the sum total of my armament. Emptying my revolver among the mob, and then being caught while reloading, would mean a lingering death by the most diabolical tortures, processes that the heathen Chinee has reduced to a refinement of cruelty unsurpassed in the old Spanish inquisition chambers.

The saucer of peanuts eaten, I pursue my way along the cobblestone path leading to the gate, without having come to any more definite conclusion than to keep cool and govern my actions according to circumstances. Ten minutes after taking this precaution I am trundling along a paved street, somewhat wider than the average Chinese city street, in the thick of the inevitable excited crowd.

The city probably contains two hundred thousand people, judging from the length of this street and the wonderful quantity and richness of the goods displayed in the shops. Along this street I see a more lavish display of rich silks, furs, tiger-skins, and other evidences of opulence than was shown me at Canton. The pressure of the crowds reduces me at once to the necessity of drifting helplessly along, whithersoever the seething human tide may lead. Sometimes I fancy the few officiously interested persons about me, whom I endeavor to question in regard to the hoped-for Jesuit mission, have interpreted my queries aright and are piloting me thither; only to conclude by their actions, the next minute, that they have not the remotest conception of my wants, beyond reaching the other side of the city. Now and then some ruffian in the crowd, in a spirit of wanton devilment, utters a wild, exultant whoop and raises the cry of "Fankwae. Fankwae." The cry is taken up by others of his kind, and the whoops and shouts of "Fankwae" swell into a tumultuous howl.

Anxious moments these; the spirit of wanton mischief fairly bristles through the crowd, evidently needing but the merest friction to set it ablaze and render my situation desperate. My coat-tail is jerked, the bicycle stopped, my helmet knocked off, and other trifling indignities offered; but to these acts I take no exceptions, merely placing my helmet on again when it is knocked off, and maintaining a calm serenity of face and demeanor.

A dozen times during this trying trundle of a mile along the chief business thoroughfare of Kan-tchou-foo, the swelling whoops and yells of "Fankwae" seem to portend the immediate bursting of the anticipated storm, and a dozen times I breathe easier at the subsidence of its volume. The while I am still hoping faintly for a repetition in part of my delightful surprise at Chao-choo-foo, we arrive at a gate leading out on to a broad paved quay of the Kan-kiang, which flows close by the walls.

Here I first realize the presence of Imperial troops, and awaken to the probability that I am indebted to their known proximity for the self-restraint of the mob, and their comparatively mild behavior. These Celestial warriors would make excellent characters on the spectacular stage; their uniforms are such marvels of color and pattern that it is difficult to disassociate them from things theatrical. Some are uniformed in sky blue, and others in the gayest of scarlet gowns, blue aprons with little green pockets, and blue turbans or Tartar hats with red tassels. Their gowns and aprons are patterned so as to spread out to a ridiculous width at bottom, imparting to the gay warrior an appearance not unlike an opened fan, his head constituting the handle.

As a matter of fact, the soldiers of the Imperial army are the biggest dandies in the country; when on the march coolies are provided to carry their muskets and accoutrements. As seen today, beneath the walls of Kantchou-foo, they impress me far more favorably as dandies than as soldiers equal to the demand of modern warfare.

Like soldiers the whole world round, however, they seem to be a good-natured, superior class of men; no sooner does my presence become known than several of them interest themselves in checking the aggressive crowding of the people about me. Some of them even accompany me down to the ferry and order the ancient ferryman to take me across for nothing. This worthy individual, however, enters such a wordy protestation against this that I hand him a whole handful of the picayunish tsin. The soldiers make him give me back the over-payment, to the last tsin. The sordid money-making methods of the commercial world seem to be regarded with more or less contempt by the gallant sons of Mars everywhere, not excepting even the soldiers of the Chinese army.

The scene presented by the city and the camp from across the river is of a most pronounced mediaeval character, as well as one of the prettiest sights imaginable. The grim walla of the city extend for nearly a mile along the undulating bank of the Kan-kiang, with a narrow strip of greensward between the solid gray battlements and the blue, wind-rippled waters of the river. Along the whole distance, rising and falling with the undulations of the bank, are ranged a continuous row of gayly fluttering banners-red, purple, blue, green, yellow, and all these colors combined in others that are striped as prettily as the prettiest of barber-poles-probably not less than five hundred flags. These multitudinous banners flutter from long, spear-headed bamboo-staves, and of themselves present a wonderfully pretty effect in combination with the blue waters, the verdant bank, and the gray walls. But in addition to these are thousands of soldiers, equally gaudy as to raiment, reclining irregularly along the same greensward, each warrior a bright bit of coloring on the verdant groundwork of the bank.

Over variable paths and through numerous villages and hamlets my way now leads, my next objective point being Ki-ngan-foo. At first a country of curious red buttes, terraced rice-fields, and reservoirs of mountain-drift water, serving the double purpose of fish-ponds and irrigating reservoirs, it develops later into a more mountainous region, where the bicycle quickly degenerates into a thing more ornamental than useful.

On a narrow mountain-trail is met a gentleman astride of a chunky twelve-hand pony. This diminutive steed is almost concealed beneath a wealth of gay trappings, to which are attached hundreds of jingling bells that fill the air with music as he walks or jogs along. In his fright at the bicycle, or me, he charges wildly up the steep mountain-slope, unseating his rider and making for the mountain-top like the all-possessed. His rider takes the sensible course of immediately pursuing the pony, instead of wasting time in unprofitable fault-finding with me.

Few people of these obscure mountain-hamlets have ever seen a Fankwae; many, doubtless, have never even heard of the existence of such queer beings. They gather in a crowd about me when I stay to seek refreshments; the general query of "What is he? what is he?" passed from one to another, sometimes elicits the laconically expressed information of" Fankwae" from some knowing villager or traveller passing through, but often their question remains unanswered, because among the whole assembly there is nobody who really knows what I am.

The wonderful industry of these people is more apparent in this mountain-country than anywhere else. The valleys are very narrow, often little more than mere ravines between the mountains, and wherever a square yard of productive soil is to be found it is cultivated to its utmost capacity. In places the mountain-ravines are terraced, to their very topmost limits, tier after tier of substantial rock wall banking up a few square yards of soil that have been gathered with infinite labor and patience from the ledges and crevices of the rocky hills. The uppermost terrace is usually a pond of water, gathered by the artificial drainage of still higher levels, and reserved for the irrigation of the score or more descending "steps" of the rice-growing stairway beneath it.

Notwithstanding the mountainous nature of the country and the dallying progress through Kan-tchou-foo, so lightsome does it seem to be once more journeying along, free and unencumbered, that I judge my day's progress to be not less than fifty miles when nightfall overtakes me in a little mountain-village. It is the first day's progress in China with which I have been really satisfied. Nevertheless, it has been a toilsome day, taken altogether, and when nothing but tea and rice confronts me at supper the reward seems so wretchedly inadequate that I rise in rebellion at once.

Neither eggs, fish, nor meat are to be obtained, the good woman at the little hittim explains in a high key; neither loan, ue, nor ue-ah, nothing but ch'ung-ch'a and mai. The woman is evidently a dear, considerate mortal, however, for she surveys my evident disgust with sorrowful visage, and then, suddenly brightening up, motions for me to be seated and leaves the house. Presently the good dame returns with a smile of triumph on her face and an object in her hand that, from casual observation, might be the hind-quarters of a rabbit. Bringing it to me in the most matter-of-fact manner, she holds it near my face and, pointing to it with the air of a cateress proudly conscious of having secured something that she knows will be unusually acceptable to her guest, she explains "me-aow, me-aow!" The woman's naivete is simply sublime, and her sagacity in explaining the nature of the meat by imitating a kitten's cry instead of telling me its Chinese name stamps her as superior to her surroundings; but, for all that, I conclude to draw the line at kitten and sup off plain rice and tea. "Me-aow, me-aow" might not be altogether objectionable if one knew it to have been a nice healthy kitten, but my observations of Chinese unsqueamishness about the food they eat leaves an abundance of room for doubt about the nature of its death and its suitableness for human consumption. I therefore resist the temptation to indulge.

A clear morning and a white frost usher in the commencement of another march across the mountains, over cobbled paths for the greater part of the forenoon. The sun is warm, but the mountain-breezes are cool and refreshing. About noon I ferry across a large tributary of the Kan-kiang, and follow for miles a cobble-stone path that leads down its eastern bank.

According to my map, Ki-ngan-foo should be about fifty miles south of Kan-tchou-foo, so that I ought to have reached there by noon to-day. All due allowance, however, must be made for the map-makers in mapping out a country where their opportunities for accuracy must have been of the meagerest kind. Small occasion for fault-finding under the circumstances, I think, for in the middle of the afternoon the gray battlements, the pagodas, and the bright coloring of military flags a few miles farther down stream tell me that the geographers have not erred to any considerable extent.

It is about sunset when I enter the gates and find myself within the Manchu quarter, that portion of the city walled off for the residence of the Manchu garrison and their families. The hittim to which the quickly gathering crowd conduct me is found to be occupied by a rather prepossessing female, who, however, looks frightened at my approach and shuts the door. Nor will she consent to open it again until reassured of my peaceful character by the lengthy explanation of the people outside, and a searching scrutiny of my person through a crack. After opening the door again, and receiving what I opine to be a statement of the financial possibilities of the situation from some person who has heard fabulous accounts of the Fankwaes' liberality, her apprehensiveness dissolves into a smile of welcome and she motions for me to come in.

The evening is chilly, and everybody is swollen out to ridiculous proportions by the numerous thick-quilted garments they are wearing. All present, whether male or female, are likewise distinguished by abnormally protruding stomachs. Being Manchus, and therefore the accredited warriors of the country, it occurs to me that perhaps the fashionable fad among them is to pad out their stomachs in token of the possession of extraordinary courage, the stomach being regarded by the Chinese as the seat of both courage and intelligence. In the absence of large stomachs provided by nature, perhaps these proud Manchus come to the correction of niggardly nature with wadding, as do various hollow-chested people in the "regions of mist and snow," the dreary, sunless land whence cometh the genus Fankwae.

But are the females also ambitious to be regarded as warriors, Amazonian soldiers, full of courage and warlike aspirations. As though in direct reply to my mental queries, a woman standing by solves the problem for me at once by producing from beneath her garments a wicker-basket containing a jar of hot ashes; stirring the deadened coals up a little she replaces it, evidently attaching it to her garments underneath by a little hook.

Among the hundreds of visitors that drop in to see the Fankwae and his bicycle is an intelligent old officer who actually knows that the great country of the Fankwaes is divided into different nationalities; either that, or else he thinks the Fankwaes have another name, said name being "Ying-yun" (English). Some idea of the dense ignorance of the Chinese of the interior concerning the rest of the world may be gathered from the fact that this officer is the first person since leaving Chao-choo-foo, upon whom the word "Ying-yun" has not been wholly thrown away.

Scenes of more than democratic equality and fraternity are witnessed in this Manchu hittim, where silk-robed mandarins and uncouth ragamuffins stand side by side and enjoy the luxury of seeing me take lessons in the use of the chop-sticks. All through China one cannot fail to be impressed with the freedom of intercourse between people of high and low degree; beggars with unwashed faces and disgusting sores and well-nigh naked bodies stand and discuss my appearance and movements with mandarins of high degree, without the least show of presumption on the one hand or condescension on the other.

Fully under the impression that Ki-ngan-foo has now peacefully come and peacefully gone from the pale of my experiences, I follow along awful stone paths next morning, leading across a level, cultivated country for several miles. Before long, however, a country of red clay hills and limited cultivable depressions is reached, where well-worn foot-trails over the natural soil afford more or less excellent going. In this particular district the women are observed to be all golden lilies, whereas the proportion of deformed feet in other rural districts has been rather small. Seeing that deformed feet add fifty or a hundred per cent, to the social and matrimonial value of a Chinese female, one cannot help applauding the enterprise of the people in this district as compared to the apathy existing on the same subject in some others. The comparative poverty of their clayey undulations has doubtless awakened them to the opportunities of increasing values in other directions. Hence they convert all their female infants into golden lilies, for whom some prospective husband will be willing to pay a hundred dollars more than if they were possessed of vulgar extremities as provided by nature.

The people hereabout seem unusually timid and alarmed at my strange appearance; it is both laughable and painful to see the women hobble off across the fields, frightened almost out of their wits. At times I can look about me and, within a radius of five hundred yards, see twenty or thirty females, all with deformed feet, scuttling off toward the villages with painful efforts at speed. One might well imagine them to be a colony of crippled rabbits, alarmed at the approach of a dog, endeavoring to hobble away from his destructive presence.

In the villages they seem equally apprehensive of danger, making it somewhat difficult to obtain anything to eat. At one village where I halt for refreshments the people scurry hastily into their houses at seeing me coming, and peep timidly out again after I have passed. Leaning the bicycle against a wall, I proceed in search of something to eat. A basket of oranges first attracts my attention; they are setting just inside the door of a little shop. The two women in charge look scared nearly out of their wits as I appear at the door and point to the basket; both of them retreat pell-mell into a rear apartment, and, holding the door ajar, peep curiously through to see what I am going to do. While my attention is directed for a moment to something down the street, one daring soul darts out and bears the basket of oranges triumphantly into the back room. For this heroic deed I beg to recommend this brave woman for the Victoria Cross; among the golden lilies of the Celestial Empire are no doubt many such brave souls, coequal with Grace Darling or the Maid of Saragossa.

Baffled and out-generaled by this brilliant sortie, I meander down to the other end of the village and invade the premises of an old man engaged in chopping up a piece of pork with a cleaver. The gallant pork-butcher gathers up the choicest parts of his meat and carries them into a rear room; with a wary yet determined look in his eye he then returns, and proceeds to mince up the few remaining odds and ends. It is plainly evident that he fancies himself in dangerous company, and is prepared to defend himself desperately with his meat-chopper in case he gets cornered up.

Finally I discover a really courageous individual, in the person of a man presiding over a peanut and treacle-cake establishment; this man, while evidently uneasy in his mind, manfully steels his nerves to the task of attending to my wants. Presently the people begin to gather at a respectful distance to watch me eat, and five minutes later, by a judicious distribution of a few saucers of peanuts among the youngsters, I gain their entire confidence.

About four o'clock in the afternoon my road once again brings me to a ferry across the Kan-kiang. Just previous to reaching the river, I meet on the road eight men, carrying a sedan containing a hideous black idol about twice as large as a man. A mile back from the ferry is another large walled city with a magnificent pagoda; this city I fondly imagine to be Lin-kiang, next on my map and itinerary to Ki-ngan-foo, and I mentally congratulate myself on the excellent time I have been making for the last two days.

Across the ferry are several official sampans with a number of boys gayly dressed in red and carrying old battle-axes; also a small squad of soldiers with bows and arrows. No sooner does the ferryman land me than the officer in charge of the party, with a wave of his hand in my direction, orders a couple of soldiers to conduct me into the city; his order is given in an off-hand manner peculiarly Chinese, as though I were a mere unimportant cipher in the matter, whose wishes it really was not worth while to consult. The soldiers conduct me to the city and into the yamen or official quarter, where I am greeted with extreme courtesy by a pleasant little officer in cloth top-boots and a pigtail that touches his heels. He is one of the nicest little fellows I have met in China, all smiles and bustling politeness and condescension; a trifle too much of the latter, perhaps, were we at all on an equality; but quite excusable under the conditions of Celestial refinement and civilization on one side, and untutored barbarism on the other.

Having duly copied my passport (apropos of the Chinese doing almost everything in a precisely opposite way to ourselves may be pointed out the fact that, instead of attaching vises to the traveller's passport, like European nations, each official copies off the entire document), the little officer with much bowing and scraping leads the way back to the ferry. My explanation that I am bound in the other direction elicits sundry additional bobbings of the head and soothing utterances and smiles, but he points reassuringly to the ferry. Arriving at the river, the little officer is dumbfounded to discover that I have no sampan—that I am not travelling by boat, but overland on the bicycle. Such a possibility had never entered his head; nor is it wonderful that it should not, considering the likelihood that nobody, in all his experience, had ever travelled to Kui-kiang from here except by boat. Least of all would he imagine that a stray Fankwae should be travelling otherwise.

At the ferry we meet the officer who first ordered the soldiers to take me in charge, and who now accompanies us back to the yamen. Evidently desirous of unfathoming the mystery of my incomprehensible mode of travelling through the country, these two officers spend much of the evening with me in the hittim smoking and keeping up an animated effort to converse. Notwithstanding my viceregal passport, the superior officer very plainly entertains suspicions as to my motives in undertaking this journey; his superficial politeness no more conceals his suspicions than a glass globe conceals a fish. Before they take their departure three yameni-runners are stationed in my room to assume the responsibility for my safe-keeping during the night.

An hour or so is spent waiting in the yamen next morning, apparently for the gratification of visitors continually arriving. When the yamen is crowded with people I am provided with a boiled fish and a pair of chop-sticks. Witnessing the consumption of this fish by the Fankwae is the finale of the "exhibition," and candor compels me to chronicle the fact that it fairly brings down the house.

It is a drizzly, disagreeable morning as I trundle out of the city gate over cobble-stones, made slippery by the rain. Walking before me is a slim young yameni-runner with a short bamboo-spear, and on his back a white bull's-eye eighteen inches in diameter; he is bare-footed and bare-headed and bare-legged. In the poverty of his apparel, the all-round contempt of personal appearance and cleanliness, and the total absence of individual ambition, this young person reminds me forcibly of our happy-go-lucky friend Osman, in the garden at Herat.

In striking contrast to him is the dandified individual who brings up the rear, about ten paces behind the bicycle. He likewise is a yameni-runner, but of higher degree than his compatriot of the advance; instead of a vulgar and rusty spear, he is armed with an oiled paper parasol, a flaming red article ornamented with blue characters and gilt women. Besides this gay mark of distinction and social superiority, he owns both shoes and hat, carrying the former, however, chiefly in his hand; when fairly away from town, he deliberately turns his red-braided jacket inside out to prevent it getting dirty. This transformation brings about a change from the two white bull's-eyes, to big rings of stitching by which these distinguishing appendages are attached.

A substantial meal of yams and pork is obtained at a way-side eating-house, after which yet another evidence of the sybaritic tastes of the rear-guard comes to light, in the form of a beautiful jade-stone opium pipe, with which he regales himself after chow-chow. He is, withal, possessed of more than average intelligence; it is from questioning him that I learn the rather startling fact that, instead of having reached Lin-kiang, I have not yet even come to Ki-ngan-foo. Ta-ho is the name of the city we have just left, and Ki-ngan-foo is whither we are now directly bound.

The weather at noon becomes warm, and the luxurious personage at the rear delivers his parasol, and shoes, and jade-stone pipe over to the slender and lissom advance guard to carry, to spare himself the weariness of their weight. Tea and tid-bit houses are plentiful, and stoppages for refreshing ourselves frequent. The rear guard assumes considerable dignity when in the presence of a crowd of sore-eyed rustics; he chides their ill-bred giggling at my appearance and movements by telling them, no matter how funny I appear to them here, I am a mandarin in my own country. After hearing this the crowd regard me with even more curiosity; but their inquisitiveness is now heavily freighted with respect.

Some of the costumes of the women in this region are very pretty and characteristic, and many of the females are themselves not devoid of beauty, as beauty goes among the Mongols. Particularly do I notice one to-day, whose tiny, doll-like extremities are neatly bound with red, blue, and green ribbon; her face is a picture of refinement, her head-dress a marvel of neatness and skill, and her whole manner and make-up attractive. Unlike her timid and apprehensive sisters of yesterday, she sees nothing in me to be afraid of; on the contrary, she comes and sits beside ine on the bench and makes herself at home with the peanuts and sweets I purchase, and laughs merrily when I offer to give her a ride on the bicycle.

The sun is sinking behind the mountains to the west when we approach the city of Ki-ngan-foo, its northern extremity marked by a very ancient pagoda now rapidly crumbling to decay. The city forms a crescent on the west bank of the Kan-kiang, the main street running parallel with the river for something like half a mile before terminating at the walls of the Manchu quarter.

The fastidious gentleman at the rear has betrayed symptoms of a very uneasy state of mind during the afternoon, and now, as he halts the procession a moment to turn the bull's-eye side of his coat outward, and to put on his shoes, he gives me a puzzled, sorrowful look and shakes his head dolefully. The trickiness of former acquaintances causes me to misinterpret this display of emotion into an hypocritical assumption of sorrow at the near prospect of our parting company, with ulterior designs on the nice long strings of tsin he knows to be in my leathern case. It soon becomes evident, however, that trouble of some kind is anticipated in Ki-ngan-foo, for he points to my revolver and then to the city and solemnly shakes his head.

The crescent water-front, the broad blue river and white sand, the plain dotted with smiling villages opposite, the tall pagodas, the swarms of sampans with their quaint sails, form the composite parts of a very pretty and striking picture, as seen from the northern tip of the crescent.

Near the old ruined pagoda the rear-guard points in an indifferent sort of a way to a substantial brick edifice surmounted by a plain wooden cross. Ah! a Jesuit mission, so help me Pius IX! now shall I meet some genial old French priest, who will make me comfortable for the night and enlighten me in regard to my bearings, distances, and other subjects about which I am in a very thick fog. Instead of the fifty miles from Kan-tchou-foo to Ki-ngan-foo indicated on my map, it has proved to be considerably over a hundred.

The sole occupant of the building, however, is found to be a fat, monkish-looking Chinaman, who knows never a word of either French or pidgeon English. He says he knows Latin, but for all the benefit this worthy accomplishment is to me he might as well know nothing but his own language. He informs me, by an expressive motion of the hand, that the missionaries have departed; whether gone to their everlasting reward, however, or only on a temporary flight, his pantomimic language fails to record. Subsequently I learn that they were compelled to flee the country, owing to the hostility aroused by the operations of the French in Tonquin.

Instead of extending that cordial greeting and consideration one would naturally expect from a converted Chinaman whose Fankwae accomplishments soar to the classic altitude of Latin, the Celestial convert seems rather anxious to get rid of me; he is evidently on pins and needles for fear my presence should attract a mob to the place and trouble result therefrom.

As we proceed down the street my appearance seems to stir the population up to a pitch of wild excitement. Merchants dart in and out of their shops, people in rags, people in tags, and people in gorgeous apparel, buzz all about me and flit hither and thither like a nest of stirred-up wasps. If curiosity has seemed to be rampant in other cities it passes all the limits of Occidental imagination in Ki-ngau-foo. Upon seeing me everybody gives utterance to a peculiar spontaneous squeak of surprise, reminding me very much of the monkeys' notes of alarm in the tree-tops along the Grand Trunk road, India.

One might easily imagine the very lives of these people dependent upon their success in obtaining a glimpse of my face. Well-dressed citizens rush hastily ahead, stoop down, and peer up into my face as I trundle past, with a determination to satisfy their curiosity that our language is totally inadequate to describe, and which our temperament renders equally difficult for us to understand.

By the time we are half-way along the street the whole city seems in wild tumult. Men rush ahead, peer into my face, deliver themselves of the above-mentioned peculiar squeak, and run hastily down some convergent alley-way. Stall-keepers quickly gather up their wares, and shop-keepers frantically snatch their goods inside as they hear the tumult and see the mob coming down the street. The excitement grows apace, and the same wanton cries of "Fank-wae. Fankwae!" that followed me through Kan-tchou-foo are here repeated with wild whoops and exultant cries. One would sometimes think that all the devils of Dante's "Inferno" had gotten into the crowd and set them wild with the spirit of mischief.

By this time the yameni-runners are quaking with fear; he of the paper parasol and jade-stone pipe walks beside me, convulsively clutching my arm, and with whiningly anxious voice shouts out orders to his subordinate. In response to these orders the advance-guard now and then hurries forward and peeps around certain corners, as though expecting some hidden assailants.

Thus far, although the symptoms of trouble have been gradually assuming more and more alarming proportions, there has been nothing worse than demoniacal howls. The chief reason of this, however, it now appears, has been the absence of loose stones, for no sooner do we enter an inferior quarter where loose stones and bricks are scattered about, than they come whistling about our ears. The poor yameni-runners shout deprecatingly at the mob; in return the mob loudly announce their intention of working destruction upon my unoffending head. Fortunately for me that head is pretty thoroughly hidden beneath the thick pith thatch-work of my Indian solar topee, otherwise I should have succumbed to the first fusillade of stones at the instance of a cracked pate. Stones that would have knocked me out of time in the first round rattle harmlessly on the 3/4-inch pith helmet, the generous proportions of which effectually protect head and neck from harm. Once, twice, it is knocked off by a stone striking it on the brim, but it never reaches the ground before being recovered and jammed more firmly than ever in its place. Things begin to look pretty desperate as we approach the gate of the Manchu quarter; an immense crowd of people have hurried down back streets and collected at this gate; fancying they are there for the hostile purpose of heading us off, I come very near dodging into an open door way with a view of defending myself till the yameni-runners could summon the authorities. There is no time for second thought, however; precious little time, in fact, for anything but to keep my helmet in its place and hurry along with the bicycle. The yameni-runners repeatedly warn the crowd that I am armed with a top-fanchee (revolver);

this, doubtless, prevents them from closing in on us, and keeps their aggressive spirit within certain limits.

A moment's respite is happily obtained at the Manchu gate; the crowd gathered there in advance are comparatively peaceful, and the mob, for a moment, seem to hesitate about following us inside. Making the most of this opportunity, we hurry forward toward the yamen, which, I afterward learn, is still two or three hundred yards distant. Ere fifty yards are covered the mob come pouring through the gate, yelling like demons and picking up stones as they hurry after us. "A horse, a horse, my kingdom for a horse." or, what would suit me equally as well, a short piece of smooth road in lieu of break-neck cobble-stones.

Again are we overtaken and bombarded vigorously; ignorant of the distance to the yamen, I again begin looking about for some place in which to retreat for defensive purposes, unwilling to abandon the bicycle to destruction and seek doubtful safety in flight. At this juncture a brick strikes the unfortunate rear-guard on the arm, injuring that member severely, and quickening the already badly frightened yameni-runners to the urgent necessity of bringing matters to an ending somehow.

Pointing forward, they persist in dragging me into a run. Thus far I have been very careful to preserve outward composure, feeling sure that any demonstration of weakness on my part would surely operate to my disadvantage. The runners' appealing cries of "Yameni! yameni!" however, prove that we are almost there, and for fifty or seventy-five yards we scurry along before the vengeful storm of stones and pursuing mob.

As I anticipated, our running only increases the exultation of the mob, and ere we get inside the yamen gate the foremost of them are upon us. Two or three of the boldest spirits seize the bicycle, though the majority are evidently afraid I might turn loose on them with the top-fanchee. We are struggling to get loose from these few determined ruffians when the officials of the yamen, hearing the tumult, come hurrying to our rescue.

The only damage done is a couple of spokes broken out of the bicycle, a number of trifling bruises about my body, a badly dented helmet, and the yameni-runner's arm rather severely hurt. When fairly inside and away from danger the pent-up feelings of the advance-guard escape in silent tears, and his superior of the jade-stone pipe sits down and mournfully bemoans his wounded arm. This arm is really badly hurt, probably has sustained a slight fracture of the bone, judging from its unfortunate owner's complaints.

The Che-hsein, as I believe the chief magistrate is titled, greets me while running out with his subordinates, with reassuring cries of "S-s-o, s-s-o, s-s-o, s-s-o," repeated with extraordinary rapidity between shouts of deprecation to the mob. The mob seem half inclined to pursue us even inside the precincts of the yamen, but the authoritative voice of the Che-hsein restrains their aggressiveness within partly governable measure; nevertheless, in spite of his presence, showers of stones are hurled into the yamen so long as I remain in sight.

As quickly as possible the Che-hsein ushers me into his own office, where he quickly proves himself a comparatively enlightened individual by arching his eyebrows and propounding the query, "French?" "Ying-yun," I reply, feeling the advantage of being English or American, rather than French, more appreciably perhaps than I have ever done before or since.

This question of the Che-hsein's at once reveals a gleam of explanatory light concerning the hostility of the people. For aught I know to the contrary it may be but a few days ago since the Jesuit missionaries were compelled to flee for their lives. The mob cannot be expected to distinguish between French and English; to the average Celestial we of the Western world are indiscriminately known as Fankwaes, or foreign devils; even to such an enlightened individual as the Che-hsein himself these divisions of the Fankwae race are but vaguely understood.

After satisfying himself by questioning the yameni-runners, that I am without companions or other baggage save the bicycle, the Che-hsein ferrets out a bottle of samshoo and tenders me a liberal allowance in a teacup. This is evidently administered with the kindly intention of quieting my nerves, which he imagines to be unstrung from the alarmingly rough treatment at the hands of his riotous townmen.

Riotous they are, beyond a doubt, for even as the Che-hsein pours out the samshoo the clamorous howls of "Fankwae. Fankwae." seem louder than ever at the gates. Now and then, as the tumult outside seems to be increasing, the Che-hsein writes big red characters on flat bamboo-staves and sends it out by an officer to be read to the mob; and occasionally, as he sits and listens attentively to the clamor, as though gauging the situation by the volume of the noise, he addresses himself to me with a soothing and reassuring "S-s-o, s-s-o, s-s-o, s-o."

Shortly after my arrival the worthy-minded Che-hsein knits his brow for a moment in a profound study, and then, lightening up suddenly, delivers himself of "No savvy," a choice morsel of pidgeon English that he has somehow acquired. This is the full extent of his knowledge, however; but, feeble glimmer of my own mother tongue though it be, it sounds quite cheery amid the wilderness wild of Celestial gabble in the office. For although the shackles of authority hold in check the murderous mob, howling for my barbarian gore outside, a constant stream of officials and their friends are admitted to see me and the bicycle.

In making an examination of the bicycle, the peculiar "Ki-ngan-foo squeak" finds spontaneous expression at every new surprise. A man enters the room, peers wonderingly into my face-squeak!—comes closer, and looks again—squeak!—notices the peculiar cut of my garments—squeak!—observes my shoes—squeak!—sees helmet on table—squeak!—sees the bicycle—squeak!—goes and touches it—squeak!—finds out that the pedals twirl round—squeak! and thus he continues until he has seen everything and squeaked at everything; he then takes a lingering survey of the room to satisfy himself that nothing has been overlooked, gives a parting squeak, and leaves the room.

The Che-hsein provides me with a chicken, boiled whole, head included, for supper, and consumes his own meal at the same time. The difference between the Che-hsein, eating little prepared meatballs and rice, with gilded chop-sticks, and myself tearing the spraggly-looking rooster asunder and gnawing the drum-sticks greedily with my teeth, no doubt readily appeals to the interested lookers-on as an instructive picture of Chinese civilization and outer barbarism as depicted in our respective modes of eating, side by side.

More than once during the evening the tumult at the gate swells into a fierce hubbub, as though pandemonium had broken loose, and the blood-thirsty mob were determined to fetch me out. Every minute, at these periodical outbursts, I expect to see them come surging in through the doorway. A sociable young man, whose chief concern is to keep me supplied with pipes and tea, explains, with the aid of a taper, that the crowd are desirous of burning me alive. This cheerful piece of information, the sociable young man imparts with a characteristic Chinese chuckle of amusement; the thought of a Fankwae squirming and sizzling in the oil-fed flames touches the chord of his risibilities, and makes him giggle merrily. The Che-hsein himself occasionally goes out and harangues the excited mob, the authoritative tones of his voice being plainly heard above the squabbling and yelling.

It must be near about midnight when the excitement has finally subsided, and the mob disperse to their homes. Six yameni-runners then file into the room, paper umbrellas slung at their backs in green cloth cases, and stout bamboo quarter-staves in hand. The Che-hsein gives them their orders and delivers a letter into the hands of the officer in charge; he then bids me prepare to depart, bidding me farewell with much polite bowing and scraping, and sundry memorable "chin-chins."

A closely covered palanquin is waiting outside the door; into this I am conducted and the blinds carefully drawn. A squad of men with flaming torches, the Che-hsein, and several officials lead the way, maintaining great secrecy and quiet; stout carriers hoist the palanquin to their shoulders and follow on behind; others bring up the rear carrying the bicycle.

Back through the Manchu quarter and out of the gate again our little cavalcade wends its way, the officials immediately about the palanquin addressing one another in undertones; back, part way along the same street which but a few short hours ago resounded with the hoots and yells of the mischievous mob, down a long flight of steps, and the palanquin is resting at the end of a gang-plank leading aboard a little passenger-sampan. The worthy Che-hsein bows and scrapes and chin-chins me along this gang-plank, the bicycle is brought aboard, the six yameni-runners follow suit, and the boat is poled out into the river. The squad of torch-bearers are seen watching our progress until we are well out into the middle of the stream, and the officer in charge of my little guard stands out and signals them with his lantern, notifying them, I suppose, that all is well. One would imagine, from their actions, that they were apprehensive of our sampan being pursued or ambushed by some determined party. And yet the scene, as we drift noiselessly along with the current, looks lovely and peaceful as the realms of the blest; the crescent moon, the shimmering water—and the slowly receding lights of the city; what danger can there possibly be in so quiet and peaceful a scene as this?

By daylight we are anchored before another walled city, which I think is Ki-shway, a city of considerable pretentions as to wall, but full of social and moral rottenness and commercial decadence within, judging, at least, from outward appearances. Few among the crowds that are permitted free access to the yamen here do not betray, in unmistakable measure, the sins of former generations; while, as regards trade, half the place is in a ruinous, tumble-down condition.

The mandarin here is a fleshy, old-fashioned individual, with thick lips and an expression of great good humor. He provides me with a substantial breakfast of rice and pork, and fetches his wife and children in to enjoy the exhibition of a Fankwae feeding, likewise permitting the crowd to look in through the doors and windows. He is a phlegmatic, easy-going Celestial, and occupies about two hours copying my passport and writing a letter. At the end of this time he musters a squad of twelve retainers in faded red uniforms and armed with rusty pikes, who lead the way back to the river, followed by three yameni-runners, equipped, as usual, each with an umbrella and a small string of tsin to buy their food. The gentlemen with the mediaeval weapons accompany us to the river and keep the crowd from pressing too closely upon us until I and the yameni-runners board a Ki shway sampan that is to convey me to the next down-stream city.

It now becomes apparent that my bicycling experiences in China are about ending, and that the authorities have determined upon passing me down the Kan-kiang by boat to the Yang-tsi-kiang. I am to be passed on from city to city like a bale of merchandise, delivered and receipted for from day to day.

A few miles down stream we overtake a fleet of some twenty war-junks, presenting a most novel and interesting sight, crowded as each one is with the gayest of flags and streaming pennants galore. The junks are cumbersome enough, in all conscience, as utterly useless for purposes of modern warfare as the same number of floating hogsheads; yet withal they make a gallant sight, the like of which is to be seen nowhere these days but on the inland waters of China. Each junk is propelled by a crew of fourteen oarsmen, dressed in uniforms corresponding in color to the triangular flags that flutter gayly in the breeze at the stern. Not the least interesting part of the spectacle are these same oarsmen, as they ply their long unwieldy sweeps in admirable unison; the sleeves of their coats are almost as broad as the body of the garment, and at every sweep of the oar these all flap up and down together in a manner most comical to behold.

All day long our modest little sampan keeps company with this gay fleet, giving me an excellent opportunity of witnessing its manoeuvres. Said manoeuvres and evolutions consist of more or less noisy greetings and demonstrations at every town and village we pass. In the case of a small town, a number of pikemen and officials assemble on the shore, erect a few flags, hammer vigorously on a resonant gong, shout out some sing-song greeting and shoot off a number of bombs and fire-crackers. The foremost vessel of the fleet replies to these noisy compliments by a salute of its one gun, and mayhap throws in two or three bombs, according to the liberality of the salutation ashore.

At the larger towns the amount of gunpowder burned and noise created is something wonderful. Bushels of fire-crackers are snapping and rattling away, the while gongs are beating, bombs exploding by the score, and salvoes of artillery are making the mountains echo, from every vessel in the fleet. Beneath the walls of a town we pass soon after noon are ranged fifteen other junks; as the fleet passes, these vessels simultaneously discharge all their guns, while at the same instant there burst upon the startled air detonations from hundreds of bombs, big heaps of firecrackers, and the din of many resonant gongs. Not to be outdone, the fleet of twenty return the compliment in kind, and with cheers from the crews thrown in for interest.

The fifteen now join the procession, adding volume and picturesqueness to the already wonderfully pretty scene, by their hundreds of brilliant-hued banners, and theatrically costumed oarsmen. About four o'clock, as we are approaching the city of Hat-kiang, our destination for the day, there comes to meet the gallant navy a pair of twin vessels surpassing all the others in the gorgeousness of their flags and the picturesqueness of the costumes. Purple is the prevailing color of both flags and crew. At their splendid appearance our yameni-runners announce in tones of enthusiasm and admiration that these new-comers hail from Lin-kiang, a large city down stream, that I fancied, it will be remembered, having reached at Ta-ho.

The officials are still abed when, in the early morning of the third day, we reach Sin-kiang, and repair to the yamen. A large crowd, however, gather and follow us from the market-place, swelling gradually by reenforcements to a multitude that surges in and out of the shanty-like office in such swarms that the frail board walls bulge and crack with the pressure. When the crowd overwhelm the place entirely, the officials clear them out by angry gesticulations and moral suasion, sometimes menacingly shaking the end of their own queues at them as though they were wielding black-snake whips. Having driven them out, no further notice is taken of them, so they immediately begin swarming in again, until the room is again inundated, when they are again driven out.

The permitting of this ebbing and flowing of the multitude into the official quarters is something quite incomprehensible to me; the mob is swayed and controlled—as far as they are controlled at all—without any organized effort of those in authority; when the officials commence screaming angrily at them they begin moving out; when the shouting ceases they begin swarming back. Thus in the course of an hour the room will, perchance, be filled and emptied with angry remonstrance half a dozen times, when, from our own stand-point, a couple of men stationed at the door with authority to keep them out would prevent all the bother and annoyance. Sure enough the Chinaman is "a peculiar little cuss," whether seen at home or abroad.

If the inhabitants of Ki-shway are scrofulous, sore-eyed, and mangy, they are at least an improvement on the disgusting state of the public health at Sin-kiang, as revealed in the lamentable condition of the crowd at the yamen and in the markets. Scarcely is it possible to single out a human being of sound and healthful appearance from among them all. Everybody has sore eyes, some have horribly diseased scalps, sores on face and body, and all the horrible array of acquired and hereditary diseases. One's hair stands on end almost at the thought of being among them, to say nothing of eating in their presence, and of their own cooking. Of my new escort from Sin-kiang all three have dreadfully sore eyes, and one wretched mortal is as piebald as a circus pony, from head to foot, with the leprosy. Added to these recommendations, they have the manners and instincts of swine rather than of human beings.

The same sampan is re-engaged to convey us farther down stream; beneath the housing of bamboo-mats, the rice-chaff leaves barely room for us to crowd in and huddle together from the rain and cold prevailing outside. The worst the elements can do, however, is far preferable to personal contact with these vile creatures; and so I don my blanket and gossamer rubbers, and sit out in the rain. The rain ceases and the chilly night air covers everything with a coating of hoar-frost, but all this is nothing compared with the horrible associations inside, the reeking fumes of opium and tobacco adding yet another abomination to be remembered.

At early morn we land and pursue our way for a few miles across country to Lin-kiang, which is situated on a big tributary stream a few miles above its junction with the Kan-kiang. Our way loads through a rich strip of low country, sheltered and protected from inundations by an extensive system of dykes. Here we pass through orchards of orange-trees bristling with the small blood-red mandarin oranges; we help ourselves freely from the trees, for their great plenteousness makes them of very little value. On the stalls they can be purchased six for one cent; like the people in the great peanut producing country below Nam-hung, the cheapness and abundance of oranges here seems an inducement for the people to almost subsist thereon.

Everybody is either buying, stealing, selling, packing, gathering, carrying, or eating oranges; coolies are staggering Lin-kiang-ward beneath big baskets of newly plucked fruit, and others are conveying them in wheelbarrows; boats are being loaded for conveyance along the river. Every orange-tree is distinguished by white characters painted on its trunk, big enough so that those who run may read the rightful owner's name and take warning accordingly.

Three more wearisome but eventful days, battling against adverse winds, and we come to anchor in a little slough, where a war-junk and several fishing vessels are already moored for the night. While supper is preparing I pass the time promenading back and forth along a little foot-trail leading for a short distance round the shore. The crew of the war-vessel are engaged in drying freshwater shrimps, tiny minnows, and other drainings and rakings of the water to store away for future use. One of the younger officers stalks back and forth along the same path as myself, brusquely maintaining the road whenever we meet, evidently bent on showing off his contempt for the boasted prowess of the Fankwaes, by compelling me to step to one side. His demeanor is that of a bully stalking about with the traditional chip on his shoulder, daring me to come and knock it off.

Considering the circumstances about us, this is a wonderfully courageous performance on his part; nothing but his ignorance of my Smith & Wesson can explain his temerity in assuming a bellicose attitude with only one man-of-war at his back. Out of consideration for this ignorance, I studiously avoid interfering with the chip.

At length the river-voyage comes to an end at Wu-chang, on the Poyang Hoo, when I am permitted to proceed overland with an escort to Kui-kiang.

Spending the last night at a village inn, we pursue our way over awful bowlder paths next morning, for several miles; over a low mountain-pass and down the northern slope to a level plain. A towering white pagoda is observable in the distance ahead; thia the yameni-runner says is Kui-kiang. At a little way-side tea-house, I find Christmas numbers of the London Graphic pasted on the walls; yet with all this, so utterly unreliable has my information heretofore been, and so often have my hopes and expectations turned out disappointing, that I am almost afraid to believe the evidence of my own senses. The Graphic pictures are of the Christmas pantomimes; the good woman of the tea-house points out to me the tremendous noses, the ear-to-ear mouths, and the abnormal growths of chin therein depicted, with much amusement; "Fankwae," she says, "te-he, te-he," apparently fancying them genuine representations of certain types of that queer, queer people.

The paths improve, and soon I see the smoke of a steamer on the Yang-tsi than which, it is needless to say, no more welcome sight has greeted my vision the whole world round. Only the smoke is seen, rising above the city; it cannot be a steamer, it is too good to be possible! this isn't Kui-kiang; this is another wretched disappointment, the smoke is some Chinese house on fire! Not until I get near enough to distinguish flags on the consulates, and the crosses on the mission churches, do I permit myself fully to believe that I am at last actually looking at Kui-kiang, the city that I have begun to think a delusion and a snare, an ignis fatuus that was dancing away faster than I was approaching.

The sight of all these unmistakable proofs that I am at last bidding farewell to the hardships, the horrible filth, the soul-harrowing crowds, the abominable paths, and the ever-present danger and want of consideration; that in a little while all these will be a dream of the past, gives wings to my wheel wherever it can be mounted, and ridden. The yameni-runner is left far behind, and I have already engaged a row-boat to cross the little lake in the rear of the city, and the boatman is already pulling me to the "Ying-yun," when the poor yameni-runner comes hurrying up and shouts frantically for me to come back and fetch him.

Knowing that the man has to take back his receipt I yield to his request, follow him first to the Kui-kiang yamen, and from thence proceed to the English consulate. Captain McQuinn, of the China Steam Navigation Company's steamer Peking, and the consulate doctor see me riding down the smooth gravelled bund, followed by a crowd of delighted Celestials. "Hello! are you from Canton" they sing out in chorus. "Well, well, well! nobody expected to ever see anything of you again; and so you got through all safe, eh?"

"What's the matter? you look bad about the eyes," says the observant doctor, upon shaking hands; "you look haggard and fagged out."

Upon surveying myself in a mirror at the consulate I can see that the doctor is quite justified in his apprehensions. Hair long, face unshaved for five weeks, thin and gaunt-looking from daily hunger, worry, and hard dues generally, I look worse than a hunted greyhound. I look far worse, however, than I feel; a few days' rest and wholesome fare will work wonders.

An appetizing lunch of cold duck, cheese, and Bass's ale is quickly provided by Mr. Everard, the consul, who seems very pleased that the affair at Ki-ngan-foo ended without serious injury to anybody.

The Peking starts for Shanghai in an hour after my arrival; a warm bath, a shave, and a suit of clothes, kindly provided by pilot King, brings about something of a transformation in my appearance. Bountiful meals, clean, springy beds, and elegantly fitted cabins, form an impressive contrast to my life aboard the sampans on the Kan-kiang. The genii of Aladdin's lamp could scarcely execute any more marvellous change than that from my quarters and fare and surroundings at the village hittim, where my last night on the road from Canton was spent, and my first night aboard the elegant and luxurious Peking, only a day later.

A pleasant run down the Yang-tsi-kiang to Shanghai, and I arrive at that city just twenty-four hours before the Japanese steamer, Yokohama Maru, sails for Nagasaki. Taking passage aboard it leaves me but one brief day in the important and interesting city of Shanghai, during which time I have to purchase a new outfit of clothes, see about money matters, and what not.

CHAPTER XIX

THROUGH JAPAN

An uneventful run of two days, and the Yokohama Maru steams into the beautiful harbor of Nagasaki. The change from the filth of a Chinese city to Nagasaki, clean as if it had all just been newly scoured and varnished, is something delightful. One gets a favorable impression of the Japs right away; much more so, doubtless, by coming direct from China than in any other way. Two days of preparation and looking about leaves almost a pang of regret at having to depart so soon. The American consul here, Mr. B, is a very courteous gentleman; to him and Mr. M, an American gentleman, instructor in the Chinese navy, I am indebted for an exhibition of the geisha dance, and many other courtesies.

Having duly supplied myself with Japanese paper-money—ten, five, and one yen notes; fractional currency of fifty, twenty, and ten sen notes, besides copper sen for tea and fruit at road-side teahouses, on Tuesday morning, November 23d, I start on my journey of eight hundred miles through lovely Nippon to Yokohama.

Captain F and Mr. B, the American consul, have come to the hotel to see me off. A showery night has made the roads a trifle muddy. Through the long, neat-looking streets of Nagasaki, into a winding road, past crowded hill-side cemeteries, adorned with queer stunted trees and quaint designs in flowers, I ride, followed by wondering eyes and a running fire of curious comments from the Japs.

Nagasaki lies at the shoreward base of a range of hills, over a pass called the Himi-toge, which my road climbs immediately upon leaving the city. A good road is maintained over the pass, and an office established there to collect toll from travellers and people bringing produce into Nagasaki. The aged and polite toll-collector smiles and bows at me as I trundle innocently past his sentry-box-like office up the steep incline, hoping that I may take the hint and spare him the necessity of telling me the nature of his duty. My inexperience of Japanese tolls and roads, however, renders his politeness inoperative, and, after allowing me to get past, duty compels him to issue forth and explain. A wooden ticket containing Japanese characters is given me in exchange for a few tiny coins. This I fancy to be a passport for another toll-place higher up. Subsequently, however, I learn it to be a return ticket, the old toll-keeper very naturally thinking I would return, by and by, to Nagasaki.

Ponies and buffaloes, laden with baskets of rice, fodder, firewood, and various agricultural products, are encountered on the pass, in charge of Japanese rustics in broad bamboo-hats, red blankets, bare legs, and straw sandals, who lead their charges by long halter-ropes. Both horses and buffaloes are shod with shoes of the same unsubstantial material as the men. When the Japanese traveller sets out on a journey, he provides himself with a new pair of straw sandals; these last him for a tramp of from ten to twenty miles, according to the nature of the road. When worn out, his foot-gear may be readily renewed at any village for a mere song. The same may be said of his horse or buffalo, although several extra shoes are generally carried along in case of need.

The summit of the pass is distinguished by a very deep cutting through the ridge rock of the mountain, and a series of successive sharp turns back and forth along narrow-terraced gardens and fields bring the road down into the valley of a clear little stream, called the Himi-gawa. Smooth, hard roads follow along this purling rivulet, now and then crossing it on a stone or wooden bridge. A small estuary, reaching inland like a big bite out of a cake, is passed, and the pretty little village of Yagami reached for dinner. The eating-house, like nearly all Japanese eating-places, is neat and cleanly, the brown wood-work being fairly polished bright from floor to ceiling.

Sitting down on the edge of the raised floor, I am approached by the landlady, who kneels down and bows her forehead to the floor. Her politeness is very charming, and her smile would no doubt be more or less winsome were it not for the hideous blackening of the teeth. Blackened teeth is the distinguishing mark between maid and matron in the flowery kingdom of the Mikados. The teeth are stained black at marriage, and henceforth a smile that heretofore displayed rows of small white ivories, and perchance was fairly bewitching, becomes positively repulsive to the Western mind.

Fish and rice (sakana and meshi) are the most readily obtainable things to eat at a Japanese hotel, and often form the only bill of fare. Sake, or rice-beer, is usually included in the Jap's own meal, but the average European traveller at first prefers limiting his beverage to tea. The sake is served up in big-necked bottles of cheap porcelain holding about a pint. The bottle is set for a few minutes in boiling water to warm the sake, the Japs preferring to drink it warm. Sake is more like spirits than beer, an honest alcoholic production from rice that soon recommends itself to the European palate, though rather offensive at first.

Every tea-house along the road is made doubly attractive by prettily dressed attendants-smiling girls who come out and invite passing travellers to rest and buy tea and refreshments. Their solicitations are chiefly winsome smiles and polite bows and the cheerful greeting "O-ai-o" (the Japanese "how do you do"). A tiny teapot, no larger than those the little girls at home play at "keeping house" with, and shell-like cup to match, is brought on a lacquered tray and placed before one, with charming grace, if a halt is made at one of these tea-houses. Persimmons, sweets, cakes, and various tid-bits are temptingly arrayed on the sloping stand in front. The most trifling purchase is rewarded with an exhibition of good-nature and politeness worth many times the money.

About sunset I roll into the smooth, clean streets of Omura, a good-sized town, and seek the accommodation of a charming yadoya (inn) pointed out by a youth in semi-European clothes, who seems bubbling over with pleasure at the opportunity of rendering me this slight assistance. A room is assigned me upstairs, a mat spread for me to recline on, by a polite damsel, who touches her forehead to the floor both when she makes her appearance and her exit. Having got me comfortably settled down with the customary service of tea, sweets, little boxed brazier of live charcoal, spittoon, etc., the proprietor, his wife, and daughter, all come up and prostrate themselves after the most approved fashion.

After all the salaaming and deferentiality experienced in other Eastern countries, one still cannot help being impressed with the spectacle of several grotesque Japs bowing before one's seated figure like Hindoos prostrating themselves before some idol With any other people than the Japs this lowly attitude would seem offensively servile; but these inimitable people leave not the slightest room for thinking their actions obsequious. The Japs are a wonderful race; they seem to be the happiest people going, always smiling and good-natured, always polite and gentle, always bowing and scraping.

After a bountiful supper of several fishy preparations and rice, the landlord bobs his head to the floor, sucks his breath through the teeth after the peculiar manner of the Japs when desirous of being excessively polite, and extends his hands for my passport. This the yadoya proprietor is required to take and have examined at the police station, provided no policeman calls for it at the house.

The Japanese Government, in its efforts to improve the institutions of the country, has introduced systems of reform from various countries. Commissions were sent to the different Western countries to examine and report upon the methods of education, police, army, navy, postal matters, judiciary, etc. What was believed to be the best of the various systems was then selected as the model of Japan's new departure and adoption of Western civilization. Thus the police service is modelled from the French, the judiciary from the English, the schools after the American methods, etc.

Having inaugurated these improvements, the Japs seem determined to follow their models with the same minute scrupulosity they exhibit in copying material things. There is probably as little use for elaborate police regulations in Japan as in any country under the sun; but having chosen the splendid police service of France to pattern by, they can now boast of having a service that lacks nothing in effectiveness.

A very good road, with an avenue of fine spreading conifers of some kind, leads out of Omura. To the left is the bay of Omura, closely skirted at times by the road. At one place is observed an inland temple, connected with the mainland by a causeway of rough rock. The little island is covered with dark pines and jagged rocks, amid which the Japs have perched their shrine and erected a temple. Both the Chinese and Japs seem fond of selecting the most romantic spots for their worship and the erection of religious edifices.

The day is warm, and a heavy shower during the night has made the road heavy in places, although much of it is clean gravel that is not injured by the rain. Over hill and down dale the ku-ruma road leads to Ureshino, a place celebrated for its mineral springs and bath. On the way one passes through charming little ravines, where tiny cataracts come tumbling down the sides of moss-grown precipices, a country of pretty thatched cottages, temples, groves, and purling rivulets.

On the streams are numerous rice-hulling machines, operated by the ingenious manipulation of the water. In a little hut is a mortar containing the rice. Attached to a pivot is a long beam having a pestle at one end and a trough at the other. The pestle is made to fall upon the rice in the mortar by the filling and automatic emptying of the trough outside. The trough, filling with water, drops down and empties of its own weight; this causes the opposite end to fall suddenly. This operation repeats itself about every two seconds through the day.

The gravelly hills about Ureshino are devoted to the cultivation of tea; the green tea-gardens, with the undulating, even rows of thick shrubs, looking very beautiful where they slope to the foot of the bare rocky cliffs. Ureshino and the baths are some little distance off the main road to Shimonoseki; so, not caring particularly to go there, I continue on to the village of Takio, where rainy weather compels a halt of several hours. Everything is so delightfully superior, as compared with China, that the Japanese village yaduya seems a veritable paradise during these first days of my acquaintance with them. Life at a Chinese village hittim for a week would well-nigh unseat the average Anglo-Saxon's reason, whereas he might spend the same time very pleasantly in a Japanese country inn. The region immediately around Takio is not only naturally lovely, but is embellished by little artificial lakes, islands, grottoes, and various landscape novelties such as the Japs alone excel in.

An eight-wire telegraph line threads the road from Takio to Ushidzu, passing through numerous villages that almost form a continuous street from one town to the other. As one notices such improvements, and sees the police and telegraph officials in trim European uniforms seated in their neat offices, an American clock invariably on the wall within, and, moreover, notes the uniform friendliness of the people, it is difficult to imagine that thirty years ago one would have been in more danger travelling through here than through China. Passing through the main streets of Ushidzu in search of the best yadoya, I am accosted by a middle-aged woman with, "Hello! you wanchee room? wanchee chow-chow." Her mother keeps a yadoya, she tells me, and leads the way thither, chatting gayly in pidgeon English, all the way. She seems very pleased at the opportunity to exercise her little stock of broken English, and tells me she learned it at Shanghai, where she once resided for a couple of years in an English family. Her name, she says, is O-hanna, but her English friends used to call her Hannah, without the prefix. Understanding from experience what I would be most likely to appreciate for supper, she rustles around and prepares a nice fish, plenty of Ureshino tea, sugar, sweet-cakes, and sliced pomolo; this, together with rice, is the extent of Ushidzu's present gastronomic limits.

The following morning opens with a white frost, the road is level and good, and the yadoya people see that I am provided with a substantial breakfast in good season. My boots, I find, have been cleaned even. They were cleaned with a rag, O-hanna apologizing for the absence of shoe-brushes and blacking in pidgeon English: "Brush no have got."

In striking contrast to China, here are gangs of "cantonniers" taking care of the road; men in regular blue uniforms with big white "bull's-eyes," and characters like our Celestial friends the yameni-runners. Troops of school-children are passed on the road going to school with books and tally-boards under their arm. They sometimes range themselves in rows alongside the road, and, as I wheel past, bob their heads simultaneously down to the level of their knees and greet me with a polite "O-ai-o."

The country hereabout is rich and populous, and the people seemingly well-to-do. The tea-houses, farm-houses, and even the little ricks of rice seem built with an eye to artistic effect. One sees here the gradual encroachment of Western mechanical improvements. The first two-handled plough I have seen since leaving Europe is encountered this morning; but alongside it are men using the clumsy Japanese digging-tool of their ancestors, and both men and women stripped to the waist, hulling rice by pounding it in mortars with long-headed pestles. It is merely a question of a few years, however, until the intelligent Japs will discard all their old clumsy methods and introduce the latest agricultural improvements of the West into their country. Passing through a mile or more of Saga's smooth and continuously ridable streets, past big school-houses where hundreds of children are reciting aloud in chorus, past the big bronze Buddha for which Saga is locally famous, the road continues through a somewhat undulating country, ridable, generally speaking, the whole way. Long cedar or cryptomerian avenues sometimes characterize the way. Strings of peasants are encountered, leading pack-ponies and bullocks. The former seem to be vicious little wretches, rather masters, on the whole, than servants of their leaders.

The Japanese horse objects to a tight girth, objects to being overloaded, and to various other indignities that his relations of other countries meekly endure. To suit his fastidious requirements he is allowed to meander carelessly along at the end of a twenty-foot string, and he is decorated all over with gay and fanciful trappings. A very peculiar trait of his character is that of showing fight at anything he doesn't like the looks of, instead of scaring at it after the orthodox method of horse-flesh in other countries. This peculiarity sometimes makes it extremely interesting for myself. Their usual manner of taking exception to me and the bicycle is to rear up on the hind feet and squeal and paw the air, at the same time evincing a disposition to come on and chew me up. This necessitates continual wariness on my part when passing a company of peasants, for the men never seem to think it worth while to restrain their horses until the actions of the latter render it absolutely necessary.

Jinrikishas now become quite frequent, pulled by sturdy-limbed men, who, naked almost as the day they were born, trot along between the shafts of their two-wheeled vehicles at the rate of six miles an hour. Men also are met pulling heavy hand-carts, loaded with tiles, from country factories to the city. Most of the heaviest labor seems to be performed by human beings, though not to the same extent as in China.

In every town and village one is struck with the various imitations of European goods. Ludicrous mistakes are everywhere met with, where this serio-comical people have attempted to imitate name, trade-mark, and everything complete. In one portion of the eating-house where lunch is obtained to-day are a number of umbrella-makers manufacturing gingham umbrellas; on every umbrella is stamped the firm-name "John Douglas, Manchester." Cigarettes, nicely made and equal in every respect to those of other countries, are boldly labelled "cigars:" thus do these curious imitators make mistakes. Had Shakespeare seen the Japs one could better understand his "All the world's a stage, and all the men and women merely players;" for most other nations life is a serious enough problem, the Japs alone seem to be merely "playing at making a livelihood." They always impress me as happy-go-lucky harlequins, to whom this whole business of coming into the world and getting a living for a few years is nothing more nor less than a huge joke.

The happiest state of affairs seems to exist among all classes and conditions of people in Japan. One passes school-houses and sees the classes out on the well-kept grounds, going through various exercises, such as one would never expect to see in the East. To-day I pause a while before the public-school in Nakabairu, watching the interesting exercises going on. Under the supervision of teachers in black frock-coats and Derby hats, a class of girls are ranged in two rows, throwing and catching pillows, altogether back and forth at the word of command. Classes of boys are manipulating wooden dumb-bells and exercising their muscles by various systematic exercises. The youngsters are enjoying it hugely, and the whole affair looks so thoroughly suggestive of the best elements of Occidental school-life that it is difficult to believe the evidence of one's own eyes. I suspect the Japanese children are about the only children in the wide, wide world who really enjoy studying their lessons and going to school. One of the teachers comes to the gate and greets me with a polite bow. I address him in English, but he doesn't know a word.

The wooden houses of Japan seem frail and temporary, but they look new and bright mostly in the country. The government buildings, police-offices, post-offices, schools, etc., all look new and bright and artistic, as though but lately finished. The roads, too, are sometimes laid out straight and trim, suggestive of an attempt to imitate the roads of France; then, again, one traverses for miles the counterpart of the green lanes of Merrie England—narrow, winding, and romantic. The Japanese roads are mainly about ten or twelve feet wide, giving ample room for two jinrikishas to pass, these being the only wheeled vehicles on the roads. Rustic bridges frequently span lovely little babbling brooks, and waterfalls abound this afternoon as I approach, at early eve, Futshishi. Rain necessitates a lay-over of a day at Futshishi, but there is nothing unendurable about it; the proprietor of the house is a blind man, who plays the samosan, and makes the girls sing and dance the geisha for my edification. Beef and chicken are both forthcoming at Futshishi, and the fish, as in almost all Japanese towns, are very excellent.

The weather opens clear and frosty after the rain, and the road to Fukuoko is most excellent wheeling; the country continues charming, and every day the people seem to get more and more polite and agreeable. A novel sight of the morning's ride is a big gang of convicts working the roads. They are fastened together with light chains, wear neat brown uniforms, and seem to regard the unconvicted world of humans outside their own company with an expression of apology. To look in their serio-comic faces it is difficult to imagine them capable of doing anything wrong, except in fun: they look, in fact, as if their being chained together and closely attended by guards was of itself anything but a serious affair.

Cavalry officers, small, smart-looking, and soldierly, in yellow-braided uniforms, are seen in Fukuoko, looking as un-Asiatic in make-up as the schools, policemen, and telegraph-operators. A collision with a jinrikisha that treats me to a header, and another with a diminutive Jap, that bowls him over like a ninepin, and a third with a bobtailed cat, that damages nothing but pussy's dignity, enter into my reminiscences of Fukuoko. The numbers of jinrikishas, and the peculiar habits of the people, necessitate lynx-eyed vigilance to prevent collisions every hour of the day. The average Jap leaves the door of a house backward, and bows and scrapes his way clear out into the middle of the street, in bidding adieu to the friends he has been calling upon, or even the shopkeeper he has been patronizing. Scarcely a village is passed through but some person waltzes backward out of a door and right in front of the bicycle.

A curious sight one frequently sees along the road is an acre or two of ground covered with paper parasols, set out in the sun to dry after being pasted, glued, and painted ready for market. Umbrellas and paper lanterns are as much a part of the Japanese traveller's outfit as his clothes. These latter, nowadays, are sometimes a very grotesque mixture of native and European costume. The craze for foreign innovations pervades all ranks of society, and every village dandy aspires to some article of European clothing. The result is that one frequently encounters men on the road wearing a Derby hat, a red blanket, tight-fitting white drawers, and straw sandals. The villager who sports a European hat or coat comes around to my yadoya, wearing an amusing expression of self-satisfaction, as though filled with an inward consciousness of inv approval of the same. Whereas, every European traveller deprecates the change from their native costume to our own.

Following for some distance along the bank of a large canal I reach the village of Hakama for the night. The yadoya here is simply spotless from top to bottom; however the Japanese hotel-keeper manages to transact business and preserve such immaculate apartments is more of a puzzle every day. The regulation custom at a yadoya is for the newly arrived guest to take a scalding hot bath, and then squat beside a little brazier of coals, and smoke and chat till supper-time. The Japanese are more addicted to hot-water bathing than the people of any other country. They souse themselves in water that has been heated to 140 deg. Fahr., a temperature that is quite unbearable to the "Ingurisu-zin" or "Amerika-zin" until he becomes gradually hardened and accustomed to it. Both men and women bathe regularly in hot water every evening. The Japs have not yet imbibed any great quantity of mauvaise honte from their association with Europeans, so the sexes frequent the bath-tub indiscriminately, taking no more notice of one another than if they were all little children. "Venus disporting in the waves"—of a bath-tub—is a regular feature of life at a Japanese inn. Nor can they quite understand why the European tourist should object to the proprietor, his wife and children, chambermaids, tea-girls, guests and visitors crowding around to see him undress and waltz into the tub. Bless their innocent Japanese souls! why should he object. They are only attracted out of curiosity to see the whiteness of his skin, to note his peculiar manner of undressing, and to satisfy a general inquisitiveness concerning his corporeal possibilities. They have no squeamishness whatever about his watching their own natatorial duties; why, then, should he shrink within himself and wave them off?

The regular hotel meals consist of rice, fish in various forms, little slices of crisp, raw turnip, pickles, and a catsup-like sauce. Meat is rarely forthcoming, unless specially ordered, when, of course, extra charges are made; sake also has to be purchased separately. After supper one is supplied with a teapot of tea and a brazier of coals.

Passing the following night at Hakama, I pull out next morning for Shimonoseki. Traversing for some miles a hilly country, covered with pine-forest, my road brings me into Ashiyah, situated on a small estuary. Here, at Ashiyah, I indulge in nay first simon-pure Japanese shave, patronizing the village barber while dodging a passing shower. The Japanese tonsorial artist shaves without the aid of soap, merely wetting the face by dipping his fingers in a bowl of warm water. During the operation of shaving he hones the razor frequently on an oil-stone. He shaves the entire face and neck, not omitting even the lobes of the ear, the forehead, and nose. If the European traveller didn't keep his senses about him, while in the barber-chair of a Japanese village, he would find himself with every particle of fuzz scraped off his face and neck, save, of course, his regular whiskers or mustache, and with eye-brows considerably curtailed.

From Ashiyah my road follows up alongside a small tidal canal to Hakamatsu, traversing a lowland country, devoted entirely to the cultivation of rice. Scores of coal-barges are floating along the canal, propelled solely by the flowing of the tide. I can imagine them floating along until the tide changes, then tying up and waiting patiently until it ebbs and flows again; from long experience they, no doubt, have come to calculate upon one, two, or three tides, as the case may be, floating their barges up to certain landings or villages.

The streets of Hakamatsu present a lively and picturesque scene, swarming with country people in the gayest of costumes; the stalls are fairly groaning beneath big piles of tempting eatables, toys, clothing, lanterns, tissue-paper flowers, and every imaginable Japanese thing. Street-men are attracting small crowds about them by displaying curiosities. One old fellow I pause awhile to look at is selling tiny rolls of colored paper which, when cast into a bowl of water, unfold into flowers, boats, houses, birds, or animals. In explanation of the holiday-making, a young man in a custom-house uniform, who knows a few words of English, explains "Japan God "-it is some religious festival these smiling, chatting, bowing, and comical-looking crowds are keeping with such evident relish.

Prom Hakamatsu to Kokura the country is hilly and broken; from Kokura one can look across the narrow strait and see Shimonoseki, on the mainland of Japan. Thus far we have been traversing the island of Kiu-shiu, separated from the main island by a strait but a few hundred yards wide at Shimonoseki. From Kokura the jinrikisha road leads a couple of ri farther to Dairi; thence footpaths traverse hills and wax-tree groves for another two miles (a ri is something over two English miles) to the village of Moji. Here I obtain passage on a little ferry-boat across to Shimonoseki, arriving there about two o'clock in the afternoon.

A twenty-four hours' halt is made at Shimonoseki in deference to rainy weather. The landlady of the yadoya understands enough about European cookery to prepare me a very decent beefsteak and a pot of coffee. Shimonoseki is full of European goods, and clever imitations of the same; a stroll of an hour through the streets reveals the extent of the Japs' appreciation of foreign things. Every other shop, almost, seems devoted to the goods that come from other countries, or their counterfeits. Not content with merely copying an imported article, the Japanese artisan generally endeavors to make some improvement on the original. For instance, after making an exact imitation of a petroleum-lamp, the Jap workman constructs a neat little lacquer cabinet to set it in when not in use. The coffee-pot in which the coffee served at my yadoya is prepared is an ingenious contrivance with three chambers, evidently a reproduction of Yankee ingenuity.

A big Shinto temple occupies the crest of a little hill near by, and flights of stone steps lead up to the entrance. At the foot of the steps, and repeated at several stages up the slope, are the peculiar torii, or "bird-perches," that form the distinctive mark of a Shinto temple. Numerous shrines occupy the court-yard of the temple; the shrines are built of wood mostly, and contain representations of the various gods to whose particular worship they are dedicated. Before each shrine is a barred receptacle for coins. The Japanese devotee poses for a minute before the shrine, bowing his head and smiting together the palms of his hands; he then tosses a diminutive coin or two into the barred treasury, and passes on round to the next shrine he wishes to pay his respects to. In the main building are numerous pictures, bows, arrows, swords, and various articles, evidently votive offerings. The shrine of the deity that presides over the destiny of fishermen is distinguished by a huge silver-paper fish and numerous three-pronged fish-spears. Among other queer objects whose meaning defies the penetration of the traveller unversed in Japanese mythology is a monstrous human face, with a nose at least three feet long, and altogether out of proportion.

Strolling about to while away a rainy forenoon I pass big school-houses full of children reciting aloud. Their wooden clogs and paper umbrellas are stowed away in racks, provided for the purpose, at the door. The cheerfulness with which they shout out their exercises proves plainly enough that they are only keeping "make-believe" school. Female vegetable and fruit venders, neat and comely as Normandy dairy-maids, are walking about chatting and smiling and bowing, "playing at selling vegetables." While I pause a moment to inspect the stock of a curio-dealer, the proprietor, seated over a brazier of coals, smoking, bows politely and points, with a chuckle of amusement, at the fierce-looking effigy of a daimio in armor. There is not the slightest hint of a mercenary thought about his actions; plainly enough, he hasn't the remotest wish to sell me anything—he merely wants to call my attention to the grotesqueness of this particular figure. He is only playing curio-dealer; he doesn't try to sell anything, but would do so out of the abundance of his good-nature if requested to, no doubt. A pair of little old-fashioned fire-engines repose carelessly against the side of a municipal building. They have grown tired of playing at extinguishing fires and have thrown aside their toys. I wander to the water-front and try to locate my hotel from that point of observation. Watermen are lounging about in wistaria waterproof coats. They want me to ride to my destination in one of their boats, very evidently, from their manner, only for the fun of the thing. Everybody is smiling and urbane, nobody looks serious; no careworn faces are seen, no pinched poverty. Wonderful people! they come nearer solving the problem of living happily than any other nation. Even the professional mendicants seem to be amused at their own poverty, as if life to them was a mere humorous experiment, scarcely deserving of a serious thought.

The weather clears up at noon, and in the face of a strong northern breeze I bid farewell to Shimonoseki.

The road follows for some miles along the shore, a smooth, level road that winds about the bases of the hills that here slope down to toy and dally with the restless surf of the famous Inland Sea. Following the shore in a general sense, the road now and then leads inland for a mile or two, for the purpose of linking together the numerous towns and villages that dot the little alluvial valleys between the hills. Passing through one large village, my attention is attracted by the sign "English Books," over a book-shop. Desirous of purchasing some kind of a guide for the road to Kobe, I enter the establishment, expecting at least to find some one capable of understanding English. The young man in charge knows never a word of English, and his stock of "English books" consists of primers, spelling-books, etc., for the use of school-children.

The architecture of the villages above Shimonoseki is strikingly artistic. The quaint gabled houses are painted a snowy white, and are roofed with brown glazed tiles of curious pattern, also rimmed with white. About the houses are hedges grotesquely clipped and trained in imitation of storks, animals, or fishes, miniature orange and persimmon trees, pretty flower-gardens and little landscape vanities peculiar to the Japanese. Circling around through little valleys, over small promontories and along smooth, gravelly stretches of sea-shore road, for thirty miles, brings me to anchor for the night in a good-sized village.

Among my visitors for the evening is a young gentleman arrayed in shiny top-boots, tight-fitting corduroy trousers, and jockey cap. In his general make-up he is the "horsiest" individual I have seen for many a day. One could readily imagine him to be a professional jockey. The probability is, however, that he has never mounted a horse in his life. In all likelihood he has become infatuated with this style of Western clothes from studying a copy of the London Graphic, has gone to great trouble and expense to procure the garments from Yokohama, and now blossoms forth upon the dazed provincials of his native town in a make-up that stamps him as the swellest of the swell He affects great interest in the bicycle—much more so than the average Jap—from which I infer that he has actually imbibed certain notions of Western sport, and is desirous of posing before his uninitiated and, consequently, unappreciative, countrymen, as an exponent of athletics. Altogether the horsey young gentleman is the most startling representative of "New Japan" I have yet encountered.

A cold drizzle ushers in the commencement of my next day's journey. One is loath to exchange the neat yadoya, with everything within so spotless and so pleasant, the tiny garden, not over ten yards square, but containing a miniature lake, grottos, quaint stone lanterns, bronze storks, flowers, and stunted trees, for the road. Disagreeable weather has followed me, however, from Nagasaki like an avenging Fate, bent on preventing the consummation of my tour from being too agreeable. Even with rain and mud and consequent delays my first few days in Japan have seemed a very paradise after my Chinese experiences; what, then, would have been my impressions of country and people amid sunshine and favorable conditions of weather and road, when the novelty of it all first burst upon my Chinese-disgusted senses?

The country round about is mountainous, snow lying upon the summits of a few of the higher peaks. The road, though hilly at times, manages to twist and wind its way along from one little valley to another without any very long hills. Peasants from the mountains are met with, leading ponies loaded with firewood and rice. Their old Japanese aboriginal costumes of wistaria raincoats, broad bamboo-hats, and rude straw-sandals make a conspicuous contrast to their countrymen of "New Japan," in Derby hats or jockey suits. Notwithstanding the rapid Europeanizing of the city-bred Japs, the government's progressive policy, the blue-coated gendarmerie, and the general revolutionizing of the country at large, many a day will come and go ere these mountaineers forsake the ways and methods and grotesque costumes of their ancestors. For decades Japan will present an interesting study of mountaineer conservatism and ultra-liberal city life. One party will be wearing foreign clothes, aping foreign manners, adopting foreign ways of doing everything; the other will be clinging tenaciously to the wistaria garments, bamboo sieve-hats, straw-sandals, and the traditions of "Old Japan."

Most farm-houses are now thatched with straw; one need hardly add that they are prettily and neatly thatched, and that they are embellished by various unique contrivances. Some of them, I notice, are surrounded by a broad, thick hedge of dark-green shrubbery. The hedge is trimmed so that the upper edge appears to be a continuation of the brown thatch, which merely changes its color and slopes at the same steep gradient to the ground. This device produces a very charming effect, particularly when a few neatly trimmed young pines soar above the hedge like green sentinels about the dwelling. One inimitable piece of "botanical architecture" observed to-day is a thick shrub trimmed into an imitation of a mountain, with trees growing on the slopes, and a temple standing in a grove. Before many of the houses one sees curious tree-roots or rocks, that have been brought many a mile down from the mountains, and preserved on account of some fanciful resemblance to bird, reptile, or animal. Artificial lakes, islands, waterfalls, bridges, temples, and groves abound; and at occasional intervals a large figure of the Buddha squats serenely on a pedestal, smiling in happy contemplation of the peace, happiness, prosperity, and beauty of everything and everybody around. Happy people! happy country. Are the Japs acting wisely or are they acting foolishly in permitting European notions of life to creep in and revolutionize it all. Who can tell. Time alone will prove. They will get richer, more powerful, and more enterprising, because of the necessity of waking themselves up to keep abreast of the times; but wealth and power, and the buzz and rattle of machinery and commerce do not always mean happiness.

CHAPTER XX

THE HOME STRETCH

During the afternoon the narrow kuruma road merges into a broad, newly made macadam, as fine a piece of road as I have seen the whole world round. Wonderful work has been done in grading it from the low-lying rice-fields, up, up, up, by the most gentle and even gradient, to where it seemingly terminates, far ahead between high rocky cliffs. The picture of charming houses and beautiful terraced gardens climbing to the very upper stories of the mountains here beggars description; one no longer marvels at what he has seen in the way of terraced mountains in China.

New sensations of astonishment await me as the upper portion of the smooth boulevard is reached, and I find myself at the entrance to a tunnel about five hundred yards long and thirty feet wide. The tunnel is lit up by means of big reflectors in the middle, shining through the gloom as one enters, like locomotive headlights. It is difficult to imagine the Japs going to all this trouble and expense for mere jinrikisha and pedestrian travel; yet such is the case, for no other vehicular traffic exists in the country. It is the only country in which I have found a tunnel constructed for the ordinary roadway, although there may be similar improvements that have not happened to come to my notice or ear. One would at least expect to find a toll-keeper in such a place, especially as a person has to be employed to maintain the lights, but there is nothing of the kind.

A few miles beyond the tunnel the broad road terminates in a good-sized seaport, whence I encounter some little difficulty in finding my way along zigzag field-paths to my proper road for the north. The rain has fallen at intervals throughout the day, but the roads have averaged good. Fifty miles, or thereabout, must have been reeled off when, at early eventide, I pull up at a village ya-doya. Before settling myself down, for rest and supper, I take a stroll through the village in quest of possible interesting things. Not far from the yadoya my attention is arrested by a prominent sign, in italics, "uropean eating, Kameya hous." Entertaining happy visions of beefsteak and Bass's ale for supper, I enter the establishment and ask the young man in charge whether the place is an hotel. He smiles, bows, and intimates his woeful ignorance of what I am saying.

The following morning is frosty, and low, scudding clouds denote unsettled weather, as I resume my journey. Much of the time my road practically follows the shore, and sometimes simply follows the windings and curvatures of the gravelly beach. Most of the low land near the shore appears to be reclaimed from the sea—low, flat-looking mud-fields, protected from overflow by miles and miles of stout dikes and rock-ribbed walls. Fishing villages abound along the shore, and for long distances a recent typhoon has driven the sea inland and washed away the road. Thousands of men and women are engaged in repairing the damages with the abundance of material ready to hand on the sloping granite-shale hills around the foot of which the roadway winds.

Fish are cheaper and more plentiful here than anything else, and the old dame at the yadoya of a fishing village cooks me a big skate for supper, which makes first-rate eating, in spite of the black, malodorous sauce she uses so liberally in the cooking.

In this room is a wonderful brass-bound cabinet, suggestive of soul-satisfying household idols and comfortable private worship. During the evening I venture to open and take a peep in this cabinet to satisfy a pardonable curiosity as to its contents. My trespass reveals a little wax idol seated amid a wealth of cheap tinsel ornaments, and bits of inscribed paper. Before him sets an offering of rice, sake, and dried fish in tiny porcelain bowls.

Clear and frosty opens the following morning; the road is good, the country gradually improves, and by nine o'clock I am engaged in looking at the military exercises of troops quartered in the populous city of Hiroshima. The exercises are conducted within a large square, enclosed with a low bank of earth and a ditch. Crowds of curious civilians are watching the efforts of raw cavalry recruits to ride stout little horses, that buck, kick, bite, and paw the air. Every time a soldier gets thrown the on-lookers chuckle with delight. Both men and horses are undersized, but look stocky and serviceable withal. The uniform of the cavalry is blue, with yellow trimmings. The artillery looks trim and efficient, and the horses, although rather small, are powerful and wiry, just the horses one would select for the rough work of a campaign.

North of Hiroshima the country assumes a hilly character, the road following up one mountain-stream and down another. In this mountainous region one meets mail-carriers, the counterpart almost of the fleet-footed postmen of Bengal. The Japanese postman improves upon nature by the addition of a waist-cloth and a scant shirt of white and blue cotton check; his letter-pouch is fastened to a bamboo-staff; as he bounds along with springy stride he warns people to clear the way by shouting in a musical voice, "Honk, honk." This cry resembles in a very striking degree the utterances of an old veteran brant, or wild-goose, when speeding northward in the spring to escape a warm wave from the south.

Among these mountains one is filled with amazement at the tremendous work the industrious Japs have done to secure a few acres of cultivable land. Dikes have been thrown up to narrow the channels of the streams, so that the remaining width of the bed may be converted into fields and gardens. The streams have been literally turned out of their beds for the sake of a few acres of alluvial soil. Among the mountains, chiefly between the mountains and the shore, are level areas of a few square miles, supporting a population that seems largely out of proportion to the size of the land. Many of these sea-shore people however, get their livelihood from the blue waters of the Inland Sea; fish sharing the honors with rice in being the staple food of provincial Japan.

The weather changes to quite a disagreeable degree of cold by the time I reach the end of to-day's ride. This introduces me promptly into the mysteries of how the Japanese manage to keep themselves warm in their flimsy houses of wooden ribs and semi-transparent paper in cold weather. An opening in the floor accommodates a brazier of coals; over this stands an open wood-work frame; quilts covered over the frame retain the heat. The modus operandi of keeping warm is to insert the body beneath this frame, wrapping the covering about the shoulders, snugly, to prevent the escape of the warm air within. The advantage of this unique arrangement is that the head can be kept cool, while, if desirable, the body can be subjected to a regular hot-air bath.

The following day is chilly and raw, with occasional skits of snow. People are humped up and blue-nosed, and seemingly miserable. Yet, withal, they seem to be only humorously miserable, and not by any means seriously displeased with the rawness and the snow. Straw wind-breaks are set up on the windward side of the tea-houses, and there is much stopping among pedestrians to gather around the tea-house braziers and gossip and smoke.

Everybody in Japan smokes, both men and women. The universal pipe of the country is a small brass tube about six inches long, with the end turned up and widened to form the bowl. This bowl holds the merest pinch of tobacco; a couple of whiffs, a smart rap on the edge of the brazier to knock out the residue, and the pipe is filled again and again, until the smoker feels satisfied. The girls that wait on one at the yadoyas and tea-houses carry their tobacco in the capacious sleeve-pockets of their dress, and their pipes sometimes thrust in the sash or girdle, and sometimes stuck in the back of the hair.

Many of the Buddhas presiding over the cross-roads and village entrances along my route to-day are provided with calico bibs, the object of which it is impossible for me to determine, owing to my ignorance of the vernacular. The bibs are, no doubt, significant of some particular season of religious observance.

The important city of Okoyama provides abundant food for observation—the clean, smooth streets, the wealth of European goods in the shops, and the swarms of ever-interesting people, as I wheel leisurely through it on Saturday, December 4th. No human being save Japs has so far crossed my path since leaving Nagasaki, nor am I expecting to meet anybody here. An agreeable surprise, however, awaits me, for at the corner of one of the principal business thoroughfares a couple of American missionaries appear upon the scene. Introducing themselves as Mr. Carey and Mr. Kowland, they inform me that three families of missionaries reside together here, and extend a cordial invitation to remain over Sunday. I am very glad indeed to accept their hospitality for to-morrow, as well as to avail myself of an opportunity to get my proper bearings. Nothing in the way of a reliable map or itinerary of the road I have been traversing from Shimonoseki was to be obtained at Nagasaki, and I have travelled with but the vaguest idea of my whereabouts from day to day. Only from them do I learn that the city we meet in is Okoyama, and that I am now within a hundred miles of Kobe, north of which place "Murray's Handbook" will prove of material assistance in guiding me aright.

The little missionary colony is charmingly situated on a pine-clad hill overlooking the city from the east. Several lady missionaries are visiting from other points, all Americans, making a pleasant party for one to meet in such an unexpected manner.

On Sunday morning I accompany Mr. Carey to see his native congregation in the nice new church which he says they have erected from their own means at a cost of two thousand yen. This latter is a very gratifying statement, not to say surprisingly so, for it savors of something like sincerity on the part of the converts. In most countries the converts seem to be brought to a knowledge of their evil ways, and to perceive the beauties of the Christian religion through the medium of material assistance provided from the mission. Instead of spending money themselves for the cause they profess to embrace, they expect to receive something from it of a tangible earthly nature. Here, however, we find the converts themselves building their own meeting-house, and bidding fair ere long to support the mission without outside aid. This is encouraging from the stand-point of those who believe in converting "the heathen" from their own religion to ours, and gratifying to the student of Japanese character.

About five hundred people congregate in the church, seating themselves quietly and orderly on the mat-covered floor. They embrace all classes, from the samurai lawyer or gentleman to the humblest citizen, and from gray-haired old men and women to shock-headed youngsters, who merely come with their mothers. Many of these same mothers have been persuaded by the missionaries to cease the heathenish practice of blackening their teeth, and so appear at the meeting in even rows of becoming white ivories like their unmarried sisters. Numbers of curious outsiders congregate about the open doors and peep in and stand and listen to the sermon of Mr. Carey, and the singing. The hymns are sung to the same tunes as in America, the words being translated into Japanese. Everybody seems to enjoy the singing, and they listen intently to the sermon.

After the sermon, several prominent members of the congregation stand up and address their countrymen and women in convincing words and gestures. Mr. Carey tells me that any ordinary Jap seems capable of delivering a fluent, off-hand exposition of his views in public without special effort or embarrassment. Altogether the Japanese Christian congregation, gathered here in ita own church, sitting on the floor, singing, sermonizing, and looking happy, is a novel and interesting sight to see. One can imagine missionary life among the genial Japs as being very pleasant.

Saturday and Sunday pass pleasantly away, and, with happy memories of the little missionary colony, I wheel away from Oko-yama on Monday morning, passing through a country of rich rice-fields and numerous villages for some miles. The scene then changes into a beautiful country of small lakes and pine-covered hills, reminding me very much of portions of the Berkshire Hills, Mass. The weather is cool and clear, and the road splendid, although in places somewhat hilly.

Fifty-three miles are duly scored when, at three o'clock in the afternoon, I arrive at the city of Himeji. The yadoya here is a superior sort of a placc, and Himeji numbers among its productions European pan (bread), steak, and bottled beer. The Japs are themselves rapidly coming to an appreciation of this latter article, and even to manufacture it, a big brewery being already established somewhere near Tokio. A couple of young dandies of "New Japan" drop in during the evening, send out for bottles of beer, and seem to take particular delight in showing off their appreciation of the newly introduced beverage before their countrymen of the "ancient regime."

Beyond Himeji one leaves behind the mountains, emerging upon a broad, level, rice-producing plain, which extends eastward to Kobe and the sea-shore. The fine level road traversing the plain passes through numerous towns and villages, and for the latter half of the distance skirts the shore. Old dismantled stone forts, tea-houses, eating-stalls, fishermen's huts, house-boats, and swarms of jinrikishas and pedestrians make their sea-shore road lively and interesting. The single artery through which the life of all the southern tributary country ebbs and flows to trade at the busiest treaty port in Japan, this road is constantly swarming with people. Over the Minato-gawa River by an elevated bridge, and one finds himself in a broad street leading through Hiogo to Kobe. These two cities are practically joined together, although bearing different names. Like many of the rivers of Japan, the bed of the Minato-gawa is elevated considerably above the surrounding plain. Confined between artificial banks to prevent the flooding of the adjacent fields in spring, the debris brought down from year to year has gradually raised the bed, and necessitated continued raising also of the levees. These operations have very naturally ended in raising the whole affair to an elevation that leaves even the bottom of the stream several feet higher than the fields around.

Kobe is one of the treaty ports of Japan, and nowadays is reputed to do more foreign trade than any of the others. One can imagine Kobe being a very pleasant and desirable place to live; the foreign settlement is quite extensive, the surroundings attractive, and the climate mild and healthful.

Pleasant days are spent at Kobe and Ozaka. Twenty-seven miles of level road from the latter city, following the course of the Yodo-gawa, a broad shallow stream that flows from Lake Biwa to the sea, brings me to Kioto. From the eighth century until 1868 Kioto was the capital of the Japanese empire, and is generally referred to as the old capital of the country. The present population is about a quarter of a million, about half of what it was supposed to be in the heyday of its ancient glory as the seat of empire.

Living at Kioto is Mr. B, an American ex-naval officer, who several years ago forsook old Neptune's service to embark in the more peaceful pursuit of teaching the ideas of youthful Japs to shoot. The occasion was auspicious, for the whole country was fired with enthusiasm for learning English. English was introduced into the public schools as a regular study. Mr. B is settled at Kioto, and now instructs a large and interesting class of boys in the mysteries of his mother tongue. Taking a letter of introduction he makes me comfortable for the afternoon and night at his pleasant residence on the banks of the Yodo-gawa. Under the pilotage of his private jinrikisha-man, I spend a portion of the afternoon in making a flying visit to various places of interest. A party of American tourists are unexpectedly met in the first temple we visit, that of Nishi Hon-gwan-ji. The paintings and decorations of this temple, one of the ladies says with something akin to enthusiasm, are quite equal to those of the great temple at Nikko. This lady appears to be a missionary resident, or, at all events, a person well versed in Japanese temples and things. Her companions are fleeting tourists, who listen to her explanations with respect, but, like myself, know nothing more when they leave the temple than when they entered. Japanese mythology, religion, temples, politics, history, and titles, seem to me to be the worst mixed up and the most difficult for off-hand comprehension of anything I have yet undertaken to peep into. The multitudinous gods of the Hindoos, with their no less multitudinous functions, seem to me to be easily understood in comparison with the weird legends and mazy mythology of the Flowery Kingdom.

Near this temple is a lovely little garden that gives much more satisfaction to the casual visitor than the temples. It is always a pleasure to visit a Japanese garden, and, in addition to its landscape attractions, historical interest lends to this one additional charm. The artificial lake is stocked with tame carp, which come crowding to the side when visitors clap their hands, in the expectation of being fed. A pair of unhappy-looking geese are imprisoned beneath an iron grating within the garden. They are kept there in commemoration of some historical incident; what the incident is, however, even the well-informed lady of the party doesn't seem to know; neither does Murray's voluminous guide-book condescend to explain. A small palace, with interior decorations of the usual conventional subjects— storks, flying geese, rising moons, bamboo-shoots, etc.—together with a small, round, thatched summer-house, where, five hundred years ago, Ashikaga Yoshimitsu, the Shogun monk, was wont to pass the time in meditation, form the remaining sole attractions of the garden.

The one place I have been anticipating some real pleasure in visiting is the Shu-gaku-In gardens, one of the most famous gardens in this country where, above all others, gardening is pursued as a fine art. This, however, is not accessible to-day, and wearied already of temples, gods, and shaven-pated priests, I give the jin-rikisha-coolie orders to return home. A mile or two through the smooth and level streets and the hopeful and sanguine "riksha" man dumps me out at another temple. Fancying that, perchance, he might have brought me to something extraordinary, I follow him wearily in. A graduate in the Shinto religion would no doubt find something different about these temples, but to the ordinary, every-day human, to see one is to see them all. My man, however, seems determined to give me a surfeit of temples, and hurries me off to yet another one, ere awakening to the fact that I am trying to get him to return to Mr. B's. The third one I positively refuse to have anything to do with.

At Mr. B's I find awaiting my coming an interesting deputation, consisting of the assistant superintendent of the young ladies' seminary, together with three of his most interesting pupils. They have been reading about my tour in the native papers, and, in the assistant superintendent's own words, "are very curious at seeing so famous a traveller." The three young ladies stand in a row, like the veritable "three little maids from school" in "The Mikado," and giggle their approval of the teacher's explanation. They are three very pretty girls, and two of them have their hair banged after the most approved American style.

Sweetcakes and tea are indulged in by the visitors, and before they leave an agreement is entered into by which I am to visit their school in the morning before leaving and hear them sing "Bonny Boon" and "The fire-fly's light," in return for riding the bicycle in the school-house grounds. "The fire-fly's light" is sung to the tune of "Auld lang syne," the Japanese words of which commemorate a legend of the tea-district of Uji near Lake Biwa. The legend states that certain learned men repaired to a secluded spot near Uji to pursue their studies. On one occasion, being out of oil and unable to procure the means of lighting their apartment, myriads of fire-flies came and illumed the place with their tiny lamps sufficient for their purpose.

My compact with the "three little maids from school" takes me down into the city on something of a detour from my nearest road out next morning. The detour is well repaid, however; besides the singing and organ-playing promised, the many departments of industrial study into which the school is divided are very interesting. Laces and embroidery for the Tokio market, dresses for themselves and to sell, are made by the girls, the proceeds going toward the maintenance of the institution. One of the most curious scholarships of the place is the teaching of what is known as the "Japanese ceremony." It seems to be a perpetuation of some old court ceremony of making tea for the Mikado. Expressing a wish to see the ceremony, I am conducted to a small room divided off by the usual sliding paper panels. A class of girls are kneeling in a row, confronting a very neat-looking old lady who sits beside a small brazier of coals. The old lady is the teacher; when she claps her hands, one of the paper screens slides gently aside and one of the scholars enters, bearing a small lacquer tray with tiny teapot and cups, a canister of tea, and various other paraphernalia. There is really very little to the "ceremony," the graceful motions of the tea-maker being by far the more interesting part of the performance. The tea used is finely powdered and comes from Uji, where it is grown especially for the use of the Mikado's household. The tea-dust is mixed with hot water by means of a curiously splintered bamboo mixer that looks very much like a shaving-brush. The result is a very aromatic cup of tea, delicious to the nostrils, but hardly acceptable to the European palate.

My jinrikisha-man of yesterday precedes me through the streets, shouting the "honk, honk, honk." of the mail-runners, to clear the way. To see him cleave a way through the multitudes for me to follow, keeping up a six-mile pace the while, swinging his arms like a windmill, one might well imagine me a real dai-mio on wheels with faithful samurai-runner ahead, warning away the common herd from my path.

At Kioto begins the Tokaido, the most famous highway of Japan, a road that is said to have been the same great highway of travel, that it is to-day, for many centuries. It extends from Kioto to Tokio, a distance of three hundred and twenty-five miles.

Another road, called the Nakasendo, the "Road of the Central Mountains," in contradistinction to the Tokaido, the "Road of the Eastern Sea," also connects the old capital with the new; but, besides being somewhat longer, the Nakasendo is a hillier road, and less interesting than the Tokaido. After leaving the city the Tokaido leads over a low pass through the hills to Otsu, on the lovely sheet of water known as Biwa Lake.

This lake is of about the same dimensions as Lake Geneva, and fairly rivals that Switzer gem in transcendental beauty. The Japs, with all their keen appreciation of the beauties of nature, go into raptures over Biwa Lake. Much talk is made of the "eight beauties of Biwa." These eight beauties are: The Autumn Moon from Ishi-yama, the Evening Snow on Hira-yama, the Blaze of Evening at Seta, the Evening Bell of Mii-dera, the Boats sailing back from Yabase, a Bright Sky with a Breeze at Awadzu, Bain by Night at Karasaki, and the Wild Geese alighting at Katada. All the places mentioned are points about the lake. All sorts of legends and romantic stories are associated with the waters of Lake Biwa. Its origin is said to be due to an earthquake that took place several centuries before the Christian era; the legend states that Fuji rose to its majestic height from the plain of Suruga at the same moment the lake was formed. Temples and shrines abound, and pilgrims galore come from far-off places to worship and see its beauties.

One object of special curiosity to tourists is a remarkable pine-tree, whose branches have been trained in horizontal courses over upright posts, until it forms a broad shelter over several hundred square yards. A smaller imitation of the large tree is also spreading to ambitious proportions on the Tokaido side.

Snow has fallen and rests on the upper slopes of the mountains overlooking the lake, little steamers and numerous sailing-craft are plying on the smooth waters, and wild geese are flying about. With these beauties on the left and tea-gardens on the right, the Tokaido leads through rows of stately pines, and past numerous villages along the lake shore.

The Nakasendo branches off to the left at the village of Kusa-tsu, celebrated for the manufacture of riding-whips. Through Ishibe and beyond, to where it crosses the Yokota-gawa, the Tokaido continues level and good. Near the crossing of this stream is a curious stone monument, displaying the carved figures of three monkeys covering up their eyes, mouth, and ears, to indicate that they will "neither see, hear, nor say any evil thing." All through here the country is devoted chiefly to growing tea; very pretty the undulating ridges and rolling slopes of the broken foot-hills look, set out in thick, bushy, well-defined rows and clumps of dark, shiny tea-plants.

Down a very steep declivity, by sharp zigzags, the Tokaido suddenly dips into the little valley of the Yasose-gawa. At the foot of the hill is a curious shrine cave, containing several rude idols, a trough with tame goldfish, and one of the crudest Buddhas I ever saw. The aim of the ambitious sculptor of Buddhas is to produce a personification of "great tranquillity." The figure in the Valley of Yasose-gawa is certainly something of a masterpiece in this direction; nothing could well be more tranquil than an oblong bowlder with the faintest chiselling of a mouth and nose, poised on the top of an upright slab of stone rudely chipped into a dim semblance of the human form.

A mile or two farther and my day's ride of forty-six miles terminates at the village of Saka-no-shita. A comfortable yadoya awaits me here, no better nor worse, however, than almost every Jap village affords; but on the Tokaido the innkeepers are more accustomed to European guests than they are south of Kobe. Every summer many European and American tourists journey between Yokohama and Kobe by jinrikisha.

At this yadoya I first become acquainted with that peculiar institution of Japan, the blind shampooer. Seated in my little room, my attention is attracted by a man who approaches on hands and knees, and butts his shaven pate accidentally against the corner of the open panel that forms my door. He halts at the entrance and indulges in the pantomime of pinching and kneading his person; his mission is to find out whether I desire his services. For a small gratuity the blind shampooer of Japan will rub, knead, and press one into a pleasant sensation from head to foot. This office is relegated to sightless individuals or ugly old women; many Japs indulge in their services after a warm bath, finding the treatment very pleasant and beneficial, so they say.

One of the most amusing illustrations of Jap imitativeness is displayed in the number of American clocks one sees adorning the walls of the yadoyas in nearly every village. The amusing feature of the thing is that the owners of these time-pieces seem to have the vaguest ideas of what they are for. One clock on the wall of my yadoya indicates eleven o'clock, another half-past nine, and a third seven-fifteen as I pull out in the morning. Other clocks through the village street vary in similar degree. Watching out for these widely varying clocks as I wheel through the villages has come to be one of the diversions of the day's ride.

The road averages good, although somewhat hilly in places, from Sakano through lovely valleys and pine-clad mountains to Yokka-ichi. Yokka-ichi is a small seaport, whence most travellers along the Tokaido take passage to Miya in the steam passenger launches plying between these points. The kuruma road, however, continues good to the Ku-wana, ten miles farther, whence, to Miya, one has to traverse narrower paths through a flat section of rice-fields, dikes, canals, and sloughs.

A ri beyond Okabe and the pass of Utsunoya necessitates a mile or two of trundling. Here occurs a tunnel some six hundred feet in length and twelve wide; a glimmer of sunshine or daylight is cast into the tunnel by a system of simple reflectors at either entrance. These are merely glass mirrors, set at an angle to reflect the rays of light into the tunnel.

Descending this little pass the Tokaido traverses a level rice-field plain, crosses the Abe-kawa, and approaches the sea-coast at Shidzuoka, a city of thirty thousand inhabitants. The view of Fuji, now but a short distance ahead, is extremely beautiful; the smooth road sweeps around the gravelly beach, almost licked by the waves. The breakers approach and recede, keeping time to the inimitable music of the surf; vessels are dotting the blue expanse; villages and tea-houses are seen resting along the crescent-sweep of the shore for many a mile ahead, where Fuji slopes so gracefully down from its majestic snow-crowned summit to the sea.

It is indeed a glorious ride around the crescent bay, through the seashore villages of Okitsu, Yui, Kambara, and Iwabuchi to Yoshiwara, a little town on the footstool of the big, gracefully sweeping cone. The stretch of shore hereabout is celebrated in Japanese poetry as Taga-no-ura, from the peculiarly beautiful view of Fuji obtained from it.

This remarkable mountain is the highest in Japan, and is probably the finest specimen of a conical mountain in existence. Native legends surround it with a halo of romance. Its origin is reputed to be simultaneous with the formation of Biwa Lake, near Kioto, both mountain and lake being formed in a single night—one rising from the plain twelve thousand eight hundred feet, the other sinking till its bed reached the level of the sea.

The summit of Fuji is a place of pilgrimage for Japanese ascetics who are desirous of attaining "perfect peace" by imitating Shitta-Tai-shi, the Japanese Buddha, who climbed to the summit of a mountain in search of nirvana (calm). Orthodox Japs believe that the grains of sand brought down on the sandals of the pilgrims ascend to the summit again of their own accord during the night.

Tradition is furthermore responsible for the belief that snow disappears entirely from the mountain for a few hours on the fifteenth day of the sixth moon, and begins to fall again during the following night. Formerly an active volcano, Fuji even now emits steam from sundry crevices near the summit, and will some day probably fill the good people at Yoshiwara and adjacent villages with a lively sense of its power. Fuji is the special pride of the Japs, its loveliness appealing strongly to the national sense of landscape beauty. Of it their poet sings:

"Great Fusiyama, tow'ring to the sky. A treasure art thou, giv'n to mortal man, A god-protector watching o'er Japan: On thee forever let me feast mine eye."

Fuji is passed and left behind, and sixteen miles reeled off from Yoshiwara, when Mishima, my destination for the night, is reached. A festival in honor of Oyama-tsumi-no-Kami, the god of "mountains in general," is being held here; for, behold, to-day is November 15th, the "middle day of the bird," one of the several festivals held in his honor every year. The big temple grounds are swarming with people, and pedlers, stalls, jugglers, and all sorts of attractions give the place the appearance of a country fair.

Leaving the bicycle outside, I wander in and stroll about among the crowds. Sacred ponds on either side of the footway are swarming with sacred fish. An ancient dame is doing a roaring trade, in a small way, in feathery bread-puffs, which the people buy and throw to the fish, for the fun of seeing them swarm around and eat.

Interested groups are gathered around veritable fac-similes of the Yankee "street-men," selling to credulous villagers little boxes of powder for "coating things with silver." Others are selling song-books, attracting customers by the novel and interesting performances of a quartette of pretty girls, who sing song after song in succession. Here also are little travelling peep-shows, containing photographic scenes of famous temples and places in distant parts of the country.

Among the various shrines in this temple is one dedicated to an ancient wood-cutter, who used to work and spend his wages on drink for his aged father, who was now too old to earn money for the purpose himself. At his father's demise the son was rewarded for his filial devotion by the discovery of a "cascade of pure sake."

A gayly decorated car and a closed tumbril, that looks very much like an old ammunition-wagon, have been wheeled out of their enclosures for the occasion. Strings of little bells are suspended on these; mothers hold their little ones up and allow them to strike these bells, toss a coin into the contribution-box, and pass on. The vehicles probably contain relics of the gods.

A wooden horse, painted red, stands in solemn and lonely state behind the wooden bars of his stall—but I have almost registered a vow against temples and their belongings, in Japan, so inexplicable are most of the things to be seen. A person who has delved into the mysteries of Japanese mythology would no doubt derive much satisfaction from a visit to the Oyama-tsumi-uo-Kami temple, but the average reader would weary of it all after seeing others. What to ordinary mortals signify such hideous mythological monsters as saru-tora-hebi (monkey-tiger-serpent), or the "Twenty-four Paragons of Filial Piety" on the architrave. Yet, of such as these is the ornamentation of all Japanese temples. Some few there are that are admirable as works of art, but most of them are hideous daubs and representations more than passing rude.

Down the street near my yadoya, within a boarded enclosure, a dozen wrestlers are giving an entertainment for a crowd of people who have paid two sen apiece entrance-fee. The wrestlers of Japan form a distinct class or caste, separated from the ordinary society of the country by long custom, that prejudices them against marrying other than the daughter of one of their own profession. As the biggest and more muscular men have always been numbered in the ranks of the wrestlers, the result of this exclusiveness and non-admixture with physical inferiors is a class of people as distinct from their fellows as if of another race. The Japanese wrestler stands head and shoulders above the average of his countrymen, and weighs half as much more. As a class they form an interesting illustration of what might be accomplished in the physical improvement of mankind by certain Malthusian schemes that have been at times advocated.

Within a twelve foot arena the sturdy athletes struggle for the mastery, bringing to bear all their strength and skill. No "hippodroming" here: stripped to the skin, the muscles on their brown bodies standing out in irregular knots, they fling one another about in the liveliest manner. The master of ceremonies, stiff and important, in a faultless gray garment bearing a samurai crest, stands by and wields the fiddle-shaped lacquered insignia of his high office, and utter his orders and decisions in an authoritative voice.

The wrestlers squat around the ring and shiver, for the evening is cold, until called out by the master of ceremonies. The two selected take a small handful of salt from baskets of that ingredient suspended on posts, and fling toward each other. They then advance into the arena, and furthermore challenge and defy their opponent by stamping their bare feet on the ground, in a manner to display their superior muscularity. Another order from the gentleman wielding the fiddle-shaped insignia, and they rush violently together, engage in a "catch-as-catch-can" scuffle, which, in less than half a minute usually, results in a decisive victory for one or the other.

The master of ceremonies waves them out of the ring, straightens himself up, assumes a very haughty expression, until he looks like the very important personage he feels himself to be, and announces the name of the victor to the spectators.

The one portion of the Tokaido impassable with a wheel commences at Mishima, the famous Hakone Pass, which for sixteen miles offers a steep surface of rough bowlder-paved paths. Coolies at Mishima make their livelihood by carrying goods and passengers over the pass on kagoa (the Japanese palanquin). Obtaining a couple of men to carry the bicycle, the chilly weather proves an inducement for following them afoot, rather than occupy a kago myself. The block road is broad enough for a wagon, being constructed, no doubt, with a view to military transport service. The long steep slopes are literally carpeted in places with the worn-out straw shoes of men and horses.

The country observed from the elevation of the Hakone Pass is extremely beautiful, the white-tipped cone of the magnificent Fuji towering over all, like a presiding genius. Near the hamlet of Yamanaka is a famous point, called Fuji-mi-taira (terrace for looking at Fuji). Big cryptomerias shade the broad stony path along much of its southern slope to Hakone village and lake.

Hakone is a very lovely and interesting region, nowadays a favorite summer resort of the European residents of Tokio and Yokohama. From the latter place Hakone Lake is but about fifty miles distant, and by jinrikisha and kago may be reached in one day. The lake is a most charming little body of water, a regular mountain-gem, reflecting in its clear, crystal depths the pine-clad slopes that encompass it round about, as though its surface were a mirror. Japanese mythology peopled the region round with supernatural beings in the early days of the country's history, when all about were impenetrable thickets and pathless woods. Until the revolution of 1868, when all these old feudal customs were ruthlessly swept away, the Tokaido here was obstructed with one of the "barriers," past which nobody might go without a passport. These barriers were established on the boundaries of feudal territories, usually at points where the traveller had no alternate route to choose.

A magnificent avenue of cryptomeria shades the Tokaido for a short distance out of Hakone village; on the left is passed a large government sanitarium, one of those splendid modern-looking structures that speak so eloquently of the present Mikado's progressive and enlightened policy. The road then turns up the steep mountain-slopes, fringed with impenetrable thickets of bamboo. Fuji, from here, presents a grand and curious sight. The wind has risen, and the summit of the cone is almost hidden behind clouds of drifting snow, which at a distance might almost be mistaken for a steamy eruption of the volcano. Close by, too, the spirit of the wind moves through the bamboo-brakes, rubbing the myriad frost-dried flags together and causing a peculiar rustling noise—the whispering of the spirits of the mountains.

The summit reached, the Tokaido now leads through glorious pine-woods, descending toward the valley of the Sakawagawa by a series of breakneck zigzags. The region is picturesque in the extreme; a small mountain-stream tumbles along through a deep ravine on the left, mountains tower aloft on the other side, and here and there give birth to a cataract that tumbles and splashes down from a height of several hundred feet.

By 1 p.m. Yomoto and the recommencement of the jinrikisha road is reached; a broiled fish and a bottle of native beer are consumed for lunch, and the kago coolies dismissed. The road from Yomoto is a gradual descent, for four miles, to Odawara, a town of some thirteen thousand inhabitants, on the coast. The road now becomes level and broader than heretofore; vehicles drawn by horses mingle with the swarms of jinrikishas and pedestrians. Both horses and drivers of the former seem sleepy, woe-begone and careless, as though overcome with a consciousness of being out of place.

Gangs of men are dragging stout hand-carts, loaded with material for the construction of the Tokaido railway, now rapidly being pushed forward. Every mile of the road is swarming with life—the strangely interesting life of Japan. Thirty miles from Yomoto, and Totsuka provides me a comfortable yadoya, where the people quickly show their knowledge of the foreigner's requirements by cooking a beefsteak with onions, also in the morning by charging the first really exorbitant price I have been confronted with along the Tokaido. Totsuka is within the treaty limits of Yokohama. A mile or so toward Yokohama I pass, in the morning, the "White Horse Tavern," kept in European style as a sort of road-house for foreigners driving out from that city or Tokio.

A fierce wind, blowing from the south, fairly wafts me along the last eleven miles of the Tokaido, from Totsuka to Yokohama. The wind, indeed, has been generally favorable since the rain-storm at Okabe, but it fairly whistles this morning. It calls to mind the Kansas wheelman, who claimed to have once spread his coat-tails to the breeze and coasted from Lawrence to Kansas City in three hours. Unfortunately I am wearing a coat the pattern of which does not admit of using the tails for sails otherwise the homestretch of the tour around the world might have provided one of the most unique incidents of the many I have encountered on the journey.

A battery of field-artillery, the smartest seen since leaving Germany, is encountered in the streets of Kanagawa, at which point the road to Yokohama branches off from the Tokaido. The great Imperial highway, along which I have travelled from the old capital almost to the new, continues on to the latter, seventeen miles farther. Since the completion of the railway between Tokio and Kanagawa, travellers journeying from the capital down the Tokaido usually ride on the train to Kanagawa, so that the jinrikisha journey proper nowadays commences at the latter city.

Kanagawa is practically a suburban part of Yokohama: one Japanese-owned clock observed here points to the hour of eight, another to eleven, and a third to half past-nine, but the clock at the Club Hotel, on the Yokohama bund, is owned by an Englishman, and is just about striking ten, when the last vault from the saddle of the bicycle that has carried me through so many countries is made. And so the bicycle part of the tour around the world, which was begun April 22, 1884, at San Francisco, California, ends December 17, 1886, at Yokohama.

At this port I board the Pacific mail steamer City of Peking, which in seventeen days lands me in San Francisco. Of the enthusiastic reception accorded me by the San Francisco Bicycle Club, the Bay City Wheelmen, and by various clubs throughout the United States, the daily press of the time contains ample record. Here, I beg leave to hope that the courtesies then so warmly extended may find an echoing response in this long record of the adventures that had their beginning and ending at the Golden Gate.

ITINERARY
GIVING THE NAME AND DATE OF EACH SLEEPING-POINT ON THE BICYCLE TOUR AROUND THE WORLD

VOLUME I. UNITED STATES. CALIFORNIA. 1884 April 23 San Francisco 23 House in the tuiles 24 Elmira 25 Sacramento 26 Near Rocklin 27-28 Clipper Gap 29 Blue Canon 30 Summit House **NEVADA.** May 1 Verdi 2 Ranch on Truckee River 3 Hot Springs 4 Lovelocks 5 Mill City 6 Winnemucca 7 Stone House 8 Ranch on Humboldt 9 Palisade 10 Carlin 11 Halleck 12 C P Section House **UTAH.** 13 Tacoma 14 Matlin 15 Salt House 16 Near Corrinne 17 Willard City 18 Ogden 19 Echo City 20 Castle Rocks **WYOMING TERRITORY.** May 21 Evanston 22 Hilliard 23 In abandoned freight wagon 24 Carter Station 25 Near Granger 26 Rocks Springs 27 Ranch 28-29 Rawlins 30 Carbon 31 Lookout June 1-2 Laramie City 3 Cheyenne **NEBRASKA.** 4 Pine Bluffs 5 Potter Station 6 Lodge Pole 7 Ranch on Platte 8 Ogallala 9 In a "dug-out" 10 Brady Island 11 Plum Creek 12 Kearney Junction 13 Grand Island 14 Duncan 15 North Bend 16 Fremont 17-18 Omaha **IOWA.** 19 Farm near Nishnebotene 20 Farm near Griswold June 21 Farm near Menlo 22 Farm near De Soto 23 Altoona 24 Kellogg 25 Victor 26 Tiffin 27 **MOSCOW-ILLINOIS.** 28 Rock Island 29 Atkinson 30 La Moile July 1 Yorkville 2 Naperville 3 Lyons 4-11 Chicago **INDIANA.** 12 Miller Station 13 Beneath a wheat shock 14 Goshen 15 Farm **OHIO.** 10 Ridgeville 17 Empire House 18 Bellevue 19 Village near Cleveland 20 Madison **PENNSYLVANIA.** 21 Roadside Hotel near Erie **NEW YORK.** 22 Angola 23 Buffalo 24 Leroy 25 Farm near Canandaigua 26 Marcellns 27 East Syracuse 28 Erie Canal Inn 29 Indian Castle 80 Crane's Village 31 Westfalls Inn **MASSACHUSETTS.** Aug. 1 Otis 2 Palmer 3 Worcester 4 Boston **EUROPE. ENGLAND.** 1885 Liverpool May 2 Warrington 3 Stone 4 Coventry 5 Fenny Stratford 6 Great Berkhamstead 7-8 London 9 Croydon 10 British Channel Steamer **FRANCE** Via Dieppe 11 Elbeuf 12 Mantes 13-15 Paris 16 Sezanne 17 Bar le Duo 18 Trouville 19 Nancy **GERMANY.** 20

Phalzburg Via Strasburg 21 Oberkirch 22 Rottenburg 23 Blauburen 24 Augsburg 25-26 Munich 27 Alt Otting AUSTRIA-HUNGARY. 28 Hoag 29 Strenberg 80 Neu Lengbach 31 Vienna June 1-3 4 Altenburg 5 Neszmely 6-7 Budapest 8 Duna Pentele 9 Szegszard 10 Duna Szekeso 11-12 Eszek 13 Sarengrad 14 Neusatz 15 Batauitz SERVIA, BULGARIA, AND TURKEY. 16-17 Belgrade 18 Jagodina 19 Nisch June 20-31 Bela Palanka 22 Sofia 23 Ichtiman 24 Near Tartar Bazardjic 25 Cauheme 26 Near Adrianople 27-28 Eski Baba 29 Small Village 30 Tchorlu July 1 Camped out 2 Constantinople

    6,000 miles wheeled from San Francisco.
ASIA.
  ASIA MINOR.
    Aug. 10 Ismidt
    11 Geiveh
    12 Terekli
    13 Beyond Torbali
    14 Nalikhan
    15 Bey Bazaar
    16-17 Angora
    18 Village
    19 Camped out
    20 Koordish Camp
    21 Yuzgat
    22 Camped out
    23 Village
    24-25 Sivas
    26 Zara
    Mar. 27 Armenian Village
    28 Camp in a cave
    29 Merriserriff
    30 Erzingan
    31 Houssenbeg Khan
    Sept. 1 Village in Euphrates Valley
    2-6 Erzeroum
    7 Hassan Kaleh
    8 Dela Baba
    9 Malosman
    10 Sup Ogwanis Monastery
  PERSIA.
    11 Ovahjik

12 Koodish Camp
13 Peri
14 Khoi
15 Village near Lake Ooroomiah
16 Village near Tabreez
17-20 Tabreez
21 Hadji Agha
22 Turcomanchai
23 Miana
24 Koordish Camp
25-26 Zendjan
27 Heeya
28 Kasveen
29 Yeng Imam
30 Teheran

VOLUME II. 1886 Mar. 10 Katoum-abad 11 Aivan-i-Kaif 12 Aradan 13-14-15 Lasgird 16 Semnoon 17 Gusheh 18 Deh Mollah 19-20 Shahrood 21 Mijamid 22 Miandasht 23-24 Mazinan 25 Subzowar 26 Wayside caravanserai 27 Shiirab 28 Gadamgah Mar. 29 Wayside caravanserai 30-Ap. 6 Meshed April 7 Shahriffabad 8 Caravanserai 9 Torbet-i-Haidorai 10 Camp on Gounabad Desert 11 Kakh 12 Nukhab 13 Small hamlet 14 Beerjand 15 Ali-abad 16 Darmian 17 Tabbas 18 Huts on desert edge AFGHANISTAN. April 19 Camp on Desert of Despair 20 Nomad camp 31 Village ou Harud 22 Ghalakua 23 Nomad camp 24-25 Furrali (arrested by Afghans) 26 Nomad camp 27 Subzowar 28 Nomad camp 29 Camp out 30-May 9 Herat May 10 Village 11 Roadside umbar 12 Camp in Heri-rood jungle PERSIA. 13 Karize (released by Afghans) 14 Nomad camp 15 Furriman 16-18 Meshed 19 Caravanserai 20 Near Nishapoor 21 Lafaram 22 Wayside umbar 23 Mazinan 24 Near caravanserai 25 Camp out 26-27 Shahrood 28 Camp out 29 Asterabad 30 Bunder Guz

Russian steamer to Baku; rail to Batoum; steamer to Constantinople and India. Renewed bicycle tour:

INDIA.
August Lahore
1 Amritza
2 Beas River 8 Jullunder

4 Police chowkee
5-6 Umballa
7 Peepli
8 Paniput
9 Police chowkee
10-14 Delhi
15 Dak bungalow
16 Bungalow
17 Muttra
Aug. 18-19 Agra
20 Mainipoor
21 Miran-serai
22-26 Cawnpore
27 Caravanserai
28 Caravanserai
29-30 Allahabad
31 Roadside hut
Sept. 1-2 Benares
3 Mogul-serai
4 Caravanserai
5 Dilli
6 Shergotti
7 D`ak bungalow
8 D`ak bungalow
9 Burwah
10 Ranuegunj
11 Burdwan
12 Hooghli
13-17 Calcutta Steamer to Canton
CHINA.
Oct. 7-12 Canton
13 Chun-kong-hi
14 Low-pow
15 Chin-ynen
16 Bamboo thicket
17-20 Aboard sampan
21 Schou-chou-foo
22 Small village
23 Do.
24 Nam-hung
25-28 Nam-ngan
29 Aboard sampan
30 Large village

31 Large village near Kan-tchou-i'oo
Nov. 1 Small mountain hamlet
2 Walled garrison city
3 Ta-ho
4 Ki-ngan foo (under arrest)
5-15 Under arrest on sampan
16 Inn near Kui-Kiang
17 Yangtsi-Kiang steamer
18 Shanghai
19-20 Japanese steamer
JAPAN.
21-22 Nagasaki
23 Omura
Nov. 24 Ushidza
25-26 Futshishi
27 Hakama
28 Shemonoseki
29 Village
30 Do.
Dec. 1 A small fishing hamlet
2 Do.
3 Do.
4-5 Okoyama
Dec. 6 Himeji
7-8 Kobe
9 Ozaka
10 Kioto
11 Saka-no-shita
12 Miya
13 Hamamatsu
14 Roadside inn
15 Mishima
16 Totsuka
17 Yokohama

DISTANCE ACTUALLY WHEELED, ABOUT 13,500 MILES.